Cultural Psychology in Clinical Research and Practices

Advances in Cultural Psychology: Constructing Human Development

Series Editor
Jaan Valsiner
Niels Bohr Professor of Cultural Psychology, Aalborg University

In the beginning of the 21st century, a new direction has been emerging at the intersection of developmental and social psychologies, anthropology, education, and sociology – which has become labeled cultural psychology. This fits the vast global social processes of most countries becoming multicultural in their social orders, and the World becoming one 'global village' – with the corresponding need to know how different parts of that 'village' function. The knowledge base of developmental psychology and education has become truly interdisciplinary, and its applications in the vast variety of cultural contexts need to be informed about varieties of cultural expectations. In that interdisciplinary synthesis, the knowledge base of contemporary developmental psychology and educational sciences is increasingly international. At the same time, any application of the knowhow of the social sciences in the areas of education and social life in any society remain local. Advances in Cultural Psychology creates an international forum for communicating key ideas of methodology, different approaches to family, relationships, schooling and social negotiations of issues of human development. New perspectives-dynamic systems theory, dialogical perspectives on the development of the self, the role of various symbolic resources in human development, and other new topics of interdisciplinary kind will figure prominently in the book series.

OTHER TITLES IN THIS SERIES

Culture and Leadership: From Approximation Towards Symbiosis. 1st Edition (2026) Enno von Fircks. ISBN 978-1-83708-975-8

Handbook of Cultural Sports Psychology. 1st Edition (2024) Natalie Jancosek and Christian Højen Bisgaard. 979-8-88730-842-5

Learning with William Stern. 1st Edition (2024) Enno von Fircks. ISBN 979-0-88730-783-1

The Semiotic Field of the Garden. 1st Edition (2024) Teppei Tsuchimoto. ISBN 979-8-88730-635-3

Culture, Work and Psychology. 1st Edition (2019) Pedro F. Bendassolli. ISBN 978-1-64113-633-4

Cultural Psychology in Clinical Research and Practices

Edited by

Audrey S. Namdiero-Walsh

Independent Scholar and Researcher, Germany

emerald PUBLISHING

United Kingdom – North America – Japan
India – Malaysia – China

Emerald Publishing Limited, Floor 5, Northspring, 21-23 Wellington Street, Leeds LS1 4DL

First edition 2026

Cover photo: iStock, prezent, GC402 and Kittapud Janpirom

Reprints and permissions service
Contact: www.copyright.com

British Library Cataloguing in Publication Data
A catalogue record for this book is available from the British Library

ISBN: 978-1-83742-214-2 (Print hardback)
ISBN: 978-1-83742-216-6 (Print paperback)
ISBN: 978-1-83742-213-5 (PDF)
ISBN: 978-1-83742-215-9 (EPUB)

Typeset by TNQ Tech

Cover design by TNQ Tech

CONTENTS

ABOUT THE EDITOR

Audrey S. Namdiero-Walsh is a passionate leader, bridge-builder, and advocate for inclusive dialogue and collaborative approaches. With over 15 years of experience in international program management and strategic partnerships, she has led impactful initiatives across education, public health, and foreign policy, often addressing complex tackling complex and intersecting challenges. She also brings a multidisciplinary approach to her work. Trained as a clinical psychologist and policy adviser, Audrey brings a multidisciplinary perspective grounded in behavioural science and cultural psychology. Her current research at the University of Hertfordshire (UK) explores complexity management and systems change, building on her longstanding interest in how cultural contexts shape psychological practice and systemic transformation. By combining practice and scholarship, Audrey works to co-create solutions that are not only effective and sustainable, but also deeply rooted in people's lived experiences. She believes that meaningful change emerges when individuals and organisations embrace authenticity, foster trust, and engage with cultural diversity as a source of insight and strength.

ABOUT THE CONTRIBUTORS

Michal Blau, MA in Clinical Psychology, is a psychotherapist and psychoanalytic candidate at the Arbeitsgemeinschaft für Psychoanalyse und Psychotherapie Berlin (APB e.V.) since 2022. She earned her Master's degree in Psychology at the International Psychoanalytic University Berlin (IPU Berlin), with a thesis on misunderstandings in psychotherapy when English is used as a lingua franca. Her clinical and research interests include intercultural psychotherapy, the therapeutic use of foreign languages, conversation analysis in psychotherapy, and the transgenerational transmission of experience and trauma. She has worked with patients with migration and refugee backgrounds in institutional, day clinic, and outpatient settings.

Erin Bulluss, PhD, is a clinical psychologist with both lived and professional experience in the area of autism. Erin's primary area of practice is supervising and mentoring Autistic mental health professionals. She also has an interest in cultural humility as it relates to Autistic Culture, and supports non-Autistic mental health professionals who work with Autistic clients to develop both their cultural competence and humility.

Pradeep Chakkarath, PhD, is a cultural psychologist born in India and an interim professor at the *International Psychoanalytic University* (IPU) in Berlin. He is also a senior researcher and lecturer in the Faculty of Social Sciences at *Ruhr University Bochum*. Furthermore, he is Co-Director of the *Hans Kilian and Lotte Köhler Centre for Cultural Psychology and Historical Anthropology* (KKC). His academic interests focus on researching human development in different cultural contexts and critically examining the dominant theoretical perspectives and methods underlying related research in the social and cultural sciences, particularly psychology. He is co-editor of the German-language journal *psychosozial* and co-founder of the online journal *HARM: Journal of Hostility, Anger, Repression and Malice.*

Janet Conti is a clinical psychologist and academic in psychology. Her research demonstrates and advocates for the prioritisation of the person/family's voice to inform therapeutic interventions and for clinicians to develop skills in tailoring treatments to the person/family. She has a particular interest in qualitative research, particularly critical discursive approaches.

Dawn Darlaston-Jones is a critical community psychologist with over 20 years experience in the university sector, she is now in private practice as a consultant researcher. Her interests focus on decolonisation at the individual, discipline and societal levels.

Maria Virginia Dazzani has a degree in Psychology (1994), a master's degree (2000) and a doctorate in Education at the Federal University of Bahia (2004). She did postdoctoral studies at Purdue University/USA (2002–2003), postdoctoral studies at Clark University/USA (2009-2010), where she was visiting professor in 2015–2016. She is currently Associate Professor III at the Institute of Psychology of the Federal University of Bahia, and the coordinator of the research group Investigations in Cultural Psychology: Culture, Language, Transitions and Developmental Trajectories (CULTS).

Cristiana Kaipper Dias holds a degree in Psychology from the Federal University of Bahia (UFBA, 2008), a Master's in History of Religions from the Portuguese Catholic University (2012, recognized in Brazil by UFJF), and a PhD in Psychology (Human Development) from UFBA (2023). She was a member of the research group Culture, Language, Transitions, and Developmental Trajectories (CULTS) from 2019 to 2023, and participated in the project Under the Sign of Poverty: Psychosocial and Educational Dynamics of Low-Income Populations from a Semiotic-Cultural Psychology Perspective. Her research interests include Phenomenological Psychology, Semiotic-Cultural Psychology, Human Development, Inclusive Education, Family, Gender, and Sexuality. She is a reviewer for Trends in Psychology, Human Arenas, and Culture & Psychology. With clinical experience since 2012, she also holds postgraduate training in Humanistic Psychotherapy and Music Therapy. Currently, she teaches and supervises clinical training at Unijorge University Center and teaches at Faculdade Santa Casa.

Patricia Dudgeon is a Bardi woman from the Kimberley and Professor of Indigenous Health and Well-Being. Her research focuses on suicide prevention and uses community engagement, consultation and responsiveness, and draws upon multidisciplinary approaches. Her large, national integrated projects map social phenomena and seek to implement transformative methods and practices.

Pablo Fossa is Director of the Cognition & Culture Laboratory (C&C Lab) of Instituto de Bienestar Socioemocional (IBEM) at the Faculty of Psychology, Universidad del Desarrollo, Chile. He received a PhD degree in Psychology from the Pontifical Catholic University of Chile. His doctoral thesis dealt with the expressive dimension of inner language in human experience. He did a postdoctoral fellowship financed by the National Commission for Scientific and Technological Research (CONICYT) of Chile, with a research project on thought trajectories from a microgenetic orientation. His lines of research are related to Cognition, Cultural Psychology and Phenomenology. He is the editor of the book *Latin American Advances in Subjectivity and Development: Through Vygotsky Route* (Springer, 2021), *New Perspectives on Inner Speech* (Springer, 2022), *Inner Speech, Culture & Education* (Springer, 2022), *Affectivity & Learning* (Springer, 2023), *Affektivität und Lernen* (Springer, 2024), *Collected Papers on Inner Speech* (IAP, 2024) and *Person & Knowledge* (Emerald, 2025). Currently, he is PhD candidate in Philosophy at the University of Navarra, Spain.

Klessyo do Espirito Santo Freire is a psychologist, Master in Education, and PhD student in psychology at the Federal University of Bahia (Brazil). Also a member of the research group *Investigations in Cultural Psychology: Culture, Language, Transitions and Developmental Trajectories* (CULTS) at the Federal University of Bahia.

Danilo Silva Guimarães is an indigenous person with Tikmu'um (Maxakali) ancestry. He is a psychologist (CRP 06/95800), lecturer, and researcher in the field of History and Philosophy of Psychology at the Institute of Psychology of the University of São Paulo. His research focuses on the indigenous roots of psychological theories and systems, colonialist projects of psychological discourse and practices, and the possibilities and limits of psychology as a territory of sharing, inclusive of epistemological diversities, ethically committed to indigenous people, communities, and ways of being. He coordinates the Indigenous Network, which hosts the USP's House of Indigenous Cultures.

Tanja Hirvonen is a Clinical Psychologist and has a double degree majoring in psychology and human research management and holds a postgraduate Masters in Clinical Psychology. Tanja has worked in academic, clinical, and executive roles. Tanja is currently the Wellbeing Director with The Healing Foundation. Tanja identifies as Jaru and Bunuba (WA).

Josephine Kirschner is a clinical psychologist currently completing her second year of training in psychodynamic psychotherapy in Berlin, Germany. She holds a master's degree in clinical psychology and is pursuing her doctoral research at Charité – Universitätsmedizin Berlin, focusing on the relationship between yoga practice and psychological health. Her research and clinical interests center on processes of recovery and integration after severe illness, with a focus on subjective theories of healing leading to new perspectives on the individual role of mind-body approaches in therapy. She works as a psychologist in palliative medicine, where she supports patients in coping with existential challenges and promotes holistic perspectives on care and healing. Alongside her academic and clinical work, she facilitates yoga-based workshops for individuals affected by chronic or mental illness, combining scientific insight with practical experience in mind–body therapy.

Daniela Lemmo, PhD (Gender Studies), is a psychotherapist and Clinical Psychology researcher at the University of Naples Federico II. Her research examines motivation and engagement in self-care among people living with chronic illness across the lifespan. She investigates emotional and narrative mechanisms shaping prevention, chronic illness management, and adherence. Her research includes gender-sensitive studies of women's health and mind–body meaning-making in oncological prevention and adaptation to breast cancer in women under 50. She has participated in international collaborations between the University of Naples Federico II and the Centre for Medical Ethics at the University of Oslo, linking medical ethics and clinical psychology. She conducts intervention research in hospital and primary care contexts, using quali-quantitative methods and narrative meaning-making models. She contributed to the MIRIADE research-action project on adherence profiles in cancer screening and currently works on the national research program 'Age' on self-care motivation and healthy ageing.

Jennifer Malecki is a psychologist supporting people in the community living with acute mental health problems. She is also a PhD researcher in clinical psychology exploring an embodied and feminist conceptualisation of trauma and anorexia.

Giuseppina Marsico is Associate Professor of Development and Educational Psychology at the University of Salerno (Italy), Visiting Professor at PhD Programme in Psychology, Federal University of Bahia, (Brazil) and Honorary Associate Professor in School of Psychology University of Sidney (Australia). She is a 20 years' experienced researcher, with a proven international research network. She is Editor-in-chief of the Book Series *Cultural Psychology of Education* (Springer), *Latin American Voices - Integrative Psychology and Humanities* (Springer), co-editor of SpringerBriefs *Psychology and Cultural Developmental Sciences* (together with Jaan Valsiner) and *Annals of Cultural*

Psychology: Exploring the Frontiers of Mind and Society (Emerald). She is also co-editor of *Human Arenas. An Interdisciplinary Journal of Psychology, Culture and Meaning* (Springer) and of *Trends in Psychology* (Springer).

Maria Luisa Martino, PhD, Assistant Researcher in Clinical Psychology at the Department of Humanities, Federico II University, Naples. Within a clinical health psychology framework, she focused on the different phases of life-threatening illness, in particular the cancer condition, as a critical and potentially traumatic experience. She deals with research-intervention in hospital institutions regarding the use and evaluation of different narrative devices, such as writing, dreams, and memories, as tools to promote adaptation, integration and recovery from critical/traumatic experiences. Adopting quali-quantitative methods, she deepens clinical models to support the construction of narrative meaning-making from illness experience. She was a researcher on the action-research project MRIADE 'An innovative model of research-intervention for the identification of adherence profiles to cancer screening,' funded by the Regional Prevention Plan (PRP Campania 2020–2025, Italy). She was Principal Investigator of the Project IMPRONTE 'Breast Cancer Women: Innovative Model For Processing Traumatic Experience' – Star Grant 2017–2019 – funded by Federico II University and San Paolo Company Foundation Bank of Naples.

María Elisa Molina is Full Professor at the Faculty of Psychology, Universidad del. Desarrollo, Chile (UDD), and Director of the Transformations and Human Agency. Laboratory (Lab-TAH) at of Instituto de Bienestar Socioemocional (IBEM). She received a PhD degree in Psychology from the Pontifical Catholic University of Chile. Member of the editorial boards of Latin American Voices: Integrative Psychology and Humanities; Human Arenas; Methodologies in Developmental Sciences, Springer, and Socioemotional Well-Being, IBEM–Springer. She is first editor of the volume of the series: Annals of Cultural Psychology, Intimacy: The Shared part of me (IAP, 2022). Her research focuses are on relational processes from the perspective of culturally situated systems, temporality, dialogue and semiotic mediation. Main areas of interest include psychotherapy, human encounters, families' and couples' relationships. https://orcid.org/0000-0002-7874-3459

Dario Marinho de Lima Neto is currently works as a clinical psychologist in Brazil. He graduated in psychology from USP (2019), where he completed his master's degree in 2023. He has been a member of the Indigenous Support Network (ISN) since 2016 and, starting in 2019, participated in the development of the clinical care initiative for Indigenous people. Today, it is a more punctual collaboration of ISN.

Lan-Sze Pang, PhD is a Registered Counselling Psychologist (HKPS) and part-time Associate Professor of Practice in the Department of Counselling and Psychology at Hong Kong Shue Yan University. She has served as Director of the PsyD programme in Counselling Psychology and was instrumental in establishing Hong Kong's first and only Master's programme in Counselling Psychology as its first Assistant Director. Dr Pang has maintained a private practice for over a decade, developing her strength-based narrative approach to career counselling. Her in-house vocational psychology training series has been consistently sought after by practitioners, alongside customized training for organizations and universities. Dr Pang holds a BA in Psychology, and MA and PhD in Counselling Psychology from Southern Illinois University at Carbondale, USA. Her clinical and research interests include psycholinguistic phenomenon in psychotherapy encounters, clinical supervision process, localization of multicultural counselling training, and career development of college students and midlife adults.

Raffaele De Luca Picione, PhD, is Full Professor of Dynamic Psychology at the Giustino Fortunato University (Benevento, Italy). He is a psychotherapist and psychoanalyst. His research focuses on subjectivity, affectivity, liminality, modelization of the mind and semiotic borders, unconscious temporality, starting from a psychoanalytic, cultural psychology and semiotic perspective. He is the author of over 200 international and national scientific works, in the various format of papers/books/essays/chapters. He is Editor and member of Scientific Board of several international journal of psychology and psychoanalysis. He is Scientific Director of *Research Laboratory on Liminality of Psychic and Collective Processes* at Giustino Fortunato University.

Paul Rhodes is an academic in psychology specialising in qualitative inquiry. His current interests include the history of peer activism and community psychiatry, eco-psychology and place-based identity, semiotics and distress, contemporary existentialism and decolonising psychotherapy. He runs a private practice specialising in supporting young people in distress.

Leonardo Rafael Leite da Rocha: Master's degree in Psychology from UFBA, with a doctorate in progress. Graduated in Psychology from the Adventist University Center of Northeast Education (UNIAENE). Affiliated with the research group 'Research in Cultural Psychology: Culture, Language, Transitions and Developmental Trajectories' (CULTS) and the Graduate Program in Psychology (PPGPSI/UFBA). Topics of interest: Developmental Psychology, Cultural Psychology, Social Identities, Race and Gender.

Tracie Rogers is a social work academic and trauma-responsive practitioner whose work sits at the intersections of Black feminist thought, decolonial social work, and arts-based inquiry. Her teaching and practice integrate culturally grounded methodologies with community-centred mental health approaches, advancing Caribbean ways of knowing and strengthening justice-oriented practice.

Sabrina Saase (no pronouns), is a psychologist and counsellor, is a PhD candidate (research interest: intersectionality-informed competency). Current position: Health & Well-being Manager at the international university ESCP Berlin (health strategy, counselling, DEI and campaigns). Work experience: academic teaching and thesis supervision, psychotherapy, psychiatric clinics, the United Nations in Geneva, queer NGOs in Yogyakarta and Berlin, accommodation for underage refugees and educational work, e.g. for GIZ (the German Agency for International Cooperation), WIDE+ (Women in Development Europe+) and the State Office for Equal Treatment – Against Discrimination Berlin (LADS). Other responsibilities: Global Affiliate of the Canadian Institute for Intersectionality Research & Policy (IIRP); Member of Scientific Advisory Boards; Mentor; Member of the German Carlo Schmid Network for International Politics & Cooperation e.V.; Former Board Member of the Berlin Committee for UNESCO Work e.V. and the Berlin Queer Raumerweiterungshalle –Selbstuniversität e.V.; Additional Training in Peace & Conflict Management (Oxford). Co-organiser of the conference www.therapie-intersektional.de

Alan Souza Pereira Silva is a Masters' graduate of Psychology. He is currently a doctoral student in Developmental Psychology at the Graduate Program in Psychology at the Federal University of Bahia (Brazil). He participates in the Center for Studies on Development and Cultural Contexts, in the line of research entitled Developmental Transitions and Educational Processes, at the Federal University of Bahia. https://orcid.org/0000-0002-5177-5944

Jasmin Spiegel, PhD, is a clinical psychologist, a psychoanalyst in training, and a postdoctoral fellow at the Martin Buber Society of Fellows in the Humanities and Social Sciences at the Hebrew University of Jerusalem. Her research focuses on the conceptual and methodological connections between dance science and psychotherapy, with a particular focus on nonverbal communication in the psychotherapeutic dyad. Currently, she is enrolled in the ISMETA Whole Movement Program in Israel to become a certified Movement Analyst (CMA).

Jovanna Ulmschneider. After completing her studies at the University of the Arts, Jovanna worked in conceptual development and coordination for an international conference focused on green energy and urban community engagement. She later pursued a degree in Psychology at SFU Berlin, specializing in conflict transformation. Currently training as a systemic psychotherapist, her work and interests continue to be shaped by a deep curiosity about the lived experiences of illness, health, and care – as well as alternative forms of care work and collective support within landscapes of politics of care.

Caroline Skov Vestbjerg is an authorized psychologist in clinical practice in Denmark, working in the field of Forensic Psychiatry. She graduated as a Cultural Psychologist at the Niels Bohr Professorship Center of Cultural Psychology at Aalborg University. Her research concentrates on cultural psychological aspects of individual and social phenomena by investigating ways of approaching otherwise clinical questions with a cultural psychological standpoint. Topics like trauma, resilience, diagnostical systems, pathology, meanings construction and life course perspectives have been main issues of her research. Besides working on her research and in clinical practice, she also concerns herself with organizational psychology where she among other things is board member of the Danish Psychological Union, Denmark.

Meike Watzlawik is Professor of Development, Education and Culture at Sigmund Freud University (SFU) Berlin, Germany. She holds a diploma in psychology and completed her doctorate and habilitation at Technische Universität Braunschweig. As a former Alexander von Humboldt Foundation fellow, she conducted research at Clark University (USA) within Jaan Valsiner's cultural-psychology network. Her research focuses on human identity development – particularly during adolescence, within sibling and twin relationships, in professional contexts, and across diverse cultural settings. A further focus of her work is sexual and gender diversity, to which she contributes through empirical research and applied scholarship. Watzlawik employs both quantitative and qualitative methods and has published widely as both editor and author. At SFU Berlin, she heads the Department of Psychology and directs the master's programme in Clinical Psychology. She is licensed as a psychotherapy practitioner and is committed to advancing interdisciplinary dialogue and fostering inclusive academic environments for students and colleagues alike.

Catherine Wilson identifies as Queer (gender and sexuality), but does not claim lived experience as a trans person. They are a Clinical Psychologist working on Gadigal land; doing mostly therapy, but also providing supervision and education; are a member of AusPATH; and a co-founder of the Gender Galaxy community of practice. They work at the bulk-bill private practice Uplift Psychological Services, predominantly with people of TGD and LGBTQIA+ experiences; and at the Sacred Heart Bereavement Counselling Service at St Vincent's Hospital.

SERIES EDITOR'S PREFACE

CLINICAL ARENAS FOR CULTURAL PSYCHOLOGY: NEW HORIZONS

This volume is long awaited – cultural psychology needs to be linked with the vast field of applications that the clinical practices call for. And there are many! The domain of heath – starting from personal negotiations of 'my well-being' in contrast to 'there is something wrong with me' – leading to the questions of macro-level societal health risk discourses ('is vaccination dangerous?') are all overdetermined by the manifold of meaning constructions that organize that domain. All reflections upon health emerge in the ongoing processes of meaning making, using various semiotic mediating devices.

An inevitable counterpart of such overdetermination by meaning of our health discourses is the continuing uncertainty of our struggle for health. It is a personal existential struggle of the whole life course. It does not need any psychology – be it clinical or scientific. Health concerns are natural part of life course personal constructions, involving imagination, fears, and appreciation of the very fact that we live, love, and feel into our worlds.

Where, then, psychology enters into human lives? And how? What new can it bring to human lives that the tumultuous human history of wars, famines, glorifications of rulers and revolutions, and devastations by epidemics have not produced by default? Human *psyche* has survived the history of its species and become resilient against many – but not all – new challenges. The primary function of the human *psyche* is its strength – resistance against the flow of incoming information, and resilience while proceeding towards one's own goals.

Psychology is a discipline that since its emergence has been characteristically ambivalent about its status between science and social practices. This ambivalence became enhanced in the 19th century when the need for knowledge for the uses in various kinds of social practices grew – while the trajectory of science historically moved into the dominance of the natural sciences (Valsiner, 2012). The result was appropriation by the natural science orientation of the whole history of psychology. Wilhelm Wundt's administrative act of opening an experimental psychology laboratory in Leipzig in 1879 was made into the key event of the birth of scientific psychology – albeit 50 years later. In parallel – much of the psychological know-how was lost in the selective representations of the discipline (Cornejo & Maturana, 2025). It was also streamlined to amount to focus on *prediction and control* of behavior – a task that is in principle impossible in the case of all open systems. If that focus were to be taken seriously, psychology would be a science of the prediction of the unpredictable and control of the uncontrollable. Not a very productive basis for a science.

Looking at psychology today, I would posit that it is the science of the basic processes of the functioning of the human soul – usually called *mind* or *self* – in its relationships with the environment. The human mind is hierarchically organized complex structure of psychological processes with high compensatory potentials within the hierarchy. Its different levels of hierarchy entail the unity of the highest creation of the mind itself – from myths, values, prejudices, etc. – down to cognitive problem-solving processes and acts of meaning construction. In their decisions to act, human lives are self-reflexively meaningful. Only at the lowest levels of this hierarchy do we find concrete behavioral acts. And even those become targets for contemplation. Human behavior is a set of actions treated as meaningful.

Psychology is a general science – similar to biology – as it deals with phenomena that exist only in living organisms. All living systems exist due to their constant exchange relations with the environment – be that of oxygen (biological systems), relations to the minds of others (psychological systems), institutions relating to other institutions (social systems, or states relating to other states = political systems). One particular feature – *intentionality of actions* – is unique to the psychology of the human species. Hence psychology deals with basic processes of human intentional actions, their consequences, and the feed-forward from these actions to future actions. The temporal feature – never-ending processes if living towards the future – makes psychology into a fundamental part of developmental science (Carolina Consortium on Human Development, 1996).

Cultural psychology occupies a special place on the mindscape of psychology – it is dedicated to the study of human meaning-making and meaning use in the context of values-based intentional actions. Cultural psychology works at the higher end of the hierarchical structure of the *psyche* – where values of the society intersect with the feelings and lead to meaningful and often passionate actions. As a result, our thinking is guided by affect, and is nonrational in its core.

What is the nature of clinical psychology as a part of psychology at large? It is a vast field of efforts to apply the general knowhow of the discipline that has historically belonged to the expertise of natural healers, palm readers, and shamans. Today it is of course the powerhouse of medical professions and pharmaceutical companies that keep the hold of all features of health maintenance and improvement – not to speak of their lucrative profits. In the last few centuries psychology has slowly entered into the field of clinical practices and carved out its place in it – two larger domains, diagnostics and therapy – are the locations where clinical psychology has taken its hold. These two differ in their epistemological *foci* – if diagnostics works on the ontological basis (e.g., claims like 'diagnosis X exists as real'), the latter is explicitly developmental. Overcoming an illness is a developmental process. Consequently, cultural psychology can contribute to clinical psychology in two directions. First of all – all diagnostic labels are signs; their representational value needs verification. This is static semiotic representation function.

More importantly, the therapeutic direction in clinical practice is open to the dynamic semiosis side of cultural psychology. Here the invention and use of signs enters into direct relation with the clinical practices and their evaluations. Nowhere else is cultural psychology more important than in the multitude of psychotherapy practices. The latter are examples of secular healing dramatisms. In the present volume the reader can get an interesting overview of ways to re-think various treatment possibilities that cultural psychology makes possible. By raising questions of power, identity, and positionality, various chapters show that culture is not a neutral background for human well-being, but a domain in which privilege and marginalization are reproduced, resisted, or transformed. Clinical work is closely intertwined with issues of social power, and the latter sets up constraints on the application of any basic knowledge in a society. Cultural psychology is a new discipline that is only beginning to find out its limits of applications. This volume can inform all of us more about those.

Jaan Valsiner
Chapel Hill, NC
November 2025

REFERENCES

Carolina Consortium on Human Development. (1996). Developmental science: A collaborative statement. In R. B. Cairns, G. Elder, & E. J. Costello, (Eds.), *Developmental science* (pp. 1–6). Cambridge University Press.

Cornejo, C., & Maturana, C. C. (Eds.). (2025). *Forgotten streams in the history of 19th century German psychology* (Vol. *1–2*). Springer.

Valsiner, J. (2012). *A guided science: History of psychology in the mirror of its making.* Transaction Publishers.

EDITOR'S PREFACE

Audrey S. Namdiero-Walsh

WHY THIS BOOK, AND WHY NOW?

Clinical Psychology stands at a crossroad. Mental health cannot be fully understood in isolation from the systems (e.g., culture and society) in which people live and make meaning. While the field has expanded globally through evidence-based protocols, digital innovations, and global mental health initiatives, its foundations remain rooted in Western epistemologies, diagnostic categories, and nonindividualised models of care that foster a gateway therapy approach that often fails to connect with patients on an individual basis or even causes harm. The result is a discipline that often struggles to meaningfully engage with the diverse social, cultural, and political contexts in which psychological distress is experienced (Henrich et al., 2010).

At the same time, global debates around equity, decolonisation, and structural injustice have intensified. Movements such as Black Lives Matter, critiques of systemic racism in healthcare (Fernando, 2017), and renewed calls to integrate Indigenous knowledge systems (Dudgeon et al., 2014), highlight the urgency of rethinking how Clinical Psychology and different psychotherapeutic approaches account for identity, power, and culture. Mental health scientists and practitioners cannot afford to remain 'neutral' in the face of these realities. To ignore them only risks reinforcing the very structures of exclusion and inequity that contribute to people's suffering (Summerfield, 2008).

This book situates Cultural Psychology as a valuable framework that broadens our understanding of the mind and illness beyond 'contextual add-ons' while interrogating the political and ethical dimensions of clinical practice. Culture, in this view, is not an optional element but the obligatory ground on which experiences of psychological distress, resilience, and transformation are built. Culture is everywhere and cannot be detangled from an individual. A Cultural Psychology perspective, therefore, provides conceptual and methodological foundations for a Clinical Psychology that is globally relevant, locally meaningful, and socially just (Patel et al., 2018).

ORIGINS OF THE VOLUME

The idea for this volume emerged from a shared recognition among researchers and practitioners of the persistent gap between mainstream Clinical Psychology and the cultural, political, and social realities that shape human suffering. What began as an interdisciplinary conversation across Clinical Psychology, Cultural Psychology, Sociology, and Psychotherapy, developed into this collaborative book volume project. Our shared objective has been to bring together voices that challenge, critique, and extend the field while offering new conceptual, methodological, and practical directions as potential solutions.

THEMES AND STRUCTURE

Although the chapters are not organised into formal sections, they can be read as contributing to four interrelated themes that run through the volume.

- *Reframing theory and foundations*: The opening chapters (Chakkarath; Freire, Pereira, Dazzani & Marsico; De Luca Picione, Martino & Lemmo) challenge Western assumptions of illness, introduce semiotic Cultural Psychology, and explore meaning-making processes in clinical and health-related contexts. Together, they set the stage by rethinking how we conceptualize mental illness, health, and its cultural underpinnings, including the sociohistorical and colonial roots of current concepts and practices.
- *Politics, justice, and intercultural practice*: Several chapters position therapy and psychology as unavoidably political. Rhodes and colleagues argue for psychology as activist practice oriented toward justice; de Lima Neto and Guimarães propose an intercultural notion of 'dwelling' grounded in Indigenous Brazilian contexts; Molina and Fossa explore psychotherapy as a cultural dynamic process of meaning-making; and I, Namdiero-Walsh, examine how whiteness, privilege, and racism manifest in everyday discourse by analysing reactions to a White woman's social media reflections during the Black Lives Matter protests. Taken together, these chapters assert that Clinical Psychology must grapple with structural inequities, power relations, and the politics of consciousness, if it is to remain relevant.

- *Identity, language, and the therapeutic encounter.* Other contributions address how identity and communication shape clinical processes. Saase examines therapist self-disclosure and intersectionality; Pang analyses bilingual counselling and linguistic identity; Blau & Spiegel study nonverbal negotiations in intercultural therapy using English as a lingua franca; and Rocha, Dias & Marsico discuss gender identity development and its clinical implications. Collectively, these chapters reveal how identity, privilege, and language are not peripheral, but central to therapeutic meaning-making and clinical relationships.
- *Embodiment, culture, and lived experience.* Finally, several chapters expand the focus of clinical psychology to include the body and lived experience. Kirchner's chapter on yoga highlights cultural healing practices as resources for clinical care. Ulmschneider's work on chronic pain conceptualises suffering as a liminal phenomenon, while Vestbjerg interrogates how 'truth' and 'delusion' are culturally constituted. Together, these studies remind us that mental health is not purely cognitive or emotional but embodied, relational, and deeply cultural.

By weaving theoretical, qualitative methodological, and empirical insights, this volume moves beyond surface-level adaptation and instead advocates a fundamental rethinking of Clinical Psychology through cultural lenses to catalyse the development of individualised treatment approaches that can be more sustainable for anyone, regardless of their background.

EDITORIAL REFLECTIONS

Editing this volume has been both intellectually challenging and deeply rewarding.

What struck me in particular was that though there was a diversity of approaches – semiotic, phenomenological, political, and psychodynamic – all chapters converged on a shared conviction: that culture is not an 'extra variable' but a constitutive force in mind, illness, and healing. Furthermore, by raising questions of *power, identity* and *positionality*, the chapters demonstrate that culture is also not a neutral backdrop but a contested space in which privilege and marginalization are reproduced, resisted, or transformed. As a psychologist working across non-Western and global contexts, I found these contributions both affirming and provocative, often pushing me to question my own assumptions about what counts as valid knowledge in clinical contexts.

EDITORIAL REVIEW PROCESS

This book project was initiated in late 2020 during the COVID-19 pandemic. The original volume editors were me (Audrey S. Namdiero-Walsh) and Josephine Jacobi, both clinical psychologists with a strong interest in cultural perspectives in Clinical Psychology. As first-time editors, Josephine and I received guidance and oversight throughout the peer review and editorial process from two senior scholars: Prof. Dr Meike Watzlawik (Professor of Developmental, Educational, and Cultural Psychology at Sigmund Freud University, Berlin) and Prof. Dr Jaan Valsiner (Series Editor and Professor of Cultural Psychology at Aalborg University Denmark).

The editorial review process focused on each submission's demonstration of the relevance of culture in the study and practice of Clinical Psychology. Manuscripts were reviewed both by the editors and Professors Watzlawik and Valsiner for conceptual clarity, originality, and alignment with the volume's interdisciplinary approach.

Biographically, Audrey and Josephine identify as cisgender Black and white women, respectively, with personal and professional ties to Kenya, Ireland, and Germany. Both come from working-class backgrounds and have navigated experiences of upward mobility in professional and academic settings, perspectives that informed their approach to this project and to fostering inclusive scholarly dialogue. Due to unforeseen personal circumstances, Josephine was unable to continue her role in this project as co-editor. Her early contributions to the conceptualisation and development of the volume were nonetheless highly valuable.

ACKNOWLEDGEMENTS

I am deeply grateful to the contributing authors, who brought scholarly depth, critical reflexivity, and practical insight to their chapters. The determination of many authors to contribute and translate their insights into a foreign language (English) added to the value of this volume. Appreciation is due to Professors Meike Watzlawik and Jaan Valsiner, whose guidance helped ensure the academic rigor and quality of the volume.

I also thank my peer reviewers, Josephine Jacobi and Max Vogel, both clinical psychologists and researchers with the Sigmund Freud University Berlin. Their thoughtful critiques strengthened the contributions in this volume.

Finally, I want to acknowledge the clients, participants, and communities whose lived experiences form the foundation of much of the research in this book. Their perspectives, too often marginalised in mainstream psychology, are central to reimagining the field in more inclusive and equitable ways.

CLOSING

This volume is both a critique and an invitation. It critiques the ways Clinical Psychology has too often neglected culture, politics, and identity. It also invites readers – whether researchers, practitioners, or students-to envision a dynamic discipline that is globally relevant, locally grounded, and ethically engaged. My hope is that these chapters will spark dialogue, unsettle assumptions, and inspire practices that honour the plurality of human experience. Clinical Psychology will only thrive when it embraces culture not as context but as core to the study of mental health.

REFERENCES

Dudgeon, P., Milroy, H., & Walker, R. (Eds.). (2014). *Working together: Aboriginal and Torres Strait Islander mental health and wellbeing principles and practice* (2nd ed.). Commonwealth of Australia.

Fernando, S. (2017). *Institutional racism in psychiatry and clinical psychology: Race matters in mental health.* Palgrave Macmillan. https://doi.org/10.1007/978-3-319-62728-1

Henrich, J., Heine, S. J., & Norenzayan, A. (2010). The weirdest people in the world?. *Behavioral and Brain Sciences, 33*(2–3), 61–135. https://doi.org/10.1017/S0140525X0999152X

Patel, V., Saxena, S., Lund, C., Thornicroft, G., Baingana, F., Bolton, P., Chisholm, D., Collins, P. Y., Cooper, J., Eaton, J., Herrman, H., Herzallah, M. M., Huang, Y., Jordans, M., Kleinman, A., Medina-Mora, M. E., Morgan, E., Niaz, U., Omigbodun, O., ... Unutzer, J. (2018). The Lancet Commission on global mental health and sustainable development. *The Lancet, 392*(10157), 1553–1598. https://doi.org/10.1016/S0140-6736(18)31612-X

Summerfield, D. (2008). How scientifically valid is the knowledge base of global mental health? *BMJ, 336*(7651), 992–994. https://doi.org/10.1136/bmj.39513.441030.AD

CHAPTER 1

CULTURE AND THE SUFFERING PSYCHE: A VIEW FROM CULTURAL AND POSTCOLONIAL PSYCHOLOGY

Pradeep Chakkarath
International Psychoanalytic University, Germany

ABSTRACT

In this chapter, I will explore, from a cultural psychological and postcolonial perspective, the practices and sociohistorical contexts through which basic and applied disciplines concerned with the study and treatment of the human psyche have developed concepts such as madness, mental or nervous illness, mental or psychiatric disorder, neurosis, or culture-bound syndromes. To this end, I will first distinguish between the cultural psychological perspective and perspectives that dominate the mainstream of the so-called 'psy disciplines.' I will then present Foucault's discourse-theoretical analysis of the intellectual fabrication of 'madness' and the emergence of therapeutic treatments and institutions as an approach that in many respects corresponds with cultural psychological views and interests. This will be followed by a short account of Freud's view of culture as a source of mental illness—a view that, according to Foucault and others, represented the most powerful discourse on this topic in the 20th century. I will then show that many of the current core issues related to this topic originated in the context of colonialism and within the practices that constituted it. Finally, I will encourage the psychological and therapeutic

Cultural Psychology in Clinical Research and Practices, pages 1–26

Published under exclusive licence by Emerald Publishing Limited
doi:10.1108/978-1-83742-213-520261001

sciences to come to terms with their problematic role in these contexts and to contribute to their own decolonisation.

Keywords: Cultural psychology; postcolonial psychology; indigenous psychology; psychoanalysis; suffering; mental health discourse

INTRODUCTION: TWO DIFFERENT VIEWS OF HUMANS AND THEIR PSYCHE

In the field of biosystematics, humans are classified as creatures of nature and products of evolution, and their relationship to other animals, especially primates, is investigated with respect to biological characteristics (e.g., anatomy, physiology, physical maturation) as well as basic behaviours. At least since Darwin's work on the origin of species, this biological classification of humans has had a great influence on modern psychology. The 19th-century founders of academic psychology—fascinated by the scientific paradigm of Newton's physics, its reductionist machine and calculation models, not to mention their predictive power—endeavoured to use the methods of physics and physiology in their own research. Thus, psychophysics, an apparatus-supported laboratory and experimental psychology became formative characteristics of the newly established discipline. This approach required that the human subjects under investigation be studied the same way physicists studied celestial bodies and elementary particles, i.e., as objects. This reductionist view of the human being has largely been preserved: Even today, many psychological subdisciplines focus on stimulus-response patterns, condition-effect relationships, biologistic explanatory models of neuropsychology while applying perspectives borrowed from computer science. The adoption of the scientific paradigm had similar effects on psychiatry, which derived its causal explanations for mental disorders from pathological-anatomical and physiological bases and thereby reduced most psychiatric research to physical sciences. It is certainly no coincidence that psychophysics, with its interest in the relationship between the physical world and measurable sensory representations thereof, is often considered the origin of modern neuroscience. Moreover, psychophysics not only had an enormous influence on academically institutionalised psychology, but also on many of the research programs Foucault called 'psy disciplines', including psychiatry and psychoanalysis (Makari, 2008; Rose, 1996).

Although it can hardly be doubted that this view has had a lasting influence on most of psychology up to the present day, in the 19th century, when it was established, there was already an alternative, but effectively ignored view. It was formulated by Giambattista Vico, Wilhelm von

Humboldt, Johann G. Herder, Johann F. Herbart, and others, including earlier predecessors (Chakkarath, 2003; Jahoda, 1993, 2011). Initially, it gained its greatest visibility in the interdisciplinary 'Zeitschrift für Völkerpsychologie und Sprachwissenschaft' ['Journal of Folk Psychology and Linguistics'], a short-lived journal founded by Moritz Lazarus and Heymann Steinthal in 1860. One of their aims was to trigger a socio-historical and linguistic turn in psychology. This was to correspond to their view of humans as beings who are not only products of nature, but also of culture, and who create and constantly modify the cultural webs in which they are living by using material *and* mental tools (Lazarus & Steinthal, 1860). Remarkably, Wilhelm Wundt, nowadays considered the 'father of experimental psychology,' was to become the most prominent representative of this alternative view because of his conviction that laboratory experiments alone do not do justice to the historical and sociocultural reality of human life. According to Wundt, to attain an understanding of the object of its research, psychology as a discipline needed to position itself as a 'dual' science between the natural sciences and the humanities with respect to content and methodology. Only then would it be able to understand psychic phenomena not only in their present manifestations, but also in the broader context of their cultural-historical development and the role of the cultural complex in humans' mental and material articulations. Consequently, psychology as a discipline would have to supplement its natural science repertoire with interpretative, hermeneutical procedures and information provided by disciplines like social anthropology and ethnology (Wundt, 1916).

Time and again, the field of Völkerpsychologie ('folk psychology'), established in the 19th and early 20th century, has been viewed as the forerunner of all recent psychological undertakings that view humans not only as biosystematically classifiable natural beings, but also as cognitively, especially linguistically, highly developed and distinctively creative cultural beings who, as such, differ considerably from other beings. Any adequate approach to studying humans must therefore do justice to the particularities of this special being (Tomasello, 2019). At the beginning of the 20th century, this insight was captured by psychiatrist and philosopher Karl Jaspers when he wrote that, whenever the object we study is the human being and not the human being as a species of animal, we come to understand that psychopathology cannot be seen as a mere branch of biology, but needs to consider itself part of the humanities, too (Jaspers, 1963/1913).

However, even though some psychological approaches now pay more attention to interdisciplinary perspectives as opposed to narrow natural science perspectives, these differences between the two paradigms outlined above still show up between so-called *culture-sensitive, culture-informed* and *culture-integrative* approaches.

A CULTURAL PSYCHOLOGICAL CONCEPTION OF CULTURE AND PSYCHE

The different approaches, internationally sometimes referred to under the collective term 'culture-inclusive psychology', are disciplines such as psychological anthropology, cross-cultural psychology, intercultural psychology, transcultural psychology, cultural-historical psychology, postcolonial psychology, indigenous psychology, and cultural psychology.[1] All these approaches aim—in their very own ways and to varying degrees—to revise internationally established psychological theories, which are highly influential for a variety of reasons, on the basis of intercultural competence, critical reflection on their inherent Euro- and Americentrism, and the academic cultivation of cultural humility. Without delving deeper into the methodological differences between and similarities of these approaches, and before focussing specifically on the cultural psychological perspective, I will just name two key differences between cross-cultural and cultural psychology:

a. the way in which they conceptualise the relationship between humans and culture, and
b. the extent to which they—dependent on these conceptualizations—move away from the natural science paradigm to perspectives taken in the humanities and social sciences to study psychological phenomena.

These differences refer particularly to the distinction between two methodological perspectives: cultural psychology—at least in its European variant—has a primarily ideographic and qualitative orientation, while cross-cultural psychology, which is Anglo-Saxon in origin, operates primarily nomothetically and quantitatively. The latter conceptualises culture as a complex set of external variables (e.g., social preferences for certain norms and standards of 'normality', self-concepts, societal orientations such as individualism or collectivism, rules of emotional expression, educational goals) that, to a certain extent, affect individuals from the outside and stimulate certain psychological processes on the inside. Cross-cultural psychologists assume that internal phenomena can be adequately measured by means of tests and/or behavioural observations to create datasets on the basis of which hypotheses are tested using various statistical tools. In order to subject results and theories to a supposedly even tougher test and thus to better argue for their universal validity (keyword 'psychic unity of humankind'), individuals from different countries or different ethnic groups are compared to each other. Here, 'culture-inclusive' essentially means that cultural phenomena are taken into account in psychological research, but mostly within a methodological paradigm borrowed from the natural sciences.

In contrast, cultural psychology does not conceive of culture as an external set of variables independent of human beings, but rather as an integral and co-constitutive component of the human psyche. Here, 'culture-inclusive' refers to a conception that is sometimes characterised by the phrase 'culture in mind' (Cole, 2003; Valsiner, 2007). It owes much to Max Weber's (1904/2012) sociological expansion of the concept of culture and its more recent reception, for example, by Clifford Geertz (1973), who spoke of culture as a semiotic web of meaning. Although it would be misleading to portray cultural psychology as a unified research field with widespread agreement on theories and methods, in the following, I will identify several commonalities of different cultural psychological perspectives to describe a theoretical and methodological framework within which cultural psychology has moved in recent decades (for a more detailed description, see Chakkarath & Straub, 2020).

All psychological phenomena are intrinsically and interdependently related to cultural contexts, ways of life, language games, and discourses. Cultures are to be understood as practical systems of signs, symbols, knowledge, beliefs, and attitudes inherent in action, inaction and omission. These systems enable humans, for example, to give meaning and significance to their world, to history, to themselves, to what they consider their own or view as foreign, to this world and the hereafter, to good and evil, life and death, nature and culture, the normal and abnormal. When people think, feel, hope, despair, judge, acknowledge, love, betray, despise, accuse, defend themselves, lie, hate, forgive, suffer, get angry, etc., they do and experience this in a corresponding network of culturally woven and interconnected supplies of interpretation, meaning and understanding.

With regard to the role of these systems in the human ability to act in a structured and purposeful way, culture can also be described as a field of action (Boesch, 1991). As such, culture—through its orientation systems—opens up possibilities for action, but it also draws normative (e.g., moral) boundaries that are difficult to overcome. Culture induces actions, but also regulates and controls them, just as it structures perceptions, intuitions, anticipations and emotions that initiate and accompany our actions. Since people constantly move between various fields of action, culture is both a structure and a process.[2]

Cultural change may also be continuous, but that does not mean the cultural network of meaning can be shaken off or completely replaced, not even after one leaves it voluntarily (or involuntarily) and becomes acquainted with a 'foreign culture'. Only against the backdrop of a familiar culture does the unfamiliar seem foreign, the supposedly disordered chaotic; only against the background of the familiar does the unfamiliar become a challenge. Belonging to several cultures at once is not only possible, but rather common, especially since most societies are culturally quite differentiated and may become even more diverse due to comprehensive globalisation and migration processes.

Cultures thus fulfil manifold and complex orientation functions for subjects who are able to act on the basis of their physical, linguistic, emotional and cognitive endowment and need cultural orientation to find their way through highly complex, often overlapping and permanently changing human life worlds.

The cultural psychological understanding of human beings and culture outlined here implies at least two things:

1. Psychological research that focuses on the human being in his or her indissoluble connectedness with his or her natural environment must be conceived as an interpretative science or as a cultural science within the humanities, and consequently as an interdisciplinary psychology. Since humans—together with their practices and ways of experiencing—are integrated, occasionally even 'entangled', in historically grown and socio-culturally transmitted systems of symbols, knowledge and interpretation, diverse narratives and discourses, a predominantly qualitative, reconstructive and interpretative repertoire of methods is required for the investigation and analysis of these connections. These include autobiographical-narrative interviews, group discussions, participatory field research, ethnographic approaches, and various procedures of text, discourse, image, film, and artefact analysis.
2. Cultural psychology also aims to reveal general structures and rules along which people create meaning in their cultural life worlds (Bruner, 1993). It sees these general facets, for example, in the universal significance that culture has for the genuinely human. However, unlike cross-cultural psychology, for example, it is not methodologically bound to pursue claims of universality. Unlike cross-cultural psychology, it gives importance to varying images of humankind, including human ethnicity, sex and gender, youth and age, body and mind, health and illness. Above all, cultural psychology is interested in investigating the psychological role of languages, language games, modes of communication, thinking styles, time concepts, world views, and associated problems of translation, interpretation, and explanation. Thus, it views the assumption of a 'psychic unity of humankind' as too presuppositional and as resting upon inappropriately simplistic conceptions of humans and culture and a correspondingly reductionist methodology. Instead, cultural psychologists assume that there is 'unity in diversity'. Thus, from a cultural psychologist's

perspective, deviations from the norm are likely to be found universally in all cultures and societies, and it would be quite surprizing if what was considered normal (or deviant, respectively) in one culture or society was widely considered normal (or deviant, respectively) everywhere. As for the connection between culture and disease, cultural psychologists assume that the ways in which individuals suffer and become ill from their culture may well be similar sometimes, but that culture-specific paths to suffering and even so-called culture-bound syndromes may also develop.[3] Moreover, a cultural psychological perspective assumes that where there is talk of human psychological suffering, this talk as well as the suffering itself is deeply embedded in culture as a practical system of signs, symbols, knowledge, beliefs, interpretations, and attitudes. Furthermore, it assumes that these complex interrelationships cannot be adequately understood if we pursue them exclusively using methods of biology and neurology.

The following critical statement made by a group of psychiatrists on the current state of their discipline, published in an editorial in the *British Journal of Psychiatry*, may help to clarify the standpoint that I will take on this subject in the subsequent sections:

> Psychiatry is not neurology; it is not a medicine of the brain. Although mental health problems undoubtedly have a biological dimension, in their very nature they reach beyond the brain to involve social, cultural and psychological dimensions. These cannot always be grasped through the epistemology of biomedicine. The mental life of humans is discursive in nature. (Bracken et al., 2012, p. 432)

CULTURE AND SUFFERING

Foucault on Discourses and the Creation of Mental Maladies

Physical and psychological suffering have been conspicuously important (Porter, 2002) themes of human reflection since the earliest documents were written. In the ancient tragedies and epics, philosophical, religious, and historical treatises, the most diverse works of art, in jurisprudence, anthropology, medicine, psychiatry, and psychotherapy, human suffering and reflections on how to alleviate or even overcome pain, misery, unhappiness and other sorts of suffering have always been central themes. In all societies, suffering has played a key role in shaping individual and collective memory, and hardly anything has left more discursive and hurtful traces than the experience of events that have caused great misery. Suffering is a theme that has mercilessly and violently carved itself into the cultural fabric of societies and individuals. This metaphorical way of imagining culture as something that physically engraves itself into one's flesh incorporates an idea that reflected a quasitechnical conception of the mind well before the emergence of modern psychophysics. Aristotle compared the mind to a 'boatsman' who navigates the psychophysical vessel across the sea. Plato and other ancient thinkers described memory as analogous to a 'wax tablet' into which experiences are etched, but in which they also become obscured over time. Descartes, comparing the development of psychological sensations to processes set in motion by the interplay of parts of a clock, proposed the idea of 'mind-body machines'. Finally, Freud, who revisited Plato's metaphor with his 'mystic writing pad' as well and proposed the 'hydraulic model' of the psyche, found that the condensation of dreams results in images resembling those created by copying the prints from photographic plates over each other. He also illustrated the subtle communication between the psychoanalyst's and the patient's unconscious by using the analogy of the telephone. More recently, psychologists have adopted cybernetic models to describe psychological thinking using technology-based metaphors. The mechanistic conception of mind and soul has also become deeply ingrained in our everyday language, for example, when we find that our mind is not 'functioning properly'. These are just a few examples of how historically and socio-culturally evolved interpretations, illustrations and associated ways of speaking are incorporated into the fabric we have previously described as culture. Taken as a whole, they are important aspects of discourse, which in turn are important struts in the scaffolding of any culture. The concept of discourse is certainly one of the most popular concepts in modern social and cultural sciences, which has also led to different uses not only in philosophy and science, but also in everyday language. Even Michel Foucault, who initiated the academic triumph of the concept, did not present a consistent definition of 'discourse'. However, it is possible to convey the extent to which the concept has an analytical potential related to the cultural psychological perspective introduced above. There is another good reason to point out the role that culturally deeply rooted discourses play in our context of discussion: Foucault's discourse- and cultural-theoretical perspective on the history of the assessment and treatment of mental illness has greatly contributed to the critical self-evaluation of clinical psychologists, psychiatrists, and psychotherapists that led to institutional reforms in Europe since the 1970s.

Generally speaking, a 'discourse' is a set of statements and assumptions, descriptions, problematisations, and judgements. Discourses determine ways of speaking and thinking that are available to people during a certain historical period, but which also change and generate follow-up discourses that can intertwine with other discourses and thus form communicative webs on which our thinking and speaking depend, but from which they can also hardly free themselves. Discourses are filters of what can be said, how things should be said, what should not be said, who may say something and who may not. They thereby cause and represent power effects in social relations and practice. To make this point clearer, Foucault borrows from Saussure, who noted that language, as a system of arbitrary signs, does not represent an objective or subjective mental reality, but creates and organizes reality according to its own rules. Accordingly, Foucault emphasised that one of the most lasting effects of discourses is that they systematically form the objects of which they speak and thus anchor themselves in the cultural fabric of human communication, thought, and knowledge (Foucault, 1966/2001). His distinction between discursive and nondiscursive practices is central here: 'Discursive practices' are conveyed through linguistic content, structures, styles, and so-called foundational texts; 'nondiscursive practices' show up in actions, techniques, technologies, architecture, and institutions. Foucault called both forms 'practices', since they cooperatively structure and generate human experience, attitudes, convictions, and behaviour as well as the various societal arenas or action fields in which they appear. Analysing discourses resembles the work of an archaeologist trying to uncover the buried discourses of past times and to discover layers that allow him to observe the genesis, fate, and sometimes longevity of certain discourses.

This brief list of key features of a discourse should sufficiently sketch how discourse creates an epistemic reality and thus can be used as a technique of control and discipline, that is, as a strategy of homogenising, standardising, and normalising, especially by those who are ascribed a powerful position in and through the discourse. Anything that does not conform to the basic propositions of the ruling discourse is branded as deviant. In his dissertation, 'Madness and Civilization' (1961/2001), Foucault began to demonstrate the discursive practices of exclusion. There, he examined the different ways in which societies have dealt with madness over history, especially in Europe and particularly from the 15th to the end of the 18th century. Drawing on a large number of historical documents, he began by describing how the late mediaeval treatment of lepers and fools became a model for the treatment of people suffering from so-called madness. While these groups were considered different, but still accepted and integrated by others in the 15th and 16th centuries, this changed in the transition from the 16th to the 17th century. First, the topic of madness largely disappeared from dominant social discourses, until the 'mad' were finally imprisoned and thus excluded not only from texts, but also from public life. In the 18th century, the age of 'enlightenment and reason', the imprisonment of the insane was considered inhumane, on the one hand, but, on the other hand, in the newly emerged discourse on reason, their insanity was considered the inability to reason and therefore a severe disease requiring healing. This reoriented discourse, which distinguished between madness and reason, resulted in the birth of psychiatry and psychotherapies along with the facilities in which patients encountered professional healers. This example of the definitional and institutional power of discourse also exemplifies how culturally embedded discursive practices in interplay with non-discursive practices can lead to the materialisation of the main tenets of a discourse in the form of prisons or mental health facilities.

Against this background, Foucault was also sceptical of the conventional historiography that exalted psychiatric reformers such as Philippe Pinel in France or Samuel Tuke in England to liberators of the insane. In Foucault's view, their methods were still aimed at exerting control over the abnormal. Both Tuke's relocation of the insane to the countryside and Pinel's conditioning-based therapies were aimed at punishing the insane, making them socially compliant, subjecting them to the prevailing moral standards and bringing about their economically desirable reintegration into the working world (Porter, 2002).

In his lectures on 'Psychiatric powers', held in the early 1970s, Foucault continued to show how the category of 'mental illness' emerged as a specific form of knowledge in the course of the profound standardisation of individuals in modern psychiatric practice. Interestingly, Foucault considered the forms of treatment in 19th-century psychiatry (e.g., administration of drugs, aversion therapies, hypnosis, and anamnestic interviews) violent methods of generating knowledge about the mentally ill. He regarded anamnestic interviews as a discursive continuation of ecclesiastical and legal confession practices that helped establish mental illness as a disease and the psychiatrists and therapists as experts in the discourse on the sufferings of the psyche.

Foucault criticised the conceptual juxtaposition fundamental to the theoretical perspectives and therapeutic practices of psychiatric and psychotherapeutic care: the supposedly obvious, natural, and universally applied distinction between sanity and insanity or—in terms characteristic of contemporary discourse—the conceptual distinction between mental health on the one hand and mental disorder, mental illness, or distress on the other. In Foucault's view, a discourse analysis of the history of madness shows that, since the emergence of occidental rationality in the early modern period, it has had an exclusionary and repressive function. For Foucault, a culture is defined in particular by the delineation of cultural boundaries and the rejection of what lies outside them. Thus, for him, dealing with madness, as well as the cognitive and practical handling of sexuality or delinquency, crime and punishment, are illuminating examples of how culture, society, and individuals make each other up and how one can also suffer from this entanglement.[4]

The methodological proximity to Sigmund Freud's conception of psychoanalysis as an archaeological endeavour was already discernible in Foucault's conception of discourse analysis as an archaeology of knowledge.

Indeed, Foucault's interest in psychoanalysis is evident in many of his major works. In 'Madness and Civilization', for example, he noted that all 19th-century psychiatry converged on Freud. In 'The Order of Things' (1966), Foucault claimed that all the knowledge within which Western culture had formed a certain image of man in one century revolved around Freud's work. He thus maintained that the discourse initiated by Freud was one of the most powerful discourses on the human psyche of the 20th century.

Freud's 'Uneasiness' With Culture

When, in the 19th century, the European social sciences like sociology, social anthropology, and psychology began to form at Western universities, social scientists already showed a pronounced interest in the subject of 'culture,' in the method of cross-cultural comparison, and in the topic of culture and health (for an overview, see Quah, 2010). In his foundational 'Rules of Sociological Method' (1895), Émile Durkheim, for example, instructed future social and cultural sciences to include the comparison of several societies in their analyses. He viewed the investigation of social facts, i.e., socially crystallised institutions along with the social and moral norms they mediate, as a key task of the social sciences, since social facts were to be seen as representations of society in the mind of the individual and thus tell us something about how the individual feels in society and culture. He assumed that ambiguities and intransparencies regarding social facts lead to a state of anomie in which individuals become psychologically confused about social and moral norms, a state which can result in deviant behaviour and even suicide. This interest in the psychological concomitants of the relationship between individual and culture can also be found in Wilhelm Wundt's 'Völkerpsychologie', Max Weber's comparative studies of world religions, Georg Simmel's reflections on the emergence and effects of a 'cultural spirit' (Zeitgeist), and continues in contemporary sociology, social anthropology, and culturally sensitive approaches within psychology. Although the subject matter had been discussed since the mid-19th century, it was another figure of the modern age who left a more lasting mark on the discourse concerning the connection between psyche and culture than anyone before him.

At the beginning of the 20th century, it was in particular Sigmund Freud who diagnosed a pathological connection between culture and the psychological condition of the individual (Freud, 1913). In one of his most-read books, 'Civilization and its Discontents' (1930a), but also in various other works, Freud expressed his conviction that culture makes us feel uncomfortable and in the long run even mentally ill. This assumption served as a breeding ground for a psychologically oriented and pessimistic analysis of society, which has had an influence on many other sceptical diagnoses of the present and on gloomy visions of the future.[5]

It should not matter that Freud did not present a unified and authoritative conception of culture over the decades of his thinking. It is sufficient to note that his respective conceptions were largely based on social-Darwinistic, anthropological and ethnological concepts of culture of his time. Simplistically, but sufficiently for our purposes, we can say that Freud understood culture—like dreams and symptoms of an illness—as expressions of drives in conflict with each other and with society. He did not doubt that cultural achievements such as religion, art, and science each have their own functions, some pathological and some useful, but he emphasised that culture essentially emerges from sexual or aggressive impulses that are denied immediate gratification. To Freud's understanding, culture requires the individual to repress and control his drives based on the *superego,* which along with the *ego* and the *id,* is one of the three instances in Freud's structural model of the human psyche. The concept of the superego refers to that part of the psychic structure in which social norms, values, obedience, restraint, and taboos are located, and which acts as the moral command-and-prohibition instance of conscience. To a fair extent, the superego's facets can be understood as culturally deeply rooted and individually internalized rules. These rules are mediated through upbringing by various educators and caregivers, first and foremost the parents, with the symbolic internalisation of the father figure serving as a formative pattern of the inner moral instance. Through these channels, culture demands that individuals suppress their urges, especially sexuality and aggression. With the help of the superego—the moral authority within—individuals direct their aggression against themselves and thereby exercise control over their psyche. At the same time, this culturally imposed repression makes them unhappy and neurotic. In principle, Freud had outlined these ideas before, in 1908, in an essay on '"Civilised" sexual morality and modern nervous illness'. Like Durkheim, he points out that cultural rules, if their meaning and usefulness is not clear to individuals, can foster the development of nervousness, neurosis, perversion, suffering from marriage, sexual inhibition, impotence, and frigidity. Fear of life and fear of death can also result.

An important component of his analyses is a sharp critique of religion (Freud, 1961/1927), in which the avowed atheist Freud assigned religion—as one of the most momentous cultural inventions in human history—a leading role among the pathogenic instances of culture. He developed one of his main arguments through a distinction whose origin Foucault identifies in the 18th century, the century of Enlightenment, namely, the opposition of reason and unreason (see above). According to Freud, religion owes its superior position in the history of ideas to its supposed ability to give life a higher meaning. It exerts, however, an exceedingly harmful influence on the individual as well as on social groups and the entire course of culture by restricting the freedom and development of reason. For the individual, the religious prohibition of the freedom of thought thus entails a neurotising influence, in a historical perspective a serious danger for the future of mankind. His aversion to the unreasonableness of religion corresponds, however, to the hope that Freud associates with science, the guardian of reason. In this respect, Freud's thinking shows the aftermath of historical models such as those left by Hegel and Comte, among others, which reconstruct the development of reason and rationality as a liberation from previous stages of magic and religion. For him, only science, of all cultural institutions and achievements, holds the utopian promise that a cultural level can be reached that is largely freed from neurotic mechanisms. This would be a culture in which the peaceful coexistence of all people is guaranteed and a system of norms and rules is created that avoids any unnecessary repression. In such a culture, people are forced to renounce their instincts and control their emotions only insofar as it is necessary for the maintenance of peaceful coexistence.

It is characteristic of Freud's psychoanalytic view of the individual's suffering from culture that he, as other thinkers before him, viewed the human being as a seeker of happiness, but as one whose lasting happiness is not contained in the plan of creation and who, on the contrary, is continually confronted with unhappiness and threatened by suffering (Freud, 1930). This means that all hope for lasting happiness is based on delusion and humans are bound to be disappointed again and again. Since humans are virtually driven to strive for happiness, their almost unswerving belief that it can be reached is due to their susceptibility to self-delusion and wishful thinking. According to Freud, the truth is that suffering is unavoidable and springs from various sources, most notably the ageing and increasing frailty of our pain-prone bodies, the relentless and destructive blows of fate from the forces of nature, and the often stressful relationships with our fellow human beings. The actual psychological source is the last one and stems from culture: Stresses that come upon us through our social relationships and the socio-cultural rules that govern them.

As stated earlier, Freud's theory on the relationship between culture and the mental constitution of the human being is one of many theories that have addressed this topic since the emergence of modern social and cultural sciences in the mid-19th century. Despite the brevity of the presentation offered here, it should be apparent that Freud's reflections at least partially show similarities to the reflections of other authors. This is due not least to the fact that Freud's interest in cultural and individual development also reflected a Zeitgeist that had its sociohistorical and political roots (Warwick et al., 2011). The striking European interest in culture arose to a certain extent from a psychological need on the part of many still young Western nations to establish their own supposedly superior cultural, political, and national identity by distinguishing themselves from the rest of the world. This need was also driven by the feeling that Europe in particular had become the centre of the world and of world history thanks to the colonisation of more and more overseas territories. This brings us to a cultural-historical theme that has provided a central framework for relations between the so-called West and the rest of the world, as well as for interpersonal relations, over the past few centuries. It is also a contextual framework that has played a major role in the development of the psychological sciences and the images of the human being that they have developed.

The Colonisation of the Psyche: How Politics and Science Construed the 'Others' and Made Them Sick

The concept of 'colonialism' is fuzzy and controversial given its multiple historical manifestations and due to the overlap with other historical key concepts like 'imperialism'. For the purposes of this chapter, however, it will suffice to distinguish between concepts like 'colonisation', 'colony', and 'colonialism' (cf. Osterhammel, 2005): 'Colonisation' refers to a process of appropriating land. 'Colony' refers to a particular form of political, economical, and social association of persons that usually develops in the course of colonisation. 'Colonialism' primarily refers to the intentional construction and maintenance of a very specific relationship of domination. Although all three terms refer to processes in human history that can be traced back to earliest times, colonialism, as a specific and largely imposed relationship of domination, animated by a very specific ideology, is commonly associated with the European expansion over the rest of the world—a process that began at the end of the 15th century and lasted at least for about 500 years. That being said, the political and ideological features of colonialism, along with its economic, sociocultural, and psychological consequences also characterise imperialist expansions by nonWestern powers, e.g., Japan, the Ottoman Empire, and China. The specific colonialist relationship of domination and its underlying ideology of justification was borne by a very specific *colonial spirit*, which can be summarised as follows: Colonialism is a relationship between collectives in which the way of life of the colonised is regulated by colonial masters who are culturally different and who show little willingness to adapt to the foreign culture (Osterhammel, 2005). This is usually associated with missionary justification doctrines based on the colonial masters' conviction that they are cognitively, emotionally, and dispositionally superior to the colonised and that their Western culture is more developed than that of nonwesterners. It should come as no surprize that the gap purposefully created here between the advanced West and the stagnating rest of the world was accompanied by a disparagement of the physical appearance and mental abilities of the colonised. This colonial spirit was by no means purely power-political in nature, but an expression of a centuries-old mindset that served the colonisers' material and psychological self-interests and spread to almost all areas of life in the Western world, including the sciences of the human psyche, which helped to keep the colonial spirit alive. Two examples will suffice to illustrate core elements of this mindset.

In the *Encyclopaedia Britannica* of 1798, one of the leading sources of the knowledge of the time and place, under the newly included entry 'Negro', we find a characterisation representative of a colonialist and racist perspective on Africans (and a Western perspective on the self and the other) as documented in countless other texts:

> [...] ugliness and irregularity of shape characterised their external appearance [...] Vices the most notorious seem to be the portion of this unhappy race; idleness, treachery, revenge, cruelty, impudence, stealing, lying, profanity, debauchery, nastiness and intemperance are said to have extinguished the principles of natural law, and to have silenced the reproofs of conscience. They are strangers to every sentiment of compassion, and are an awful example of the corruption of man when left to himself. (cited in Ishay, 2008, p. 113)

Moreover, leading scholars of the so-called Enlightenment, such as Linnaeus, Buffon, Locke, Hobbes, Voltaire, Hume, Kant, Forster, Meiners, Blumenbach, and Hegel, spearheaded European discourse about dark-skinned people, degrading them to biologically and mentally retarded specimens of the human genus or to creatures of another world (Park, 2013). In doing so, they gave welcome intellectual legitimacy to colonialist, and often even violent, 'educational' measures. This affected not only Black Africans but anyone who was not considered 'white'. Since the 1800s, for instance, French doctors attributed the criminal behaviour of indigenous people in French North Africa to their ethnicity and the climate's influence on cognitive impairment. As Keller (2007) demonstrates, until the 1930s, North African Muslims were widely regarded as inherently violent, sexually fixated, irrational, superstitious, morally deficient, and dangerous to society. Even in the 1950s, French hospitals and research centres in North Africa were renowned internationally for their contributions to so-called colonial psychiatry. However, racist assumptions about the alleged inferiority of the local population remained fundamental there. Thus, psychiatry continued serving as an instrument for maintaining colonial control by portraying the local mentality as pathological. Many psychiatrists upheld the racist foundations of colonialism, even though biological racism was increasingly joined by cultural racism. The idea that cultural traditions prevent North Africans and other nonEuropeans from successfully integrating into European civilization remains an influential concept among Western politicians to this day. We will see that this concept has not entirely disappeared from Western science either.

Another example paradigmatic of the colonial spirit is the famous devaluation of nonWestern intellectuality and knowledge by the British parliamentarian Thomas Babington Macaulay. In his recommendations for a more effective arrangement of colonial rule over India, Macaulay developed a plan for clearing the clouded minds of the colonised subjects with the enlightened minds of their colonial masters. After claiming that 'all the historical information which has been collected from all the books written in the Sanskrit language is less valuable than what may be found in the most paltry abridgements used at preparatory schools in England' (Macaulay, 1835/1935, p. 359), he enfolds his vision for the future:

> We must at present do our best to form a class who may be interpreters between us and the millions whom we govern; a class of persons, Indian in blood and colour, but English in taste, in opinions, in morals, and in intellect. To that class we may leave it to refine the vernacular dialects of the country, to enrich those dialects with terms of science borrowed from the Western nomenclature, and to render them by degrees fit vehicles for conveying knowledge to the great mass of the population.

With a seemingly generous attitude, Macaulay expressed what was characteristic of the colonial spirit and ideally suited to sell it as a charitable mission: A central and almost missionary task of colonialism consisted in 'normalising' the others according to Western standards of mental normalcy by subjecting the colonised to a kind of brainwashing for their own good and, of course, for the benefit of the colonial power. In the vocabulary of postcolonial critique, such colonialist conduct is termed 'epistemic violence' (Spivak, 1988). The effects of such conduct are strikingly apparent even in today's neocolonialist era and a vivid reminder of how colonialism pursued not only the settlement and exploitation of geographic territories, but also the colonisation of the mind. As mentioned earlier, from a cultural-psychological perspective, the colonialist practice of replacing the languages of the colonised with those of the colonisers is not trivial, but rather a drastic intervention in the cognitive system of the colonised individuals' world appropriation and the formation of meaning, which is largely linguistically constituted. The explicit focus on refining the country's vernacular dialects and 'enriching them with scientific terms borrowed from Western nomenclature' has led to the gradual disappearance of competing scientific languages as well as the concepts and the knowledge traditions rooted in them. This naturally includes nonWestern views on human suffering, physical and mental illnesses, and methods of therapy.

These brief notes on the colonialist spirit point to some of its most important discursive elements: the supposedly almost unbridgeable differences between colonialists and the colonised; the supposed mental deficits of nonwhites; the supposed universal superiority of Western (and uselessness of others') knowledge systems; the white member of the enlightened Western culture as the gold standard for judging the physical and psychological qualities of dark-skinned people and their educability. These elements served the justification of an asymmetrical power structure and the West's claim to hegemony over others. As indicated above, these elements of the colonialist spirit also found their way into psychiatry and the clinical psychological disciplines, which in turn further promoted it.

In 'The question of lay analysis' (1926), Freud maintained that we know less about little girls' sexual life than of little boys'—and that the adult females' sexual life is also a 'dark continent' yet to be explored by psychology.[6] By using the English term 'dark continent', Freud took up a characterisation of Africa established especially by Victorian authors like the colonial administrator Henry Morton Stanley. Africa was the continent that the Europeans, who were eager to conquer it, regarded as still completely unaware of the light of the Enlightenment, therefore dark, ignorant—and dangerous due to the uncivilised psyche of its peoples. The fact that Freud resorted to colonialist stance and parlance to describe the status quo of psychological research into female sexuality has not gone unnoticed, especially by feminist critics of psychoanalysis. At intersections at which feminist, gender-theoretical, and postcolonialist perspectives meet and constructively complement each other, several authors have recently pointed out that an entanglement of concepts like 'femininity', 'primitivity', 'retardedness', skin-colour constructs like 'white/bright', 'black/dark', and 'race' can be traced again and again back to psychological, including psychiatric and psychoanalytic, statements (e.g., see Brickman, 2003; Doane, 1999, Khanna, 2003). Through attentive reading and interpretation, to which psychoanalysis has inspired even its critics, this entanglement can also be found in Freud's writings: The psyche of women apparently was as enigmatically dark and inaccessible to men's psychological urge for knowledge as African territories were to Europeans' urge for conquest. Moreover, compared to the development from boy to man, the development from girl to woman is, according to Freud, rather insignificant. In this regard, he claimed, it resembles the developmental psychological limitations of the 'primitives' about whom Freud and other psychological theorists of his time—informed by contemporary sociobiology, anthropology, and ethnology—repeatedly wrote and whom they frequently characterised as infantile and neurotic. As Brickman (2003) pointed out, the formation of the psychoanalytic subject requires the continuous psychological exclusion of qualities associated with primitivity and femininity, which are then projected onto subordinate people like the colonised peoples in Africa, Asia, and the Americas. Their psychological makeup is conceived of as a natural and almost museum-like exemplification of these very qualities, enabling the superior peoples and their soul-searchers to conquer dark continents and dig into the dark past of humanity, or—as Freud, the believer in stage models of human and cultural development, wrote in a letter to Romain Rolland in 1930—to engage in 'an embryology of the soul' (Freud, 1930b, p. 393).

In the same letter and with regard to Indian philosophy and spirituality, Freud also asserted that the European terrain was closer to him than nonEuropean landscapes of the soul, confessing that 'an uncertain blending of Hellenic love of proportion, Jewish sobriety, and philistine timidity' had prevented him from 'penetrating into the Indian jungle' (Freud, 1930b, p. 392). Freud's conspicuous use of sexualising language may not be mere coincidence. Descriptions of colonial entry into foreign territories as invasion, conquest, or subjugation by white colonial masters brimming with masculinity were not uncommon in Freud's day. Nor was it unusual to depict the nonwhite, subjugated men as demasculinised, feminised prey or as woman-like, in the sense of women being the weaker sex, thus sexually marking power differences (cf. Sinha, 1995). Freud had already expressed his secret admiration of the colonial-type masculine adventurer shortly after the publication of his 'Interpretation of Dreams', in which he himself, as it were, had entered new territory. In a letter to his confidant Wilhelm Fliess, written on 1 February 1900, he compared himself to a conqueror, again resorting to the vocabulary of colonial history: 'I am by temperament nothing but a conquistador, an adventurer [...] with all the curiosity, daring, and tenacity characteristic of a man of this sort' (cited in Freud, 1900/1985, p. 398).

Freud made an almost obsessive effort to characterise psychoanalysis as a terrain more or less independently explored and conquered by him alone. This resulted in his notorious difficulty accepting dissenting views from colleagues from his own European discourse environment; at best, he repressed them as hostile spin-offs. Convinced of the largely universal validity of his theory, he also held little regard for suggestions from nonEuropean critics who doubted some of the principles of psychoanalysis due to profound cultural differences in the conditions of socialisation and human relational structures in nonEuropean societies. This can be seen, for example, in the correspondence he had with Girindrasekhar Bose, the early Indian psychoanalyst who had started to discuss his own theory of repression, in which he took into account the peculiarities of Indian, especially Hindu, experience. What fascinated Freud about the Indian psychoanalyst's communications was not so much the insight into the Indian world of experience, which he found to be as unaccessible as a 'jungle', but the indication that his theory was conquering the world for him. In a letter written to Bose in December 1931, he maintained, with regard to psychoanalysis, that he will always recall 'the proud conquests it has made in foreign countries and the kind feelings for me it has aroused in some of my contemporaries at least' (cited in Ramana, 1964, p. 128).

One might consider the reverberations of 'colonial spirit' found in Freud's Eurocentric thought subtle, but his writings still bear unmistakable traces of a white conquistador's mindset. His were unquestionably not the only ones.

In 1988, an article by Farhad Dalal appeared in the *British Journal of Psychotherapy*, in which he suggested, based on a number of statements, that C. G. Jung was a colonialist racist. Indeed, Jung's publications contain many disparaging statements about nonwhite people he had encountered, especially in North America, Africa, and India (e.g., see his autobiography, Jung, 1995/1962). Although, in some writings, Jung appears to feel a certain romantic nostalgia reminiscent of Rousseau, for example, when lamenting that scientific knowledge had dehumanised the world, torn man from nature, and isolated him in the universe. Jung also appears to be well aware of the moral dubiousness of colonialism when he speaks of the true psychological nature of the West, which found its expression in eagles and other predatory animals on European coats of arms. However, other writings contain clearly disparaging passages like the following:

> Even today, the European, however highly developed, cannot live with impunity among the negroes of Africa; their psychology goes into him unnoticed and unconsciously he becomes a negro. There is no fighting against it. In Africa there is a well-known technical expression for this: 'going black.' It is no mere snobbery that the English should consider anyone born in the colonies, even though the best blood may run in his veins, 'slightly inferior.' There are facts to support this view. (Jung, 1970/1927, CW10, paragraph 249)

Occasionally, as in the foregoing passage, and surprisingly with regard to the unconscious, Jung warned the reader of the danger of 'infection' that existed for white people on the dark continent. He thereby incorporated a central theme of tropical medicine and microbiology, which in the service of colonialism endeavoured to protect colonial rulers from dangerous diseases, such as malaria and tuberculosis. This was primarily accomplished by means of human experiments on the indigenous population. Jung also spoke of layers of consciousness and understanding, of which, in his opinion, fewer could be found in black people than in white people. Statements like these can also be found among physicians—for example, Robert Koch, the famous co-founder of modern bacteriology—who tried to justify their questionable experiments with African populations in similar ways. Their animalistic 'bushman soul' moved the blacks into the proximity of animals anyway—and these, according to Jung, were 'facts'.

In 2018, frustrated that in the 21st century, and 30 years after Dalal's article was published, there had been no noteworthy debate about Jung's racist remarks and their consequences for their guild, over 30 psychologists close to Jung's Analytical Psychology published an open letter in the *British Journal of Psychotherapy* (Baird et al., 2018). The letter's authors called for a serious confrontation of psychologists, clinicians, and therapists with the consequences of the continuing colonialist spirit for their work. Dalal had warned that Jung's statements should not be dismissed as the quirky slips of a man who was just a child of his time. Rather, the fact that Jung's work links relevant statements about other cultures and ethnicities to the fundamental concepts of individuation and the collective unconscious gives cause to question how unabashedly concepts such as the collective unconscious and individuation can continue to be used without seriously questioning and examining their possible colonialist and racist roots.

The letter's authors also pointed out institutional issues that can be understood as ongoing effects of an ethnocentric and racist science of the psyche. They sought to encourage more nonwhite students, clinicians, and researchers to participate in the study of the human psyche and help promote a more sophisticated attitude towards human differences than is exhibited by the majority of white researchers who have inherited and perhaps still internalise the colonialist spirit. It was no surprize, they said, that persons of African descent and other populations who have been similarly maligned and demeaned would rarely consider training to become Jungian analysts. What was articulated in the open letter, and certainly not only addressed to Jungians, is one of the clearest moral dissociations from the colonialist spirit of psychology in the clinical field that has been heard from a larger group of its representatives in recent times. It suggests a change in perspective that stems from a desire for a psychological awakening that must be different from the programme of the European Enlightenment and its deep involvement in the colonisation of minds and the resulting traumatisation of the colonised that countless people still suffer from today.

There are many examples that illustrate how almost all elements of the 'othering' discourse of the Enlightenment and colonialism, especially distinctions along the concept of race, still play a prominent role in the natural and social sciences.[7] Continuing a tradition of psychological theorising that goes back to Western scholars such as Gustave Le Bon, Lewis Terman, Carl Brigham, Raymond Cattell, William Shockley and Arthur Jensen, Murray and Herrnstein's famous 'The Bell Curve' (1994) did not remain the last attempt to link racist psychological views with pedagogical and educational policy recommendations. In 2007, Nobel laureate James Watson made headlines with his thesis that Africans and African-Americans have a genetically determined low intelligence when compared to white people (Watson, 2007; for a defence of Watson's views, see Malloy, 2008). He also made use of another topos, that was still influential from colonial times, with his assertion that dark-skinned people also have a more pronounced and unbridled libido (Hilliard, 2012). In the racialising demarcations as well as in the psychometric and molecular biological methods on which these and similar views are based, theories and methods that had already served to legitimise racial psychiatry and therapy in the 19th and early 20th century live on in a modernised form. While this colonial mentality may help some to scientifically ground their privileged positions of knowledge and power for the purpose of self-valorisation, it imposes a colonial mentality on the 'others' that makes them not only strangely different, but also sick (see Ward, 2013). This damaging mentality was imposed by colonialism with the help of various scientists, among them many representatives from the psychological disciplines, and it has been passed on discursively over generations, and is still being internalized by countless people worldwide. It manifests itself as an internalized attitude of ethnic or cultural inferiority and as a discursively imposed and burdening urge to constantly reflect on whether the colonisers' cultural values and theories about the 'others' may perhaps be justified, since the colonisers' sciences, scientific instruments, and scientific textbooks have, after all, for several centuries provided the standard of epistemological quality against which the 'others' must now evaluate themselves. Thus, the colonial spirit has left traces of traumatisation in the colonised and their descendants, which Ashis Nandy (2009) has so aptly described as the 'intimate enemy'. That enemy is still very much alive, even though the majority of Western social scientists, including psychologists and therapists, believe it to be buried.

CONCLUDING REMARKS

The preceding examples were intended to draw attention to how a perspective on human psychological suffering that is not primarily biological, medical, or neurological can help expose the cultural conditions of what we call 'mental illness' and what is deeply embedded in a socio-historically grown system of signs, language games, knowledge, beliefs, attitudes, and human experiences. Important elements of this discursive and nondiscursive network, which was already firmly established in the 19th century, include evolutionary and social-Darwinian theories of development and recapitulation, theories of race and eugenics, sociological stage models of human development, perceptions of crises and the corresponding European fear of degeneration and doom as well as a wealth of anthropological and ethnographic reports, including travelogues, about almost inconceivably different and alien worlds with inconceivably different people. In all of these fields of the natural sciences, the humanities, and the social sciences, as well as in art and literature, notions of civilization versus primitivity and a classification and hierarchisation of people according to race, anatomy, skin colour, gender, religion, and language based on these notions played a central role. In symbiotic coexistence, the political zeitgeist in the era of colonialism promoted the implementation and popularisation of corresponding theories, while the scientific zeitgeist helped to legitimise and prolong the colonial spirit.

The effects of what I have tried to characterise as 'colonial spirit' are still evident in numerous social domains where many oppressed minorities around the world are struggling for liberation from colonially established constant states of violation. They also show up in the clinical setting, where, however, they are more palpable and significant to the patients, who suffer in one form or another from internalized colonialism and the colonial mindset, than they are to their therapists. This contributes to the general and frequently discussed problem of asymmetry of power and experience between therapist and client. If therapists wish to reduce these asymmetries, they need to consider the perspectives presented above seriously. This is especially true for a world in which the so-called 'others' no longer dwell in distant places on their 'dark continents.' The urgent need to expand therapeutic knowledge and skills in order to cater for the growing number of migrants changing familiar demographic conditions worldwide is only gradually being recognized and addressed (see, for example, Santambrogio et al., 2024).

An interdisciplinary cultural psychological perspective informed by anthropological, sociological, and postcolonial findings encourages the development of an understanding of how culture shapes illness as an experience, but also of how we conceive of illness and identify, describe, classify, and treat its various manifestations.

This perspective also encourages more attentive reflection on how the theories, procedures, and instruments of the diagnosis and treatment of mental illness continue to be situated in a highly problematic tradition in which they are shown to be a means of ongoing ethnocentric regulation and control of the 'other' that is still infused with hegemonic ambitions. As a much-discussed and much-criticised example, see for instance the controlling power emanating from the Diagnostic and Statistical Manual of Mental Disorders (DSMs) of the American Psychiatric Association (2022; see also Horwitz, 2021).

For the diversity of human being and suffering to become accessible to the therapeutic eye, the decolonisation of psychological thinking, especially where it has practical and therapeutic consequences, is imperative. This effort, which more and more authors have called for in recent times (e.g., see Beshara, 2021; Okazaki et al., 2008), involves not only recognising how colonialist the history, theories, and methods of psychology are, but also how so-called mainstream psychology continues to make alternative psychologies, so-called indigenous psychologies developed outside Western-dominated intellectual traditions, invisible in teaching, research, and writing—thereby still exercising epistemic violence instead of improving its intercultural competencies and its psychological literacy (Chakkarath, 2012).

A final word on the broader societal significance of the issues discussed in this chapter. As we have seen, understandings of mental health and illness are discursively intertwined with conceptions of many other central aspects of human social life such as debates about gender and sexuality, primitiveness and civilization, ethnicity and race, potential threats and protective measures. All of these dimensions continue to serve as means of legitimising and reinforcing existing power structures as well as the discriminatory practices and injustices they entail and perpetuate. Of course, this applies not only in the context of colonial and ongoing postcolonial conditions, but also within the internal dynamics of every society. The interrelations outlined above thus concern not only the social sciences, but all those who, across a range of societal domains, are confronted with human suffering and seek to identify, acknowledge, alleviate, and perhaps even heal it: social workers, therapists, counsellors, physicians, educators, legal professionals, politicians, and many others within administrative structures. For all of them, just as for the psychological sciences, the following holds true: Insofar as they are committed to helping those who suffer, they would do well to recognise that the best way to meet this concern is to understand the human being—whether scientist, social worker, therapist, teacher, client, migrant, refugee, policymaker, perpetrator and victim—in their entirety, that is, as beings who cannot comprehend their own nature except through the lens of their culture.

NOTES

1. I consider myself a cultural psychologist, but one who believes that the basic scientific concerns of cultural psychology cannot be realized without the integration of postcolonial and indigenous perspectives (see Chakkarath, 2012, Chakkarath et al., 2024).
2. Boesch's perspective on culture as a field of action also enables us to move away from the influential notion that cultures are primarily synonymous with countries or nations. Rather, we can understand any hierarchically organized, norm- and rule-based institutions such as families, companies, the courts, hospitals, refugee camps, the military, schools, universities, or domains such as the workplace, religion, migration management, or competitive sports as cultures—from which people are also known to suffer and to which their psyche can fall victim.
3. In some respects, this view is in line with that of ethnopsychiatry, for example as developed by Devereux (1980) since the 1930s. From a cultural-psychological perspective, it is not only a question of whether one is possibly more susceptible to certain mental peculiarities in some socialization contexts than in others, but also of how these peculiarities are judged in the respective contexts and what consequences this has, both for the patients and for larger society. For example, certain mental features that are considered illnesses in most Western societies can be understood as accompanying symptoms of valued spiritual abilities in other societies (see Dhar, 2019).
4. Ian Hacking's concept of the 'looping effect' is based on similar analyses. It refers to how classifications of people can change the classified people, their self-perception, and their behavior, and how this can in turn lead to changes in the classification itself, thus simultaneously altering broader cultural attitudes toward certain people (Hacking, 1986, 1995). This creates a feedback loop between the classifier and the classified. To this day, large parts of clinical psychology and psychiatry fail to recognize that their categorizations do not simply describe reality 'objectively' but also shape it significantly.
5. For similarly famous and psychoanalytically influenced accounts, see, for example, Wilhelm Reich's *Mass psychology of fascism*, 1933; Adorno's and Horkheimer's *Dialectic of enlightenment*, 1947; Lasch's *Culture of narcissism*, 1979; or Žižek's *Sublime object of ideology*, 1989.
6. In the following paragraphs, I partially refer back to one of my earlier essays (see Chakkarath, 2021).
7. Although I focus here on exclusionary strategies based on the concept of race, I would argue that Western social scientists *generally* tend to exploit some of their key concepts for the formation of European and North American identities through complacent cultural comparisons. Even today, key terms such as 'individuality', 'modernity' and 'progress' are used to describe what are supposedly specifically European achievements (Chakkarath, 2024a).

REFERENCES

American Psychiatric Association. (2022). *Diagnostic and statistical manual of mental disorders* (5th ed.). APA.

Baird, D., Beebe, J., Brewster, F., Brooke, R., Carta, S., Duckworth, M., Flowers, B. S., Formaini, H., Franco, L., Hejinian, C., Heuer, B., Heuer, G. M., Holifield, B., Lanfranchi, A. M., Kimbles, S., Luci, M., Maitra, B., Mills, J., Morgan, H., ... Zoja, L. (2018). Open letter from a group of Jungians on the question of Jung's writings and theories about "Africans". *British Journal of Psychotherapy, 34*, 673–678.

Beshara, R. (Ed.). (2021). *Critical psychology praxis. Psychosocial non alignment to modernity/coloniality.* Routledge.

Boesch, E. E. (1991). *Symbolic action theory and cultural psychology.* Springer.

Bracken, P., Thomas, P., Timimi, S., Asen, E., Behr, G., Beuster, C., Bhunnoo, S., Browne, I., Chhina, N., Double, D., Downer, S., Evans, C., Fernando, S., Garland, M. R., Hopkins, W., Huws, R., Johnson, B., Martindale, B., Middleton, H., ... Yeomans, D. (2012). Psychiatry beyond the current paradigm. *British Journal of Psychiatry, 201*(6), 430–434. https://doi.org/10.1192/bjp.bp.112.109447

Brickman, C. (2003). *Aboriginal populations in the mind: Race and primitivity in psychoanalysis.* Columbia University Press.

Bruner, J. S. (1993). *Acts of meaning. Four lectures on mind and culture.* Harvard University Press.

Chakkarath, P. (2003). *Kultur und Psychologie. Zur wissenschaftlichen Entstehung und zur Ortsbestimmung der Kulturpsychologie* [*Culture and psychology. On the scientific genesis and localization of cultural psychology*]. Kovac.

Chakkarath, P. (2012). The role of indigenous psychologies in the building of basic cultural psychology. In J. Valsiner (Ed.), *The Oxford handbook of culture and psychology* (pp. 71–95). Oxford University Press.

Chakkarath, P. (2021). Der dunkle Kontinent: Kolonialisierung und Dekolonialisierung der Psyche und der Psychologie [The dark continent: Colonization and decolonization of the psyche and psychology]. *Psychosozial, 165*, 75–85.

Chakkarath, P. (2024a). Is the individual an enlightened westerner? Some skeptical remarks on Eurocentric notions of self and the development of individualism. In A. Dueck & L. Sundararajan (Eds.), *Values and indigenous psychology in the age of the machine and market.* Palgrave Macmillan.

Chakkarath, P. (2024b). The indigenous-psychological perspective. In U. Wolfradt, L. Allolio-Näcke, & P. S. Ruppel (Eds.), *Cultural psychology. An introduction.* Springer.

Chakkarath, P., & Straub, J. (2020). Kulturpsychologie [Cultural psychology]. In G. Mey & K. Mruck (Eds.), *Handbuch Qualitative Forschung in der Psychologie* (Vol. *1*, pp. 284–304). Springer.

Cole, M. (2003). *Cultural psychology. A once and future discipline* (6th ed.). Harvard University Press.

Dalal, F. (1988). Jung: A racist. *British Journal of Psychotherapy, 4*, 263–279.

Devereux, G. (1980). *Basic problems of ethnopsychiatry.* Chicago University Press.

Dhar, A. (2019). *Madness and subjectivity. A cross-cultural examination of psychosis in the West and India.* Routledge.

Doane, M. A. (1999). Dark continents: Epistemologies of racial and sexual difference in psychoanalysis and the cinema. In J. Evans & S. Hall (Eds.), *Visual culture: The reader* (pp. 448–456). Routledge.

Foucault, M. (1966/2001). *The order of things: An archaelogy of the human sciences.* Original French edition, 1966. Routledge.

Foucault, M. (2001). *Madness and civilization: A history of insanity in the age of reason.* Original French edition, 1961. Routledge.

Freud, S. (1900/1985). Letter from Freud to Fliess, February 1, 1900. In J. M. Masson (Ed.), *The complete letters of Sigmund Freud to Wilhelm Fliess, 1887–1904* (pp. 397–398). Harvard University Press.

Freud, S. (1913). Totem and taboo. In J. J. Strachey (Ed.), *The standard edition of the complete psychological works of Sigmund Freud* (Vol. *XIII*). The Hogarth Press.

Freud, S. (1926). The question of lay analysis. In J. J. Strachey (Ed.), *The standard edition of the complete psychological works of Sigmund Freud* (Vol. *XX*). The Hogarth Press.

Freud, S. (1927/1961). The future of an illusion. In J. J. Strachey (Ed.), *The standard edition of the complete psychological works of Sigmund Freud* (Vol. *21*, pp. 1–56). The Hogarth Press.

Freud, S. (1930a). Civilization and its discontents. In J. J. Strachey (Ed.), *The standard edition of the complete psychological works of Sigmund Freud* (Vol. *XI*). The Hogarth Press.

Freud, S. (1930b/1961). Letter from Sigmund Freud to Romain Rolland, January 19, 1930. In E. L. Freud (Ed.), *Letters of Sigmund Freud 1873–1939* (pp. 392–393). The Hogarth Press.

Geertz, C. (1973). *The interpretation of cultures. Selected essays.* Basic Books.

Hacking, I. (1995). *Rewriting the soul: Multiple personality and the sciences of memory.* Princeton University Press.

Hacking, I. (1986). Making up people. In T. Heller, M. Sosna, & D. Wellberry (Eds.), *Reconstructing individualism* (pp. 222–236). Stanford University Press.

Hilliard, C. (2012). *Straightening the bell curve. How stereotypes about Black masculinity drive research on race and intelligence.* Potomac Books.

Horwitz, A. V. (2021). *DSM: A history of psychiatry's bible.* Johns Hopkins University Press.

Ishay, M. (2008). *The history of human rights: From ancient times to the globalization era.* California of University Press.

Jahoda, G. (1993). *Crossroads between culture and mind: Continuities and change in theories of human nature.* Harvard University Press.

Jahoda, G. (2011). Past and present of cross-cultural psychology. In F. J. R. van de Vijver, A. Chasiotis, & S. M. Breugelmans (Eds.), *Fundamental questions in cross-cultural psychology* (pp. 37–63). Cambridge University Press.

Jaspers, K. (1963). *General psychopathology* (transl. by J. Hoenig & M. W. Hamilton; original German edition, 1913). Manchester University Press.

Jung, C. G. (1970/1927). Woman in Europe. In R. F. C. Hull (Ed.), *Collected works of C. G. Jung* (Vol. *10*, pp. 113–133). Princeton University Press.

Jung, C. G. (1995/1962). *Memories, dreams, reflections* (A. Jaffé, Ed.; R. Winston & C. Winston, Trans.). Fontana Press.

Keller, R. C. (2007). *Colonial madness: Psychiatry in French North Africa.* University of Chicago Press.

Khanna, R. (2003). *Dark continents: Psychoanalysis and colonialism.* Duke University Press.

Lazarus, M., & Steinthal, H. (1860). Einleitende Gedanken über Völkerpsychologe, als Einladung zu einer Zeitschrift für Völkerpsychologie und Sprachwissenschaft

[Introductory thoughts on Völkerpsychologe, as an invitation to a Journal of Folk Psychology and Linguistics]. *Zeitschrift für Völkerpsychologie und Sprachwissenschaft, 1*, 1–73.

Macaulay, T. B. (1835/1935). Minute of the 2nd of February. In G. M. Young (Ed.), *Speeches by Lord Macaulay with his minute on Indian education* (pp. 345–361). Oxford University Press.

Makari, G. (2008). *Revolution in mind: The creation of psychoanalysis*. Harper & Collins.

Malloy, J. (2008). James Watson tells the inconvenient truth: Faces the consequences. *Medical Hypotheses, 70*, 1081–1091. https://doi.org/10.1016/j.mehy.2008.03.041

Nandy, A. (2009). *The intimate enemy. Loss and recovery of self under colonialism* (2nd ed.). Oxford University Press. with a postscript by the author; originally published in 1983).

Okazaki, S., David, E. J. R., & Abelmann, N. (2008). Colonialism and psychology of culture. *Social and Personality Psychology Compass, 2*, 90–106.

Osterhammel, J. (2005). *Colonialism: A theoretical overview*. Markus Wiener Publishers.

Park, P. K. J. (2013). *Africa, Asia, and the history of philosophy. Racism in the formation of the philosophical canon, 1780–1830*. State University of New York Press.

Porter, R. (2002). *Madness. A brief history*. Oxford University Press.

Quah, S. (2010). Health and culture. In W. C. Cockerham (Ed.), *The new Blackwell companion to medical sociology* (pp. 27–46). Wiley-Blackwell.

Ramana, C. (1964). On the early history and development of psychoanalysis in India. *Journal of the American Psychoanalytic Association, 12*, 110–134.

Reich, W. (1933/1946). *The mass psychology of fascism*. Orgone Institute Press.

Rose, N. (1996). *Inventing our selves. Psychology, power and personhood*. Cambridge University Press.

Santambrogio, J., Ciscato, V., Lorusso, O., Wisidagamage, D. P., Leon, E., Miragliotta, E., Capuzzi, E., Colmegna, F., & Clerici, M. (2024). The challenge of diagnosing cultural syndromes: A narrative review. *International Journal of Social Psychiatry, 70*(6), 1016–1027.

Sinha, M. (1995). *Colonial masculinity. The 'manly Englishman' and the 'effeminate Bengali' in the late nineteenth century*. Manchester University Press.

Spivak, G. (1988). Can the subaltern speak? In C. Nelson & L. Grossberg (Eds.), *Marxism and the interpretation of culture*. University of Illinois Press.

Tomasello, M. (2019). *Becoming human. A theory of ontogeny*. Harvard University Press.

Valsiner, J. (2007). *Culture in minds and society*. Sage.

Ward, A. (2013). Understanding postcolonial traumas. *Journal of Theoretical & Philosophical Psychology, 3*, 170–184.

Warwick, A., Jenson, D., & Keller, R. C. (Eds.). (2011). *Unconscious dominions, psychoanalysis, colonial trauma, and global sovereignties*. Duke University Press.

Watson, J. (2007). *Avoid boring people and other lessons from a life in science*. Random House.

Weber, M. (2012). The 'objectivity' of knowledge in social science and social policy In H. H. Bruun & S. Whimster (Eds.), *Max Weber: Collected methodological writings* (pp. 100–138). Original German edition 1904. Routledge.

Wundt, W. (1916). *Elements of folk psychology: Outlines of a psychological history of the development of mankind* (E. L. Schaub, Trans.). George Allen & Unwin. (Original German work published 1912).

CHAPTER 2

CONTRIBUTIONS OF SEMIOTIC CULTURAL PSYCHOLOGY FOR INTERVENTIONS IN CLINICAL PSYCHOLOGY

Klessyo do Espirito Santo Freire†
Federal University of Bahia, Brazil

Alan Souza Pereira Silva‡
Federal University of Bahia, Brazil

Maria Virginia Dazzani§
Federal University of Bahia, Brazil

Giuseppina Marsico||
University of Salerno, Italy

†https://orcid.org/0000-0001-5189-1278
‡https://orcid.org/0000-0002-5177-5944
§https://orcid.org/0000-0001-5303-3576
||https://orcid.org/0000-0002-8683-2814

Cultural Psychology in Clinical Research and Practices, pages 27–35

Published under exclusive licence by Emerald Publishing Limited
doi:10.1108/978-1-83742-213-520261002

ABSTRACT

This chapter explored how Semiotic Cultural Psychology conceptualises interventions in clinical psychology, through the interconnected concepts of semiosis, agency, catalysis, and ambivalence. From this perspective, mental suffering arises from dilemmatic situations-fields where multiple, often conflicting, possibilities of choices coexist. These fields encompass cognitive, ethical, and affective dimensions, all of which contribute to a person's distressing experience.

Clinical psychology practice should be based on understanding an individual's lived experiences and meaning-making processes. The psychologist's role is to collaboratively explore, with the individual, multiple possible choices within a given dilemmatic field, and facilitate a path towards greater self-understanding and agency.

Keywords: Cultural psychology; clinical psychology; semiosis; agency; catalysis; ambivalence

This chapter explores interventions in clinical psychology through the lens of Semiotic Cultural Psychology, highlighting their potential to foster agency. To establish a foundation for this discussion, we will first define the broad field of clinical psychology, acknowledging its diverse definitions and theoretical approaches. According to the American Psychological Association, Clinical Psychology integrates research, assessment, and intervention. It aims to understand, predict, and alleviate suffering associated with emotional, cognitive, biological, psychological, social, and behavioral factors that contribute to psychological difficulties and mental health problems. (Teachman et al., 2021)

The APA definition is one of the most widely accepted and adopted in many countries throughout the world. It states that clinical psychology seeks to understand and address mental suffering as it manifests in various problems in people's lives. Mental suffering is therefore understood differently depending on the chosen theoretical framework.

According to Holzhey-Kunz (2018), there are two major approaches to understanding mental suffering: one based on a Cartesian model of cause and effect, and the other on a hermeneutic perspective. The former, derived from a biomedical model, aims to identify the social, biological, and psychological factors underlying mental suffering. The latter, conversely, stems from Freudian psychoanalysis and existential-phenomenological psychotherapy approaches, viewing mental suffering as an expression of certain meanings and significance within a person's life (Holzhey-Kunz, 2018).

The hermeneutic perspective posits that a person and society are interdependent in the construction of meaning, a process underlying various psychological states. This view aligns with the semiotic cultural view in psychology (Valsiner, 2012, 2014a), and emphasises that mental life unfolds through signs that mediate individuals' relationship with the world. These signs emerge precisely from the collective culture, forming a personal culture related to a system of semiotic regulation of human behaviour (Valsiner, 2012, 2014a).

This interpretative dialogue between the person and the world, through signs, is called semiosis. In the field of Biosemiotics (Jämsä, 2008), the process of semiosis always occurs within an Umwelt, involving an organism that interprets its environment through signs and their meaning-making. The Umwelt represents the experienced environment, individuals' life history, and the social cues provided by their historical and cultural context (Carriere, 2013).

Semiosis includes an affective dimension, in which a person acts on the environment to activate certain affective states connected to their Umwelt. From this perspective, the person is an interpreter of their cultural contexts with the ability to act over their life according to environmental cues (Carriere, 2013; Cornejo et al., 2018). Thus, mental suffering may emerge from difficulties in semiotic regulation and agency development, rather than merely from isolated problems of sign interpretation. Exploring the concepts of agency and catalysis would provide a better understanding of mental suffering, from a Semiotic Cultural Psychology perspective.

AGENCY AND SEMIOTIC CULTURAL PSYCHOLOGY

Agency is an important concept for understanding human psychological life and can be understood as a person's ability to act and transform their cultural contexts (Giddens, 2003). While animals also possess the capacity to act, only in humans is this ability mediated by complex semiotic processes that give meaning and purpose to their actions (Valsiner, 2012). Thus, agency implies a semiotic agent who actively interacts with the world.

Semiotic Cultural Psychology emphasises the active role of individuals in interacting with others and shaping their environment. It challenges the notion of a passive person, who merely reacts to social cues (Valsiner, 2014a). Instead, individuals are active agents capable of thinking, choosing, improvising, and acting in different ways within social interactions. Thus, agency is the uniquely human form of action.

However, having the capacity for agency does not necessarily imply that one exercises it well. Just as the ability to speak does not guarantee that one will be a good speaker-although this competence can be developed-the mere fact of being an able agent does not ensure that one will exercise agency successfully. A person may, for example, remain in unsatisfying relationships, struggle at work, or experience creative blocks due to impairments in their agency.

To better understand agency, we must explore its key characteristics: intentionality, decision-making, creativity, and regulation. *Intentionality* implies that every human action has some meaning (Valsiner, 2014a). When people act, they affect others and the environment in order to achieve their desired goals. For example, people build houses to provide shelter, clear forests to plant crops, and negotiate prices for discounts. It is important to note that intentionality does not mean that goals will be achieved nor does it imply strict rationality, as choices always have an affective dimension (Giddens, 2003). We know, for instance, that negotiating prices will not guarantee the desired discount; that deforestation, even if intended for agriculture, contributes to climate change; and that relationship choices are always strongly influenced by emotions. Although full awareness of the consequences of one's actions is impossible, intentionality, as an inherent characteristic of human action, guides decision-making.

Decision-making refers to our ability to reflect and evaluate our actions considering a range of possibilities. When we interact with people, we create spaces for negotiation where we can accept or deny suggestions (Marsico & Tateo, 2018). Naturally, people are not always fully aware of the various affective, ethical, and cognitive elements involved in decision-making, nor are they strong enough to resist social pressures. They may also be caught in 'semiotic traps' (Valsiner, 2012) which push them in different directions from those intended. Sometimes, people make decisions that seem rational when in fact they are essentially emotional. Gambling games, such as the lottery, are an example of actions that go against the mathematical probability of winning, in favour of the desire to get rich. In other cases, people make illogical decisions based on misunderstandings, or insufficient or false evidence. Heuristics, studied in Cognitive Psychology, along with fallacies and fake news exemplify decisions based on flawed premises. However, even in these situations, a person actively makes choices - even if they are 'forced' or defer the decision to others, the capacity to choose is always present.

Agency enables diverse choices, and consequently, the ability to transform various cultural contexts. *Creativity* refers to the acts of imagining, creating, inventing, and innovating. Technological advances and global transformations result from individuals actively resisting and challenging existing situations; such changes arise from nonconformity. If human action were passive, people would invariably act in the same way and there would be no room for spontaneity, improvisation, innovation, or overcoming difficulties (Stetsenko, 2020). Although people's behaviour is often controlled and directed, the potential for creation, in the form of latent agency always exists.

Meanings permeate human psychological life, *regulating* both an individual's and other's actions. Agency, therefore, involves two interacting processes: self-regulation and hetero-regulation (Valsiner, 2012). Self-regulation involves actions that people take when planning, executing, and evaluating their decisions. For example, a writer must think, analyse, articulate, and clearly write words to communicate their ideas to the reader. Hetero-regulation involves actions performed when, for instance, seeking help or persuading others of a personal point of view. Co-authoring a text, for example, requires some hetero-regulatory activity, such as discussing ideas, delegating tasks, and relying on everyone's collaboration. These interactions involve negotiation, adjustment, reorganization, and compromise. The more effectively a person exercises agency the more appropriate their decisions tend to be. This is relevant to clinical practice, where individuals often seek assistance for suffering in their professional, personal, or academic lives, suggesting potential difficulties in the regulating these interactions.

Another important aspect of agency is the inherent unpredictability of human interaction. Human's capacity for innovation, transformation, and transgression of established social patterns make it difficult to predict the effects of interventions. Prediction implies anticipation and a belief that doing '*x*', invariably results in '*y*'. This type of reasoning requires isolating intervening factors to determine causal relationships. While this logic may be more applicable in the hard sciences, it proves insufficient and limited when applied to human and psychological phenomena. Therefore, this study adopts the concept of catalysis, developed within Semiotic Cultural Psychology, to address psychological phenomena (Cabell & Valsiner, 2014).

CATALYSIS

From its inception, psychology research has generally used a linear model of cause-and-effect to analyse psychological phenomena. This approach is based on the normal statistical curve, which establishes causal relationships between events and psychological aspects. In contrast, Semiotic Cultural Psychology adopts the concept of catalysis from chemistry to analyse the conditions of emergence, maintenance, inhibition, and transformation of psychological phenomena (Cabell & Valsiner, 2014).

The concept of catalysis transformed chemistry into the science that studies the reactions of a substance through its subcomponents. Chemical reactions are explained by a chain of relations that produce a specific result.

This science focuses on the conditions that enable a substance to transition from one state to another, and the elements that can inhibit or promote a particular chemical reaction (Valsiner, 2014b).

Therefore, the analysis of psychological phenomena through a Semiotic Cultural Psychology lens, focuses not solely on their causes, but rather the conditions for their emergence, inhibition, maintenance, and disappearance. Within this perspective, signs, in a context-dependent and future-oriented manner, regulate an individual's relationship with the world and catalyse specific psychological states. Through semiosis, the environment provides social cues that catalyse the emergence of meanings for the individual (Innis, 2018). These catalytic signs are essential for meaning construction and semiotic regulation, and empower an individual to act as an agent, negotiating their actions within their cultural context (Innis, 2018). Consequently, the issue is not what causes psychological suffering, but rather what conditions enable its emergence and persistence as a psychopathological state, manifested in the process of semiosis and impacting the individual's relationship with their cultural contexts.

From this perspective, psychological suffering stems from the type of relationships an individual establishes with their cultural contexts. Catalytic signs, in this context, attribute meaning to uncomfortable affective states, resulting in difficulties in people's daily activities. Consequently, individuals struggle to exercise their agency and deal with various life situations, especially those involving ambivalence (Innis, 2018; Valsiner, 2014b).

From a Semiotic Cultural Psychology perspective, clinical psychology should not base its interventions on a causal linear model or perspectives based on a normal statistical distribution. Interventions should be planned according to the unique way each person acts in their daily lives. To address mental suffering, Semiotic Cultural Psychology seeks to understand how people immersed in this psychological state negotiate and construct meanings in their cultural context.

We return to a hermeneutic model of clinical practice (Holzhey-Kunz, 2018) that seeks to understand people's worldviews, recognising them as unique expressions of their cultural contexts and the plurality of meanings and actions within the world. Some of these actions are catalysed in semiotic processes, and when their affective nature is particularly potent, mental suffering can arise.

States of mental suffering are generally linked to dilemmatic situations. According to Tateo (2018), ambivalence is inherent to human experience, since all meaning-making involves coexisting meanings. We frequently have to make decisions within a field of overlapping meanings. Tateo (2018) further explains that ambivalence can create dilemmatic fields where overlapping meanings exist, and the possibility of becoming something necessitates *not* becoming something else. These situations are permeated by cognitive, affective, and ethical dimensions that define the action field and can persist for a considerable time in an individual's life.

Consider, for example, the issue of guilt. A past decision, such as choosing not to pursue a specific course of study, losing a loved one (accompanied by feelings that they could have prevented the loss), or entering a particular relationship, can continuously present current and future choices in distressing ways. Depending on the current life situation, these situations can lead the person to ethical conflicts manifested as suffering.

Mental suffering, therefore, often arises from dilemmatic situations (Tateo, 2018), where the tendency to make one choice is countered by the pull of its opposite. The potentially distressing nature of this internal conflict can lead to paralysis and impaired agency. The whole interpretative process of semiosis becomes restricted to a single field of meanings, impairing the person's daily activities.

From a cultural semiotic perspective, clinical psychology aims to understand individuals' dilemmatic situations and help them expand agency. The goal is not to eliminate dilemmatic situations, as they are part of human psychological life, but rather to reduce their distressing nature.

HERMENEUTIC AND CULTURAL SEMIOTIC PERSPECTIVES ON CLINICAL PSYCHOLOGY INTERVENTIONS

From a hermeneutic and cultural semiotic perspective, interventions in clinical psychology are focused on personal experience with inherent dilemmatic situations. Consequently, psychotherapy should embrace a phenomenological approach that allows the emergence and expression of dilemmatic phenomena, and prioritising understanding them as they appear, rather than attempting to explain them (Asworth & Chung, 2006).

In studying the history of philosophy, Heidegger (2015) proposed that phenomenology be hermeneutic. That is, that it should seek to understand how phenomena are expressed within a historical context and the associated meanings. Subsequently, a phenomenological investigation focuses on the meanings people attribute to the world, within their daily actions. This notion is aligned with the idea that ambivalence and dilemmatic situations are a human existential condition (Tateo, 2018). Targeted interventions must, therefore, consider an existential field, in which cognitive, ethical, and affective dimensions are immersed. The entire process of human semiosis and bi-directional sensemaking (Valsiner, 2014a) is fundamentally experiential.

Therefore, clinical interventions for mental suffering should focus on people's accounts of their everyday experiences and identify the ethical, cognitive, and affective dimensions of the various dilemmatic situations, in order to identify the different potential and coexisting choices within their dilemmatic field. By understanding the various choices and their possible meanings, the psychotherapist can work with the individual to reduce the distress associated with dilemmatic situation, and help the individual recover their agency.

Semiotic Cultural Psychology can not only help investigate the effectiveness of psychotherapeutic intervention but also illuminate the psychological mechanisms underlying the psychotherapist's actions. Understanding dilemmatic situations, their associated mental suffering, and the processes of semiosis and agency can provide valuable insights for improving clinical psychology interventions.

CONCLUSION

This chapter explored how Semiotic Cultural Psychology conceptualises interventions in clinical psychology, through the interconnected concepts of semiosis, agency, catalysis, and ambivalence. From this perspective, mental suffering arises from dilemmatic situations-fields where multiple, often conflicting, possibilities of choices coexist. These field encompass cognitive, ethical, and affective dimensions, all of which contribute to a person's distressing experience.

In clinical work, this perspective invites the psychotherapist to map the person's dilemmatic field, identify the signs that catalyse affective meanings, and collaboratively explore alternative meanings and courses of action that may expand the person's agency.

This process disrupts the fluid functioning of semiosis and agency processes, thereby impacting daily functioning across different cultural contexts. Therefore, clinical psychology practice should be based on understanding an individual's lived experiences and meaning-making processes. The psychologist's role is to collaboratively explore, with the individual, multiple possible choices within a given dilemmatic field, and facilitate a path towards greater self-understanding and agency.

In conclusion, Semiotic Cultural Psychology offers a valuable epistemological framework for advancing both theory and practice in clinical psychology, grounded in hermeneutic and interpretative approaches. It provides a compelling alternative to the dominant biomedical models, which often operate within a rigid cause-and-effect logic that ultimately disregards the crucial human and existential dimensions of psychological experience.

ACKNOWLEDGEMENTS

Maria Virginia Machado Dazzani acknowledges the financial support from the following Brazilian research agencies: National Council for Scientific and Technological Development (CNPq-PQ, Brazil/Process number:

307784/2022-3 and CNPq, Brazil/Process number: 435602/2018-7) and Foundation for the Coordination of the Improvement of Researchers (CAPES-PRINT/ Federal University of Bahia, Brazil/ Process number: 88887.568332/2020-00).

Giuseppina Marsico acknowledges Federal University of Bahia, Brazil (Editoral Professor Visitante and CAPES-PRINT for the financial support).

REFERENCES

Asworth, P. D., & Chung, M. C. (2006). *Phenomenology and psychological science: Historical and philosophical perspectives.* Springer.

Cabell, K. R., & Valsiner, J. (2014). Systematic systemics: Causality, catalysis and developmental cybernetics. In K. R. Cabell, & J. Valsiner, (Eds.), *The catalyzing mind:beyond models of causality* (pp. 3–16). Springer.

Carriere, K. (2013). Making a place into a home: The affective construction of the feeling <> Differentiation. *Psychology & Society, 5*(3), 87–103.

Cornejo, C., Marsico, G., & Valsiner, J. (2018). I activate you to affect me: Affectivating as a cultural psychological phenomenon. In C. Cornejo, G. Marsico, & J. &Valsiner (Eds.), *I activate you to affect me* (pp. 1–14). IAP.

Giddens, A. (2003). *A constituição da sociedade.* Martins Fontes.

Heidegger, M. (2015). *Ser e tempo.* Editora Vozes.

Holzhey-Kunz, A. (2018). *Daseisanálise: o olhar filosófico- existencial sobre o sofrimento psíquicoe seu tratamento.* Rio de Janeiro. Via Verita.

Innis, R. E. (2018). Affectivating signs: On semiotic interruptions. In C. Cornejo, , G. Marsico, , & J. Valsiner, (Eds.), *I activate you to affect me* (pp. 49–72). IAP.

Jämsä, T. (2008). Semiosis in evolution. In M. Barbieri (Ed.), *Introduction to biosemiotics: The new biological synthesis* (pp. 69–100). Springer.

Marsico, G., & Tateo, L. (2018). Introduction: The construct of educational self. In G. Marsico & L. Tateo (Eds.), *The emergence of self in educational contexts* (pp. 1–14). Springer. Cultural Psychology of Education. https://doi.org/10.1007/978-3-319-98602-9_1

Stetsenko, A. P. (2020). Critical challenges in cultural-historical activity theory: The urgency of agency. *Cultural-Historical Psychology, 16*(2), 5–18.

Tateo, L. (2018). Tensegrity as existential condition: The inherent ambivalence of development. In I. Albert, E. Abbey, & J. Valsiner (Eds.), *Trans-generational family relations: Investigating ambivalences* (pp. 3–20). Information Age Publishing. Perspectives on Human Development.

Teachman, B. A., Olatunji, B. O., & Lilienfeld, S. O. (2021). *Introduction to clinical psychology: Bridging science and practice* (9th ed.). Cambridge University Press.

Valsiner, J. (2012). *Fundamentos da psicologia cultural: Mundos da mente, mundos da vida* [Foundations of cultural psychology: Worlds of mind, worlds of life] (A. C. S. Bastos, Trans.). Artmed.

Valsiner, J. (2014a). *An invitation to cultural psychology.* Sage.

Valsiner, J. (2014b). Breaking the arrows of casuality: The idea of catalysis in its making. In K. R. Cabbel, & J. Valsiner, (Eds.), *The catalyzing mind: Beyond models of casuality* (pp. 17–32). Springer.

CHAPTER 3

SEMIOTIC AND PSYCHODYNAMIC FUNCTIONS OF AFFECTIVE SEMIOSIS. MODAL ARTICULATION PROCESSES IN NARRATIVES FROM A CLINICAL HEALTHCARE CONTEXT: EXAMPLES OF LONGITUDINAL, QUANTITATIVE AND QUALITATIVE ANALYSES

Raffaele De Luca Picione
Giustino Fortunato University, Italy

Maria Luisa Martino
University of Naples Federico II, Italy

Daniela Lemmo
University of Naples Federico II, Italy

Cultural Psychology in Clinical Research and Practices, pages 37–63

Published under exclusive licence by Emerald Publishing Limited
doi:10.1108/978-1-83742-213-520261003

ABSTRACT

The chapter explores the semiotic and affective dimensions of human sensemaking processes, emphasising the role of modal articulation in shaping subjective experience. Drawing from cultural psychology, semiotics, and clinical research, the authors propose a dynamic model where modal operators – such as necessity, possibility, will, and duty – serve as mediators that connect affectivity, cognition, and relational systems. The model highlights the fluidity and context-dependence of experience, illustrating how modal configurations evolve over time and across different life phases, particularly in health-related narratives. Empirical analysis of longitudinal cancer patient narratives demonstrates how modal categories fluctuate, reflecting shifts from uncertainty and dependence to agency and self-determination. The research underscores the importance of integrating quantitative and qualitative methods to capture the complexity of sensemaking. Clinically, the framework offers valuable insights for understanding patient narratives, facilitating therapeutic interventions that address affective, sensemaking and relational dimensions. Overall, the study advances a comprehensive semiotic approach to human experience, emphasising its relational, affective, and cultural embeddedness, and providing methodological tools for analysing the dynamic construction of meaning in health and psychological contexts.

Keywords: Modal articulation model; oncological narratives; cultural psychology; clinical psychology; sensemaking process; quali-quantitave method analyisis

INTRODUCTION

Cultural psychology teaches us that human experience is characterised by incessant sensemaking activity based on inherent affectivity. This process constitutes a value dimension of experience, shaping how individuals interpret and engage with their surroundings. It is deeply intersubjective and enables transformative actions with one's symbolic-material environment. These processes should not be considered as static and permanent 'states of facts', but rather as dynamic trajectories of development that continuously transform over time.

From a semiotic perspective, we propose that the human sensemaking process manifests these characteristics through the articulation of the modal operators (e.g. the categories of necessity, possibility, will, duty, power, knowledge, etc.). These operators significantly enhance the flexibility and variability of experience, according to contextual factors, relationships with others, and uncertainties about the future. Modal predicates facilitate different semiotic operations, including: (1) '*connection*' between affects and language; (2) '*mediation*' between subjectivity and otherness; (3) '*vectorisation*' in the temporal orientation of an action.

The concept of modal articulation has important implications for clinical psychology research and therapeutic contexts. It provides a framework for addressing and integrating dialectical tensions-such as normality versus abnormality, dynamism versus rigidity, process versus content, stability versus transformation, and continuity versus crisis-in a constructive manner.

In this chapter, we present semiotic models of analysis based on modal articulations in narratives from cases of oncological experience. Our observations indicate that: a) each subject organizes specific configurations of modal articulation; and b) different levels of modal articulations can be identified based on parameters such as flexibility versus rigidity, and descriptive accounts versus subjective implications.

In conclusion, the modal articulation model provides valuable intersections between cultural psychology and clinical psychology, bridging theory, practice and research. This perspective enhances our understanding of human experience, emphasising its fluid and context-dependent nature while offering a useful methodological framework for both analysis and intervention.

SENSEMAKING AS A DYNAMIC PROCESS OF RELATION-CONSTRUCTING

Human experience is based on an infinite network of relationship systems that develop, grow, transform, reconfigure, and decay over time. These systems are conveyed through different physiological and sociological activities through sensemaking processes. Beyond common sense, we must acknowledge that sensemaking is not an individual psychic operation, but rather entails somatic-biological and socio-cultural processes and activities. From the study of biological organisms by biosemiotics (Barbieri, 2008; Favareau, 2010; Hoffmeyer, 1996; Kull, 2009; Neuman, 2008; Sebeok & Danesi, 2000) through to the study of cultural systems (Bhabha, 1994; De Luca Picione, 2015a; Lotman, 2005; Salvatore, 2016; Valsiner, 2007, 2014, 2021; Wheeler, 2006), life is made possible by processes of sensemaking, which work as translation of events and connections of different systems. The sensemaking process in semiotic terms is a process of construction, connection, mediation, and regulation of relational systems. In fact, signification – in the perspective we adopt – is a way of relating different systems through operations carried out through signs. In human experience, semiotic mediation – by means of signs – transcends the level of the '*here and now*' and allows us to project ourselves into the future and reconsider past experiences (Valsiner, 2007, 2014, 2021). This perspective is strongly relational. It considers that the identity of objects, people, states of the world are not taken-for-granted, but that they are instantiated and made available by *pertinentization*, through sensemaking. A sign, therefore, is not a mental object that indicates or represents something already constituted and given, but it is a relational device that configures different systems (i.e., subject, object, and world) under some relevance (Salvatore et al., 2021). Such considerations certainly have a long history and debate as far as philosophical disciplines are concerned. Let's think, for example, of the Kantian distinction between *noumenon* and *phenomenon*, or of Wittgenstein's idea of *linguistic games*. Beyond the due differences, we find the very general idea that the essence of things is not graspable, localisable or representable and that the experience is entirely based on a relational and interactional processes.

From the specific semiotic point of view that we adopt, the sign is simultaneously the result of a system of relations that differentiate it from other signs (such as de Saussure's (1921) structuralist perspective showed us), and also a temporary element within a continuous process of semiosis in which signs that follow define the preceding signs (as in the semiotic interpretative perspective that Peirce (1931–1935) and Eco (1976) argue).

The idea of a relational and dynamic semiosis has great relevance for the development of the psychology, as it allows us to overcome some fallacies around the thinking of the mind in exclusively individualistic, naturalistic or computational/representational terms. The development of cultural psychology through a dynamic semiotic approach has offered significant contributions to theoretical modelling where the psyche is viewed as a recursive, intrainter-subjective, dynamic and interconnected system with the world, thereby overcoming old dualisms such as mind-body, individual-society, subject-object (De Luca Picione & Freda, 2016a, 2016b, 2016c; De Luca Picione, 2021).

Psychology becomes cultural not so much because it is believed that there is a specific cultural baggage of knowledge and information transmitted between generations and to which each new unborn child gradually accesses; but because of the view that there is a continuous semiotic mediation by cultural signs from the process of subjectivation of experience, the construction of relationships with others, the symbolisation of experience, and the flexibility of choices in contextual frames. In short, psychology is cultural since the semiotic mediation frees human beings from the rigidity of cause-effect linearity and the determination of reactions to stimuli, and puts them in the position to confront the responsibility of choice and indeterminacy, the awareness of one's own limits, and the ambivalent identity condition of being simultaneously different and similar to others (De Luca Picione, 2020a, 2021b).

Psychology – through a theoretical and methodological framework based on a semiotic, cultural, and dynamic perspectives – frees itself from the risks of the notions of 'information' and 'representation'. These notions have had great relevance since the second half of the last century both about the development of mathematical models for communication

(Shannon & Weaver, 1949) and about the development of the cognitive science paradigm of psychology, for artificial intelligence, neuroscience, etc. However, with a careful look, the ideas of information and representation risk keeping separate the constitutive and dynamic function of the subject, their interdependence with the environment and with the others, and their living body. One of the most disabling and debilitating implications for the development of psychology can be identified in neglecting or minimising the importance of affective processes, reduced to noise, interference or irrationality in a reductionist vision by pure informational and cognitivist models.

We observe that important developments in the direction of recognition of the body, affectivity, and subjectivity can be found in the perspectives of *enactment, embodied cognition* and in the re-evaluation of emotions underlying cognitive processes (Barsalou, 1999, 2008; Borghi & Caruana, 2015; Maturana & Varela, 1980; Salvatore et al., 2021).

AFFECTIVISATION OF EXPERIENCE AT THE BASIS OF SENSEMAKING PROCESSES

The recognition of the preeminence of affect in the experience is a fundamental point of the agenda for the development of psychology.

Affectivisation is a process by which affect and emotions frame, shape, and ground cognitive processes, therefore influencing how human beings interpret and engage with their socio-cultural experiences (Innis, 2020; Salvatore & Freda, 2011a, 2011b; Salvatore & Zittoun, 2011; Salvatore et al., 2021).

Affect pertains to the corporeality of the individual who experiences what is happening starting from a basic thymic polar differentiation: pleasant/unpleasant, active/passive, attraction/repulsion, expansion/contraction, etc. This bodily modification process is recursively connected with the context in a co-defined way – see the 'structural coupling' notion by Maturana and Varela (1980). It is important to note that affect neither implies an individual/solipsistic bodily state, nor an intrapsychic transformation. Affect and its processualism constitutes a semiotic matrix from which an experience is endowed with value on the basis of subjectivity and contextuality. Affect gives consistency and value to the experience, cuts out a pertinent frame from a potential and indistinct background, and generates a first prereflective person/environment configuration by providing intentionality and directionality.

> Affect can and should be considered in relation to the actions that the affected organism establishes with its environments. Thus, instead of being a

> passive happening into the individual organism, affect is tightly bonded with the actions the same organism performs in relation to others. In the case of humans, affectivating reveals the two-sided (Person→Environment and Environment→Person) process of relating—treating that relating as primarily an affective (and secondarily cognitive) process. A person is affected by aspects of their environments that previously have been made meaningful and therefore salient by that very person. So, people actively make certain aspects of their environment become affectively significant for them, and that significance feeds forward to their further relating with their Umwelts. (Cornejo et al., 2018, p. 2)

Traditionally, affectivisation was considered a passive process. In fact, the etymology of 'affect' concerns the Latin term '*affectus*', namely '*being affected, being touched, being struck*'. However, we can observe that the notion of affect is that of '*interest*' and can be understood as the way individuals connect with their environment by defining a local and contingent space of *interest* with a certain directionality. According to Argentine psychoanalyst Luis Chiozza (2012), when an '*interest*' arises, it interweaves several systems of relationship and coexistence with the world. The etymology of the term '*interest*' from Latin consists of the words '*inter*' and '*esse*' (namely *between* and *being*), referring to the meaning of '*being among things*'. Interest is, therefore, connected to affective activation, which triggers a field of relationships starting from the construction of a system of pertinences. Furthermore, in William James' (1890) '*Perception of realty*' (a chapter of his work '*Principles of Psychology*') he argues that 'the vividness, pungency and emotional interest are at basis of the constitution of realty'.

Affectivisation is therefore a dynamic and multifaceted semiotic process that serves a variety of purposes, contributing to a rich and complex understanding of human behaviour and experience. Salvatore and Zittoun (2011, pp. 20–21) elaborate on this:

> 1. Somatic activation as embodied appraisal. Affects are dynamics of generalised bodily activation; that is, the basic way of prereflexively experiencing the world in terms of embodied meanings, in terms of hedonic basic values (positive versus negative or exciting versus relaxing) qualifying and constructing the experience.
> 2. Self–other regulation. The immediate appraisal of experience as an inherent motivational and communicative valence, thereby making affects powerful, situated, preconventional semiotic regulators of the social bond.
> 3. Symbolisation as subjectivisation. The patterns of sense–motor activation sustaining arousal are subject to a continuous and recursive process of symbolisation (sometimes called mentalisation). One can consider this process of symbolisation as a process of

incorporating the embodied meanings within an associative chain of signs (Green, 1973), thereby transforming raw experience (Bion, 1962) into representations: the sub symbolic into the symbolic.

4. Feelings. These are the self-reflective output of the affective process, resulting from the introduction of the body into the realm of the secondary process, mainly through language. These feelings can then, in turn, enter the whole dynamic again, for instance, as triggers for further affective activation (Salvatore & Zittoun, 2011, pp. 20–21).

Recursive cultural semiotic processes are activated by affective processes (De Luca Picione & Valsiner, 2017). The process of symbolisation (De Luca Picione, 2021; De Luca Picione & Freda, 2014; Salvatore, 2016; Salvatore & Freda, 2011a, 2011b; Valsiner, 2007, 2014) translates into the signs of the affective experience of the subject. Affects instantiate the sense of the subjective experience of the world as a totality. Affective symbolisation is a holistic process that constructs a meaningful framework. Within this framework, individual signs acquire specific values – values that are always local and context-dependent, never absolute. This framework emerges through a dynamic interplay between generalisation and abstraction, alongside pertinentization, contextualisation, and discretisation. As Jaan Valsiner has emphasised over the past three decades, semiotic mediation, rooted in affective processes, enables the dynamic, recursive, and irreversible configuration of sign hierarchies. These hierarchies, in turn, guide and orient human conduct, action, thinking, and feeling (De Luca Picione & Valsiner, 2017; Valsiner, 2021). In other words, through the process of semiotization, objects and experiences within a specific social and cultural context, are assigned meaning (Schutz, 1945).

Another important implication of cultural affective semiotic processes that is worth discussing concerns the overcoming of a static representational plane in which interaction with the world is mediated by an abstract idea, concept, representation or scheme. Affective semiosis, through primary embodiment and relationality, works by realizing the '*presentification*' of the world, rather than its '*representation*' (De Luca Picione & Salvatore, 2023).

Signs are therefore not conceptual mediators existing apart from experience. Rather they are devices that are integral to experience itself, embodying the subject's experience as inherently charged with value, sense and direction. By introducing a sort of *principle of complementarity of semiosis* we acknowledge on one hand a relational perspective on signs as knots of a network in constant transformation of relationships. On the other hand, we gain a 'quasiontologising' perspective that considers signs as entities that reify experience, by giving it consistency and a sense of reality. These two sides always work simultaneously and complementarily and cannot be separated. If a sign performed purely a relational function, we would face an infinite regress in attempting to trace the origin of the associative network. Any attempt to define the infinite relationships within a given context would quickly prove impossible. Consider, for example, the postmodernist tenet that there is no ultimate source of reality, a relativism often taken to its extreme consequences. A major implication of this is the idea that everyone can assert their own local truth and connect anything with everything else. This fluidity of connections prevents the establishment of any fixed points of reference to orient and guide individual experience.

Concurrently, if a sign possessed a real identity, it could flexibly linked in multiple ways, overdetermining experience and constantly shifting its meaning through metaphorisation, polysemy and generalisation. The sign would then have a one-to-one relation with the things and states in the world, as in a mechanical system that simply encodes and decodes stimuli or input. Therefore, a sign's '*relational valence*' allows the continuous transformation of an experience, whilst its '*reifying valence*' offers a reduction of the experience's complexity, polysemy and overdeterminement (Neuman, 2010). This bivalence guarantees the sign's local stability within an experience. The semiotic function of affectivisation implies keeping together a sign's 'relationality' and 'thingness' (De Luca Picione, 2020b; De Luca Picione & Freda, 2023a).

By summarising, affective semiosis does not have a purely referential or denotative function of the world. It does not represent something separate from the subject through signs. Affective semiosis presents the world by making it experienceable, connected, consistent and shareable with others. This process is therefore by no means detached from the cultural dimension of the psyche. The signs do not only indicate specific states of the world but directly implicate a 'subjectivity in motion' within the scenario represented (De Luca Picione & Salvatore, 2023).

Affective semiosis, therefore, creates a field of experience where the subject lives, moves, and interacts with others. Through this semiotic mediation, subjectivation, relationships with others, and the agency of experience is enabled. As Valsiner states:

> Human beings are a passionate species for whom affect is in the center of the developing *psyche*. We focus on inventing terms that reference meaningful affect. On that primacy of the affective life by the notion of *affectivating*—relating to everything we do, think, or imagine. We not only *understand* the World—we *relate to* it with the flow of our feelings extended into it—and then attempt to change it. (Valsiner, 2021, p. 20)

Building on this foundation of cultural psychology background, we will now examine the functions of 'the modal articulation' as a semiotic process. This process constructs experience in different ways – through what we term 'modalities' – which generally correspond to categories such as necessity, obligation, possibility, permission, will, power, and knowledge.

MODAL ARTICULATION – A CONCEPTUAL AND METHODOLOGICAL DEVELOPMENT OF AFFECTIVE SEMIOSIS

Consider the different meanings conveyed by modal operators in sentences such as 'I must eat,' 'I want to eat,' 'I can eat,' 'I am forced to eat,' and 'I am allowed to eat'. These examples demonstrate how subjectivity navigates a range of meaning transformations within a semiotic configuration. There is a significant difference between the feeling of '*want*', '*can*', '*must*', '*being forced*', '*having permission to*', '*knowing to*' act in a certain way. We consider that each syntagm can be conjugated with different tenses and ways, and negation can also be added. Furthermore, we observe often periphrases can be used to construct the modal sense beyond the direct and explicit servile verbs, for which the modal tension is constructed through a broader syntagmatic and paraphrastic construction. For example, '*I was not able to pursue my goals*', or '*I have to improve my life style inasmuch there is need*'.

Modal articulation has a constitutive relationship with the positioning assumed by the subject within a context, in affective, modelling/shaping, cognitive and performative terms. In this sense, every modal articulation can be understood as a '*marker of the sense of the subjective position*' experienced by the subject within her semiotic relational systems. We refer to this semiotic process as '*modal articulation*', defining the process of recursive semiotic configuration between the different modal operators. Note that for a subject, the choice of one does not exclude the consideration of others. We believe that a certain modal positioning implies the consideration of the other modalities (in the background or implicitly).

The important semiotic capacity of human beings to imagine possible worlds (Bruner, 1986; Leibnitz, 1704; Peirce, 1931–1935; Sebeok, 1986; Valsiner, 2021) cannot be reduced to a simplistic, neutral and aseptic '*as if*'. The projection in different times of the same subject (possible futures and different reconstructions of past scenarios) is connected to a modal mediation (affectively experienced) as necessary, possible, desirable, unacceptable, due, required, etc.

It is worth noting that the modalisation of experience relates to the uncertainty of a context and the difficulty of predicting the future (De Luca Picione, 2021). This is distinct from the focus of modal formal logic, which concerns modalities such as *aletic* (possibility of truth), *epistemic* on the (certainty of a proposition), *temporal* (truth-value over time), and *deontic* (duty and permission). The fundamental and central dimension of the modal movement we are highlighting here is the affective one. As Greimas (1983) argues in his studies of 'semiotics of the passions', the modalisation process is the first step from full emotional undifferentiation between a subject and object to the differentiation between the two.

Furthermore, for the physician, psychologist and philosopher Weizsäcker, the subject's experience is always affective (in his terms: '*pathic*', namely *passionate* – De Luca Picione, 2024a, 2024b) and it is expressed through a continuous modalisation towards the world to which she is inextricably connected in a constant cycle of breaking and repairing of the living balance. Weizsäcker describes a sort of pentagram-like structure in which there is a changing relationship between five *modal-pathic* forms. The five modalities are always connected to a dynamic search for equilibrium with the world, which is patently instantiated (in the sense of passion):

> If I want (*wollen*) something, then it is something that is not, otherwise I would not have been able to want it; if I can (*können*) something, it is something that is possible, however, not (yet) real; likewise, if I may (*dürfen*) something, it is allowed; if I have to (*sollen*), it is necessary; if I must (*müssen*), it is inevitable. (von Weizsäcker, 1956, p. 554)

In cultural psychology, the great importance of modal categories as dynamic semiotic mediators has been widely highlighted and developed by Jaan Valsiner (2014):

> Once the I AM stem concept is established, it serves as the basis for binding different predicates to itself, while maintaining its own stability. (p. 19) [...]
>
> Yet, as the person operates at the border of time (PAST | FUTURE), the primary stem concept I AM is not sufficient for existing in a world of constant changes. If the person were limited to I-AM → {predicate X} → I-AM... system only, no action upon the world would follow. The person would be a hostage to the environmental conditions, registering new qualities of oneself under the influence of the environment. The self would be self-centered as an end point in itself, while the stem concept IAM makes it possible for the person who reflects upon one's being only and is not active towards the world. The scenario of a fully functioning I-AM → {predicate X} → I-AM... system in responding to the input from the environment is that of a passive self-labelling that does not relate to any action. (p. 20)
>
> [...] The person operating within the system is endlessly self-descriptive *without the predicates becoming semiotic mediators for action.* Yet the potential to turn to action is prepared through these concepts. The I-AM needs to become complemented with other stem concepts.
>
> The stem concept I-NEED is likewise a cycle of self-maintaining kind (like I-AM in Figure 1.9), yet it is oriented to an *object that is not present* at this time. The I NEED stem concept introduces the move

> from the present towards the future, yet it remains framed by the I AM concept: I AM {I NEED→ I DESIRE} → X. The recognition of a need is oriented to the future, but is not necessarily leading to action that fulfils the need. It is the I WANT stem concept that brings a need to self-reflexivity. I WANT is likewise oriented to the future, but is not action-prone. A person can operate in a cycle of attaching predicates to the I WANT cycle (e.g. "I want to go to the Moon", "I want to be a millionaire", "I want children", "I want peace for the whole world"), yet without any action other than talk about what one wants. This is similar to talk about needs: "I need X, Y, Z" does not mean that the person moves beyond the process of attaching predicates to the stem concept. Finally, the I WILL stem concept links the person with some (promised, but not necessarily carried out) action. (p. 21) [...]
>
> The four basic stem concepts can be combined in many ways, and each can grow a complex structure of meanings around their primary role—the binding of predicates. It is into this relationship of the stem concepts that social norms23 become inserted, either prohibiting or enforcing an action. (Valsiner, 2014, p. 21)

Using the above arguments, we developed a three-function modal articulation model (for a full review of this, see De Luca Picione, 2021; De Luca Picione et al., 2018, 2019) described below:

1. The *function of connection* between affective and linguistic processes. Affective/embodied activation predisposes action and forms the basis of symbolisation processes. As discussed above, from basic bodily forms of pleasure/displeasure to more sophisticated forms of what??? modal articulation is mediated through culture, language, and modal categories such as necessity, power, will and knowledge. It performs the important function of mediation through translation of the plane of prereflexive affectivity in specific modal ways, thereby enabling a dynamic intentionality of subjective experience in the world. Modal devices, therefore, work as semiotic mediators of affective processes.
2. The *function of mediation* of intersubjective positionings. The modalisation of experience allows a subject to define themselves in relations with the other social actors. Responding to a systemic and intersubjective logics, modal articulation is a process that configures modal positionings between social relations. Where there are duties or prohibitions for someone, there are complementary rights or obligations for others. For example, where I am not allowed to pass over a barrier, someone else will have the permission instead. The function of mediation works within social normative frames (De Luca Picione, 2021) but it can be very plastic and dynamic. There can be many simultaneous contextual modal configurations. A

subject can be at same time father, son, nephew, and so on. Each social role has different modal configuration (in terms of duty, permission, limitation, opportunity, power, and exercise of freewill), that develop over time and occur concurrently.

3. The *function of vectorisation* between agency and temporality. Modal operators work as dynamic organisers of agency in relation to the temporal frames of an experience. They orient the sense of action in time. This function is essential, inasmuch time is not a static frame within which actions are performed. People in their transformations and developments struggle with the ever-chaning nature of time and unpredictability of the future. This inherent gap between ta presumed objective reality plane of facts (ideally knowable and referenceable world-states), the contingency and irreversibility of events, and the human process of meaning-making fuels an agentive dynamism directed towards hypothetical future scenarios. Human semiosis represents a radical departure from the animal world. It enables individuals to dynamically, flexibly, plastic and innovatively guide their actions across diverse contexts of interaction and experience. Modal articulation is a key aspect of this semiotic flexibility.

A POSSIBLE USE OF MODAL ARTICULATION IN CLINICAL PSYCHOLOGIC INTERVENTION

The aforementioned theoretical assumptions have implications for both clinical psychology practice and clinical psychology research. From a clinical practice point of view, attention to modal articulation focuses on the processes of sensemaking in affective, relational and agentive terms. In his paper, Caston (2011, p. 930) – in the section titled «*'I Must', 'I Can't ', Etc. as a Clinical Markers*» highlights the significant role that these '*verbal expressions of inhibitions, constraints and pushes*' can play in both therapeutic treatment and in the analysis of the verbatim transcripts from therapy session recordings. These expressions can reveal transformations in the patient's narrative processes.

Modal articulation centres on the subject and their 'ways' of experiencing and engaging in intersubjective relationships. For example, a psychotherapeutic journey (Freda et al., 2012) can be understood as a transformation of relational modes-a process of expanding the possibilities for developing one's subjectivity and relational systems. Our focus is not on '*who*' or '*what should be transformed*' in psychotherapy. Rather we emphasise 'how' we feel and perceive (which actively and concretely shapes our relationships) is the key to understanding possible transformative aspects of clinical intervention.

A focus on modal articulation therefore allows a structural/relational perspective, rather than a semantic view. Our intention is not to reject the semantic perspective but rather add an understanding of its relational/affective/agentive configuration that shapes it contents. We propose that semantics acquire meaning through semiotic connections (De Luca Picione, 2015a, 2020c; Salvatore, 2016) that are contextual and oriented over time. In addition, modal articulation involves the interplay of different modalities, including the concealment of some modalities by others, the disguise of modalities, the persistence of certain modalities, the dynamic shifts in salience among modalities, and the background between the relationships between them.

Modal articulation is also not built solely through a linear and progressive time process, such as in this sentence: '*I want a new and expensive car, I cannot afford it with my economic efforts, I am forced to steal it because I want it!*'; or, 'I *have to go to school if I want to become an engineer to be able to build houses*'. Rather, there can be multilevel configurations of generalisation and scope of relevance. Take for example these levels of broad generalisation and abstraction: '*we can be free only when we do our duty*'; '*every time I want something there is always some circumstance that forces me/obliges me to make sacrifices in order to achieve my goal*'; '*if I hadn't had to cook for so many people, I would have had time to be able to dedicate myself to the decorations of the party I wanted to prepare*'; '*I don't want to go to him but I have to because otherwise I can't collect my sum of money*'.

It would be naïve to assume that a modal category used in verbal expression always perfectly reflects a person's true feeling or intention. We often observe, for example, that an expressed will can mask an underlying feeling of necessity, or that expressions of inability ('I can't', 'it is not possible') can conceal a lack of desire ('I do not want'). While modalisation is conceptualised as a fundamental aspect of action, the modal content expressed linguistically may not precisely correspond with actual behaviour. This discrepancy does not invalidate the analysis of the modal articulation or render it incapable of revealing patterns; rather it emphasises the need to situate modal articulation within a broader sensemaking process shaped by cultural, affective, cognitive, and intersubjective dynamics. The analysis should focus on the overall configuration of the modal framework and not on a simplistic correspondence between language and facts.

Therefore, if a person consistently states they *must* do something, yet never does it, this does not necessaritly demonstrate an inconsistency of the modal value or a disconnect between feeling, thought, and action. Instead, it points to a complex modal configuration where the explicit dimension of duty (expressed verbally) interacts with other implicit modal positions (for example, 'I don't want', 'I can't', 'I have to realize a more important duty'). Such configurations warrant careful consideration in a clinical, psychotherapeutic, or health contexts.

MODAL ARTICULATION IN A LONGITUDINAL STUDY ON NARRATIVES OF WOMEN WITH CANCER

Study Background

This section presents examples of modal articulation in narrations of young women with cancer who had completed their planned medical treatment. These narratives were collected as part of a larger longitudinal study of the cancer experience (Lemmo et al., 2020; Martino et al., 2019a, 2019b, 2019c; 2021). The research was conducted at the National Cancer Institute '*Fondazione G. Pascale*', Naples, Italy-a national referral centre for neoplastic disease treatment and care – as part of the STAR Programme, funded by *UniNA* and *Compagnia di San Paolo*. The study was co-designed in collaboration with the hospital's psychology service and breast surgery unit and approved by the institutes medical committee. The hospital's psychology service provided space and resources for project meetings and ongoing psychotherapeutic support for the women involved. Study participants were identified from medical records and met the following criteria:

- *Inclusion criteria*: First hospital visit before age 50; diagnosis of infiltrating ductal breast cancer; voluntary participation.
- *Exclusion criteria*: Metastatic disease (stage IV); ongoing psychotherapeutic treatment

Recruitment involved a one-day meeting at the hospital to explain the study's aims and procedures. All participants provided informed consent, and the study's privacy policy was approved by the hospital. 50 women were recruited during the prehospitalisation phase. Due to changes in healthcare resources, treatment plans, or declining interest, participant attrition occurred. Of the initial 50, 10 women participated in the longitudinal study, spanning four phases: During the study the women underwent four longitudinal phases as follows: prehospitalisation phase (T1: 40–60 days before surgery), postoperative counselling phase (T2: 30–40 days after surgery, coinciding with their histological results), adjuvant therapy phase (T3: 25–35 days after starting chemotherapy, radiotherapy, or hormone therapy) and at follow-up phase (T4: approximately 8 months after completing treatment). The average age of these 10 participants was 44.4 years. During each meeting, participants were asked to freely share their experiences with the illness, including significant events, subjective experiences (emotions, fears, hopes, fantasies), relationships with others, and any transformations were undergoing or had experienced.

Study Approach

The subsequent section analyses the longitudinal narratives of three of these women to illustrate the modal articulation process during their illness experience. These analyses aim to demonstrate the application of our semiotic-psychological construct within clinical and health psychology (De Luca Picione et al., 2017, 2018, 2019). Two different analytical approaches were used: a quantitative approach and a semiotic approach focused on the sensemaking process. These approaches are not considered mutually exclusive but rather mutually informative, and potentially representing two steps in a single analytical procedure.

Measurement of the Modal Articulation

In order to study the modal articulation in illness narratives, we focused on narratives from three participants who completed the four phases of the study.

The quantitative analysis allowed us to assess the frequency and variance of modalisation in each phase, while the qualitative analysis assessed the subjective-contextual changes of modalisation. Modal verbs, synonyms, and linguistic expressions that refer to a 'modal meaning' (e.g. *I am not able to tolerate the sadness* → *I cannot tolerate the sadness*; *I wish vividly to go out* → *I want to go out*) (De Luca Picione et al., 2017) were considered. All modal expression in the participant narratives were grouped into four abstract categories of our theoretical model – I Will, I Can, I Must, and I Know. Each category was further subdivided into negative and positive formulations (I Will Not, will, I Cannot, I Must Not, I Don't Know), in order to preserve relevant information on the kind of modalisation.

The Table 3.1 below shows the frequency of text changes in each narrative, and enabled comparison between narratives along a longitudinal axis.

The initial analysis considered key variations in: (a) the frequency of modal categories; (b) the presence or absence of specific modal forms; and (c) the changing prominence of particulat modal categories across the study phases.

A key finding from the quantitative analysis of modality changes over time was the consistently high incidence of the *duty* modality (MUST) in all illness narratives:

- Narrator A: Phase I, 11 times; Phase II, 13 times; Phase III, 13 times; Phase IV, 5 times.
- Narrator B: Phase I, 2 times; Phase II, 16 times; Phase III, 11 times; Phase IV, 21 times.
- Narrator C: Phase I, 13 times; Phase II, 23 times; Phase III, 23 times; Phase IV, 29 times.

This first result has a relevant clinical implication: in the face of a health crisis, the MUST modality appears reassuring and orients choices, decisions and actions. In fact, communicating the diagnosis generates a fracture in the person's system of meaning and generates a confusing and disturbing emotional impact. Relying on a normative definition of behaviours allows one to find an organising direction in a chaotic dimension.

The WILL modality generally increases in prominence in later phases of the therapeutic process:

- Narrator A: Phase I, 1 time; Phase II, 0 times; Phase III, 3 times; Phase IV, 1 time;
- Narrator B: Phase I, 3 times; Phase II, 10 times; Phase III phase, 0 times; Phase IV, 9 times;
- Narrator C: Phase I, 9 times; Phase II, 3 times; Phase III, 3 times; Phase IV, phase 15 times.

The increase of the frequency of WILL modality attests the re-appropriation of a subjective position in the relation to one's life.

From point of view of CAN modality frequency, we observe an oscillatory trend: in the narratives of time 2 and 3 the NO-CAN modality increases and then decreases at time 4. This tendency clearly shows how there is a difficulty during the path to consider oneself a subject with a sense of agency, while instead at the end of the therapeutic path this feeling of impotence is reduced.

- Narrator A: Phase I, 4 times; Phase II, 4 times; Phase III, 3 times; Phase IV, 3 times;
- Narrator B: Phase I, 2 times; Phase II, 11 times; Phase III, 3 times; Phase IV, 0 times;
- Narrator C: Phase I, 2 times; Phase II, 13 times; Phase III, 11 times; Phase IV, 6 times.

Similar to the previous observation, this trend suggests a gradual re-appropriation of one's relationship with their own choices and sense of agency.

Generally, the high incidence of the *duty* modality (in terms of must, need, in relation to prescriptions and medical compliance), suggests the participant's strong sense of obligation and dependence to the medical context – i.e. participants must submit themselves to the therapeutic protocols of lifesaving treatment. They do not find themselves in a position of desire, possibility and subjective choice. However, it is worthy to note that the modalisation of the 'Must' modal category is very important in the first period of the illness, which is generally highly traumatic and disorienting.

TABLE 3.1 Variations of Modal Verbs in the Positive and Negative Form Over Different Phases of the Medical Treatment.

	NO-WILL	WILL	NO- CAN	CAN	NO- MUST	MUST	NO-KNOW	KNOW
Narrator A – I phase (Tot. 1,371 words)	3	1	4	2	1	11	22	4
Narrator A – II phases (Tot. 981 words)	1	0	7	1	0	13	7	0
Narrator A – III phase (Tot. 1,609 words)	0	3	3	1	0	13	7	1
Narrator A – IV phase (Tot. 1,045 words)	0	1	3	1	0	5	2	1
Narrator B – I phase (Tot. 983 words)	0	3	2	4	0	2	5	2
Narrator B – II phase (Tot. 1,768 words)	5	10	11	5	4	16	2	2

(Continued)

TABLE 3.1 Variations of Modal Verbs in the Positive and Negative Form Over Different Phases of the Medical Treatment. (Continued)

	NO-WILL	WILL	NO- CAN	CAN	NO- MUST	MUST	NO-KNOW	KNOW
Narrator B – III phase (Tot. 1,009 words)	2	0	3	3	1	11	1	1
Narrator B – IV phase (Tot. 2,050 words)	0	9	0	6	1	21	5	3
Narrator C – I phase (Tot. 2,105 words)	3	9	2	11	2	13	5	7
Narrator C – II phase (Tot. 3,366 words)	1	3	13	7	1	23	16	15
Narrator C – III phase (tot. 2,616 word)	4	3	11	10	1	23	6	8
Narrator C – IV phase (Tot. 4,078 words)	9	15	6	12	3	29	14	6

It offers a sort of semiotic scaffolding for orienting the patient's behaviour towards their treatment needs.

A quantitative semiotic approach to understanding sensemaking processes reveals a temporal variation in modal articulations related to different phases of the illness experience. These phases include: the initial shock of the diagnosis (characterised by '*I cannot*' and '*It is not possible*'); a period of confusion and uncertainty ('*not wanting*', and '*not knowing*'); gradual acceptance of the disease and treatment ('*must* undergo treatment'); and the eventual assertion of agency and desire for recovery ('*will*' and '*can*').

This quantitative approach is particularly useful for analysing long textual and narrative data, such as lengthy psychotherapy transcripts or focus group discussions. It can be applied, for example, to evaluate how agentive semiotic constructions evolve over time, within individuals, groups, or communities.

Qualitative Analysis of the Modal Articulation

This analytic procedure involves a close reading of each narrative, tracing how sensemaking unfolds and develops over time. This allows us to identify fluctuations in modal articulation, tensions between modalities, modal ambivalences regarding critical issues, and how future scenarios are constructed in relation to the past and the present. This idiographic approach (De Luca Picione, 2015b) reveals the development of subjectivity, the affective matrix of experience, the temporal trajectory of sensemaking, and the interplay between imagination or creativity and the unpredictability of the future. Each '*as if*' scenario is a modal construction, involving a fictional process in which modal operators of necessity, possibility, impossibility and contingency are implicitly linked (De Luca Picione, 2021; De Luca Picione et al., 2018).

Qualitatively, this analysis examines the flexibility, stability, and rigidity of the modal configurations, focussing on how narrative continuity and discontinuity organise the relationship between the individual and their context – emotionally, relationally, and cognitively (De Luca Picione & Freda, 2023a, 2023b). Dynamically stable modal articulations can support individual agency by providing scaffolding (De Luca Picione, 2021; De Luca Picione et al., 2019). This stability exists on a continuum between excessive flexibility (fragmentation and dispersion) and complete rigidity (blockage, stasis). Illness narratives often reveal redundant modal articulations, sometimes repeated across narratives, while at other time, we observe the beginnings of transformation.

A focus exclusively on contents, as in thematic or phenomenological interpretative analysis, would overlook these crucial nuances and variations. Analysing modal articulation allows us to examine the construction of the narrative objects (stories, events, actions, characters, and times) specifically focussing on modes and syntax.

Our analysis emphasises '*sense*' – a dynamic process evolving over time (referencing Peirce's semiotics his concept of unlimited semiosis involving the interpretant between the sign and object-rather than '*meaning*' which is considered static, dyadic and referential (De Luca Picione, 2020c; De Luca Picione & Freda, 2023a, 2023b). The following examples of modal articulations are drawn from the different narratives:

Narrator A – phase 1:

> ... I still *don't have to understand*, but until you*know*, you *don't know*, that's how the doctor said before, until *we really know* what entity it is, what reality it is, *I don't know* what to think, and do everything and think, beautiful and ugly but in fact *you do not know*, you say "you suffer from this thing, you have to do this" *we don't know yet*, we are still in limbo ...
>
> ...it makes you nervous, it makes you tense, it makes you nervous, it makes you feel., ... waiting for something *you can't control*, *you don't know*, you don't ... the difficulty of ... that's it ... not to point out many of those things, because there is a little girl who turns around you... and so ... you *can't show yourself*...

This modal articulation movements show a position of rigidity in the first phase of the illness, characterised by medical investigations to determine the extent of the disease and suitable therapeutic course. This position is characterised by the dominant use of the '*not knowing*' and '*not being able*' modalities, thus attesting to a position of uncertainty, expectation and dependence in relation respect to the medical context, and a sense of being in 'limbo'.

Narrator B – phase 2

> ...fortunately, *I must not have* chemo, but until now it has been wa*iting to know if I should have chem*o, and so ... and you just wait, *you cannot fight*, you wait. Well, even if you *had to have* chemo, what are you fighting? You decide nothing! And ... it's not that ... fighting means that *you have power* over something, but *you have no power over* anything, you just watch the succession of events, you don't have a ... *you can't do anything*! You just *have to ... let* things flow around you, it's not that *you have power over* anything, *you have no power over* anything. So it is this sense of helplessness that does not belong to me, I am used to acting, if something, there is something wrong, I ... I try to do something. In this situation, *I have no power over anything*. That's what bothered me ... bothered me the most ... because *you must wait*, that is it, *you can't do anything*.
>
> ... there are things *you must do* in the role of mother, in the role of daughter, but you *don't want to do anything* because *you just want to think* about yourself but *you can't do it*, and ... there are people *who want to help you* but not *you don't even know* what *you want*.

The observed changes in modal articulation indicate a movement from one phase another. The second is characterised by stable modalities over time (‘*not being able*’ and ‘*not knowing*’), where uncertainty, expectations, dependencies and helplessness continue to remain as prominent positions. However, the modality of ‘wanting’ begins to emerge, accompanied by a growing concern with articulating a subjective desire and emotional connection to their context.

Narrator C – phase 3.

> …I told him here it is written that I must have 4 specialist visits, he told me it is a “thing to write”, then if *you need* … .. I told him *I need to know if I can hug* my son, if *I can have sex* with a man , if *I can go home* without a car, that is, *I must know how* I am!…

The above shift in modal articulation highlights a growing flexibility in the individual’s relationship with their context, which is expanding the medical and illness sphere to include other aspects of life and of emotionally significant relationships. This expansion is accompanied by a desire for knowledge, a drive to rebuild life’s continuity, and a growing sense of agency in planning and self-determination.

Narration C – phase 4

> … then the fact that I told you before maybe, that first of all you must love each other, more,. (uhm) yourself. (uhm) Uhm…. I said one thing at the beginning, to trust and trust, but never too much. (uhm) I told her: “I *must trust* and I *must* trust.” But then, for the things that have happened, even in here, obviously I have always been …. perplexed, right? (of course) we also talked about it in the radiotherapy phase, uhm … so always with … with the who goes there. Um … I already temperamentally, I am a person who unfortunately, very suspicious, very uhm … or maybe I am then, here, I have become more, paradoxically, (uhm) it is as if … *I wanted more*, give him others. (Uhm) eh … But if, now the others don’t give this thing to me, because I think that precisely, *I don’t have to ask for* certain things, because one requires … (smiles) but not friendship or affection, in short, it *could not be a request*, in my opinion. So, if there isn’t, there isn’t, that’s enough. *I don’t want to get* mad at these things. (uhm) When … maybe on books it says: “Turn the page”, eh, *I must turn* the page, *I can’t apply* myself.

This shift in modal articulation reveals a dynamic movement towards increasing flexibility. As the individual returns to daily life and routines, their relationships with desire and choices shifts from passive dependence to active agency and self-protection. Accessing a realm of desire allows for an internal re-evaluation of the relationships with oneself, others, and one’s own emotions.

These examples illustrate how specific modal articulation configurations can be identified within narratives. These configurations often recur within a single highlighting how the narrator makes sense of critical, emotionally charged experiences. These configurations can be stable or in transformation. From a clinical point of view, they serve as valuable markers for the clinical psychologist and provide material for reflection and elaboration within the therapeutic setting.

CONCLUSION

This study presented a *semiotic model of the modal articulation*, exploring its characteristics and implications. We demonstrated that:

- Modal articulation emerges from the interplay of emotion/affect and agency within a tive relational context.
- It serves key functions: *connection* (connecting affect and sensemaking); *mediation* of intersubjectivity;, and *vectorisation* (directing and orientating action).
- Modal articulation is a dynamic process that fluctuates over time, reflecting the temporal nature of human experience.
- Modal articulation always manifests as a modal composition (Bertrand, 2002). This means that employing a specific modal category in the sensemaking process simultaneously invokes other modal categories. Similar to a musical composition, modal articulation can be monotone (repetitive use of a single modal operator) or 'symphonic' where the sensemaking process involves a rich interplay of modal operators, acting in counterpoint, harmonisation, and thematic variation, fostering novelty and transformation.

Crucially, modal articulation follows a gradual dimensional approach in its transformative processes. In other words, modal categories in sensemaking are not used in a rigid or formal manner, but rather in an idiosyncratic, context-dependent, and culturally embedded way. The construct of modal articulation does not focus on isolated modal categories but rather on the interactive dynamics of the subject within a social context. It encompasses 'feeling, thinking, and acting' in relation to the transient and evolving forms of meaning that shape experience.

We also considered two possible approaches to modal analysis: a quantitative and a qualitative approach. Rather than viewing them as conflicting, we argue that their integration enriches the methodological landscape of mixed qualitative-quantitative research methods.

In the field of clinical psychology, psychotherapy and health psychology, the construct of modal articulation offers various contributions by: (1) reinforcing the role of cultural psychology a semiotic framework centred on sensemaking processes; and (2) bridging the gap between clinical practice, research, and theoretical development.

Analysing narratives through a modal lens allow us to observe how the process of sensemaking unfolds as a dynamic semiotic organisation, revealing varying intensities and nuances. This process configures the relational field where subjectivity and otherness interact. Modalisation constitutes a dynamic movement that shapes the construction of meaning.

We argue that categorising different modal configurations in a rigid taxonomic manner would be counterproductive. Doing so would contradict the idea of sensemaking as a continuous becoming of while imposing a static classification framework (De Luca Picione, 2015b; De Luca Picione & Salvatore, 2023). Instead, we propose considering different levels of modal articulation processes.

One distinction is between '*the absence versus the presence of modal articulation*' in narratives. Some narratives lack modal operators or exhibit a notable absence of certain modal elements, resulting in a flat, purely descriptive and emotionally detached account of experience. In such cases, temporalisation may be blocked (in the case of traumatic events) or constructed in a monotonously linear fashion, where time is merely a succession of events, without deeper semiotic connections.

Another level concerns '*the presence of modal operators in first person versus in impersonal terms*'. For example the contrast between 'I must' *versus* 'it is necessary', 'I can' *versus* 'it is possible that', 'I desire' *versus* 'it is desirable that', or 'I know' *versus* 'it is known that … ', reveals a tension between subjective agency and impersonal determinism. This distinction highlights the emergence of subjectivity within narratives, reflecting the affective and dialogic expression of one's position.

A further level pertains to the '*re-configurational capacity of the modal articulations*'. Here, modal articulation moves beyond a rigid and habitual structure of sensemaking to exhibit plasticity, adapting to relational contexts and shifting meanings. At this stage, modal articulation serves as a semiotic device that individuals use in reflexive processes, shaping their active positioning within social interactions (De Luca Picione, 2019; De Luca Picione & Freda, 2023b; Esposito et al., 2016; Freda et al., 2015).

REFERENCES

Barbieri, M. (2008). Biosemiotics: A new understanding of life. *Naturwissenschaften, 95*(7), 577–599.

Barsalou, L. W. (1999). Perceptual symbol systems. *Behavioural and Brain Science, 22,* 577–609.

Barsalou, L. W. (2008). Grounded cognition. *Annual Review of Psychology, 59,* 617–645.

Bertrand, D. (2002). *Basi di semiotica letteraria.* Meltemi.

Bhabha, H. K. (1994). *The location of culture.* Routledge.
Bion, W. R. (1962). *Learning from experience.* Seven Servants.
Borghi, A. M., & Caruana, F. (2015). Embodiment theory. In J. D. Wright. (Ed.), *International encyclopedia of the social & behavioral sciences* (pp. 1–7). Elsevier.
Bruner, J. S. (1986). *Actual minds, possible worlds.* Harvard University Press.
Caston, J. (2011). Agency as a psychoanalytic idea. *Journal of the American Psychoanalytic Association, 59,* 907–938. https://doi.org/10.1177/0003065111422541
Chiozza, L. (2012). *El interés en la vida: Solo se puede ser siendo con otros* [*The interest on the life: it is possible to be only by being among others*]. Los Libros del Zorzal.
Cornejo, C., Marsico, G., & Valsiner, J. (2018). "I activate you to affect me": Affectivating as a cultural psychological phenomenon. In C. Cornejo, G. Marsico, & J. Valsiner (Eds.), *"I activate you to affect me". Annals of cultural psychology: Exploring the frontiers of mind and society* (Vol. 2). Information Age Publishing. Charlotte, N.C.
De Luca Picione, R. (2015a). *La mente come forma. La mente come testo: Un'indagine semiotico-psicologica dei processi di significazione* [*The mind as form. The mind as text: A semiotic-psychological research of sensemaking research*]. Mimesis Edizioni.
De Luca Picione, R. (2015b). The idiographic approach in psychological research. The challenge of overcoming old distinctions without risking to homogenize. *Integrative Psychological and Behavioral Science, 49*(3), 360–370.
De Luca Picione, R. (2019). Mirrors and Reflexive processes: From looking oneself in the mirror to sensemaking one's own experience. Insidious paths between semiotics, cultural psychology and dynamic psychology. In W. J. Silva Filho & L. Tateo (Eds.), *Thinking about oneself. The place and value of reflection in philosophy and psychology* (pp. 123–139). Springer.
De Luca Picione, R. (2020a). The semiotic paradigm in psychology. A mature Weltanschauung for the definition of semiotic mind. *Integrative Psychological and Behavioral Science, 54*(3), 639–650. https://doi.org/10.1007/s12124-020-09555-y
De Luca Picione, R. (2020b). Models of semiotic borders in psychology and their implications: From rigidity of separation to topological dynamics of connectivity. *Theory & Psychology.* https://doi.org/10.1177/0959354320947184
De Luca Picione, R. (2020c). The double faces of each semiotic process. The multiple dynamics of the mind between form and text. In R. Innis (Ed.), *Between philosophy and cultural psychology* (pp. 107–119). Springer. (author).
De Luca Picione, R. (2021). The dynamic nature of the human psyche and its three tenets: Normativity, liminality and resistance. Semiotic advances in direction of modal articulation sensemaking. *Human Arenas.* https://doi.org/10.1007/s42087-021-00212-3
De Luca Picione, R. (2021b). Metapsychology of borders: Structures, operations and semiotic dynamics. *European Journal of Psychotherapy & Counselling, 23*(4), 436–467.
De Luca Picione, R. (2024a). Viktor von Weizsäcker's Gestaltkreis theory. The dynamic and subjective relationship of perception and movement. *Integrative Psychological and Behavioral Science, 58*(1), 35–45.
De Luca Picione, R. (2024b). Viktor von Weizsäcker's notion of pathic: Affective liminality, modalisation of experience and illness. *Integrative Psychological and Behavioral Science, 58*(1), 46–58.

De Luca Picione, R. & Freda, M. F. (2014). Catalysis and morphogenesis: The contextual semiotic configuration of form, function, and fields of experience. In K. R. Cabell, , & J. Valsiner, (Eds.), *The catalyzing mind. Beyond models of causality. Annals of theoretical psychology* (Vol. *11*. pp. 149–163). Springer.

De Luca Picione, R., & Freda, M. F. (2016a). Borders and modal articulations. Semiotic constructs of sensemaking processes enabling a fecund dialogue between cultural psychology and clinical psychology. *Journal of Integrative Psychological and Behavioral Science, 50,* 29–43.

De Luca Picione, R., & Freda, M. F. (2016b). The processes of meaning making, starting from the morphogenetic theories of Rene´ Thom. *Culture & Psychology, 22*(1), 139–157.

De Luca Picione, R., & Freda, M. F. (2016c). Possible use in psychology of threshold concept in order to study sensemaking processes. *Culture & Psychology, 22*(3), 362–375.

De Luca Picione, R., & Freda, M. F. (2023a). The contribution of semiotics for psychological disciplines: A focus on dynamic sensemaking processes. In A. Biglari (Ed.), *Open semiotics* (pp. 217–230). L'Harmattan.

De Luca Picione, R., & Freda, M. F. (2023b). The semiotic forms of continuity and discontinuity in the narrative process. In S. Salvatore & J. Valsiner (Eds.), *Ten years of idiographic science* (pp. 47–69). Information Age Publishing.

De Luca Picione, R., Luisa Martino, M., & Freda, M. F. (2017). Understanding cancer patients' narratives: Meaning-making process, temporality, and modal articulation. *Journal of Constructivist Psychology, 30*(4), 339–359.

De Luca Picione, R., Martino, M. L., & Freda, M. F. (2018). Modal articulation: The psychological and semiotic functions of modalities in the sensemaking process. *Theory & Psychology, 28*(1), 84–103.

De Luca Picione, R., Martino, M. L., & Troisi, G. (2019). The semiotic construction of the sense of agency. The modal articulation in narrative processes. *Integrative Psychological and Behavioral Science, 53*(3), 431–449.

De Luca Picione, R., & Salvatore, S. (2023). Mind is movement. We need more than static representations to understand it. In J. Valsiner (Ed.), *Farewell to variables.* Information Age Publishing.

De Luca Picione, R., & Valsiner, J. (2017). Psychological functions of semiotic borders in sense-making: Liminality of narrative processes. *Europe's Journal of Psychology, 13*(3), 532–547.

de Saussure, F. (1921). *Course in general linguistics.* McGraw-Hill, 1966.

Eco, U. (1976). *A theory of semiotics* Trans. W. Weaver. Indiana University Press.

Esposito, G., Freda, M. F., & De Luca Picione, R. (2016). Reflexivity or "Reflexivities" in Higher Education: Conceptualizing unique reflexive process. In M. F. Freda, , J. Gonzàlez-Monteagudo, , & G. Esposito, (Eds.), *Working with underachieving students in higher education: Fostering inclusion through narration and reflexivity* (pp.32–42). Routledge.

Favareau, D. (2010). An evolutionary history of biosemiotics. In D. F. Favareau (Ed.), *Essential readings in biosemiotics* (pp. 1–77). Springer.

Freda, M. F., De Luca Picione, R., & Di Stazio, F. (2012, September). L'articolazione modale come indicazione del rapporto tra soggettività e relazionalità [Modal articulation as indicator of subjectivity-relationality]. In *Paper presented at IX Congresso Nazionale sulla Ricerca in Psicoterapia, Università degli Studi di Salerno, Fisciano, Italy.*

Freda, M. F., De Luca Picione, R., & Esposito, G. (2015). Reflexivity. Applying a reflexive process to an educational context. In P. Marsico, R. Ruggeri, & S. Salvatore (Eds.), *Reflexivity and psychology* (pp. 195–225). Information Age Publishing.

Green, A. (1973). *Le discours vivant.* Presses universitaires de France.

Greimas, A. J. (1983). *De la modalisation de l'être. Dusens II [On themodalitazation of the being. The sense II]*. Seuil.

Hoffmeyer, J. (1996). *Signs of meaning in the universe. Advances in semiotics.* Indiana University Press.

Innis, R. (2020). *Between philosophy and cultural psychology.* Springer.

James, W. (1890). *The principles of psychology.* Harvard University Press, 1983.

Kull, K. (2009). Vegetative, animal, and cultural semiosis: The semiotic threshold zones. *Cognitive Semiotics, 4*(Suppl. ment), 8–27.

Leibnitz, G. W. (1704). *New essays on human understanding* Langley translation 1896. Cambridge University Press.

Lemmo, D., Martino, M. L., Nunziante Cesàro, A., & Solbakk, J. H. (2020). Idiosyncratic ambivalence: A three-dimensional interpretative model to understand the non-adhesion of women to breast and cervical cancer screening. *Mediterranean Journal of Clinical Psychology, 8*(3), 1–19.

Lotman, Y. M. (2005). On the semiosphere. *Σημειωτκή-Sign Systems Studies, 33*(1), 205–229.

Martino, M., Gargiulo, A., Lemmo, D., & Margherita, G. (2019c). Cancer blog narratives: The experience of under-fifty women with breast cancer during different times after diagnosis. *Qualitative Report, 24*(1), 158–173.

Martino, M. L., Gargiulo, A., Lemmo, D., Dolce, P., Barberio, D., Abate, V., Avino, F., & Tortriello, R. (2019a). Longitudinal effect of emotional processing on psychological symptoms in women under 50 with breast cancer. *Health Psychology Open, 6*(1), 1–9.

Martino, M. L., Lemmo, D., Gargiulo, A., Barberio, D., Abate, V., Avino, F., & Freda, M. F. (2021). Changes of narrative meaning-making markers during the different phases of breast cancer treatment for women below 50 years old. *Health Psychology Report, 10*(1), 58–67.

Martino, M. L., Lemmo, D., Gargiulo, A., Barberio, D., Abate, V., Avino, F., & Tortoriello, R. (2019b). Under fifty women and breast cancer: Narrative markers of meaning-making in traumatic experience. *Frontiers in Psychology, 10*(618), 1–12.

Maturana, M. R., & Varela, J. F. (1980). *Autopoiesis and cognition. The realization of the living.* Reidel Publishing Co.

Neuman, Y. (2008). *Reviving the living: Meaning making in living systems.* Elsevier.

Neuman, Y. (2010). Penultimate interpretation. *The International Journal of Psychoanalysis, 91*(5), 1043–1054.

Peirce, C. S. (1931–1935). *Collected papers of Charles Sanders Peirce.* Harvard University Press.

Salvatore, S. (2016). *Psychology in Black and White: The project of a theory-driven science.* Information Age. Publisher.

Salvatore, S., De Luca Picione, R., Cozzolino, M., Bochiccio, V., & Palmieri, A. (2021). The role of affective sensemaking in the constitution of experience. *Integrative Psychological and Behavioral Science.* https://doi.org/10.1007/s12124-020-09590-9

Salvatore, S., & Freda, M. F. (2011a). Affect unconscious and sensemaking. A psychodynamic semiotic and dialogic model. *New Ideas in Psychology, 29,* 119–135.
Salvatore, S., & Freda, M. F. (2011b). Affect, unconscious, and sensemaking: A psychodynamic, semiotic and dialogical model. *New Ideas in Psychology, 29*(2), 119–135.
Salvatore, S., & Zittoun, T. (2011). Outlines of a psychoanalytically informed cultural psychology. In S. Salvatore & T. Zittoun (Eds.), *Cultural psychology and psychoanalysis in dialogue. Issues for constructive theoretical and methodological synergies* (pp. 3–46). Information Age Publishing.
Schutz, A. (1945). On multiple realities. *Philosophy and Phenomenological Research, 5*(4), 533–576.
Sebeok, T. A. (1986). *I think I am a verb. More contributions to the doctrine of signs.* Plenum.
Sebeok, T. A., & Danesi, M. (2000). *The forms of meaning: Modeling systems theory and semiotic analysis.* Walter de Gruyter.
Shannon, C. E., & Weaver, W. (1949). *The mathematical theory of communication.* University of Illinois Press.
Valsiner, J. (2007). *Culture in minds and societies: Foundations of cultural psychology.* Sage.
Valsiner, J. (2014). *An invitation to cultural psychology.* Sage.
Valsiner, J. (2020). *Sensuality in human living. The cultural psychology of affect.* Springer.
Valsiner, J. (2021). *General human psychology: Foundations for a science.* Springer.
Weizsäcker, von V. (1956). *Pathosophie* [*Pathosophy*]. Vandenhoeck and Ruprecht.
Wheeler, W. (2006). *The whole creature: Complexity, biosemiotics and the evolution of culture.* Lawrence & Wishart.

CHAPTER 4

THERAPY AS CRITICAL CONSCIOUSNESS RAISING: A COMPENDIUM OF POLITICS IN PRACTICE

Erin Bulluss
Clinical Psychologist, Australia

Janet Conti
Western Sydney University, Australia

Dawn Darlaston-Jones
University of Western Australia, Australia

Patricia Dudgeon
University of Western Australia, Australia

Tanja Hirvonen
Clinical Psychologist, Australia

Jennifer Malecki
University of Sydney, Australia

Paul Rhodes
University of Sydney, Australia

Cultural Psychology in Clinical Research and Practices, pages 65–88

doi:10.1108/978-1-83742-213-520261004

Tracie Rogers
University of the West Indies, Jamaica

Catherine Wilson
Clinical Psychologist, Australia

ABSTRACT

Contemporary psychology, dominated by the cognitive paradigm is cut off from politics, remaining at best neutral in the face of issues related to social justice and at worst complicit in the maintenance of oppressive structures and the separation of subjects from each other. In this paper we write a critique of the practice of contemporary psychology, drawing on a variety of thinkers, including de Beauvoir, Santos, Martin-Baro and Fanon, arguing for a profession that places justice as its central precept. Each author then accounts for their own practices which embrace this value, recasting psychology as a form of activist-practice, predicated on a variety of knowledges; feminist, gender-diverse, neuro-diverse, indigenous and decolonial. Concepts, practice and examples are provided from each of these positions.

Keywords: Activism; consciousness-raising; decolonial; aboriginal; contemporary psychology critique; an ethical & political psychotherapy

PSYCHOLOGY AS EPISTEMICIDE

> There must exist a paradigm, a practical model for social change that includes an understanding of ways to transform consciousness that are linked to efforts to transform structures. ——(bell hooks, 1996, p. 186)

The sociologist Boaventura de Sousa Santos coined the word epistemicide to describe how academia grants 'to modern science the monopoly of the universal distinction between true and false to the detriment of … alternative bodies of knowledge' (Sousa Santos, 2007, p. 47). In doing so an abyss is created, a line past which the insider, indigenous, storied, cultural, land-based, knowledge is made invisible. In this colonial cartography one part of humanity is sacrificed for the dominance of another, a form of radical exclusion, rendering any dialectic impossible (Fig. 4.1).

While Santos was referring to physical geography, North and South, he also implied the colonisation of the mind, whereby '*cognitive-instrumental rationality*' (Sousa Santos, 2014, p. 71) forms a monolith which cannot be questioned. While Santos did not write explicitly about the state of clinical psychology his position captures our discourse community clearly, given the dominance of Cognitive Behaviour Therapy (CBT) since the cognitive revolution in the sciences in the 1950s. This revolution, which abandoned both Freud and the humanistic/existential, interpersonal, transpersonal and transactional traditions that followed him, has dominated with the incarnation of repeated cognitive waves.

A wide variety of fields participated in the cognitive revolution from 1950s, including psychology, linguistics and philosophy and the new fields of computer science and neuroscience (Miller, 2003). Within this context, Psychology as a discipline was faced with the conceptualisation of humans as interpretative beings, as was being taken up by some other disciplines (such as sociology and anthropology), or through the metaphor of the mind as an information processor (Bruner, 1990). This coinciding of the computer revolution with the cognitive revolution was influential in psychology's central metaphor for the mind as a machine '*based on the hypothesis that the processing and representational capabilities of the computer can serve as a basis for understanding the mind*' (Friesen, 2010, p. 87). With the mind now constructed as a modular cybernetic processor, psychology became a system of command and control. The history of psychology from this point, has remained cognitive, but with a variety of iterations permitted to both deepen and then soften the paradigm. In the late 1970s Mahoney (1995b) introduced the constructivism of Guidano and Maturana, allowing for a more tacit hermeneutics, embracing a complexity beyond the crude computations of Beck (Ruggiero et al., 2018). Next came the inclusion of schematic structures, organising mental operations at the level of personality, deepening the cognitive metaphor, without returning to the relative amorphism of psychotherapy (Markus & Sentis, 1982). And now presently a challenge to structuralism, in a wave allows for an emphasis on process, acceptance, dialectics and compassion, whilst still maintaining a central role for the regulation of cognitive-emotional dynamics (Kahl et al., 2012).

Built on dominant white western ideologies, the role of the psychologist has been constrained through the construction of psychological distress and suffering within individualistic frameworks of specific reified disorders. Psychological treatments to 'cure' disorders are therefore predominantly built upon clinical formulations where relational and social determinants of distress become background factors with the focus on restructuring perspectives, altering schema and acceptance. In this sense these methods focus on first-order, rather than second-order change (Watzlawick et al., 1974), on social regulation, rather than social emancipation (Sousa Santos, 2007). This cognitive hegemony is further reinforced by the commitment to postpositivist empiricism, which remains blind to its precepts, focussing on hypothesis-testing within the cognitive paradigm. This type of research serves to maintain tradition rather than engage in radical inquiry. Alternative methods, such as ethnography, narratology or discourse analysis are marginalised, serving as threats to power.

The diversity agenda (Wood & Patel, 2017) or the commitment to cultural competence (Greene-Moton & Minkler, 2019) has not challenged the fundamental whiteness of our field. These are initiatives of the status quo, 'happy talk' (Bell & Hartmann, 2007) which fail to address decolonisation and structural inequalities. We need humility, not competence, and the capacity to engage with our own shame and colour-blindness as a field.

PSYCHOLOGY AS ACTIVIST-PRACTICE

In 2019 Erin Shandle posted an article *Political fatigue: Four ways to keep your cool* on the site BehaviourTherapist.com, run by a collection of private practices dedicated to CBT. A series of tips were provided to readers, based on cognitive principles, including Limit Exposure to Media, Remember Your Personal Values and Don't Forget Self Care. The last tip Get Involved, stated

> ...perhaps you can pick one specific way to get involved. Maybe this means volunteering for your favourite candidate. It might mean choosing a social issue to focus on, like picking up trash in your neighbourhood, or volunteering with a local animal shelter.

This post serves as a fitting symbol for clinical psychology's abyssal response to politics and justice. The cognitive paradigm, siloed in the sciences, conducts its operations in a vacuum, building and reinforcing a rational-emotive epistemology and then colonising the vulnerable. At best the population is told to calm down in the face of injustice; at worst the injustice simply does not exist. Separating values from practice in the name of professionalism does not equate to neutrality, but instead collusion. Sitting on the cognitive fence in Trump's America or Bolsonaro's Brazil amounts to collective psychopathology (Abdennur, 1982).

In 2018 Santos called for the end of the cognitive empire, firstly through the Foulcauldian (Foucault, 1969) externalisation of the unspoken paradigm of logical-empiricism, and secondly through the archaeology of knowledge that is doubly hidden, a plurality of epistemologies of the South. If we are to build an activist-practice in psychology, focused on criticality not constructivism, sociopolitics not schematics, emancipation not acceptance, then we must reject the exceptionalism of Beck, Ellis, Young and Hayes in favour of other voices.

CONSCIOUSNESS-RAISING AS THERAPY

> Authentic liberation–the process of humanization–is not another deposit to be made in a person. Liberation is a praxis: action and reflection upon the world in order to transform it. Those truly committed to the cause of liberation can accept neither the mechanistic concept of consciousness as an empty vessel to be filled, nor the use of banking [pedagogical] methods of domination (propaganda, slogans–deposits) in the name of liberation. (Paulo Freire, Pedagogy of the Oppressed, 1970, p. 74)

For a Western audience the term consciousness-raising is most commonly associated with 1960s second-wave *feminism, where, under the slogan 'the personal is political'* (Hanisch, 2006, p. 196) *'women's discontent is not the neurotic lament of the maladjusted, but a response to a social structure in which women are systematically dominated, exploited, and oppressed'* (Hartmann, 1997, p. 175). This position, of direct relevance to the renewal of psychology, took its lead from the feminist existentialism of Simone de Beauvoir, explicated in The Second Sex (de Beauvoir, 1949). For Beauvoir women are socialized to develop self-sacrificial identities, those not based on predetermined feminine traits but, instead those created by patriarchy. Central to her thesis is the idea of the objectifying male gaze, which once internalized, means the woman produces her body as objects for others. Given that this identity is created, it can be refashioned through the dismantling of a lifetime of socialisation (Curthoys, 2000; de Beauvoir, 1949).

Frans Fanon, leading black existentialist developed a similar thesis regarding race in his seminal book Black Skin, White Masks (Fanon, 1967). Fanon's decolonised Sartre's existentialism, demonstrating the totalising project of colonialism in the erasure of black identity. Black nonbeing was achieved through the internalisation of racism, the epidermalization of inferiority (Song, 2013). The negrified subject can then only navigate society through whiteness, taking on colonial identities and habits. The liberation of black subjectivity can only ever be achieved through a resistance to imperialism. For Fanon psychological emancipation cannot be separated from sociopolitical emancipation. Black authenticity and freedom are a question of black consciousness.

Both de Beauvoir and Fanon were inspired by Sartre in the development of their political praxis, willing to develop complete theories regarding oppression and identity. Sartre, of course, influenced Simone de Beauvoir's feminist existentialism, despite her vehement critiques (Simons, 1986). Sartre also influenced Frans Fanon's black existentialism, particularly his book AntiSemite and Jew (1948). Both demonstrate the capacity for mainstream ideas to be challenged, modified and according to feminist and decolonial principles.

No discussion of consciousness-raising can be complete, however, without deviating more fully from Western existential roots to an epistemology that originated in the South (Sousa Santos, 2014). Liberation psychology, founded by Ignacio Martin-Baro (1983) began in Latin America in the 1970s, geared specifically for those peoples oppressed under dictatorial regimes. The term Concientización, coined by radical pedagogist Paulo Freire, refers directly to the liberative power of socio-political awareness, the psychic freedom that comes from an understanding of the structural inequalities that lead to subjugation. Martin-Baro (1983) coined the term '*de-ideologising*,' the process by which a psychologist might help a marginalised person to understand the unjust nature of social reality by revealing the dominant ideology. This in turn opens up possibilities for ideologies to be endorsed which support empowerment and self-determination.

A COMPENDIUM OF PRACTICE

> We also arrive at a fusion, a making into one, of 'philosophy and politics, of thinking and action, in other words we arrive at a philosophy of praxis'. (Gramsci, 1971, 1891–1937, Notebook 7, p. 35)

The following compendium of practice is written by clinicians and scholars in psychology and related disciplines, activist-practitioners who do not comply with the hegemony of the cognitive-individualistic paradigm. Their writing provides evidence for a thriving, ethical, political psychotherapy, aimed at critical consciousness raising and liberation. The first two pieces are feminist, firstly from a narrative tradition, inspired by Foucault, and secondly focussing on issues on the discursive materiality of embodiment.

Feminism and Narrative Therapy

In 2021, thousands of young Australian women voiced their experiences of sexual assault in an anonymous online petition initiated by a young Australian woman, Chanel Contos. Today, 14 March 2021, this Petition For Consent To Be Included In Australian Schools Sex Education Earlier has 3,340 testimonies of young Australians, predominantly women, who have written about their experiences of sexual assault during and soon after their high school years. This petition highlights the feelings of 'sadness' and 'anger' of these young people, predominantly women, as well as '*the long lasting impacts that sexual assault at a young age* …' (https://www.teachusconsent.com, retrieved 14 March 2021). How do we as psychologists respond to this significant issue that arises out of gendered power imbalances impacting upon young people in our community? Do our current dominant therapeutic paradigms, built on individualistic assumptions that construct psychological distress as a disorder that exists within the person (Gergen & McNamee, 2000), adequately address sexual assault, its prevention and the lasting legacies on a person's sense of identity and place in the world? And more broadly, how comprehensively do these therapeutic interventions address power imbalances in relationships that are built upon gender, sexualities, race, social status and culture?

Narrative therapy (White, 2007; White & Epston, 1990), has been developed with the intention to provide therapists with a map to deconstruct dominant discourses (or taken for granted cultural assumptions) that, on being inadvertently taken up, are the language materials from which a person constructs a version of their reality and identity narratives. Furthermore, according to Jerome Bruner (2004), '*we become the autobiographical narratives by which we "tell about" our lives*' (p. 694); in other words, we perform the meaning of our identity narratives. Most renowned for the practice of externalisation of the problem, narrative therapy proposes a shift from dominant disorder constructions that locate psychological distress within the person; instead people, families and communities are understood as existing in relationship with problems they face and moves us to consider psychological distress within an interpersonal social and cultural context. Dominant discourses construct and are mobilised by institutions to support privileged social groups and are inadvertently taken up by persons to build and perpetuate problematic narratives; these dominant discourses are deconstructed in narrative therapy (White & Epston, 1990). Through this process of deconstruction or unpacking of the meaning of problematic narratives, openings are generated for the person, family and/or community to re-author alternative storylines that more comprehensively depict their life and identity (White, 2007). The person is then in a position of agency to both choose their preferred storylines and take steps to live out or perform the meaning of these.

Returning to Contos' petition, I recently saw a young woman who talked about how, in the context of reading these young Australians' testimonies, she was again faced with her own memories of an experience that she now terms 'sexual assault'. This young woman had experienced a number of symptoms that would meet diagnostic criteria for anorexia nervosa and social anxiety, neither of which handle the complexities of the social reality within which she had and currently lives. In the context of the narrative therapeutic work in which she has engaged over a number of years, naming this experience as 'assault' was a shift from the narratives of her first disclosure. Nevertheless, she talked about her ongoing struggles in naming the experience 'assault' because part of her at that time was also curious and excited at the time in light of this being her first sexual experience. As she swung between these contradictory meanings, what was consistent across her narrative was the feeling of shame that she felt at the time and continues to feel to the present day. Through the deconstructive work of narrative therapy (and more recently with the addition of Eye Movement Sensitisation and Reprocessing (Shapiro, 2017)), this young woman has shifted from locating the shame primarily within herself to a deeper knowing that the shame is not hers to hold but rather the perpetrator's. This young woman's journey highlights the importance of psychological interventions that specifically address how power relations are imbued within interpretative processes. Imbalances of relational power led to a silencing of those who have been abused in the interest of perpetrators whose privileged place remains intact and their refusal to take responsibility for their abuse continues unquestioned. A narrative approach might equally be considered as a preventative intervention in working with young Australians to unpack gendered power relations and generate a map towards respect and equality in gendered relationships.

Narrative therapy continues a marginalised therapy in the context of the dominant discourse of evidence-based practice that elevate the status of scientific research evidence and marginalise the other two arms of evidence-based practice (Sackett et al., 1996), that is client preferences and values and clinician experience of what works with the client group within which they work and collaborate. Narrative therapy provides a map to address gendered power relations in the therapy room, in addition to power dynamics that relate to race and culture, sexualities and social status.

Feminism and Embodied Resistance

As early as the 1960s, feminist activists from a range of ideological positions emphasised the importance of psychologists introducing consciousness-raising into research and clinical practice (Ruck, 2015). When consciousness-raising strategies focus women's attention on their experiences of living in and perceiving the social world from the material realities of the body, it opens possibilities to use the body to convey a new message of embodied resistance (Fahs & Swank, 2015). The following article describes the use of body mapping - a form of arts-based consciousness raising - to explore women's embodied resistance in the context of early life sexual, emotional, and physical abuse and living with anorexia nervosa. Body mapping uses tracings of the body that are overlaid with symbols, colours, and text. The maps and symbols signify the social aspects of power and oppression on the material body; the discursive symbolic aspects of culture on the body; and the intrapsychic aspects of women's identities and sexual identities (Ussher & Ussher, 2011). The finished map makes visible to both artist and audience embodied histories.

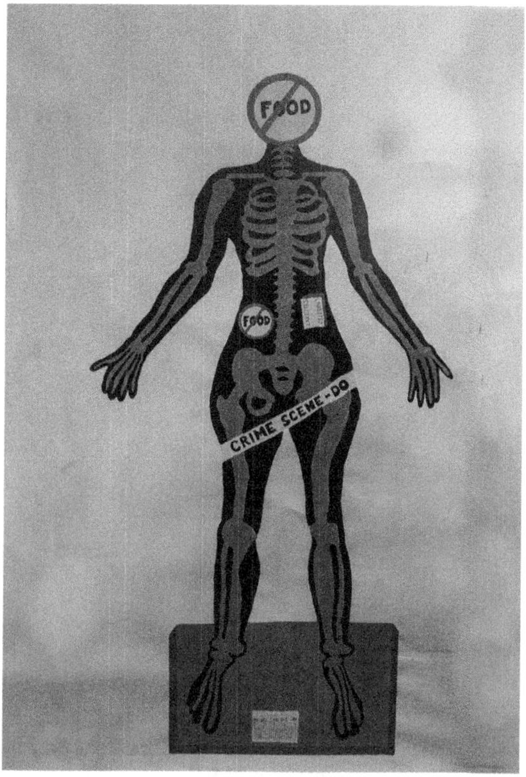

Fig. 4.1. Childhood Abuse in Anorexia. *Note:* The visual representation of childhood abuse in anorexia. It shows how anorexia is not a surface appearance; it discloses the underlying truth. *Source:* Malecki et al. (2023).

An embodied approach to consciousness-raising acknowledges the multiple intersections of gendered oppression on girls and women's bodies. May (not her real name) has deliberately drawn the audience towards the gendered aspects of embodied oppression and food meanings to show how they have become entangled with her feminine subjectivities. The simplistic form of the objects and use of colour magnifies meaning and shifts the audience's attention from the corporeal body to interrelated objects or symbols. Black and grey colour representing decay and toxicity embodied in her flesh and bones (Fig. 4.1), are juxtaposed against yellow and red colour representing violence of sexual abuse. The yellow police tape alerts the audience to the crime and marks out the boundaries of her body under protection. As food crosses the boundary to constitute the body, it takes on the 'toxic' symbolic meaning that she attached to her body. The portrait of May's head (Fig. 4.2) symbolise different parts of her identity that emerged

Fig. 4.2. Visual Expression of Dual Identities. *Note:* The visual expression of childhood abuse in anorexia brings the audience into the artist's inner world. *Source:* Malecki et al. (2023).

during adolescence when she began to question the norms and scripts around her sexuality, and the duplicitous nature of others. May reflected on her child/adult sexual identities and how she resisted abuse as a young adolescent by using her body and clothing to mark out her own regimes of sexuality. Although May had visited psychologists for therapy, she was excluded from opportunities to have her story of abuse heard in the public sphere. In 2012, with the energised political will driving reform in institutional settings, the then Prime Minister of Australia announced her obligation to protect children in institutions from sexual and other forms of abuse. May seized the opportunity in 2018 to speak publicly for the first time at the Australian Royal Commission into Institutional Responses to Child Sexual Abuse (2017), and at a private session heard by a panel of representatives from the institution where the abuse occurred. May's map disclosed to the audience her embodied distress in a visual material form, which she used as a prompt to prevent herself from becoming caught in the grips of a dissociative state. May said of the experience, '*It has been life changing...I see my power to choose what I do with my body...and rediscovered my creativity*'.

May's engagement with the state on gendered oppression was a '*dynamic and co-constructive*' (Chappell, 2002, p. 3) process that led to profound personal and social change, '*simply, to have a voice is to heal.*'

Gender

People of transgender and gender diverse (TGD), including nonbinary, experiences have been present, and often highly valued, throughout history across cultures (Feinberg, 1997). Western societies' broader recognition of these experiences has come with greater medicalisation and legalisation of people's experiences of gender (Stone, 1987). While this has allowed people access to affirming medical interventions, crucial for people of some TGD experiences to thrive (Hyde et al., 2013; Riggs et al., 2015), it has framed TGD experiences as a medical problem to be fixed, rather than personal, material and relational experiences to be celebrated (Blumer Markie et al., 2013; Stop Trans Pathologization, 2010). Binary gender has been naturalised, regulated and institutionalised (Ellis, 2020; Stone, 1987).

This reductionist approach is perpetuated in psychotherapy, where individuals' experiences of distress are explained as intrapsychic and bodily pathology (Ansara & Hegarty, 2012). The Diagnostic and Statistical Manual of Mental Disorders IV-TR (2013) uses the term Gender Identity Disorder, modified in 2013 to Gender Dysphoria. These pejorative terms position pathology internally, rather than in wider social structures and discourses, including cissexism, cisgenderism, and heteropatriarchy (Blumer Markie et al., 2013; Ellis, 2020; Riggs et al., 2015).

Equitable mental health support for TGD individuals and communities begins with affirmative care grounded in social justice and critical perspectives. To counter the harm done to TGD bodies and identities we must problematise power dynamics and challenge oppression (Blumer Markie et al., 2013; Ellis, 2020). This process starts with us and the exploration of our own cisgenderist biases (Blumer Markie et al., 2013). Affirmative therapy that comes from such a critical stance, can succeed in creating safer spaces for expression and exploration, assisting a sense of agency to confront systemic oppression.

When Carla, 25 years old, came to therapy, the barriers to accessing affirming mental health support (Haire et al., 2021) were clear. The referral from their General Practitioner used the name 'Trang' and male pronouns, and the request to *Assess for Gender Disorder.* Carla looked visibly anxious and wary. They offered me their name as '*Trang*' with low voice and downward eyes. After explicit prompting, they instead offered '*Carla*'. '*It's really nice to meet you Carla*' - they looked up and met my eyes tearfully. I acknowledged the journey Carla had already taken to get into this room, including the difficulty of passing through a medical referral system in order to financially access the session, and the erasure created by assuming their name and gender.

Carla shared previous experiences with psychologists who, when Carla raised the topic of gender, had asked intrusive body and gender presentation questions, while also deadnaming and misgendering them, or had assumed a binary trans experience. '*I'm sorry it hasn't felt safe in the past. I hope, with your guidance, I can find ways to make it safer for you here. And if I'm not the right person for you, I'll help you find someone else.*'

As we proceeded gently, I asked Carla about their experience of gender. Therapeutic dialogue can be empowering if it allows exploration of the individual's language through which they may understand their lived experience '*rather than narrow diagnostic or fixed binary ideas*' (Ellis, 2020, p. 8). For many people of TGD experience, the power imbalance inherent in formal therapy contexts has been heightened by the gatekeeper approach, whereby TGD people have been expected to perform their 'transness' in particular ways for health professionals, lest they be pathologised or blocked from accessing medical attention (Ellis, 2020; Howe et al., 2019; Stone, 1987). Confronting this '*legacy of distrust*' (Murjan & Bouman, 2017, p. 126, quoted in Ellis, 2020, p. 3) directly is essential to building a sense of safety. Carla became able to say that they were struggling to find a label to describe themself; that they/them pronouns felt most appropriate; and that they were unsure what external gender expressions fitted best. I offered the safety of my therapy room as a place to explore language and test the fit of gender expression.

Carla also shared that they find relationships difficult, have had few close relationships, and they feel '*different*'. We talked about the role that being trans in a cis world might play in this feeling of difference. Carla questioned whether they were '*on the spectrum*'. They described having difficulty understanding people's meaning at times and becoming sensorily overwhelmed. We talked through and affirmed experiences of difference that might fit in this frame, and the struggles of marginalisation in an Allistic world. I was clear that being Autistic does not negate one's gender, and that they are not alone if they have Autistic TGD experience (Strang et al., 2018). Threats to self-determination regarding gender have been heightened by paternalistic ableist views of neurodivergence (Strang et al., 2018).

As we continued to spend time together across a number of sessions, Carla became confident in their ability to direct our interactions to places that met their needs. They chose to explore language and external gender presentation in this shared space, to pursue hormone therapy with a General Practitioner who works within an informed consent model (Cundill et al., 2020), and to join a online support group for queer autistic people. Carla expressed that having someone alongside them in naming and navigating the contextual and structural barriers that they face, had allowed a new degree of self-determination.

Indigenous Psychology

Indigenous psychologies are 'critical' in that they contest the normative assumptions of a mainstream western worldview that underpins traditional psychology. Critical psychology is about the analysis of power relationships and how these impact marginalised communities and persons. Indigenous psychology is a growing area that speaks back to the Western hegemony and makes space for Indigenous populations.

Indigenous Psychology is an intellectual movement across the globe, based on a reaction against the colonisation/hegemony of Western psychology. Practitioners, activists, and researchers from nonWestern cultures can solve their local problems through indigenous practices and applications, using indigenous philosophies and concepts to generate theories and recognise this knowledge in the constructs and practices of psychology.

The imposition of mainstream western psychology as a universal strategy for addressing mental health has arguably been the biggest contributor to the exclusion of minority groups. This is especially so for Indigenous peoples whose worldviews and cultural norms reside in opposing ontological realms to westerns perspectives (Moreton-Robinson et al., 2003). Aboriginal and Torres Strait Islander peoples experience higher levels of psychological distress, self-harm, and suicide than do their nonIndigenous counterparts (Australian Institute of Health & Welfare, 2020). The cause of this disparity has been linked to the contemporary impacts of colonisation, entrenched racism, and failure of successive government policies and practices to understand the importance of the social determinants of health World Health Organization (2021). The centrality of the social determinants of health was also recognised in the Australian Productivity Commission Report, released by the Commonwealth government in November 2020 (Productivity Commission, 2020). Two key recommendations in the report are relevant to this paper; first, the importance of viewing health as more than just the absence of illness; and this includes understanding the social, political, and economic impacts on people and communities and how these relate to health outcomes. Second, the call for far greater recognition of the critical importance of early intervention and prevention and here the commission specifically referenced with explicit reference to social and emotional wellbeing (SEWB). The Productivity Commission identifying these essential aspects of health and wellbeing reflects the call for different approaches from those working in health and particularly Indigenous mental health (Dudgeon et al., 2020).

Social and Emotional Wellbeing (Gee et al., 2014a, 2014b, see Fig. 4.3.) has emerged as one of the most important theoretical and conceptual models in recent times. Grounded in cultural knowledges, the SEWB model articulates a holistic understanding of health and its interconnection with self and others as well as country, community, and spirit.

Connection to Body, Mind, and Emotion. This domain captures the intersection of the individual, interpersonal, and intrapsychic experiences including coping skills, self-esteem, and how external experiences are interpreted and framed by the person.

Connection to Spirituality, Country, and Culture. Spirituality in Aboriginal and Torres Strait Islander contexts is a vastly different concept to westerns interpretations, which are often associated with religiosity. Indigenous interpretations refer to the suite of knowledges, worldviews, traditions, values, and lore that define the collective ways of knowing being and doing for each particular group. These traditions vary across language and cultural groups, but they share some common elements such as the importance of country, the physical and spiritual connection to the land is central to all communities. Culture is an important element and needs to be considered in the delivery of health services. Aboriginal and Torres Strait Islander peoples are the oldest living culture and have continuous connection with their lands for over 60,000 years with some estimates extending to 120,000 years. That deep connection is transmitted through song lines, stories, and dance to contemporary times. The connection to traditional ways of knowing, being, and doing are intertwined with modern practices which reflect the renaissance of global Indigenous knowledges and culture in recent times.

Connection to Family, Kinship, and Community. The importance of family and kinship connections in Aboriginal and Torres strait Islander

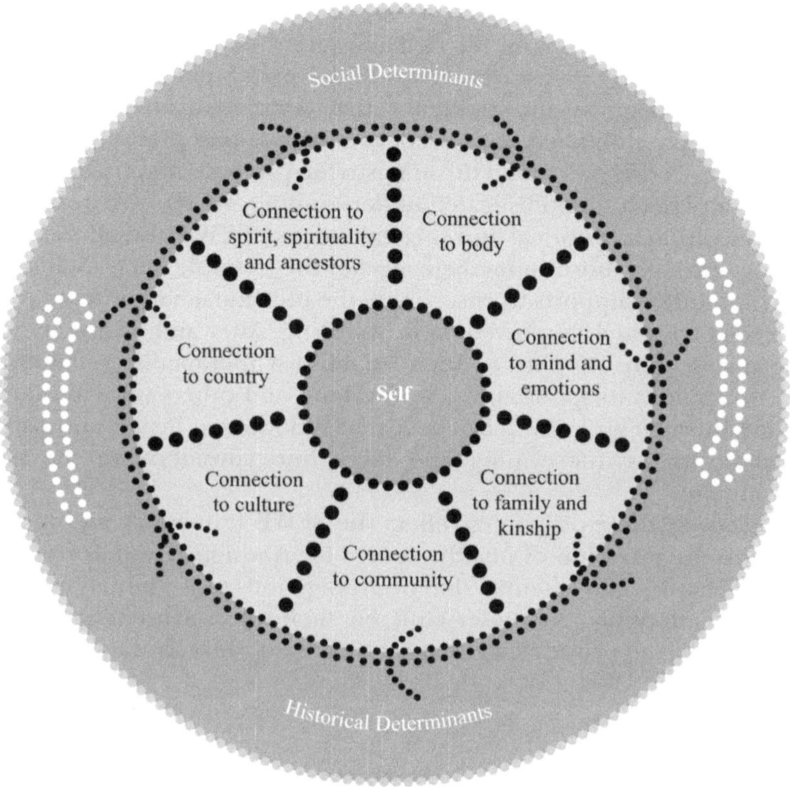

Fig. 4.3. Social and Emotional Wellbeing. *Source:* Gee et al. (2014).

experiences cannot be overstated. Like other collectivist cultures concepts such as self-determination are grounded in the roles and responsibilities that a person has within their group. Self-concept, mastery and autonomy, which in a western context refer only to the person, take on far greater importance in a collectivist context because it is intrinsically linked to how connected the person feels to the group and the degree to which they can meet the expectations of the group. While connection to community is a protective factor it can also place a burden on a person if they lack the resources to fulfil these obligations. The SEWB diagram takes into account history, social determinants and cultural determinants.

When one of the authors, Tanja an Aboriginal clinical psychologist, started working therapeutically within community and clinical settings, she realised that the mainstream psychology training had not adequately prepared her for working with Aboriginal and Torres Strait Islander individuals, families, and communities. The mainstream models that were available did not encompass the cultures of Aboriginal and Torres Strait Islander peoples. She heard firsthand the rich and varied stories of people, and stories of trauma and loss for Aboriginal and Torres Strait Islander peoples. Despite the strengths and resilience that Aboriginal and Torres Strait Islander people embodied, there were at times complex presentations. This complexity needed more than the mainstream psychology approach. SEWB provides a richer and sophisticated understanding and seeks to understand concerns within a historical and societal context. SEWB also advocates for working through more immediate needs, for example such as housing, safety, and other supports to ensure that the individual had primary practical needs met, which improved their wellbeing. After and during meeting these needs, were we able to then establish a therapeutic relationship. The connections to spirituality, identity, land and others were also key to working through an individual's needs. SEWB looks at health and psychological health as intertwining and takes into consideration the social determinants.

Collectively these principles reflect the SEWB framework and must be central to the provision of health services for Aboriginal and Torres Strait Islander peoples. It is essential that nonIndigenous professionals who work with First Nations peoples understand that their role is to listen to the voices of the people and provide care that is reflective of the cultural needs of the population.

Decolonising Caribbean Psychotherapy

Hickling (2020) forwards that the mental health challenge for Caribbean people is '*to reverse the psychological impact of 500 years of European racism and colonial oppression and create a blueprint for the decolonisation of mental health*' (p. 19). The task that supersedes this, is the engagement of therapists in decolonising their practice. With training that spans psychotherapy and social work, my practice choices are informed by a recognition of micro-macro connections and an attunement to structural vulnerabilities with a distinctive social justice orientation. Nonetheless, my training is based in theory that does not place importance on Caribbean socio-political history, namely the recognition of and engagement with colonial trauma, race, and understandings of the spirit world.

The helping professions are relatively young areas of practice in the English-Speaking Caribbean, with the commencement of regional tertiary level education in social work in 1961, psychiatry in 1965 and psychology in 1995 (Hickling et al., 2013). Theorising for practice in our context are in its formative stages, and there is a strong reliance on theory and practice models from Euro-American sources. Riley-Richardson (2021) based on a qualitative study that investigated ways in which Trinidadian social workers perceive the principles of casework and their relevance to Social Work practice, found that participants encountered challenges in operationalising their training. Within the local context, mental health interventions were perceived as '*white people thing*.' The author's questioning of the cultural relevance of intervention models and principles is echoed throughout the limited literature across the disciplines (Sutherland et al., 2013). In addition to the novelty of the field, cultural stereotyping, and associated avoidance of services among Caribbean people is well substantiated in the research literature (Amuleru-Marshall et al., 2013; Hickling, 2020; Greenidge & Daire, 2010).

With a keen awareness of the limitations of my training as well as the cultural stereotyping that exists in this practice setting, my approach to psychotherapy is deliberate in the ways it privileges meaning making for my clients who are primarily Trinidadians of African and Indian heritage. While there is much I can draw from in the literature on African and Black psychology, the Caribbean is a unique cultural space steeped in traumas which include but are not limited to, the genocide of indigenous people, African enslavement, Indian indentureship and centuries of colonialism. Our ways of knowing includes layers of disconnection, an understanding of the spirit world that is racialised at times yet transcends racial bounds at other times.

Clinical practice in this context requires holding space for disclosures outside the conventions of my psychotherapeutic training. I will draw an example from my therapeutic engagement with a client I will call Pree. During a session with Pree, I found myself in that familiar place where fear, and urgency to make a disclosure intersects. I held the silence with presence, reassuring Pree that I was ready to hold the disclosure. There was a long pause. '*Sometimes it just won't let me sleep*', she let the words quickly tumble into the space between us the way a child would in response to a dare. She continued to describe the experience of a malevolent spirit that would disturb her sleep at night and the ways in which she managed the interloper. At the end of the session, I was most moved by what Pree described as '*the feeling of being believed*' and the release that came thereafter. Believing my client goes beyond the notions of respecting the client's story found in many approaches to psychotherapy. Although Pree and I differ in racial identity as well as religious orientation, we share a knowing that is a distinct part of our cultural context. Holding space for Pree to disclose her interactions with a malevolent spirit is not about rapport building or creating a therapeutic alliance. Instead, it is about making space for our legitimate way of knowing to be witnessed and interrogated with regard. It is a political act as much as it is a therapeutic act that signals proprietorship of the healing process.

Disability Rights and Autism

Disability rights activists have long been advocating for the phenomenon of being disabled to be understood within a broader context of social oppression (Oliver, 2013). The therapeutic importance of recognising these oppressive forces - historical, contemporary, and ongoing - is highlighted when working with Autistic people. Autism existed long before it was named as such in the 1930s; it is a natural variation of the human mind, often referred to as a '*neurodivergence*' (Walker & Raymaker, 2020). However, the spuriously narrow conceptualisation of autism by early researchers, and subsequent focus on causes and cures has resulted in autism becoming a vastly misunderstood, pathologised, and stigmatised phenomenon (Silberman, 2015). As such, it perpetuates the pattern of oppression when this legacy remains unspoken and unexplored in clinical contexts. It is a goal of therapy, then, to acknowledge the significant wound left by historical and contemporary autism research and highlight harmful concepts and practices that remain to this day. Only with this awareness can Autistic people begin to see, acknowledge, and process the harm that has been done as a result of society viewing our natural ways of being through a paradigm of pathology.

As we begin therapy, we are invariably confronted by both the impact of the pathologisation of autism on the client's sense of self and the mismatch between the client's needs and the way society operates. Take the example of Molly, a 28-year-old woman who was recently formally identified as Autistic. She presents following a long history of contact with the psychiatric inpatient system, including a string of mis-diagnoses and the additional label, '*treatment resistant*'. When identified as Autistic, Molly felt her experiences '*finally make sense*' and was hopeful that this diagnostic framework would foster understanding in herself and those around her. However, both her treating psychiatrist and family expressed doubt around her diagnosis, suggesting she is too social and doesn't '*look Autistic*'. This resulted in Molly experiencing an increase in self-punitive thoughts, self-harming behaviour, and suicidal ideation.

Immediately, we can see wounds inflicted by the legacy of autism research and practice emerging in her experience of the mental health system, her delayed diagnosis, and the scepticism of those around her. This is explored candidly with Molly, as we take a consciousness-raising approach in order to shift attributions from internal ('*I am broken, difficult, intrinsically wrong*') to external

> I have experienced oppression, I feel the pain of the wounds that have been inflicted upon me and the entire Autistic community, I feel the consequences of living in a society that expects me to change who I fundamentally am rather than being flexible in meeting my needs.

Exploring childhood, we see numerous examples where Molly was misunderstood and mistreated while growing up, often by well-meaning people in positions of power. Examples include being reprimanded for fidgeting, held responsible for social misunderstandings, and expected to tolerate painful sensory sensations across both school and home contexts. We explore these experiences through a lens of autism and rewrite the narrative to include ways by which her younger self was failed by the systems surrounding her, thus developing self-compassion and shifting the sense of brokenness from within herself to the society around her, where it belongs.

We explore her current living circumstances and find she now expects herself to tolerate painful sensory input on a daily basis, feeling intense shame at the idea of establishing sensory accommodations. Molly pushes herself to match the pace and intensity of her nonAutistic counterparts, leading to periods of burn-out that have been framed as depression by her psychiatrist. When passionately engaged with her interests, her psychiatrist had erroneously diagnosed her as hypomanic, so she no longer allows herself to indulge in areas of interest. We intentionally disengage from the medical model of mental health, and, instead, work on understanding and accepting her Autistic ways of being in the world. We then explore her current needs, drawing on the compassion we developed for her younger Autistic self. We acknowledge the ways society continues to oppress and disable Autistic people while finding ways Molly can intentionally construct a lifestyle that better meets her needs.

CONCLUSION

> a psychology of liberation requires a prior liberation of psychology. (Martín-Baró, 1996, p. 32)

We began this paper with reference to psychology as epistemicide, as term coined by Sousa Santos (2007) to describe the abyssal erasure of all knowledge that contradicts cognitive instrumentality, closing down dialogue in favour s of a monolithic discourse. For Sousa Santos (2007) the alternative is cognitive justice, the right for a pluriverse of knowledge to exist, a counter-hegemony built on social justice and human rights. This paper presents evidence for an activist and affirmative psychology focussed on empowerment and liberation rather than pathologisation and remediation. Any form of psychology that remains neutral in the face of structural inequalities participates in those inequalities, engaging in a form of epistemic oppression that deepens, rather than heals the wounds. We have aimed here to present multiple perspectives, focussed on identities related to sex, gender, race and neurodiversity while being fully aware that clinical and personal reality is intersectional in nature. Each of the positions presented here share the common commitment to social justice, rejecting the pathologisation of difference in favour of the raising of a consciousness. The liberated psyche has no room for internalised hate and celebrates unique personal and collective cultures. The aim of this paper is the amplification of voices, both our own through collective writing and others through a recognition of our joint participation in an ecology of knowledge (Barreto, 2014). We provide a discursive and practical resource to support further acts of resistance.

REFERENCES

Abdennur, A. (1982). A cognitively induced collective psychopathology. *International Journal of Social Psychiatry, 28*(4), 274–281.

Amuleru-Marshall, O., Gomez, A., & Neckles, K. O. (2013). Psychology, spirituality and wellbeing in the Caribbean. In P. Sutherland, R. Moodley, & P. Chevannes (Eds.), *Caribbean healing traditions: Implications for health and mental health* (pp. 215–226). Routledge.

Ansara, Y. G., & Hegarty, P. (2012). Cisgenderism in psychology: Pathologising and misgendering children from 1999 to 2008. *Psychology & Sexuality, 3*(2), 137–160.

Australian Institute of Health & Welfare. (2020). *Social determinants of Indigenous health.* https://www.aihw.gov.au/reports/australias-health/social-determinants-and-indigenous-health

Barreto, J.-M. (2014). Epistemologies of the south and human rights: Santos and the quest for global and cognitive justice. *Indiana Journal of Global Legal Studies, 21*(2), 395–422.

Bell, J. M., & Hartmann, D. (2007). Diversity in everyday discourse: The cultural ambiguities and consequences of "happy talk". *American Sociological Review, 72*(6), 895–914.

Blumer Markie, L., Gavriel, A. Y., & Watson, C. M. (2013). Cisgenderism in Family Therapy: How everyday clinical practices can delegitimize people's gender self-designations. *Journal of Family Psychotherapy, 24*, 267–285.

Bruner, J. (1990). *Acts of meaning.* Harvard University Press.

Bruner, J. (2004). Life as narrative. *Social Research, 71*(3), 691–710.

Chappell, L. (2002). *Gendering government feminist engagement with the state in Australia and Canada.* UBC Press.

Cundill, P., Brownhill, A., & Locke, P. (2020). *Protocols for the initiation of hormone therapy for trans and gender diverse patients V2.0.* Thorne Harbour Health. https://equinoxdotorgdotau.files.wordpress.com/2020/08/protocol-for-the-initiation-of-hormone-therapy-v2-aug-2020.pdf

Curthoys, A. (2000). Adventures of Feminism: Simone de Beauvoir's Autobiographies, Women's Liberation, and Self-Fashioning. *Feminist Review,* (64), 3–18.

de Beauvoir, S. (1949). Le deuxième sexe (The Second Sex). NRF essais (in French). *Les Faits et les Mythes (Facts and Myths)*. Gallimard. Springer Publishing Company, Inc and American Psychological Association.decent life. Lexington Books. Lanham

Diagnostic and statistical manual of mental disorders (DSM-5®). (5th ed.). (2013). American Psychiatric Association.

Dudgeon, P., Boe, M., & Walker, R. (2020). Addressing inequities in Indigenous mental health and wellbeing through transformative and decolonising research and practice. *Research in Health Science, 5*(3). https://doi.org/10.22158/rhs.v5n3p48

Ellis, J. (2020, December). "Gender dysphoria": Therapist negotiations of oppressive practices. *Special Issue on Anti-Oppressive Practice in Psychotherapy and Counselling, 8*(2).

Fahs, B., & Swank, E. (2015). Unpacking sexual embodiment and embodied resistance. In *Handbook of the sociology of sexualities* (pp. 149–167). Springer International Publishing.

Fanon, F. (1967). *Black skin, white masks* (C. L. Markmann, Trans.). Grove Press.

Feinberg, L. (1997). *Transgender warriors: Making history from Joan of Arc to Dennis Rodman*. Beacon Press.

Foucault, M. (1969). *L'Archéologie du Savoir*. Gallimard.

Freire, P. (1970/2000). *Pedagogy of the oppressed*. Bloomsbury.

Friesen, N. (2010). Mind and machine: Ethical and epistemological implications for research. *AI & Society, 25*, 83–92. https://doi.org/10.1007/s00146-009-0264-8

Gee, G., Dudgeon, P., Schultz, C., Hart, A., & Kelly, K. (2014a). Aboriginal and Torres Strait Islander social and emotional wellbeing. In P. Dudgeon, H. Milroy, & R. Walker (Eds.), *Working together: Aboriginal and torres Strait islander mental health and wellbeing principles and practice* (pp. 55–68). Commonwealth of Australia.

Gee, G., Dudgeon, P., Schultz, C., Hart, A., & Kelly, K. (2014b). Aboriginal and Torres Strait Islander social and emotional wellbeing. In P. Dudgeon, H. Milroy, & R. Walker (Eds.), *Working together: Aboriginal and Torres Strait Islander mental health and wellbeing principles and practices* (pp. 55–68). Australian Government.

Gergen, K. J., & McNamee, S. (2000). From disordering discourse to transformative dialogue. In R. A. Neimeyer & J. D. Raskin (Eds.), *Constructions of disorder. Meaning making frameworks for psychotherapy* (pp. 333–349). American Psychological Association.

Gramsci, A. (1971, 1891–1937). *Selections from the prison notebooks of Antonio Gramsci*. International Publishers.

Greene-Moton, E., & Minkler, M. (2019). Cultural competence or cultural humility? Moving beyond the debate. *Health Promotion Practice, 21*, 152483991988491. https://doi.org/10.1177/1524839919884912

Greenidge, W. L., & Daire, A. P. (2010). The relationship between emotional openness and the attitudes towards seeking professional counseling of English-Speaking Caribbean college students. *International Journal for the Advancement of Counseling, 32*(3), 191–201.

Haire, B. G., Brook, E., Stoddart, R., & Simpson, P. (2021). Trans and gender diverse people's experiences of healthcare access in Australia: A qualitative study in people with complex needs. *PLoS One, 16*(1), e0245889. https://doi.org/10.1371/journal.pone.0245889

Hanisch, C. (2006, January). *The personal is political: The Women's Liberation Movement classic with a new explanatory introduction.* Retrieved 2014-09-07.

Hartmann, H. (1997). The unhappy marriage of Marxism and feminism: Towards a more progressive union. In L. J. Nicholson (Ed.), *The second wave: A reader in feminist theory* (p. 100). Routledge. ISBN 9780415917612.

Hickling, F. W. (2020). Owning our madness: Contributions of Jamaican psychiatry to decolonizing Global Mental Health. *Transcultural Psychiatry, 57*(1), 19–31. https://doi.org/10.1177/1363461519893142

Hickling, F. W., Doorbar, R., Benn, J., Gordon, E., Morgan, K., & Matthies, B. K. (2013). The roles and responsibilities of clinical psychologists in the Caribbean. In F. W. Hickling, B. K. Matthies, K. Morgan, & R. C. Gibson (Eds.), *Perspectives in Caribbean psychology.* Jessica Kingsley Publishers.

Hooks, B. (1996). *Killing rage.* Holt.

Howe, R., Harper, A., & Hammoud-Beckett, S. (2019). Uncovering Games of Truth: A collaborative exploration of the ways transgender and non-binary young people access health care and support. In D. Baines, B. Bennett, S. Goodwin, & M. Rawsthorne (Eds.), *Working across difference: Social work, social policy and social justice.*

Hyde, Z., Doherty, M., Tilley, P. J. M.,McCaul, K. A., Rooney, R. & Jancey, J. (2013). *The first Australian national trans mental health study: Summary of results.* Curtin University,

Kahl, K. G., Winter, L., & Schweiger, U. (2012). The third wave of cognitive behavioural therapies. What is new and what is effective? *Current Opinion in Psychiatry, 25*, 522–528.

Mahoney, M. J. (1995b). Theoretical developments in the cognitive and constructive psychotherapies. In M. J. Mahoney (Ed.), *Cognitive and constructive psychotherapies. Theory, research, and practice* (pp. 103–120). (1974). *Cognition and Behavior Modification.* Ballinger.

Malecki, J. S., Rhodes, P., Ussher, J., & Boydell, K. (2023). The embodiment of childhood abuse and anorexia nervosa: A body mapping study. *Health Care for Women International, 44*(9), 1192–1217. https://doi.org/10.1080/07399332.2022.2087074

Markus, H., & Sentis, K. (1982). The self in social information processing. In J. Suls (Ed.), *Social psychological perspectives on the self* (pp. 41–70). Erlbaum.

Martín-Baró, I. (1983). *Acción e Ideología. Psicología Social Desde Centroamérica.* UCA Editores.

Martín-Baró, I. (1996). *Writings for a liberation psychology* (A., Aron & S., Corne, Eds.). Harvard University Press.

Miller, G. (2003). The Cognitive Revolution: A historical perspective. *Trends in Cognitive Sciences, 7*, 141–144. https://doi.org/10.1016/S1364-6613(03)00029-9

Moreton-Robinson, A., Ahmed, S., Castaneda, C., Fortier, A., Sheller, M. (2003). I still call Australia home: Indigenous belonging and place in a white postcolonising society. In R. Uprootings, (Eds.), *Questions of home and migration* (pp. 23–40). Berg.

Murjan, S., & Bouman, W. P. (2017). Psychiatry. In C. Richards, W. P. Bouman, & M. J. Barker (Eds.), *Genderqueer and non-binary genders, critical and applied approaches in sexuality, gender and identity* (pp. 125–140). Palgrave Macmillan.

Oliver, M. (2013). The social model of disability: Thirty years on. *Disability & Society, 28*(7), 1024–1026.

Productivity Commission. (2020). *Mental health.* Report no. 95. https://www.pc.gov.au/inquiries/completed/mental-health/report/mental-health.pdf

Riggs, D. W., Ansara, G. Y., & Treharne, G. J. (2015, February). An evidence-based model for understanding the mental health experiences of transgender Australians. *Australian Psychologist, 50*(1), 32–39.

Riley-Richardson, A. (2021). I is this "white people ting"? Exploring perceptions of cultural relevance of social work principles in. *Trinidad and Tobago Caribbean Journal of Social Work, 14.*

Royal Commission into Institutional Responses to Child Sexual Abuse. (2017). *Final report: Beyond the Royal Commission.* Australian Government Publishing Service.

Ruck, N. (2015). Liberating minds: Consciousness-raising as a bridge between feminism and psychology in 1970s Canada. *History of Psychology, 18*(3), 297–311. https://doi.org/10.1037/a0039522

Ruggiero, G., Spada, M., Caselli, G., & Sassaroli, S. (2018). A historical and theoretical review of cognitive behavioral therapies: From structural self-knowledge to functional processes. *Journal of Rational-Emotive and Cognitive-Behavior Therapy, 36,* 378–403. https://doi.org/10.1007/s10942-018-0292-8

Sackett, D. L., Rosenberg, A. M. C., Muir Gray, J. A., Haynes, R. B., & Richardson, W. S. (1996). Evidence based medicine: What it is and what it isn't. *British Medical Journal, 312,* 71–72.

Sartre, J. (1948). *Anti-Semite and Jew.* Schocken Books.

Shapiro, F. (2017). *Eye-Movement Densitization and Re-processing (EMDR) therapy* (3rd ed.). Guilford.

Silberman, S. (2015). *Neurotribes: The legacy of autism and how to think smarter about people who think differently.* Allen & Unwin.

Simons, M. A. (1986). *Beauvoir and Sartre: The philosophical relationship.* Stanford University Press.

Sousa Santos, B. de (2007). Beyond abyssal thinking: From global lines to ecologies of knowledge. *Eurozine, 33,* 45–89.

Sousa Santos, B. de (2014). *Epistemologies of the South: Justice against epistemicide.* Routledge.

Stone, S. (1987). *The Empire Strike Back: A posttranssexual manifesto, revision 4.0, 9 April 2014.* https://uberty.org/wp-content/uploads/2015/06/trans-manifesto.pdf

Stop Trans Pathologization. (2010). *Best practices guide to trans health care in the national system.* Spanish Network for Depathologization of Trans Identities. http://www.stp2012.info/guia/STP_guide_health.pdf

Strang, J. F., Powers, M. D., Knauss, M., Sibarium, E., Leibowitz, S. F., Kenworthy, L., Sadikova, E., Wyss, S., Willing, L., Caplan, R., Pervez, N., Nowak, J., Gohari, D., Gomez-Lobo, V., Call, D., & Anthony, L. G. (2018). "They thought it was an obsession": Trajectories and perspectives of autistic transgender and gender-diverse adolescents. *Journal of Autism and Developmental Disorders, 48,* 4039–4055.

Sutherland, P., Moodley, R., & Chevannes, P. (Eds.) (2013), *Caribbean healing traditions: Implications for health and mental health* (1st ed.). Routledge.

Ussher, J. P., & Ussher, J. M. (2011). The Madness of Women: Myth or experience? In *The madness of women: Myth and experience* (p. 8). Routledge.

Walker, N., & Raymaker, D. M. (2020). Toward a neuroqueer future: An interview with Nick Walker. *Autism in Adulthood.* ahead of print. https://doi.org/10.1089/aut.2020.29014.njw

Watzlawick, P., Weakland, J. H., & Fisch, R. (1974). *Change: Principles of problem formation and problem resolution.* W. W. Norton.

White, M. (2007). *Maps of narrative practice.* Norton.

White, M., & Epston, D. (1990). *Narrative means to therapeutic ends.* Norton.

Wood, N., & Patel, N. (2017). On addressing 'Whiteness' during clinical psychology training. *South African Journal of Psychology, 47,* 12–24.

World Health Organization. (2021). *Social determinants of health.* https://www.who.int/health-topics/social-determinants-of-health

CHAPTER 5

DWELLING AND OTHERNESS: A PROPOSAL TO CLINICAL PRACTICE BASED ON INTERCULTURAL RELATIONSHIPS

Dario Marinho de Lima Neto[1]
Universidade de São Paulo, Brazil

Danilo Silva Guimarães[2]
Universidade de São Paulo, Brazil

ABSTRACT

The chapter presents reports concerning the first author's experience in two *Mbya Guarani Tekoa* (the places where the culture is lived or villages) in São Paulo, Brazil. We built reflections on the possibility of constructing a *sense of dwelling*, defined here as the person's feeling that a place/moment is worthy of trust and serenity, and its importance to the clinical practice. We discuss two conditions required for the of the psychologist to build places for dwelling, that is, *sustain alterity*, in an effort to being open to the otherness and available for its elaboration and *be welcomed* by the other, helping oneself to cope with the otherness. Without this, the psychologist may close itself off to the experience and may not find a place for dwell. It is proposed that the psychologist, in the clinic context, must be trained through being exposed to

Cultural Psychology in Clinical Research and Practices, pages 89–108

Published under exclusive licence by Emerald Publishing Limited
doi:10.1108/978-1-83742-213-520261005

the alterity of the otherness, envision constructing a dwelling place from it, therefore becoming available to increase its potential to dwell multiple others. The psychotherapeutic encounter is, then, seen as the encounter between others in exchange, where the construction of trust and serenity in this relationship is essential. However, the opening to the experience of alterity need to be elaborated, addressing the continuity and amplification of the dwelling process.

Keywords: Dwelling; clinical practice; Mbya Guarani; semiotic-cultural constructivism; otherness; alterity

The objective of this chapter is to discuss how the elaboration of alterity relationships, in the intercultural meetings, contribute to the work of the psychologist in the context of the clinical and other practices. To support the argument, the chapter focuses on two experiences of the first author in two different places, in two different contexts and personal moments and leading to two different attitudes towards the other. The elaboration of these experiences raised questions about the role of alterity in the clinical practice and the possible gains and challenges that the relationship with alterity can bring to it.

The reflections are made under the perspective of the Semiotic-Cultural Constructivism (SCC), as a 'theoretical-methodological, epistemological, and ethical perspective within psychology' (Silva Guimarães, 2024, p. 1124). This perspective is highly influenced by the cultural and dialogical psychologies of Boesch, Valsiner and Markova. There are other authors and other dialogs that the SCC made over the last years that can see better view in the latter works of Simão and Silva Guimarães (cf. Simão e Silva Guimarães, 2021), however, from the beginning of this framework, 'Dialogism's philosophical underpinnings, in turn, connect the SCC to the philosophy of language of Bakhtin, the hermeneutics of Gadamer, and the ethics of Levinas' (Silva Guimarães, 2024, p. 3). The SCC helps us to construct comprehensions about the relationship with the other and the alterity dimensions that emerges in psychotherapy.

Clinical practice, here, addresses a broad conception, which goes beyond its restricted medical origins concerning the attention to visible and the invisible signs of pathology and the normalisation of the medical profession (cf. Foucault, 1977). At the scope of the SCC, regarding the issue of the alterity in the I-Other relationship, primary in the works of Simão (1992, 2000); Simão e Sato (1996), the clinical practice focuses the constructivist approach regarding the co-authorship in meaning construction between psychologist and patient[3] and the alterity dimensions that is inherent to the I-Other relationship. The *co-authorship in meaning construction* is an epistemological position of the SCC about the relation between researcher and research participants, in which the goal is not the sought of reliability and precision in portraying an objective external reality, but create 'new forms of apprehension, in the empirical event, of aspects through which reality is manifested' (Bettoi e Simão, 2002, p. 613). The focus on the co-constructive approach in knowledge construction is vastly discussed in the works of Simão concerning the researcher and participant of research relation. Here, we propose that the clinical practice relationship between psychologist and patient can be comprehend by this co-constructive perspective.

In this work, we made an important distinction between otherness and alterity that is not usual. The concept of otherness in this work embraces the idea of the unknown, the not familiar, the new that are not yet comprehended and will never be fully comprehended: the knowledgeable and the unknowledgeable (never knowledgeable) (cf. Simão, 2007) – it is a broad concept. Alterity, meanwhile, which is included in the scope of the otherness, is comprehend here as the unknown who urges us to surpass ourselves 'in the tension among what is, what is not, and what could come to be in the relationship with the other' (Simão, 2007, p. 22). Otherness addresses here all the aspects a person does not feel fully familiar with, it is anything that escapes from oneself, which is strange or unknown but not necessarily uncomfortable or disturbing. Nevertheless, otherness can manifest itself as alterity when it provokes disquieting experiences, something that hurts our *expectances*, urging us to feel, think and act towards solving the impasse (Simão, 2003). Otherness is present in all places of our day-to-day lives, because it is inherent to it, as the relation with the other is the place of *non-coincidence* (there will be always a feeling of nonadjustment to the other), the *solitude of the I* (as none of them, the I and the other, can live the life of other) and the other as a *mystery* (Simão, 2007). Alterity refers to something that moves, intrigues us, something that needs action, whether if you move away from it or if you work to find a way to elaborate it. 'Alterity is not an entity, but a particular nature of the I–other relationship, where the key aspect for its occurrence is a prereflective disposition of the subject to relate to someone who exceeds him/herself' (Simão, 2003, p. 456). In other words, alterity is not inherent of something or some experience, but emerges from the relationship with the other. Besides, what is felt as alterity to one person is not necessary alterity for someone else.

For example, when we go to the bakery buy the everyday bread, we know the path, the bakery, the attendant, the dog that always bark at us on the way, the cars all around etc. But, besides that, there will always be an element of ignorance and newness in the environment, could be another dog that we never saw crossing the street, new cars in the parking spots, people we never saw before at the bakery, a new type of ham etc, all of this could be named as otherness, the things that exceeds the known and the familiar. Otherness does not need to be new things or new people, even when we talk with the attendant, there is always a portion of misunderstand between us and s/he, but that does not bother us:

> [...] what the participants coconstruct is the belief in the possibility of sharing something: the interactors treat their environment as if they would be sharable. Intersubjectivity would be, then, a coconstructed illusion by the participants of an interaction. A very relevant illusion for dealing with the reality, indeed. It would allow both, involving oneself in the interaction and clarifying some of its meanings, while hiding other. (Simão, 2007, p. 22)

However, this illusion does not necessarily close oneself to the contact with the Mystery of the Other:

> On the other hand, to assume the constructed illusion of intersubjectivity does not mean necessarily to give up of relating to the Mystery of the Other. On the contrary, from this perspective, it means to try to be nearer to that Mystery trough the dialogue, as a tentative—never completely accomplished—for clarifying the opacity and nebulosity of the Other's messages. It is the core of the intersubjective striving and quest for the future. (p. 19)

Walking through the future is the encounter with the unknown and relating with the other is a *quest for the future*, as stated by Simão (2007). Therefore, in the relation with the other, there will aways be uncertainty, blind spots, misunderstands, *mystery*, *noncoincidence* and *solitude*: they will always be the otherness. The otherness is not something special, is something that is present in the everyday life and that we have mechanisms to cope with it.

In the other hand, imagine if you are at a strange country, with other rituals and culture, and you do not quite know how to behave, people look at you in a strange way, they do not behave as you expect, and even something that you *feel* as strange, but you can not name it yet, some discomforts that is not yet elaborated. This still part of the otherness, because it is different, is new, is something unfamiliar, unknown, but is not an everyday cat or dog, is something that hits you differently, which *urges you for movement*, which, even if you just walk your way off it, the discomfort will remain inside you as an issue to be elaborated. Alterity encompasses this kind of experience, which demands movement, which is not just new, but is intriguing and *disquieting* (Simão, 2003) and leads to transformation. Nevertheless, a person does not need to be beyond his/her familiar's country's borders to experience alterity: as discussed earlier, alterity is about the relation between a person and his/her experience, so it is very idiosyncratic, differing from person to person. In that sense, going to the local bakery can provoke alterity experiences to someone, as being a foreigner could not provoke it to another person. Alterity hits you as a felling of displacement, misunderstanding, as a feeling we do not have a name to label it, demanding us an effort in order to create meaning.

This study will reflect on the first author's experiences with local communities during his graduate study internship from 2016.[4] The exerts will be based on two written reports, both when the first author participated in the service of the *Rede de Atenção à Pessoa Indígena* (Indigenous Support Network, ISN) as a graduate student enroled in a university extension project.

THE INDIGENOUS SUPPORT NETWORK

The ISN is an extension service coordinated by Associate Professor Danilo Silva Guimarães, linked to the Department of Experimental Psychology at IPUSP (Psychology Institute of the University of São Paulo), which proposes the development of projects that aim to contribute to the study of psychosocial vulnerabilities of the indigenous people. Psychosocial care services are integrated into initiatives that aim to respect the process of ethnic self-assertion, promote forums for equitable interethnic dialogue between indigenous knowledge and Brazilian society and promote the visibility of indigenous culture that remains strongly active in the contemporary world. It is situated in IPUSP at Laboratory of Verbal Interaction and Knowledge Building (LIVCC) and linked to the disciplines related to Community Actions.

About the Internship and Its Methods

The students usually visit a community (that the ISN have a previous relationship or they help to build the relationship from the ground up) and in co-authorship with the community develop a project (new or current) and/or experience an event (as a student, the first author, at *Takoa* A, experience the *Nhemongaraí*[5] while was working in a audiovisual project with the community; and he visit the *Takoa* B while was working in another project that was about building a dry toilet). After the visits and working with the projects, the students write reports about the experience, writing about the feelings that emerged, the experiences that was lived and how it can compare with the expectations that they had before the visit. The report's excerpts that we will debate bellow are products of this internship: one talks about the experience at Tekoa A and the other at Tekoa B.[6]

It is important to state that the visits at the communities was not organised with the intent to produce material to research or to collect data in this regard. From the hermeneutic methodology (Silva Guimarães et al., 2019), the members of ISN first discuss what are the expectations concerning the next visit, planning the goals of the activity (to film, to participate in an event, to create a new project with the community etc.) and what the team expect as the outcome. The experience at the communities cause ruptures into these expectations and to the preconceptions about the communities. This rupture is further elaborated after the experience, with reunions with the members of the ISN, when they exchange and talk about the experience together and writing reports afterwards. From these reports, we pick two of them from the first author and relate them with the elaborated memories of himself to create this piece of science. At the time, at the communities and with the group, the first author did not expect the visit to turn into an essay, article, or any kind of academic text, but the outcomes of the experience can be fruitful to construct knowledge in psychology and its process.

REPORTS FROM THE EXPERIENCE OF A PSYCHOLOGIST UNDER FORMATION

This chapter presents the two visits at *Tekoa* A and *Tekoa* B and the respective excerpts of the reports written little time after the visits. The reports are close in time and they can be viewed as a whole process (instead of two different ones) if you consider the process in between connecting them - of the elaboration of the previous experience and the preparation for the next one.

Experience at Tekoa A

The first report concerns the experience at the *Nhemongarai Xeramoi Mbaraete*[7] event. A group of five people, members of the ISN, arrived at *Tekoa* A. It was the first time for many of them to spend two days and one night in an indigenous *Tekoa*. The first author (at that time, a psychology student in training; will be referred from this point as just 'the student') knew very little about the way of life of that community: who the leaders were, where he would sleep, what he would eat, who he would find and how the encounters should take place. He was not familiar with the pace and organisation of these activities. He felt powerless, even though he was curious and interested in having that experience. He was with the intention of being more observant, with a more passive attitude towards events, for fear of doing something wrong. Besides his wish to live the experience, his attitude was very reserved. As a member of the ISN, one of the objectives was to participate at the rituals and to record the event with a digital camera, to later edit it and present it back to the community.

At the arrival, the student was curious about what would be found there. He was anxious to know where he would eat, with whom he would interact and even with what language they would communicate with him – if it were the language of Guarani,[8] he would not understand it. He also remembers how strange it was to drive the car into the *Tekoa*: at that moment he realized that there was very little differentiation between what was inside and what was outside of that community, he expected to have a fence, a gate. So, as soon as he got out of the car, he realized that he was already inside the community, he was in the 'backyard' of some families. While he felt as if he was invading the territory of the indigenous people, he also felt that they *welcomed him with such good will* that it seemed more of a discomfort from the side of the author than probably from them. His feelings were that it was always very difficult to know what he should do and what could be potentially offencive. However, in a moment, he had his first certainty of what to do:

> The first ceremony, in the morning, could not be seen by the students of the [ISN], only one member, who already had more time in contact with the village, was able to enter and even participate. One of the young people explained to us that this choice was because it was something very sacred to them. When we could get in, he would let us know. This became the usual during our stay. (Lima Neto, 2016a, p. 1)

The student points out that he does not remember feeling distressed or displaced when he was barred from the ceremony. The feeling was that *he finally had had some certainty* of where he could stay and where he should not, a certainty of the place that he could belong and act without harming or being harmed, without crossing limits or making mistakes.

Throughout that same day, until late at night, Guarani Mbya music was a constant:

> More songs started, sung by men and women, both lined up separately and facing each other. There was also music in the afternoon, before the big celebration in the evening. *Xeramoi* was passing through them. The people around were singing too. (Lima Neto, 2016a, p. 1)

The student was gradually feeling acclimated, yet not with all the confidence of being able to act and make mistakes, but more comfortable. As depicted in the following reflection:

> I started filming and a young [indigenous] Guarani [Mbya] repressed me saying that I couldn't be filming at that moment because it was sacred. I didn't know how to distinguish the sacred moments or not from there, so the doubt was greater than the courage to register now on. I stayed with the camera, from that moment on, in my hands and next to the children who were lying around me. They were curious and I also entertained them with jokes and with the camera, but always with the camera off, because I didn't know when

> I could shoot or not. It is worth saying that I managed to have a lot of freedom with the children, a freedom that with the teenagers I could not access: they were very busy and I also did not force the meetings too much. (Lima Neto, 2016a, p. 2)

The student's first close interactions with the community that day was with the younger members of that community - the children. Free from the camera, he was able to be present in other places. The camera was a kind of barrier preventing the author from living the experience at the *Tekoa*. As the day progressed, without any concerns to academic duties or tasks might have thought he needed to do as an internship in the field, the student's confidence grew so that he could participated in the dance of the *Xondaro*, the young Guarani warriors, at the end of the day:

> Anyone who danced would surely come out of the dances tired. I only participated in the last one, reserved for men. In this dance there were always two or three young [indigenous] Guarani [Mbya] who hindered us with wooden sticks so that we couldn't get through. It was all with reasonable difficulty. Anyone who tried would pass without any major problems and whoever got in the way of the stick would leave with some falls. There was also a moment when a Guarani person invited another one to duel him inside the circle, until someone fell; whoever won stayed and challenged one more. I managed to challenge a nonindigenous and win (take someone down) and then a Guarani came to fight and managed to win me out. All to the sound of a guitar that ceaselessly played. (Lima Neto, 2016a, p. 1)

We can see how the student was reluctant to interact with the indigenous people at the *Tekoa A*, afraid to make mistakes – mistakes that the student didn't even know what they could be. But, after being well received at the community, from the very beginning, passing through the relation with the children and at the final with the dance with the *Xondaro*, and with the sustaining of his presence at the *Tekoa*, remaining open to the experience, trying to deal with the alterity dimensions that constantly hit him, he was able to push his limits a little further: he managed to dance and play with the other people present at the *Tekoa* at the last moments of the visit. Both positions, being welcomed by the people at the community and opening himself to the experience, helped the student to outcome his tension and restlessness to live the experience and to be comfortable and safe there.

The Process in Between

After the experience at *Tekoa A*, the members reunited at the University to discuss the experience and talk about it, as usual in the ISN work method. They exchanged how were the expectations before the visit in face of what really happened, sharing the fears, the joys, the moments of anxiety, displacement etc., trying together to understand, sharing the experiences and theoretical interpretation. Parallel with this, the members themselves, outside of the University facilities, shared their sentiments regarding the last experience between them, because of the friendship and closeness with one another. The elaboration continued in each member as they prepared themselves to go to the next experience, at *Tekoa B* (not necessarily everyone who was at A went to B).

The student felt different, felt as he could get used to the Guarani rituals and that spending a whole day and night at an Tekoa felt very different then just going and visiting in a few hours' window. He felt, too, that experience changed the way he saw the world outside the Tekoa, that something had changed. For example, somethings that seemed banal, were then felt in a different way, and the other way around. What really changed may never be fully comprehended; however, analysing this experience from today's point of view, we can make some considerations about what was going on that will be fully debated further on.

Experience at Tekoa B

The objective of this visit was to accompany the sharing of knowledge between *Tekoa B* and another *Tekoa*, from the coast of São Paulo, in which the people from this other *Tekoa* would instruct and accompany the community from B how to make a dry toilet, necessary to promote community-based tourism at the *Tekoa* B, a common desire of both communities. This experience happened a couple weeks after the preview experience reported at *Tekoa* A.

This immersion lasted three days: a group of people from ISN arrived on Friday morning and departed on Sunday afternoon, after a major part of the toilet was built. Because there were fewer people at the community and there were no important events going on, compared to when we visited *Tekoa* A, the student was less worried and could interact with more people at the community. He had lunch and dinner at the *Opy'i*,[9] he bent irons, he put cement, and he shared the same experiences with the *Tekoa*'s residents, while working with the toilet building. Sometimes community members spoke to each other in the language of Guarani, which made the student suspicious about the content of those communications. But his general attitude was a little more relaxed, less concerned, he felt more comfortable playing and making mistakes with them than when he was at the beginning of his experience at *Tekoa* A.

In one afternoon, we went to the river, which passes close to the *Tekoa* B, to bathe. The river was more rough than normal, which made it difficult to pass it to reach the group's desired section of the river, which forms a small calm lake:

> Almost all the men went down the river to bathe. I was afraid to cross because I didn't know how to swim. Everyone noticed my hesitation, and everyone encouraged me. I passed without difficulties. There, I was no longer able to differentiate who was a Guarani and who was a nonGuarani [who was Indigenous and nonIndigenous]. Personally, I am very concerned with respecting differences, but every now and then I try to forget and become more unconcerned. At these times, when I assume my nonindigenous side, I feel that the Guarani seem to welcome me more than when we try to be very respectful and keep our distance. We, from the (...) [ISN], have a lot of freedom there, gained by the years of interaction. This is very valuable, and I feel, as a newcomer to the (...) [ISN], the ease with which I can approach. It helps a lot, even though I feel like I haven't enjoyed everything yet. They seem to me to be tolerant about our slips, demanding our respect and nothing more. (Lima Neto, 2016b, p. 1)

The student felt more at ease to dance, to talk, to make jokes, to disagree, to agree because he was able to confuse the borders of the places in which he could occupy, and this opened doors to feel at home where was previously mostly alterity experiences. The people at the community were very welcoming too, they encouraged the author to cross the river, they were tolerant with his hesitation and lack of courage – they were willing to get together and have a nice afternoon. The student was then comfier with the space, as when he went to speak in front of *Opy'i*, a very important moment in *Mbya Guarani* culture:

> On the second day I also went ahead in front of the *Opy'i* to speak. [An indigenous *Mbya Guarani* friend] (...) helped me, before I went ahead, whispering to me *ka'aruju*,[10] reminding me what to say before I started speaking up front. The night before, I had said that I didn't know how to speak Guarani. He and I were very similar people, it seemed to bring us closer and create a good bond. (Lima Neto, 2016b, p. 1)

This is another example of the *welcoming* he received at the *Tekoa*, when one of the indigenous people at that moment, whom he had the closest friendship with, helped him to present his speech in front of everyone. The next day from this experience, the student woke up with the feeling that he wanted to go to *Opy'i* to drink mate (a traditional *Mbya Guarani* herbal tea) and stay near the fire. Some of the indigenous people were sharing photos with their cell phones, with each other, and some of them were talking in a low voice. The student stayed there and rapidly was his turn to enjoy the mate, that was being shared with everyone around the fire. He remembers that moment as one of the cosiest he has ever had in a *Tekoa* or at any trip he has ever taken. He enjoyed the heat of the fire, it was warm, given the cold it was in the morning, the voice of the people, the light entering the cracks of the *Opy'i*, it was all very beautiful and welcoming to him.

It was cold and the student likes rituals like this, where he drinks milk or tea on cold days and remains silent, or watching TV, or listening to people at home talking. The *Mbya Guarani* rite, of waking up and staying around a fire drinking mate, was then familiar with the student's rites and desires. The experience in the *Tekoa*, along with the bond created with the people and the familiarity of the morning rituals, made the act of sitting around the fire and taking the mate a safe and potent place. Imbued with pleasure and confidence, the author went to the *Opy'i*, greeted everyone with a loud *javy ju*[11] and sat by the fire without the need to be invited.

A CLOSE LOOK TO THE REPORTS

This further analysis and discussion aim to highlight the process of transformation of the author through the two experiences regarding his relationship with alterity. The tension and shift moments narrated in the reports will be emphasised and discussed. Adding up to the reports, the memories and feelings of the author is analysed through introspection. Inspired by William James introspection method (Araújo e de Souza, 2015; James, 1890), we understand here that it is not possible today to apprehend the flow of the conscious that emerged at the time the experience at the *tekoas* were lived, however its memories, that are already a transformation of it, and the feeling that the student, now a psychologist, today experiences regarding his contact with alterity are possible. This addition in the analysis complements the reports, bringing to discussion rawer feelings, in contrast with the reports that are already organised in words: with the introspection method, the author is able to go through his memories and the feelings that emerge when he tries to go back to them, looking to them with another perspective, bringing a new understanding to the experience of his first visits. With only the reports we do not have the student to dialogue with it, to expand and go deep in its analysis. With the first author (the student today) exploring his memories and feelings, we can expand the scope of the analysis and its outcomes.

We can see a difference in the availability of the student towards otherness when we compare the visits between *Tekoa* A and *Tekoa* B. In the first experience, at A, because of the fear of doing something wrong, he initially closed himself to the contact with the alterity in order to protect himself, holding him back to live the experience, but once he insisted to support the discomfort and was welcome by the people at the *Tekoa*, he was able to transform habitat the experience in a less worried way.

At the second experience, at *Takoa B*, he was initially more available to it because he had already had an experience of transformation at the visit to *Tekoa A*, where he managed to elaborate the disquieting experiences (Simão, 2003) provoked by the open contact with alterity, in the period in between the two visits. The rites are not that strange anymore, he knew then (at *Tekoa B*) what places he could occupy and feel comfortable, which limits he could trespass with the other in that context and he create an understanding about what kind of feelings he might face and, however still yet very rudimental, he knew how to cope with this kind of experience better than before. Another reason is the type of experience itself at the *Tekoa B* which was more familiar for the student then at *A* was: the cold and raining weather, the familiar people, the quiet environment – i.e., things that the author already felt comfortable with in other contexts. Being able to feel safe and serene at the beginning of this experience (at *A* took until the final moments to occur) encouraged the student to go further into the otherness and to feel and deal with alterity in a more confident and creative way, transforming himself and elaborating more undemanding.

When the indigenous people at *Tekoa* A made clear the student's prohibition to enter the *Opy'i*, in a sacred ritual, he started to feel more at ease, as if they had put him in a limited place and, by denying his participation in one place, they were affirming his participation in another. In the same way, when they forbade him to film a ritual, he shifted his uncomfortable role of recording the ritual to observe and act in other places, as he played with the children by his side for, then, releasing the camera once and for all, so he could finally dance with the music and participate more vividly in the event. These young children welcomed him with patience, care, and joy, taking the student out of his university duties (to film) to be present at that time with the community. The bond was strengthened, and the author was transformed in order to embrace those new rites and affections he experienced. He could see possibilities for his actions that were not as evident as before. Without the attitude of openness to the alterity from either him and the community's members (who welcomed him without knowing who he was), the author could have simply returned to his old places of comfort (as be silent, be alone, just watch, do not interact) to feel relaxed, but he threw himself (and was thrown) into the experience in the desire to establish a dwelling in this new meeting.

Figueiredo (1995), creating approximations between the works of Foucault and Heidegger in the studies of ethics, comprehends ethics as dwelling and habitat. From Figueiredo (1995), we understand dwelling as an experience of feeling at home, safe, serene, a subjective place where we feel confident to play, to jest, to experience life in a more unworried way. The concept of dwelling emerged from the elaborations of the first author experiences reported and helped him to understand and deal with his relationship with alterity and the transformations that took place afterwards. Dwelling is an important concept for our work, as it represents the feeling and place that helps us to deal with alterity, which can be itself, a consequence of a previous relation with alterity. Dwelling is a place where you feel potent, feel safe and confident to go further in the experience, as it is a place where you can relax, be more at ease, enjoy the moment without concerns. A life without moments of dwellings is a life full of anxieties and turbulence that can block a person from living and elaborating his/her experiences.

The author, at *Tekoa B*, inhabited the river, he inhabited those new friendships, he inhabited the partnership, he felt he was building a dwelling within that new space, which made him build a safe place so that he could venture into these relationships in a deeper way. It was possible to confuse the borders of the places in which he could occupy (to dance, talk, make jokes, disagree, agree, hug, drink, eat with the once strangers) and this opened doors to shelter what was previously alterity dimensions and, with this, to relate in different attitudes towards the otherness. Leão e Silva Guimarães (2021), in a dialogical perspective, discuss this transformation process that take place in the dialogical relation with the other:

> [The] dialogical relations are filled with opposition speeches, and [...] the dialogue with the strangeness of the other requires the availability for the involvement of the other who is different. These relationships, although they can be of conflict, create a process of maturation resulting from the expansion of our capacity to shelter what exceeds us. (Leão & Silva Guimarães, 2021, p. 8)

Leão and Silva Guimarães (2021) notion of shelter is parallel with the notion of dwelling. It is important to emphasize that the dwelling is never a definitive state, but the cultivation of 'serenity and trust' subjective, intersubjective and interobjective places in which we can rely on to engage with relationships with ourselves and the others. Creating places for dwelling, nevertheless, does not mean merge with the other and erase the differences – the dwelling helps us to deal with the alterity, not to avoid it. The elaboration of the contact with the other transforms us and this transformation (as the creation of places of dwelling) can move us to go further, towards growth, into the alterity experiences:

> In the relationship with the other, the 'I' is intertwined, loses its original contours, and with this, it can also create new contours that no longer define it as the 'I' it was before. On the one hand, the strangeness on the other can inhibit, intimidate, coerce and repress the 'I'; on the other hand, the encounter with it can generate growth; a knowledge to be added and assimilated, which one could offer to the other in the construction of a partnership as a possibility of development. We note, therefore, that in relationships of otherness, something of itself always remains, at the same time that changes occur that allow the constitution of a subjectivity affected by interlocutions, verbal or nonverbal. The 'I' changes, but doesn't merge with the other. (Leão & Silva Guimarães, 2021, p. 9)

Being available to transform oneself from the relation of alterity depends on an ethical opening stance, being able to lose yourself into the experience (Siqueira, 2005). It is not through inertia that the relation with alterity is made. Because it is a disquieting experience, the disruptive contact with alterity requires elaboration and a transformation of the person's internal structures, in order to organise this disturbance and elaborate it (Simão, 2003). This elaboration, at the best, can lead to the built of dwelling subjective places, but it not always like that:

> The self does not merge with the other, but assimilates it, expands and, consequently, morphs. Although there are changes that can occur violently, without respect or responsibility for the other, producing more pain and suffering than growth and expansion. (Leão & Silva Guimarães, 2021, p. 9)

That is why it is crucial that the environment is welcoming and open to the other so a good relationship with alterity can take place. If not, it might create a situation of violence and neglection without fertile soil to elaboration. As stated before, the experience acknowledged as alterity or not, disquieting or not, depends on the perspective of the person who experience it. The same is valid for the construction of the dwelling, as the elaboration and paths someone goes across to accomplish it, is not technical or totally predictable. Nevertheless, the availability to live the alterity is necessary to elaborate experience and to build a dwelling place, which made room to live other disquieting experiences and so on. This is, thus, the process that we consider important in the clinical practice: the process of how to cope with alterity, its challenges and its expected outcome, the dwelling.

OTHERNESS AND THE LIMITS OF NAMING EXPERIENCES AND TRANSLATING

A form of encounter that predominates the assimilable will always be loneliness as stated at Coelho Jr. (2008), who discuss the concept of alterity from Lévinas from philosophical and psychoanalytical approaches. For him, being with the other implies a certain displacement, division, or modification by the person, therefore, to be with the other implies an experience of alterity. Coelho Jr. (2008) claims that a person should never just assimilate the other, however, should learn how to live and to be transformed in the face of what in principle would be excluded. 'What is ignored or rejected, what is repelled, is precisely what differs from me and could make me another, in my radical openness to alterity' (Coelho Jr., 2008, p. 217). Besides, alterity being inherent to the intersubjective relations, imply movement: from the openness to the other, someone could try to move back to the sameness, closing him/herself to the relation with the other '[such as] Odysseus, whose adventure in the world was nothing more than a return to his native land - a complacency in the Same, an ignorance of the Other'. (Lévinas, 1972, p. 40).

To be open to the experience of alterity is to allow ourselves to be affected by the other, as the ethnographer Favret-Saada (Siqueira, 2005) proposes, when talking about her experience in the field. To be available to the other is not to identify ourselves with the point of view of the other (in her case, the 'native'), nor to use the field experience to exercise our narcissism, to confirm our beliefs. Being affected, being open to the other and to the experience as a whole, is to take the risk of the dismounting of our objectives and expectations. Being available means assuming the risk to lose ourselves in the experience, to be transformed, putting our own beliefs at stake and allowing the other to touch us from the inside out. At the indigenous communities, the first author exposed himself to the disquieting experience (Simão, 2003) of the relation with alterity, not fully and all at once at first, but as he perceived that the risk was worthwhile and kept opening himself up to the experiences.

A few words/expressions of the indigenous Guarani Mbya tradition were presented in this chapter, as *Tekoa, Nhemongarai* and *Xondaro*, for example. From the reflections about the issues surrounding the translation of indigenous expressions to another language (and another culture, inevitably), the Brazilian anthropologist Viveiros de Castro (2018) proposes the method of controlled equivocation (*equivocação controlada*, in Portuguese). By proposing this method, Viveiros de Castro (2018) states that the equivocation is not a 'subjective failure, but an objectivation tool' (p. 256) that helps us to transit between different cultures and languages. 'To translate is to situate yourself in the space of equivocation and dwell there' (p. 254) and '(...) [to] presume that the equivocation already exists; (...) [to translate] is to communicate through the differences, rather than silence the Other presuming an univocality' (p. 255). Finally, Viveiros de Castro (2018) affirms that the labour of translating is not to find synonyms, but to avoid losing sight of the equivocations that will be present in our communication between our language and the other, whereas both different cultures are never talking about the same things.

Therefore, when we try to translate a Guarani Mbya word or expression to Portuguese (the authors' of this chapter mother tongue) and then to English (this chapter's language), what we are trying to do is to create another meaning (different from the original) in the hope to approximate the English reader to what us and the people from our culture, as another psychologists and anthropologists, that made the contact with Guarani culture, understood about their word/expression in sight. What is important to know is that we do not hope to be exact and precise (there will always be a portion of equivocation) with the translations, but we hope to get the closest we can (controlled) to the original meaning. To get close it is not necessary to bring a word in English, for example, that better translates another word in Guarani Mbya, as hoping to find a synonym. However, to translate is to work around, create another meaning, make turns, add interpretations to what we think is a better comparison about what might be the meaning of that word/expression for this another culture using our own words/expressions to represent it.

For example, Viveiros de Castro (2018) talks about, in his article, about the expression *txai* from the Kaxinawá culture, that was once translated to 'brother', in Portuguese (*irmão*). But, if we want to be more precise about what it means to the Kaxinawá people, brother-in-law, for example, would be a better translation (because *txai* presumably is an expression that cannot be used to relatives with blood relationship). Although, when we look at how the expression *txai* is used in the Kaxinawá culture and how the brother is used in the Brazilian culture, maybe to translate *txai* to brother makes more sense than to brother-in-law. The point is, in order to translate a feeling/expression from one culture to another, to avoid the equivocation (*txai* is not brother) might not be the ideal move. To assume the equivocation as a constant (there is not really a word that can translate *txai*), we are able to work around it, expanding and adding new meanings to the original word/expression, being able to create a new understanding of it, without assuming the fully veracity and housing the contradictions. Another example is: when we often translate *Opy'i* as House of Prayer in Brazil, we are less talking about how Guarani Mbya people understand it, and more about how the *Opy'i* as a sign or an object, would mean to us with our own culture/language background.

THE ROLE OF ALTERITY AND DWELLING AT THE CLINICAL PRACTICE

Assuming that alterity is present in the intersubjective relations and that the clinical practice requires this type of relation, it is inevitable for the professional to be able to deal with the alterity that will emerge in the therapist-patient relation. From the reflections on the reports about the experiences in the *Tekoa* and the introspective analysis of the first author's memories and feelings, we propose an approach to the clinical endeavour where coping with alterity is the main focus.

Both, psychologist and patient face the inevitable relation with alterity at the therapeutic process. Therefore, if both are in contact with the disquiet experience of alterity, both are in the position of *demanding to change* themselves to deal with it. So, both of them are not passive, and both will not get out of this relation intact if they relate with alterity. The psychologist should not be a sterile entity that does her/his work and goes home as they came, untransformed. If this occurs, something is not happening in the relationship, as the therapist might be avoiding facing the consequences of alterity. On the other hand, the patient being active result in the necessity of he/she to move and act too, being the therapeutic process a work of both parts. The patient is not passive and s/he is also responsible for his/her own process.

To help dealing with the alterity, we saw that the student, at the *Tekoa* A and B, insisted in the relation with the other despite the discomforts, not by just forcing himself to do it, but letting the experience hit him, trying to figure out how he, with his particularities, could make that a place to stay. Parallel to his posture, the people at both *Tekoa*, mainly the children at *Tekoa* A and the indigenous friends of the student at *Tekoa* B, made an effort to welcome the student at the community and tried to make him comfortable, or, at least, included in the activities. After that, the student perceived a feeling that he afterwards named as dwelling, this feeling of safety and joy that instigated him to go further in the experience.

We propose that this dwelling experience can be an indicative of how someone is dealing with their alterity experiences and how alterity hits them. It is hard to describe or bring examples of it because both alterity and dwelling are very intimate feeling that are not necessarily attached to words and are very particular from person to person. And that is why we think that these concepts are important to the clinical practice, because it is necessary to construct theoretical-methodological strategies to cope with phenomenal that emerges in the clinical practice that is not simply understandable with words or practical schemes. Concepts that provoke us to make introspection analyses of ourselves, to pay attention to what intrigues us, of what escapes our expectations of what the clinical encounter should be. For example, the psychologist might ask themselves at the therapeutic process 'Am I too comfortable with this process? Am I gatekeeping out of this clinical process dimensions of the patient because they are too disquieting to me? Am I rushing to a diagnosis to deal with the uncertainties?'. This questions can be seen as tools to the psychologist to keep track and question themselves if they are avoiding the contact with alterity and, therefore, reducing the complexity of the patient's feelings and expressions to a scope that is comfortable to the psychologists: to welcome the other is to be able to deal with the unexpected and the strange, that through the constantly elaboration of this discomforts, both psychologist and patient start to be able to create a dwelling place (that work for both of them) at the psychotherapy space (and outside of it) to strengthen their ability to cope with the alterity experiences that keeps coming to them. The psychotherapy space might be a tool that helps the patients to create dwelling places outside the clinical encounter, assuming that they could experience the transformation of places of alterity into dwelling at the therapy space.

The experience with the *Tekoa* A and B generated the experience of feeling both comfortable and uncomfortable for the student and a pathway to transit between them. The careful approach to the experience, that was promoted by the ISN, with the ethical posture and afterwards elaboration of the experience, prepared the first author, as a student, to have an intimate relation with the feelings and transformation process that took place at the alterity experience. The condition of a student at an internship made it possible for the first author to take risks and act more unconcern at the community, considering the lack of other obligations besides the ethical posture of respect towards the people at the community: the author can even be seen as the patient that was taken care of by the indigenous people, not the researcher that executes an academic objective. We believe that understanding internally how to cope with alterity helps the therapist to have empathy with the same process that is happening with the patient, while being watchful of his/her own feelings at the clinical process. For the psychology researchers, we believe that it is important to go through the experience of alterity, be welcomed, elaborate it and create dwelling places from it. This course might be understood as the course of a psychotherapy process, as the patient tries to elaborate his/her disquiet feelings in a (ideally) safe place, building his/her own dwellings. Passing through this experience, the psychologist her/himself helps the patient understand the process on a personal level, translating into a better understanding/interpretation of these processes in the clinical practice.

The relationship of psychotherapist and patient is not horizontal, and the same is valid to the intercultural relation with a white psychologist and a indigenous patient. To make room for alterity is also to make room for the expression of the patient of what the psychologist may not be comfortable with or what s/he does not know at first what it is about. Trying to learn and transform with the patient, getting away from the posture of knowledge holder of the relationship, is a possible way to alleviate the unbalanced relationship between psychologist and patient. If the patient can build places for dwelling at the therapeutic process, s/he would be able to go deeper in themes that could once be too sensitive - as the student was able to go further in the experience in the *Tekoa* after being welcomed and finding places of comfort and pleasure in the face of otherness, the dwelling.

Considering the clinical space, among other things, as a transformation space, the psychologist needs tools to promote it in the relation with the other. As this relation is a place of alterity, knowing strategies to deal with it might be helpful. The introduction of the dwelling conception, as a counterpoint to the concept of alterity and as this feelings that empowers us to go further in the experience with the otherness, it can be an analytical and practical tool: analytical in the sense of observing how the patient is dealing with the dwelling (on and off the time at the meetings) in relation with how s/he deals with the alterity experiences, and as practical tool in the sense of trying to make the clinical encounter a place of dwelling, a place of safety and action towards the transformation. The same is valid to the psychotherapist, which should pay attention to how s/he is coping with the alterity present in the therapeutic relationship and how, therapist and patient, are being able to build together a place for dwelling (together).

The first author, as a student, went to both *Tekoa* with an expectation to execute a formal project and left there after having been taught by the indigenous people how to be cared for and to be helped in the face of alterity.

ACKNOWLEDGEMENTS

We thank CNPq (*Conselho Nacional de Desenvolvimento Científico e Tecnológico*) for founding Dario Lima Neto's Master's Scholarship and Danilo Silva Guimarães' Research Productivity Grant which made this chapter possible.

NOTES

1. CNPq Master's Scholarship.
2. CNPq Research Productivity Grant.
3. For now, without a better word to define the person who seeks psychological attention (this expression is too big for the rhythm of the text), we will use patient. The problem with the word patient is that is comes from a tradition of thinking the patient as a passive part in the clinical relationship, which this chapter does not corroborate.
4. The event of Nhemoguaraí Xeramoi Mbarete at Tekoa A took place on October 8th and 9th, 2016 and the event of the Construction of the Dry Toilet at Tekoa B took place from October 21–23, 2016. Both tekoas are located in the City of São Paulo, SP, Brazil.
5. Nhemongarai can be understood as a baptism event, it is the event where the Xeramõi (which can be translate as the wise elder of the community), among other things, reveals the indigenous (in our perspective) name of the people present at the event. It was an event at the Tekoa A, promoted by the Xeramõi of the same community, in which we, students and teacher, were invited to participate.
6. For more details about the ISN theoretical and methodological framework see Silva Guimarães et al. (2019).
7. Xeramoi Mbaraete approximately means reunion of the wise elders. At this event, several Xeramoi from different Guarani communities, came to this event to participate. It is an important opportunity to the Xeramoi to communicate with the young members of the community.
8. Guarani here refers to the Guarani Mbya traditional language.
9. For the purpose of this chapter, we can relate the Opy'i a kind of house/space/construction that is a place for gathering, playing and dancing ritual songs, making important decisions, talking about dreams and life collectively, in the Mbya Guarani culture, that is, a sacred place for the people.
10. Ka'ruju is something like 'Good Afternoon' in Mbya Guarani language.
11. Something like 'Good Morning', in the Mbya Guarani language.

REFERENCES

Araújo, S. de F., & de Souza, R. M. (2016). "... to rely on first and foremost and always": Revisiting the role of introspection in William James's early psychological work. *Theory & Psychology*, *26*(1), 96–111. https://doi.org/10.1177/0959354315619495

Bettoi, W., & Simão, L. M. (2002). Entrevistas com profissionais como atividade de ensino-aprendizagem desejável na formação do psicólogo. *Psicologia: Reflexão e Crítica, 15*(3), 613–624.

Coelho Junior, N. (2008). Da fenomenologia à ética como filosofia primeira: Notas sobre a noção de alteridade no pensamento de E. Lévinas. *Estudos e Pesquisas em Psicologia, 8*(2), 213–223. http://pepsic.bvsalud.org/scielo.php?script=sci_arttext&pid=S1808-42812008000200007&lng=pt&tlng=pt

Figueiredo, L. C. (1995). Foucault e Heidegger: A ética e as formas históricas do habitar (e do não habitar). Tempo Social. *Rev. Sociol. USP, 7*(1–2), 139–149.

Foucault, M. (1977). *O Nascimento da Clínica*. Forense Universitária.

Leão, M. E. do A., & Silva Guimarães, D. (2021). Perspectiva poética da alteridade: diálogos entre Rimbaud e Bakhtin. *Fractal: Revista De Psicologia, 33*(1), 2–11. https://doi.org/10.22409/1984-0292/v33i1/5693

Lévinas, E. (1972). *Humanisme de l'autre homme*. Fata Morgana.

Lima Neto, D. M. (2016a, October). *Nhemoguaraí xeramoi mbarete*. Rede de Atenção à Pessoa Indígena.

Lima Neto, D. M. (2016b, October). *Oficina banheiros secos*. Rede de Atenção à Pessoa Indígena.

Silva Guimarães, D. (2021). Where is semiotic-cultural constructivism in psychology heading? Contemporary reflections on the trajectory of an approach to cultural psychology. *Culture & Psychology, 27*(4), 523–538. https://doi.org/10.1177/1354067X211017300

Silva Guimarães, D. (2024). Theoretical-methodological implications for research from the ethical standpoint of semiotic-cultural constructivism in psychology. *Integrative Psychological and Behavioral Science, 58*, 1123–1137. https://doi.org/10.1007/s12124-021-09671-3

Silva Guimarães, D., Lima Neto, D. M., Soares, L. M., Santos, P. D., & Carvalho, T. S. (2019, August 15). Temporalidade e Corpo numa Proposta de Formação do Psicólogo para o Trabalho com Povos Indígenas. *Psicologia: Ciência e Profissão, 39*(spe), e221929. Epub. https://doi.org/10.1590/1982-3703003221929

Silva Guimarães, D., & Simão, L. M. (2021). Dialogical metapsychology in semiotic-cultural constructivism: Open perspectives for an Indigenous psychology. *Hu Arenas*. https://doi.org/10.1007/s42087-021-00246-7

Simão, L. M. (1992). Interação verbal e construção de conhecimento: Aspectos do diálogo pesquisador-sujeito. *Psicologia: Teoria e Pesquisa, 8*(2), 219–229.

Simão, L. M. (2000). The role of the other in the process of knowledge construction during interactions: Developments from the symbolic action theory of Ernst Boesch. Conference Presentation. In *3rd conference for sociocultural research*. São Paulo.

Simão, L. M. (2003). Beside rupture – Disquiet; beyond the other - Alterity. *Culture & Psychology, 9*(4), 449–459.

Simão, L. M. (2007). Why "otherness" in the research domain of semiotic-cultural constructivism? In L. M. Simão & J. Valsiner (Eds.), *Otherness in question: Labyrinths of the self* (pp. 11–35). Information Age.

Simão, L. M., & Sato, T. (1996). Structural organization of verbal actions in teacher-students interactions. *International Journal of Psychology, 31*(3/4), 224.

Siqueira, P. (2005). Ser afetado. *de Jeanne Favret-Saada. Cadernos De Campo, 13*(13), 155–161. https://doi.org/10.11606/issn.2316-9133.v13i13p155-161

Viveiros de Castro, E. (2018). A Antropologia Perspectivista e o método da equivocação controlada. Tradução de Marcelo Giacomazzi Camargo e Rodrigo Amaro. *Aceno – Revista de Antropologia do Centro-Oeste, 5*(10), 47–264.

CHAPTER 6

PSYCHOTHERAPY AS A CULTURAL DYNAMIC: SIGNS, CONNECTION AND TRANSFORMATION IN MOTION

Maria Elisa Molina
Universidad del Desarrollo, Chile

Pablo Fossa
Universidad del Desarrollo, Chile

ABSTRACT

The purpose of this article is to demonstrate clinical psychology practice as a field within Cultural Psychology. In this vein, psychotherapy is analysed as a semiotically oriented process in which people engage in sense-making of their experiences through culturally mediated dynamics, namely semiosis, dialogue, and temporality. First, psychotherapy is understood as a cultural practice. Second, the construction of signs and meanings takes place as a mediational activity between the self and environment. Third, psychotherapeutic practice unfolds in a temporal field of transitions, transformations, and learning processes that are constantly in motion. Fourth, it develops within relational scenarios, through dialogical and communicative dynamics occurring both at the external and internal loci of the person and in relation

Cultural Psychology in Clinical Research and Practices, pages 109–125

Published under exclusive licence by Emerald Publishing Limited
doi:10.1108/978-1-83742-213-520261006

to oneself and to others. Finally, psychotherapy unfolds as an encounter constituted through co-joint communicative action in a shared space. The article discusses the theoretical implications of these premises, aiming to articulate general assumptions within a field characterised by singularities, intersubjectivity, and emergent phenomena in psychotherapeutic practice.

Keywords: Psychotherapy; sense making; semiotic mediation; temporality; dialogue; cultural psychology

INTRODUCTION

The field of Cultural Psychology is considered here as a foundation for making theoretical distinctions that arise from questions about the object of psychology and its basic psychological processes. In this vein, psychotherapy is analysed as a social process – a goal-oriented, local expression of human communication – rather than as a domain possessing ontological autonomy (Salvatore, 2011). That is, psychotherapeutic practice unfolds as a social phenomenon through its functions, devices, and tools, enacting the inherently cultural, social, and relational dynamics of human life.

From this perspective, the following sections outline the main conceptual dimensions through which psychotherapy can be understood as a cultural process. Among these, the first concerns psychotherapy as a social and cultural practice. It is a service, an occupation, or a craft carried out by a person skilled in an applied art. This practice develops under local conditions, using forms and actions shared within a particular community, in relation to its physical organisation and specific verbal and nonverbal language, all regulated by explicit and implicit rules. Second, once psychotherapy is understood as a cultural phenomenon, it unfolds through semiosis -that is, the co-construction of meaning among participants. The process relies on the interpretation of signs that emerge and become visible in conversation. These signs, therefore, operate as cultural tools that mediate psychological elaboration. Third, psychotherapy unfolds within temporal fields. It concerns transformation, as well as the uniqueness and irreversibility of experience and consciousness. Thus, temporality gives distinctiveness to every experience (Valsiner, 2008). Fourth, it is a dialogical process. It draws on the notion of the dialogical self, a socially multivoiced system composed of different I-positions, which include internalized and imaginary others' voices within self-narratives, as well as fields of possibility (Hermans & van, 1992). Furthermore, the dialogical self develops through relations and their qualities, which take shape at the boundaries between self and others (Valsiner, 2002). Fifth, the notion of encounter defines psychotherapy as a situated event in space and time. It is characterised mainly by intersubjectivity, that is, an activity involving two or more subjects engaged in a relational process that results in transformation for each participant (Salvatore & Freda, 2011).

PSYCHOTHERAPY AS A CULTURAL AND SOCIAL PRACTICE

Affective bonds, as well as everyday practices and identities, are co-created, organised, and negotiated within the social platform where cultural context defines the constraints and opportunities for human development (Salvatore, 2011; Salvatore & Freda, 2011; Valsiner, 2014). Within this framework, psychotherapy emerges as a vocation, a profession, and even an art; yet, from a distinct standpoint, it strives to advance in a scientific manner. To deepen this understanding of psychotherapy as a cultural practice, Werner's distinction between geometric–technical and physiognomic perception offers a useful framework for thinking about how therapists engage with experience and meaning in clinical work. The theorist of human development, Heinz Werner (1955), differentiated these two types of human perception: the first refers to concrete descriptions of objects' characteristics, whereas the second concerns a holistic, organismic involvement with the world (Werner, 1955; Werner & Kaplan, 1963).

From this perspective, psychotherapy as a cultural practice entails, on the one hand, the use of techniques and strategies taught to psychotherapists during their training. On the other hand, these tools are embodied and reinterpreted during actual encounters with psychological phenomena in clinical practice. This implies that therapists' learning processes carry an embodied dimension that integrates conceptual knowledge with subjective experience, thereby shaping their professional identity and understanding of their role.

This dual movement serves to reveal clinical practice as an integrated whole – where theory and practice intertwine -for both therapist and consultant. Specifically, while the consultant tends to experience psychotherapy in a holistic or physiognomic manner, the therapist-in-training initially focuses more on techniques and tools. Yet, at a certain point in the professional's development, in the lived experience of expert action, therapeutic exchange can no longer be explained in terms of discrete or repeatable components. Pointing to this wholeness, or physiognomic experience, studies show that therapists' descriptions of what they do in therapy often differ from those of external observers, particularly in how they frame processes of change (Ziem & Hoyer, 2020).

In a complementary way, Wittgenstein's (1953) notion of *language-games* helps to frame psychotherapy as a rule-governed cultural practice. Meaning in therapy arises within the boundaries of shared communicative forms, professional conventions, and implicit expectations that define what can be said, felt, or done. In this sense, psychotherapy operates as a socially situated language-game through which participants negotiate meanings and transform experience under culturally mediated conditions.

Hence, psychotherapy can be conceived as a culturally mediated dialogical practice. It takes place within rule-governed forms of communication but remains open to novelty, ambiguity, and transformation. Through dialogue, participants engage in the ongoing construction of meanings that give shape to their experience and to the relational world they inhabit.

From this dialogical view, psychotherapy unfolds as a semiotic process. As an open, evolving movement in which signs mediate the creation of meaning and the transformation of experience.

PSYCHOTHERAPY AS A CULTURAL SEMIOTIC PROCESS

As previously stated, psychotherapy is a cultural practice, and its main tools (language, signs, and meanings) are culturally based devices. Signs facilitate human adaptation and mediate encounters between the person and their environment. They are cultural in two complementary senses: on the one hand, a sign is the outcome of cultural development, functioning as a mediational tool for human growth and progress; on the other hand, signs themselves evolve in movement and transformation, embodying the ongoing process through which culture expresses itself (Valsiner, 2014).

The semiotic process unfolds in dialogue as a recursive chain of sign interpretation that leads to the creation and co-construction of meaning. Sequences of co-construction form dynamic chains of signs and meanings that enact dialogical relations – negotiating between oppositional and consensual positions. Meaning co-construction, therefore, is an open-ended process, as the relations among signs continually give rise to new possibilities (Peirce, 1984; Salvatore, 2011).

The notion of meaning in semiotic processes: In order to properly appreciate semiotic processes, it is essential to consider the notion of meaning. In psychotherapy, the notion of meaning is closely related to signs as their semantic dimension, which together constitute language and narrative. For Vygotsky (1934), meaning represents the cross functional unity between thought and language. It is thus partly linguistic and partly conceptual. Meaning is directly connected with the word and, at the same time, with the deepest layers of thought. This dual relation highlights the ambiguous and dynamic nature of meaning-making.

Ambiguity and ambivalence are intrinsic to signs and meanings, giving rise to their generative and transformative properties. Meanings emerge and evolve through continuous transformation. When a meaning is expressed, it is never complete; rather, it unfolds within the flow of its own genetic development (Vygotsky, 1934).

Another aspect of meaning concerns its place within a broader structure of sense, which entails an integration of cognition, affect, and values in lived experience. For Vygotsky (1934), if meaning is the unit of analysis for thought and language, sense is the unit of analysis for human consciousness as a whole. Sense constitutes the innermost dimension of meaning, while the word is its external expression. As Vygotsky beautifully illustrated, the relation between word and meaning is like that between a stone and a building, while meaning relates to sense as an atom to the entire universe.

We have stated that meaning evolves through a dynamic process; therefore, as it emerges, it remains unfinished. Discourse provides the context for meaning construction, where an author speaks within a social field of response and understanding that continues its elaboration (Bakhtin, 1981). From this perspective, a static or purely objective notion of meaning loses relevance.

The person is always subjectively positioned within dialogical chains, so meaning exists primarily for the one who asserts and interprets it (Cornejo, 2004). Meaning, therefore, points to a first-person stance of understanding and apprehension. Yet, it is most often treated from a third-person perspective, neglecting the lived, situated nature of meaning-making.

Taken together, these perspectives reveal meaning as an unfinished, dialogical, and situated process. Meaning making is an ongoing mediation between cultural forms, discursive interaction, and the subject's personal position.

The semiotic model and the co-construction of meaning: The semiotic model underlines the function of dialogue as the space where signs are displayed, bringing with them their own demands to be further interpreted. It follows, then, that the main process of semiotic construction is representing rather than the representation of a fixed thing or content. Meaning is always under construction. It is not prior to dialogue but unfolds through it. In its trajectory, meaning performs responses to previous voices, seeks to resolve emerging tensions, and anticipates new replies in an ongoing attempt to continue its development (Josephs et al., 1999; Molina et al., 2015; Valsiner, 2002).

In this process, meaning cannot be regarded as a static content of the mind, as if thoughts, feelings, or ideas were stored somewhere in an inner world. When a therapist asks a consultant, 'What do you mean by your words?' the appropriate understanding is that the meaning has not yet been co-constructed and the conversation itself remains unfinished (Pearce, 1994). Meaning construction is therefore processual and social: it cannot be produced by the individual alone but only through co-construction with others.

At every moment of interaction, meaning elaboration remains incomplete; meanings do not reside in individuals' minds but in the social encounter. This points also to the semiosphere as a cultural field in continuous transformation and evolution (Valsiner, 2014).

The Sign: At the origins of Cultural Psychology lie the works of Lev Vygotsky, particularly his developments concerning the notion of the sign. This construct was elaborated in relation to the learning process and, more profoundly, to its impact on higher psychological functions, the construction of the self, and the individual's relation to the environment. Among Vygotsky's central arguments relevant to the therapeutic process is the principle that interpsychological functioning precedes and shapes intrapsychological functioning. Moreover, the sign operates as a cultural tool that enables the emergence of higher psychological functions. As a symbolic resource, it promotes psychological transformation, modifying both the learning process and the structure of mental operations and functions (Vergel, 2014; Wertsch, 1985).

The sign, as a cultural and external tool, becomes a means for inner activity, allowing individuals to influence both others and themselves. Through its mediational function, the sign participates in social, cultural, and individual trajectories, shaping the person's relation to self and others (Vergel, 2014). The transforming role of signs establishes a relation of sense, knowledge, and reciprocal transformation between subject and object, where the object may be one's own experience, a particular event, or another person. This mediational principle is organised through a triadic process (subject–sign–object), with the sign serving as the psychological tool that mediates activity. In the therapeutic scene, therefore, it is not the therapist who acts as the mediator, but the sign itself. The sign is recursively positioned in dialogue by each participant.

The therapeutic system constructs this triadic relation through a chain of references: problems, recollections, complaints, interpretations, or suggestions, around which signs and meanings are negotiated. In psychotherapy, individuals engage in a process of regulating and transforming their experience. According to Vygotsky, this transformation of experience leads to the development of higher psychological functions.

Semiotic tension and the dynamics of the sign: The semiotic process is characterised by dialectic and opposite dynamics of meaning construction (Fossa & Molina, 2017; Valsiner, 2012, 2014). The sign places its dialectic dynamics each time that it emerges, bringing to the process its countersign [A NonA] (Josephs et al., 1999). Moreover, the opposite dynamics are the principle for dialogue and creativity, the functions that sign take forward in the signification and transformation of experience. The meanings constructed in dialogic chains create tension among them, that are expressed in states of rivalry, ambivalence, or harmony. Some are reconstructed while others are overcome or absorbed (Josephs et al., 1999). This process proceeds through tension between contrasts. Opposition and imbalance are the bases for change, as they create tension as a dynamic that challenges the state of quasistability of the person, generating movement and pushing the process of signification towards different paths (Molina et al., 2015).

Together with words, preverbal and inner speech act in the self-dialogue and are kept as the not said in encounter with the other, enabling tension to arise. Semiotic tension that emerges from the differences between the meanings, from the here and now in relation with past meanings and interpretations. That tension is proposed as a powerful dynamic for the meaning construction and the progress of knowledge and creativity. Nevertheless, according to Marková (2003) the mere co-presence of different positions, is not enough to activate the action, which does not arise as a logical consequence of the differences between meanings. For example, a complementary relationship does not necessarily generate tension. There are the different forces in interaction, which involve affects and intentions, displayed in opposition – in every relationship of conflict or collaboration – pushing one against the other, but at the same time demanding a solution that includes them, where the actions of one without the other are not contemplated. There, tension arises that awakens an impulse towards the future and seeks to resolve it and establish a feeling of balance.

Contextualisation and decontextualisation as semiotic dynamics: At the level of the sign, a particular dialectical dynamic takes the form of contextualisation and decontextualisation, which mediates tension. The symbolic quality of signs allows them to distance themselves from objects and immediate contexts, functioning beyond nonlinguistic referents. Through everyday language exchanges, new contexts of meaning are continuously created. Words possess the ability to relate to one another in decontextualised ways, enabling the person to regulate how they engage with the problems or situations that bring them to therapy.

This psychological distancing allows individuals to avoid being overwhelmed by the emotional intensity that accompanies problems in their immediate, contextualised form. At the same time, the process of contextualisation and decontextualisation enables the transformation of concrete experiences (problems, suffering, or needs) into abstract or conceptual relations of value and meaning. Thus, by decontextualising a problem, a person may reach a more reflective, generalised form of understanding. However, when one relies excessively on abstraction rather than connecting with specific feelings or momentary states, the variability of lived experience may be underestimated. Both dynamics are therefore necessary: they regulate each other dialectically. Valsiner (2014) emphasises that novelty emerges precisely at the borders of decontextualisation, where the immediacy of time and space is transcended, and new meanings are generated.

Wertsch (1985), in his interpretation of Vygotsky's work, highlights the role of context in children's development and how its influence decreases as linguistic and symbolic capacities mature. Language, with its signs and meanings, assumes the regulatory role of culture, shaping experience and guiding decision-making throughout life. An illustration of this process is how emotions themselves become objects of decontextualisation. The vivid immediacy of the here-and-now experience, with its sensations and meanings, gradually transforms as life unfolds. Original experiences move into the past, and each act of remembering involves new linguistic re-elaborations that reshape memory. Through this mediation of signs and their new linguistic relations, self-transformation occurs. Narrative and communication thus emerge as central processes of transformation.

Sense construction and the horizon of experience: The semiotic process is also defined as a process of sense construction. According to Wertsch (1985), sense changes across different contexts in a more dynamic way than meaning. From his perspective, semiotic mediation acts upon the contextual dimension at the moment of meaning's emergence. Thus, the process relies on the prevalence of sense over meaning, and of speech as a communicative act. Moreover, for Wertsch, sense is also the most significant semantic property of inner speech.

In the intertwined processes of meaning- and sense-making, the concepts and dialogs do not merely refer to specific situations to which speakers address their narratives there and then, but rather constitute a new action that realizes the situation about which the dialogue takes place (Salvatore, 2011). The subject, in this view, displays agency in the here-and-now of the meaning-action, as a moment of the whole experience of sense, where feelings and thoughts converge, blending the real and the imagined, the false and the true. Semiotic construction thus occurs at the border point of the horizon of experience.

> Experience is the emergent result of the recursive interplay between sense-making and the contextual semiotic field that sustains it. (Salvatore, 2011, p. 466)

BECOMING AS A PROCESS AND AIM OF PSYCHOTHERAPY

One of the key significances of temporality in life and development lies in its quality of movement, the ongoing renewal of each here-and-now moment into a new present. The process of transformation concerns both the relation to the environment and to oneself, involving a redefinition of self and world in continuous becoming. A major theoretical contribution to this view comes from Bergson (1959), who proposed emergence as the core of human adaptation. He argued that what is perceived in the past is projected towards an imaginary future, forming a new order of recalled events and meanings. Through its constructive capacity, memory allows movement beyond the immediate present, enabling the emergence of new forms of perception, meaning, and action. Psychotherapy, as a co-creative activity, thus takes place at the horizon of the future, where both interlocutors share an awareness of what is coming into being.

Accordingly, the psychotherapeutic process involves transitions, transformations, and learning. At the core of these processes lies chronogenesis – the creation of psychological time (Sato & Valsiner, 2010; Valsiner, 2008). Time makes life continually unfold and transform, carrying motion into experience. The quality of emergence makes each moment unique and novel in relation to the past. This can be understood as experiential or existential time, related to the Greek notion of Kairos. For Bergson, emergent experience draws on both intelligence and intuition to live time as flow, resisting attempts to measure or fix it. Reflecting on lived time allows us to grasp its wholeness and unrepeatable character, a moment of continuous becoming and decision towards the next future (Valsiner, 2008).

From this perspective, temporality is inherent to psychotherapy and offers a framework for understanding the psychological processes it entails. Motion and time shape the co-construction and sense-making of life situations through notions such as transition, uncertainty, and constructive memory. Life transitions represent durations that follow experiences of rupture. In rupture, what once felt like a stable epoch of life comes to an end. Sometimes through anticipated events, such as completing a degree, and sometimes through intrusive incidents, such as a robbery or a change of boss.

In all experiences of rupture, the sense of stability and predictability is lost, and the future can no longer be harmonised with the meanings and practices of the recent past. The future is perceived with uncertainty, while awareness of motion, transformation, and becoming becomes prominent. Accidents, illness, dismissal, death, pregnancy, a job promotion, or falling in love, are all experiences of rupture. They may elicit surprize, admiration, creative impulse, or crisis. Yet, the affective valence of these events, whether positive or negative, is not what defines them as ruptures. Rather, their constitutive feature is uncertainty and the transitions that follow. As Zittoun et al. (2012) argue, rupture is a condition that favours transformation and creativity. In semiotic terms, ruptures direct attention towards the relation among meanings, prompting new connections, counteractions, and creative reorganization.

Uncertainty is not a property of time itself but of human experience, emerging from the felt need for stability and predictability, the very opposites of change and transformation. The search for certainty thus becomes a meaning-making process that reflects our relation to time, a semiotic construction that unfolds through the inclusion and negotiation of opposites.

Time and memory: Memory is a key process that organizes the experience of time. As previously discussed in relation to Bergson's ideas, within irreversible time the past and the way a person elaborates it, plays a crucial role in constructing future possibilities (Bergson, 2011). From this perspective, memory is reconstructive, in contrast to reproductive conceptions. The latter understands remembering as the retrieval of an original event from the past in the most exact form possible, emphasising its unitary and relatively fixed characteristics. Such a view underlies notions of accuracy, distortion, and the opposition between true and false narratives (Christiaansen et al., 1983).

The reconstructive view, on the other hand, emphasises the continuous transformation of experience and meaning making, developed within social and cultural contexts. From this standpoint, G. H. Mead (2002) states:

> The past is such a construction that the reference that is found in it is not to events having a reality independent of the present, which is the seat of reality, but rather to such an interpretation of the present in its conditioning passage as will enable intelligent conduct to proceed. (p. 57)

This view highlights the present as passage of dynamic integration of past and future through the interpretive activity of the present moment. The present, in this sense, embodies emergence.

Bergson (1959) similarly conceives of reconstructive memory as the primary mechanism linking all phenomena within the experience of time. The past can never be repeated in the future; rather, through its residual images, it triggers the action of memory, allowing continuity and transformation of life. For Bergson, consciousness operates in the present as the active process that brings this connection forward. As he writes:

> Consciousness, then, illuminates, at each moment of time, that immediate part of the past which, impending over the future, seeks to realize and associate with it. (Bergson, 2011, p. 194)

Temporal resources in semiotic construction: The way in which a person subjectively elaborates and interprets experience often involves temporal categories or symbols functioning as semiotic devices. Their use reflects the attempt to manage and regulate the experience of time. One such strategy is the use of time as a resource (for example, to have time, give time, take time) or its treatment as a measurable entity, as in expressions such as 'time narrows' or 'the future is shortened'. Other examples include the demand for certainty ('who can assure me that it will not happen again?'); the condensation of time ('the great project of our entire life', 'my years of youth', 'the time of quarantine'); temporal ruptures ('we have to finish this', 'suddenly he is gone', 'I stopped talking to her'); and personalised time ('time will decide', 'implacable time'). Metaphors also emerge as symbolic constructions of temporality; for instance, 'the unpaid account' or 'I feel like paddling and paddling in this relationship'.

Considering temporality as both subjective and metaphorical, psychotherapy draws from it the potential for understanding and elaborating emergent experiences. The semiotic approach to psychotherapy regards these experiences as both the object and the criterion of therapeutic progress, nurturing creativity within the process (Molina et al., 2017). Three key qualities of temporality allow this connection with emergence:

- Time of experience – the connection with oneself and with the other in conscious practice. It entails awareness of the present moment as a locus of emergence and novelty, while recognising the lived and lost past from the standpoint of the present. It emphasises meanings and ideas that centre on the in-course experience and the realization of being with.
- Irreversible time (Bergson, 1959) – this dimension becomes evident in therapeutic dialogue when experiences of transformation, becoming, or irrevocable loss emerge. Examples include reflections such as 'Our relationship advances here on the road, but we still need to face our sorrows to rebuild trust', or 'I'm becoming a boring person'.
- Time of sense (nonsense) – this refers to the affective, cognitive, and holistic integration of meanings. Temporality plays a crucial role in sense construction, as it organizes different meanings in relation. When a temporal break or rupture occurs, meaning making often turns towards questioning the past and facing a sense of blockage towards the future. The relation between present and past becomes disrupted, and the feeling of sense may be lost. Conversely, the experience of duration (Bergson, 1959) illustrates the time of sense – as in listening to music, or becoming aware of the precise moment when a meeting ends and one realizes they must leave.

These temporal qualities highlight the relational nature of time in psychotherapy – the interweaving of past, present, and future meanings that sustains movement and allows life to continue forward.

PSYCHOTHERAPY OCCURS IN DIALOGUE

The psychotherapeutic process is relational. Not only in the obvious sense of verbal interaction or physical encounter, even though online practice has become increasingly common since the Covid-19 pandemic. It is dialogical because it involves the exchange of meanings and perspectives between the consultant and the therapist, and also within the consultant's own dialogical self. Thus, stating that meaning co-construction is social does not imply that a person cannot create meaning and sense individually. Within the dialogical self, the other may be internalized or imaginary, taking different I-positions in inner dialogue.

The dialogical assumption emphasises otherness as constitutive of subjectivity (Salvatore & Gennaro, 2012). The relational concept therefore differs from the merely interactional process. While the latter involves mutual influences between separate individuals, the relational perspective concerns the process of internalisation through which the self is constructed. This process was originally proposed by Vygotsky (1934) as the main system for the formation of the psyche. Psychological functions first appear in an interpsychological context and only later move into the inner space. In other words, psychological processes advance from the external to the internal. Internalisation and externalisation thus become central processes in constructivist and cultural psychology, driving both psychological and human development (Valsiner, 2007; Vygotsky, 1934).

At the micro genetic level, negotiation takes place through the processes of internalisation and externalisation, whereby socially suggested meanings enter into a dialogical relationship with the personal sphere. Through this dynamic, the social becomes personal, undergoing transformation across different hierarchical levels of internalisation. The catalytic action of certain signs and their affective qualities facilitates movement through these levels. These semiotic catalysts modulate the tension between differing meanings, enabling them either to become part of the inner self or to manifest in social interaction. The catalytic function of signs thus generates a dynamic of psychological distancing that supports meaning- and sense-making, as well as the regulation of semiotic tension.

Dialogue, otherness, and the expansion of experience: In psychotherapy, as in meaning construction, the subject continually positions and repositions themselves within dialogue (Bakhtin, 1981). The present experience often emerges as a rupture that demands a new self-positioning in relation to otherness, as previously discussed in connection with temporality. Likewise, the therapeutic dialogue performs a transformative function whose nature is not only temporal but also spatial, extending from the self towards the other (Simão et al., 2015).

Uncertainty, therefore, also pertains to spatial dimensions of meaning, giving rise to ambivalence, hesitation, and questioning directed towards the other; dynamics that propel the elaboration of meaning and the expansion of self-horizons. From this perspective, both experience and action are intentional, oriented towards the other through a desire for relationship, response, and engagement. The other actively participates in co-construction by counter-positioning the interlocutor's voices, introducing sufficient difference and strangeness to sustain the process of elaboration with diversity, novelty, and complexity. This process keeps meaning construction in motion, in an unending chain of sense-making.

Expanding the horizons of experience is itself one of the central aims of psychotherapy. As Salvatore and Gennaro (2012, p. 3) observes, this view 'leads definitively to decoupling subject and individual–the subject is extended and concerns not the individual, but the constitutive work of otherness on it'. Thus, communicative dynamics are constitutive of the subject's agency.

Vergel (2014), in his analysis of Vygotsky's work, notes that the author refers to communicative activity not in terms of message exchange or accuracy of speech, but in terms of the communicative function of any semiotic act – understood as a partially negotiated coordination within every day, ordinary language. This function encompasses the dialogical and relational practices of human life, involving expressive, responsive, and requesting actions. Relating these ideas to those of Bakhtin, Vergel writes:

> The I cannot be integrally understood without the presence of the other, without the action of the other, without the discourse of the other. Identity loses its egocentric and monologic axis; it becomes heterologic. Identity and alterity are understood, then, as interdependent, complementary concepts of a relational, relative nature. (p. 71)

AN ENCOUNTER, THE BEING TOGETHER IN THERAPY

The concept of encounter addresses the intersubjective and temporal nature of experience, understood as a process in continuous construction and co-construction with others. It refers to a co-creative act in which both material and immaterial elements, such as values, ideas, and beliefs, converge in ongoing innovation (Valsiner, 2014). The encounter entails a co-phenomenological coordination of cognitive and affective aspects, expressed through verbal meanings emerging in interaction and manifested in bodily postures and gestures (Cornejo, 2008).

The temporality of the encounter refers to its occurrence in the present and to its emergent character. It thus carries an inherent uncertainty, shaping its quality as an experience of unpredictability in relation to past meanings and future expectations (Molina et al., 2017). This applies both to the specific therapeutic relationship and to the relational self, more broadly.

From a phenomenological perspective, the encounter is an immediate I–Other experience that arises within a 'common communicative environment'. In Schutz's (1970) words:

> We share together the same vivid present—in one word, we grow old together… This present, common to both of us, is the pure sphere of the 'We'… We participate without an act of reflection in the vivid simultaneity of the We. (pp. 166–167)

According to Cornejo (2008), this encounter is directly perceived by those who experience it in the first person, as a synchronized co-feeling, whose minimal intersubjective unity requires a triadic convergence – a shared phenomenological experience between two people within a common world. This can be understood as a realm of intimacy that generates intersubjectivity, where the semiotic system enables meaning refractions and affective resonances of otherness within the self. It involves dynamic processes of continuous tension and transformation, guided by the mental possibilities of being-with-others and the-other-in-me (Assis Pinheiro, 2022).

Thus, the encounter constitutes a phenomenon of intersubjectivity that, in terms of semiosis and chronogenesis, traverses multifurcation points that open up different ways of being and imagining future trajectories. It invites the person to position herself in relation to the emergent otherness. The psychotherapeutic relationship is, therefore, an encounter – at the microprocess level – between two ways of being, and simultaneously a shared experience, a We, in which sameness (the shared) and otherness (the strange) meet and continue dialogically.

CONCLUSION

We have discussed some key principles for understanding psychotherapy from the perspective of cultural psychology, as a goal-oriented, local expression of human communication (Salvatore, 2011). From this view, psychotherapy constitutes a cultural practice in which human encounters unfold as ordinary social exchanges oriented towards the construction of the future. It therefore provides a suitable setting for the exercise of higher psychological functions through processes such as the exchange of values, reflection, empathy, affective attunement, collaboration, negotiation, and persuasion.

However, psychotherapy as a clinical expression within the field of psychology also engages with notions of health, crisis, pathology, suffering, and problems. This implies that, alongside the understanding of psychotherapy as a practice, clinical psychology addresses the meanings of difficulty and suffering in human life, which depend largely on how we define normality and abnormality.

As discussed throughout this article, particularly regarding the notion of living as a process of becoming, which harmonises with the view of experience as contextual, relational, and whole, we adopt a relational perspective characterised by heterogeneity and variability. From this standpoint, the notions of normality and abnormality become social representations and meanings within the semiosphere, guiding social contingencies and practices in interaction within the community. Even though individuals seek to understand what they are living, such understanding is always co-constructed in dialogue; it is not previously elaborated or categorically defined to be applied across a set of subjects.

This reflection leads naturally to a broader epistemological consideration about psychotherapy itself, that is, its historical foundations, its scientific aspirations, and the paradigms that continue to shape its understanding of human change.

On the other hand, psychotherapy, as an entity that emerged in the 20th century with psychoanalysis, behaviourism, and cognitivism, has been concerned with the need for measurement in order to guarantee its outcomes in terms of well-being. Its origins lie in a positivist and deterministic modernity, situated within a specific historical and philosophical era.

The perspective adopted in the present article, a semiotic approach, aligns better with a counter-modern stance, through its critique of categorisation and of the assumptions of homogeneity underlying psychological phenomena. This perspective is consistent with Husserl's phenomenology, Vygotsky's constructivist theory, and the sociogenetic ideas that began with James Mark Baldwin and were further elaborated by Heinz Werner (Valsiner & Van Der Veer, 2000). These approaches focus on idiographic phenomena that reveal individual subjectivities in intersubjective connection, embedded in their historical and local significance. The theoretical framework adopted here addresses dynamic, open-ended psychological processes rather than static contents. It moves beyond the intrapsychic domain and causal explanations of mental problems, towards their social, relational, and above all, cultural properties.

From this viewpoint, the epistemic shift is not only historical but conceptual. It challenges the binary foundations that have long organised psychological thought. Classical theories are grounded in oppositions such as health versus disease, or adaptive versus maladaptive trajectories. Even humanistic theorists like Rogers and Gendlin, though distant from the positivist stance, remained committed to the search for the most accurate theoretical framework to explain mental pathology.

From a cultural perspective, however, the very notion of maladaptation shifts focus: it refers not merely to an individual's deviation from normative functioning, but to their relationship with the environment and to the responses shaped by cultural constraints. For instance, what was once considered a sexual disorder of orientation is now recognized as a human condition; or the diagnostic category of hysteria, no longer in use, once reflected specific cultural and historical understandings of subjectivity and gender.

In this sense, modern categorisations of normative and nonnormative crises stem from culturally authorised assignments of behaviour and meaning, which vary across time and place. Within the modern paradigm, such constructs are interpreted through dysfunction or pathology. Yet cultural psychology invites a different set of questions: how do we define the phenomena that clinical psychology studies and intervenes upon? What are their semiotic and relational properties? And, above all, how can they be understood as processes rather than fixed states? These questions open an attractive field for further reflection and theorising, pointing towards a culturally grounded, meaning-oriented understanding of human suffering and transformation.

REFERENCES

Assis Pinheiro, M. (2022). Written under the skin: Challenges of intimacy in contemporary culture. In M. E. Molina, C. Cornejo, G. Marsico, & J. Valsiner (Eds.), *Intimacy: The shared part of me. Volume in the series: Annals of cultural psychology.* Information age Publishing. ISBN:978-1-64802-901-1.

Bakhtin, M. M. (1981). *The dialogic imagination: Four essays* by M. M. Bakhtin. (M. Holquist, Ed.; C. Emerson & M. Holquist, Trans.. University of Texas Press.

Bergson, H. (1959). *Materia y Memoria. En Obras escogidas* (pp. 209–429). Aguilar.

Bergson, H. (2011). *Matter and memory.* The Macmillan Co.

Christiaansen, R. E., Sweeney, J. D., & Ochalek, K. (1983). Influencing eyewitness descriptions. *Law and Human Behavior, 7,* 59–65.

Cornejo, C. (2004). Who says what the words say? The problem of linguistic meaning in psychology. *Theory & Psychology, 14*(1), 5–28. https://doi.org/10.1177/0959354304040196

Cornejo, C. (2008). Intersubjectivity as co-phenomenology: From the holism of meaning to the being-in-the-world-with-others. *Integrative Psychological and Behavioral Science, 42,* 171–178. https://doi.org/10.1007/s12124-007-9043-6

Fossa, P., & Molina, M. E. (2017). El debilitamiento del vínculo terapéutico: Un análisis de microproceso en psicoterapia. *Revista Argentina de Clinica Psicologica, 26*(1), 31–46.

Hermans, H., Kempen, H. J., & van, L. (1992). The dialogical self: Beyond individualism and racionalism American. *Psichologit, 47*(1), 23–33.

Josephs, I., Valsiner, J., & Surgan, S. (1999). The process of meaning construction. In J. Branststätdter & R. M. Lerner (Eds.), *Action & self development* (pp. 257–282). Sage.

Marková, I. (2003). Constitution of the self: Intersubjectivity and dialogicality. *Culture & Psychology, 9*(3), 249–259.

Mead, G. H. (2002) *The philosophy of the present. Greats books in philosophy.* Prometheus Books.

Molina, M. E., del Rio, M. T., & Tapia, L. (2015). El diálogo en la psicoterapia: Protocolo para un análisis de micro-proceso. *Revista Argentina de Clinica Psicologica, 24*(2), 121–132.

Molina, M. E., Tapia-Villanueva, L., & Fossa, P. (2017). Temporality as the co-construction of couple relationship: The regulation of experiential time. *Culture & Psychology, 24*(4), 512–528.

Pearce, W. B. (1994). Nuevos modelos y metáforas comunicacionales: El pasaje de la teoría a la praxis, del objetivismo al construccionismo social y de la representación a la reflexividad. In D. Fried Schnitman (Ed.), *Nuevos paradigmas, cultura y subjetividad. Bs As.* Paidós.

Peirce, C. S. (1984). *Writings of Charles S. Peirce: A chronological edition* (Vol. 2, pp. 1867–1871). Indiana University Press.

Salvatore, S. (2011). The reciprocal inherency of self and context: Notes for a semiotic model of the constitution of experience. *Integrative Psychological and Behavioral Science, 45*(4), 457–473. https://doi.org/10.25755/int.2840

Salvatore, S., & Freda, M. F. (2011). Affect, unconscious and sensemaking: A psychodynamic, semiotic and dialogic model. *New Ideas in Psychology, 29,* 119–135.

Salvatore, S., & Gennaro, A. (2012). The inherent dialogicality of the clinical exchange: Introduction to the special issue. *International Journal for Dialogical Science, 6*(1), 1–14.

Sato, T., & Valsiner, J. (2010). Time in life and life in time. *Ritsumeikan Journal of Human Sciences, 20,* 79–92.

Schutz, A. (1970). *On phenomenology and social relations.* H. Wagner (Ed.). The University of Chicago.

Simão, L., Silva Guimarães, D., & Valsiner, J. (2015). *Temporality: Culture in the flow of human experience.* Emerald Publishing Limited.

Valsiner, J. (2002). Forms of dialogical relations and semiotic autoregulation. *Theory & Psychology, 12*(2), 251–265.

Valsiner, J. (2007). Semiotic fields in action: Affective guiding in the internalization/externalization process. Cap. 7. In *Culture in minds and societies: Foundations of Cultural Psychology.* Sage.

Valsiner, J. (2008). Chronogenesis: Breaking the linearity of infinity. In *Paper presented at the 29th International Congress of Psychology: Time, space and culture: Chronogenesis in human life course.*

Valsiner, J. (2012). *The guided science: History of psychology in the mirror of its making.* Transaction Publishers.

Valsiner, J. (2014). *An invitation to cultural psychology.* Sage Publications.

Valsiner, J., & Van Der Veer, R. (2000). *The social mind: Construction of the idea.* Cambridge University Press.

Vergel, R. (2014). El signo en Vygostsky y su vínculo con el desarrollo de los procesos psicológicos superiores. *Folios Segunda Época, 39,* 65–76.

Vygotsky, L. S. (1934). *Pensamiento y Lenguaje.* Paidos.

Werner, H. (1955). A psychological analysis of expressive language. In H. Werner (Ed.), *On expressive language* (pp. 11–18). Clark University Press.

Werner, H., & Kaplan, B. (1963). *Symbol formation.* Lawrence Erlbaum Associates.

Wertsch, J. (1985). *Vygotsky and the social formation of mind.* EBSCO.

Wittgenstein, L. (1953). *Philosophical investigations: The German text, with a revised English translation* (p. vii). ISBN 9780631231592.

Ziem, M., & Hoyer, J. (2020). Modest, yet progressive: Effective therapists tend to rate therapeutic change less positively than their patients. *Psychotherapy Research, 30*(4), 433–446. https://doi.org/10.1080/10503307.2019.1631502

Zittoun, T., Aveling, E., Gillespie, A., & Cornish, F. (2012). People in transitions in world in transition: Ambivalence in the transition to womanhood in world ward II. In A. Bastos, K. Uriko, & J. Valsiner (Eds.), *Cultural dynamics of women's lives. A volume in, advances in cultural psychology: Constructing human development Ch. 3* (pp. 59–78).

CHAPTER 7

WHEN THERAPISTS NEED TO BE THEIR OWN CLIENTS: THE INFLUENCE OF INTERSECTIONAL PRIVILEGE AND DISCRIMINATION ON THERAPY AND THE NEED TO TALK ABOUT IT THROUGH THERAPEUTIC SELF-DISCLOSURE

Sabrina Saase
Technical University Braunschweig, Germany

ABSTRACT

Culture shapes society, individuals and therapy itself through its norms, expectations, attitudes and beliefs. This can result in social injustices entering the therapy room that need to be addressed. Drawing on literature and five case studies from a qualitative study conducted in Germany, in which novice therapists acted as experts on inequalities and an intersectional perspective in therapeutic training and therapy (Saase, 2019a, 2019b), this article explores

Cultural Psychology in Clinical Research and Practices, pages 127–154

doi:10.1108/978-1-83742-213-520261007

how social inequalities, conveyed through self-other positioning, fluid intersectional privilege, and discrimination permeate the therapy room and affect therapeutic processes. Furthermore, it presents recommendations on how to address these social inequalities through self-positioning in therapy. Therapeutic self-disclosure (TSD) and its associated effects, such as emotions, play a central role in the discussion of an intersectionality-informed therapeutic process. Existing international TSD concepts are discussed, along with suggestions for its use. Finally, the concept of intersectional therapeutic self-disclosure (ITSD) is introduced as a means of equalising the therapeutic relationship, acknowledging social injustices, affirming identities and life realities, and increasing clients' collaboration and agency, all while maintaining therapeutic abstinence. This article provides hands-on guidance on how to use ITSD as a therapeutic intervention to prevent the reproduction of oppression in the therapeutic setting and can be used to train future therapists. Furthermore, it aims to encourage further intersectional reflection among therapists, therapeutic trainers, supervisors and researchers. ITSD has the potential to shape not only therapeutic relationships, but also how we live together through role modelling. Therefore, culture influences therapy and is influenced by it in turn.

Keywords: Intersectionality; privilege; discrimination; counsellor self-disclosure; intersectional; psychotherapy; allyship

Culture brings joy, exchange and diversity as well as traditions, norms and social hierarchies which not only shape societies and their practices, but also their minds, self and body archives. These can lead to inequalities on the individual, structural and discursive levels, with psychological impacts relevant for clinical research and practice. The concept of intersectionality (Crenshaw, 1989) rooted in Black Women's Movement (e.g. Combahee River Collective, 1977) illustrates the conjunction of different discrimination dimensions which produce new qualities of experiences. This view helps to analyse social inequalities and coping strategies based on intersectional socially constructed identity categories of difference and similarity.[1] From a psychological perspective intersectionality deepens the understanding of complex mental processes involving attitudes, emotions, decision-making, social roles, group belongings, prejudices, perceptions, experiences, development and competencies. Thus, intersectionality and related concepts such as social positioning, and privileging and discrimination pushed forward in and by social movements and brought into interdisciplinary academy, have been used in US-oriented psychology and psychotherapy for a long time (see Watts-Jones, 2010). They are slowly being adopted into recent Eurocentric psychology and psychotherapy practices (Saase, 2019b, 2020a; Tißberger, 2013). Group identities and related thinking and behaviour, decision-making processes, interpretations of reality, and world views – with values, biases and assumptions – all influence psychotherapy including their orientations and theories and subsequent therapeutic relationship (Sue & Sue, 2008). It is especially (multidimensional) marginalised professionals who initiated and promoted the importance of considering various social identity influencers in therapeutic practices such as culture, ethnicity, gender, race, class, sexual orientation, age etc. Watts-Jones (2010) gives a detailed overview about how mental health professionals of colour and other feminist theorists and therapists challenged traditional therapeutic views and cultural identity frameworks that enforce issues of hierarchy, power and social injustice in therapy, and begun developing therapy approaches which address these same issues of oppression. Although the impacts of oppression and social identities for mental health and therapy are increasingly recognized, existing therapeutic approaches address these issues with different methodology (Watts-Jones, 2010). The intersectionality-informed therapeutic competence model (Saase et al., 2024; Saase, 2025) is an empirically and theoretically based model that was recently developed to teach therapists how to apply intersectionality to their practice, regardless of their therapeutic approach. Although the relevance of *whiteness*[2], maleness, and class privileges were already disputed by Du Bois (1935) and privilege awareness was academically mainstreamed by McIntosh (1988), recent analysis of inequalities mainly focus on discriminated positionings although (Saase, 2020a). Subsequently, the role of privilege and privilege awareness for psychology and psychotherapy is increasingly highlighted (Chang et al., 2018; Saase, 2020a) and examined (Phillips & Lowery, 2018). Considering privileges as gatekeeper to resources and civic participation, for example through voting, working, or housing rights, it is not surprizing that social movements aim at sharing privileges. Privilege awareness is scientifically related to activism and collective responsibility for social justice (see Saase, 2020a). Regardless of the discrimination or privilege focus, emancipatory and solidary interventions and related research are challenged by the continued use of constructed social categories that split whole identities and simplify complex life experiences and underlying processes of subjectification, thereby risking essentialist views and leading to further discrimination. Hence, following queer theory constructed social categories of difference and similarity also need to be deconstructed resulting in an identity de- and reconstructing spiral of dilemmas (Saase, 2020b, p. 211): Social categories used in social movements often result in identity politics for emancipatory demands such as women rights leading to invisibility or exclusions of further identities such as queers whereby also emancipatory demands of queer identities using more deconstructed social categories produce new constructed social categories and exclusions themselves and so on. For overcoming simplistic and exclusive identity politics, identity is understood as intersectional, dynamic and fluid over lifetime and geo-political contexts meaning that no one is only privileged or discriminated. Thus, discrimination and privileging are framed as intersectional and fluid too. Social categories of difference and similarity are seen as helpful metaphors like tarot cards to communicate specific experiences, needs and desires inside and outside the therapy room aiming at equal rights and resources for everyone in order to leave no one behind.

Based on literature and case vignettes from a German-based qualitative study with novice therapists informed about inequalities and their intersectionality in therapeutic training and therapy (Saase, 2019a, 2019b), this article examines how social inequalities transmitted through self-other positionings and fluid intersectional privilege and discrimination permeate the therapy room and influence therapeutic processes. Furthermore, recommendations on how these social inequalities can be addressed through self-positioning in therapy are presented. The role of therapeutic self-disclosure (TSD) and related effects such as emotions for an intersectional sensible therapy process are core topics of this article. Internationally existing concepts and conditions for TSD are discussed and guiding suggestions for TSD usage are presented. In addition, I introduce the concept of intersectional therapeutic self-disclosure (ITSD) and its usage. For illustrating the role of TSD and ITSD for therapeutic process, clients and therapists themselves, translated case vignettes from interviews with five German novice therapists with self-chosen pseudonyms (Ela, Xx, Penis, R, Fahimi) will be used.[3]

HOW INTERSECTIONAL PRIVILEGE AND DISCRIMINATION SHAPE PSYCHOTHERAPY

In my interviews Ela shared her understanding of therapy being: 'like a repetition of life. [...] It is like life in a nutshell'. Thus, understanding therapy as life in a nutshell, existing societal, and social inequalities can be found in therapeutic practice on different levels. Therapy itself is meant for helping and healing but can produce crises itself like shown for psychiatric practice (Foucault, 1993) through pathologising, disciplinary techniques, traditional euro-, andro- and heterocentric norms, individualisation of structural problems like discrimination and neoliberal paradigms of productivity (see Saase, 2019b). Following the minority stress model (Meyer, 2003), experienced discrimination can lead to psychological distress being a potential reason or topic for therapy. Additionally, discrimination can be experienced in therapy itself due to complex identities and other positionings of all participants with potential prejudices and hierarchies, and due to the structure of therapeutic support and training with related access and financing. Moreover, across history actions of resistance to discrimination were often diagnosed as disease such as in the cases of hysteria[4] or drapetomania[5] or homosexuality[6] (Mader, 2015; Saase, 2019b; Wolf, 2014). Thus, a critical and steady reflection of social inequalities, self-other positionings and socially ascribed roles and responsibilities is needed in counselling.

Similar to the analysis of social inequalities focussing marginalised over privileged groups, the analysis of social injustices in therapeutic contexts has mainly focused discriminations among clients (Watts-Jones, 2010) making the existing diversity of therapists invisible. This phenomenon can also be found amongst marginalised therapists themselves as therapist Xx points out: 'Often I have the feeling ok therapists are the ones without any problems. [...] Thinking on therapists, I don't know, it's not me who is not *white* who comes on my mind at first'. Examining why therapists with all their diverse intersecting social identities and geo-political and historic backgrounds are mainly overseen and therefore multiple perspectives must be taken into consideration.

First, norms are usually not visible especially for those who fit that norm (McIntosh, 1988). Norms are also pushed actively into invisibility by privileged subjects by masking them as neutral (Eggers et al., 2009) resulting in individual motivated blindness[7] and societal herd invisibility to privileges (Phillips & Lowery, 2018). Accordingly, cloaking strategies are often used to avoid negative feelings – such as shame or guilt through cognitive dissonance (Festinger, 1957) when being opposed to social injustice – while allowing the individual to continue enjoying certain privileges without having to take any responsibility for societal inequalities. This mental state of lacking in privilege awareness parallels that of lacking awareness of discrimination as described in Ogette's (2019) 'happyland', where discrimination is perceived as the other's fault. From a western perspective, compared to their clients, therapists are considered to live in 'happyland' being privileged as a result of their expert status, putative mental health, and their role as a gate-keeper for (end of) therapeutic treatment. For example, in Germany, most therapists are perceived as *white*, female, heterosexual, and able, resulting in privileges regarding ethnicity, gender, sexual orientation and ability. Therefore, considering that a therapist is in a privileged position, the concepts of motivated blindness and herd invisibility not only help explaining the invisibility of the therapist's intersectional identities but also raise awareness of the potential avoidance strategies blocking the therapeutic process or reproducing discrimination in therapeutic sessions. Thus, steadyintersectional privilege awareness has been suggested as a general posthappyland strategy (Saase, 2020a) which needs to be adapted for psychotherapy, potentially as part of TSD.

Second, due to the invisible and automatic and repetitive nature of societal norms, the resulting inequalities are learnt and can become internalized.

Thus internalized oppression (David, 2013) might explain why Xx didn't visualise herself as a typical therapist. Moreover, realities of harsh academic and financial access conditions to therapeutic training might add to the feeling of not being represented by typical therapists.

A third explanation for overseeing the diversity of therapists is given by the concept of chosen invisibility due to vulnerability of marginalised therapists. However, this strategy also represents a privilege as not all marker used for discrimination can be hidden, thus, not all therapists who experience discrimination can choose invisibility.

Fourth, the classical psychoanalytic stance that therapists should act like a blank slate without disclosure of personal information to enable transference where clients' transfer conflicted feelings onto the therapist further enforces the invisibility of nonnormative therapists. This blank-slate-stance is an example for the privilege of chosen invisibility as not all therapists can choose to be a blank slate. It also contradicts antidiscriminatory and affirmative therapy strategies which ask to state solidarity and allyship. Thus, Humanistic therapy approaches, for example often disagree with the therapeutic tabula rasa (blank state) practice and also modern psychoanalysis is softening this habit.

In summary, a detailed examination of therapists' intersectional self-other positionings and their resulting impacts for therapy would help to shed light upon the diversity among therapists, dismantle therapist's avoiding strategies, and reduce reproductions of discrimination in therapy. Subsequently, the findings should be incorporated into therapeutic reflections and trainings. In line with international research on therapist's self-other positioning (see Watts-Jones, 2010) my interviews indicate that social inequalities and resulting privileges and discrimination are not an explicit topic in therapeutic training which might be explained, but not justified, by the four mentioned concepts of: motivated blindness to social norms and privileges; internalized oppression resulting from learnt societal inequalities; the privilege of chosen invisibility due to vulnerability; and the therapist assuming a blank slate position. Hence, therapists need to be their own clients and find strategies to feel comfortable in addressing oppressions with intersectional fluid privileges and discrimination in therapy while reflecting on their own privileged and discriminated experiences and how these interact and/or affect the therapeutic process.

TSD has been discussed and used for centuries to address social inequalities and their impacts on the therapeutic process. However, therapists' attitudes towards TSD vary as also found in my interviews. For example, Fahimi perceived TSD as a standard part of therapeutic practice:

> [TSD] is totally important. I developed the attitude through this [additional queer therapeutic] course that, in the beginning of therapy, I always directly

> say 'hello my name is, my pronoun is she, I am cis and I define myself as queer'. This helps people totally. At least this is the feedback I get

Therapist R viewed it as an organic component of the therapeutic process:

> I think this happens automatically with me. Saying something. Of course I consider telling something personal and then I like doing it. In the therapeutic alliance if the patient provokes something like anger or sadness or compassion I give feedback about it as it helps in my opinion

Therapist Penis on the other hand felt TSD should be used reservedly:

> Difficult topic I think. Generally, specific boundaries need to be maintained. Some people are radical without any disclosure. Possible. I think self-disclosure supports the therapeutic process sometimes due to making yourself more approachable. [...] But you need to be careful having always the question on your mind 'Is it still about the patient or is it about me.

In the following section TSD as a concept with potential positive effects and challenges will be introduced and intersectionally specified through the concept of ITSD. Recommendation for TSD use in addressing intersectional experiences in therapy will also be presented.

THERAPEUTIC SELF-DISCLOSURE

For psychotherapy a good therapeutic relationship is core element. The therapeutic alliance is a special relationship with own characteristics but still based on communication. Thus, looking into social psychology and communication theory benefits the understanding and improvement of therapeutic relationships. Early communication theories included a self-disclosure dimension (Bühler, 1934; Schulz von Thun, 1981) enhancing the development of relationships which are shaped by social hierarchies, sympathies, antipathies and group belongings (Decker, 2018). This benefit of self-disclosure to relationships in general can be explained with interdependence theory (Thibaut & Kelley, 1959) whereby self-disclosure plays a role for affective interdependence leading to trust, acceptance, appreciation and the feeling of being understood. Taking into account that therapy is based on a trustful and accepting relationship and that a relationship is always shaped by all participants, it is surprizing that self-disclosure in therapy was seen as a helpful behaviour only on the part of clients for a long time.

Historically, self-disclosure in therapy was long discussed only as responsibility and helpful strategy for clients asking them to disclose much personal information making them feel vulnerable when therapists were often unwilling to reveal anything about themselves. Although efforts were undertaken to separate therapy from psychiatry (Saase, 2019b), therapists' voyeuristic habit of letting clients disclose while staying in the closet can be read in tradition of early psychiatric practices. Through detention of so-called madness humans were constantly examined, controlled and disciplined (Foucault, 1993) which can be framed as forced client self-disclosure. Up to today, therapists are not only working with voluntary clients but also with clients in (semi)residential treatments as well as in penal institutions.

Considering existing power hierarchies in therapeutic relationships shaped by social injustices, it is not surprizing that feminist therapists who have focused interacting oppressions steadily take a stand for TSD (Greenspan, 1986; Mahalik et al., 2000; Watts-Jones, 2010). Feminist therapy and cross-cultural counselling suggest TSD of values, social positionings and political beliefs as a powerful intervention to equalise and strengthen the therapeutic relationship, demystify therapy, acknowledge cultural and oppressive issues, affirm marginalised identities, increase trust, perceived therapist's credibility and client's cooperation (Roberts, 2005; Sue & Sue, 2008; Watts-Jones, 2010). Moreover, TSD potentially increase client's agency regarding the choice of therapist (Watts-Jones, 2010) but not all clients have the social status position offering choice due to class (Ziemba, 2001), residence status or (residential) treatment setting.

Recently, a paradigm change regarding TSD can be found internationally (Farber, 2006) and slowly also in Germany (Göth & Ralph Kohn, 2014; Vill, 2019) acknowledging evidence-based positive effects of TSD for therapeutic process and outcome perceived by therapists (Berg et al., 2017; Burkard et al., 2006; Goldfried et al., 2003; Watts-Jones, 2010) and clients (Hill et al., 1988; Knox et al., 1997; Roberts, 2005). The positive effects of TSD go beyond general self-disclosure benefits such as enhanced trust found in communication theory. Within these specific positive effects of TSD are new perspectives for clients catalysing behavioural change, improved therapeutic relationships due to a more equalised and understanding relationship, normalisation of experiences, reduced fears, reassuring, and enhanced positive expectations and motivation. In addition, also mixed perceptions regarding TSD are found (Berg et al., 2017; Moore & Jenkins, 2012) indicating that specific external factors such as therapeutic orientation, frequency, intimacy, and timing as well as internal factors such as perceived similarity, personality and motivational type as well as degree of experienced discrimination, degree of mental disorder, or prior clinical experience influence the impacts of TSD. Regarding TSD explicitly focussing social identity dimensions or oppression, similar to general TSD positive but conditional results can be found. Depending on the cross-cultural constellation, TSD regarding cultural similarities and differences and related oppression experiences decrease cultural mistrust, create trust and strengthen the therapeutic relationship as well as support clients' disclosure about experiences of social injustice and beyond (Burkard et al.,

2006). TSD of sexual orientation for instance may have positive effects in a therapeutic relationship with a shared minority sexual orientation (Mahalik et al., 2000; Pearlman, 1996) while also having potential negative effects when homosexual therapists disclose to heterosexual clients (Moore & Jenkins, 2012) due to increased vulnerability and anticipated or experienced discrimination and internalized homonegativity.

Early international preoccupation with TSD can be found using a variety of concepts and terminology to describe the process of getting personal on the part of therapists such as use of self, joining, mutuality or transparency (Roberts, 2005) or immediacy (Hill et al., 2018; Norcross & Lambert, 2018). While internationally TSD is now an established term in research and therapeutic practice, in Germany still many terms are used such as authenticity (Plitt, 2019) or giving up abstinence as Ela called it in the interview. Thus, many different terms and definitions of TSD are found in literature and practice (see Hill et al., 2018) not only challenging therapists as well as researchers but also showing the novelty of reflecting TSD in therapy and therapeutic training.

Taking intersectionality into account, common definitions of TSD (e.g. Hill & Knox, 2001) are insufficient due to focussing mainly intentional and verbal statements ignoring unintentional visibility of social identities. But visibility of perceived social identities reveals a lot of assumed personal information which can influence the therapeutic relationship, therapy process and therapy outcome. Framing unintentional visibility of social identities as unintentional TSD, definitions of TSD which exclude shared nonverbal and unintentional personal information have a potential for discrimination as not all therapists can choose the privilege to not self-disclose due to inevitable visibility of some identity marker. This privilege of chosen invisibility is illustrated by a case vignette from Roberts (2005): 'Being able to pass as White had given me "White privilege." I had a choice to make: keep my pseudo-White privilege or acknowledge my Mexican ethnicity and face the negative assumptions that some clients made about Mexicans' (p. 54). In my interviews Xx couldn't choose this privilege of invisibility and experienced the impossibility of avoiding TSD regarding skin colour:

> ...skin colour, often I don't perceive myself as different. I almost forget. But clients notice. Once a client said 'My husband always say Black people are bad and criminal and you helped me so much'. Of course this is a nice compliment but true you perceive me as Black. I didn't think about this one time.

Thus, agreeing with Roberts (2005) I define TSD as any (un)intentionally or (non)verbally shared information that reveal something personal about the therapist inside and outside the therapy room. Room and body decoration are seen as nonverbal TSD. In order to take existing TSD guidelines into account, in contrast to Roberts (2005) and Farber (2006) but in line with Watts-Jones (2010), transparency about models of therapy, methods of work, beliefs and values and personal experiences which potentially influence therapists' approaches and therapeutic alliance is integrated in my definition of TSD. Especially from an intersectional perspective experiences due to social positionings create situated knowledge (Haraway, 1988) informing therapists attitudes, knowledge and approaches. In line with a collection of metaanalyses by an APA task force (see Norcross & Lambert, 2018) my TSD definition also integrates thoughts and feelings about the concrete therapist-client encounter but TSD goes beyond authentically stating immediate feelings about clients or the therapeutic alliance or own behaviour.

Based on my earlier introduced concepts of intersectional privileges, intersectional discrimination and intersectional privilege awareness (Saase, 2020a), I additionally suggest the concept of intersectional TSD (ITSD) extending the concept of location of self (Watts-Jones, 2010). The definition of ITSD includes therapists' sharing of own divers social positionings, related intersectional experiences of privileging and discrimination as well as clear statements regarding social justice to explicitly give space for discussing social inequalities inside and outside the therapy room. Similar to TSD, ITSD can be used (un)intentionally or (non)verbally. ITSD especially focuses how social positionings of therapists and clients intersect, discussing both similarities and differences, and how these intersections might benefit or limit the therapy process. However, only slowly research on TSD includes intersectionality reflecting how social identities of clients and therapists interlock with TSD regarding if, when and how to self-disclose such as regarding differences and similarities in culture (Burkard et al., 2006), sexual orientation (Göth & Ralph Kohn, 2014; Moore & Jenkins, 2012) and intersectional interlockings (Göth & Ralph Kohn, 2014; Roberts, 2005; Watts-Jones, 2010). Thus, this paper adds up to this rising research field examining ITSD including social injustices and hierarchies, vulnerabilities and the need to feel secure.

CHALLENGES FOR IMPLEMENTING TSD: DEATH MATCH OR HEALING POWER?

Despite positive TSD effects, TSD usage greatly varies among psychotherapy orientations (Miller & McNaught, 2018) indicating challenges asking for reflection to ease the way for confident TSD usage.

TSD Facing Therapeutic Principles of Abstinence and Neutrality

One challenge for implementing TSD in therapeutic practice arise from contradictory interpretated existing therapeutic principles.

Often TSD is mistaken for giving up abstinence. When explicitly asked about TSD and if own social positionings in relation to clients make a difference for therapy, Ela answered: 'Absolutely, this is important. In terms of abstinence I am very reserved about disclosing'. Penis described a therapy situation illustrating the challenge of keeping demanded abstinence:

> ...a possible effect is creating friendship and this is not appropriate [...] One of my early patients was a film nerd and I also like movies. I don't have a problem disclosing that I also like watching movies having a broad knowledge which helps therapy through creating analogies. [...] But then he tried to build a friendship and I needed to explicitly discuss that he is centred here, not films.

For client's protection the principle of abstinence is not only widely known and in Germany obligatory across all state-approved therapeutic approaches but was also hard fight for to avoid abuse. Ignoring social boundaries in therapy is associated with sexualised violence or mixing roles through participation on private occasions, thus, therapists must not meet clients' needs beyond treatment or create private or dual relationships or satisfy their own needs (Kontny et al., 2019). While German professional rules for therapists regulate abstinence allowing personal client contact only one year after finished treatment, self-disclosure is not explicitly mentioned (BPtK, 2025). TSD understood as revealing something personal about the therapist related to client's needs can support therapy outcome, is not implementing private or dual relationships and therefore don't harm the therapeutic principle of abstinence. In line with this, even psychoanalytic congresses recently softened and clarified the therapist's tabula rasa approach declaring that therapists need to be present with their whole self in therapy without ignoring the principles of abstinence and neutrality (Vill, 2019).

Therapeutic neutrality is another valued principle as Ela mentioned: 'Psychotherapist law declares we need to meet patients as neutral as possible. Independent from origin, political, gendered [assumptions]'. Also, R advocated for neutrality: 'In a good therapeutic alliance the patient feels comfortable disclosing without being negatively judged. Patient's issues might be extraordinary or contradicting norms or scare others but therapists mustn't judge'. TSD might be seen as conflicting with nonjudging neutrality, especially when working with oppressed clients demanding solidarity and allyship with affirming judgements (Bishop, 2015; Chang et al., 2018; Sue & Sue, 2008). Considering cultural mistrust, a concept from cross-cultural counselling indicating that oppressed clients might mistrust therapists perceived as part of the oppressive group, ITSD might be necessary to create a trustful therapeutic alliance (Burkard et al., 2006; Sue & Sue, 2008). Thus, agreeing with affirmative therapy, I suggest prioritising ITSD containing a disclosure of solidarity over the principle of neutrality especially when experiences of discrimination come up in therapy. Moreover, the possibility of therapeutic neutrality can be questioned itself due to our situated knowledge and related experiences and values based on our social positionings. These therapist assumptions not only manifest in verbal but also nonverbal self-disclosure such as clothing, styling, room decoration and website exposing personal beliefs and internalized norms even or especially when trying to avoid them and might be perceived as unneutral judgements. Additionally, performativity of identities arguing that social constructed identity dimensions are defined and maintained through performative speech acts and nonverbal communication (Butler, 1990) might make neutrality impossible. Thus, performative defined and maintained social positionings might be perceived as judging by clients due to similar or different performative acts. I theorise awareness of identity-based situated knowledge and performativity not only as part of ITSD but also as part of therapist's awareness of own assumptions which is classified as one form of cultural competence (Sue & Sue, 2008). Disclosing identity-related aspects is therefore theorized as part of cultural competence. As cultural adaptations and therapists' multicultural competence enhance effectivity of mental health treatment (Soto et al., 2018) ITSD as part of cultural competence is especially an important technique.

TSD Facing Avoidance Strategies When Falling Out of Happyland

Awareness of own identity-based assumptions often brings awareness of social injustices, self-positionings and responsibilities potentially resulting in avoidance strategies regarding TSD, especially ITSD. Blame, shame, fear or anger are possible defensive reactions to privilege awareness in order to stay in Ogette's (2019) happyland, keep privileges, ignore responsibilities and preserve the self-concept due to reducing cognitive dissonance (Festinger, 1957) resulting in Phillips and Lowery's (2018) motivated blindness (see Saase, 2020a). Before mentioned privilege of therapists' chosen invisibility might be questioned by ITSD resulting in potential avoidance strategies in order to reduce cognitive dissonances. In addition, using ITSD might bring up additional privileges the therapist was not aware of or comfortable with and therefore might further facilitate motivated blindness performed by avoidance strategies regarding TSD in general.

Avoidance strategies regarding ITSD can be illustrated by class differences between clients and therapists often entering the therapy room without being discussed due to defensive emotional reactions (Hilgers, 2010; Göth & Ralph Kohn, 2014). Fahimi described that class is mainly discussed when clients are perceived as lower-class-members:

> Regarding understanding other life realities, some [therapists] can't relate being timid coming into contact. I was often said I had too extreme cases

> which I find discriminating not for me but my patients. Why is a methamphetamine addicted transman from [lower class district] more extreme than your cokehead from [higher class district].

Hilgers (2010) discusses defensive reactions for both ways of potential class differences between clients and therapists among them regarding richer clients with class privilege: attempts of ignoring inequality, denigration of the privileged position 'rich but unhappy is not what I want' (p. 520), upgrading the own de-privileged position and values 'modesty is a virtue' (p. 520), feelings of enmity, envy and shame. Avoidance strategies when therapists hold class privilege: idealising and romanticising life without money, latently blaming the clients, fascination seeking in low-class associated dissolution and violence, feelings of disgust, scorn, shame and guilt, self-upgrading due to therapeutic career and patronising patience to work with lower-class-clients (Hilgers, 2010). As these defensive reactions are clearly not helpful nether for a good therapeutic relationship nor the therapy outcome Hilgers (2010) suggested to explicitly use this inequality as an example to discuss coping with unfortunate life realities. Thus, naming inequality and self-positionings within as the elephant in the therapy room which it is can be interpretated as ITSD offering new perspectives for clients and helping therapists to avoid defensive reactions which endanger a good therapeutic alliance. A quote from Xx presents a constructive and conscious handling of potential avoidance strategies deciding for an intentional, nonverbal ITSD of class privilege:

> Social origin, thinking about the women shelter. [...] I am always aware that I often enter from a privileged situation. I reflect my appearance for example is it appropriate, maybe it sounds ridiculous, to wear gold jewelry, appear neat, relaxed and happy. [...] Usually, I opt to do so. When I search help I feel good if this person is not pretending to feel bad herself.

This ITSD reflects intersecting systems of oppression such as class and sexualised violence based on gender as well as fluidity in the position of getting help. The implied vulnerability of therapists leads us to another challenge for implementing TSD.

TSD Facing Own Vulnerability

TSD of self positionings or experiences therapists feel vulnerable about might be risky as illustrated by Xx referring shared Blackness with clients: 'I felt I need to try out how I formulate self-disclosure because first it paralysed me'. The feeling of getting paralysed in therapeutic relationships with perceived similarity is a common challenge (Göth & Ralph Kohn, 2014) equivalent to vulnerability and anxiety among marginalised therapists with privileged clients (Moore & Jenkins, 2012) indicating that ITSD potentially increase therapist's vulnerability risking re-traumatisation if not reflected.

Thus, avoidance strategies of TSD can not only be interpretated as motivated blindness to protect privileges but also as self-protection to avoid discrimination. As repetitive confrontations of traumatic events might cause posttraumatic stress disorder, therapists are not only vulnerable for secondary trauma (Schulten, 2020) but also for direct re-traumatisation as Xx's quote indicate. Thus, TSD exercise as well as reflecting on and coping with own experiences of discrimination are necessary to prevent re-traumatisation through ITSD and its negative impacts on therapy. The recommendations for TSD usage in the next section will give further advice.

In sum, despite a paradigm shift towards TSD, despite positive effects of TSD, and despite showing that TSD is not necessarily contradicting therapeutic principles of abstinence and neutrality as well as despite existing approaches to meet other challenges of implementing TSD, both internationally and in Germany, little to none explicit guidelines exist on weather, how and when to disclose yourself with which topics in therapy. Especially explicit guidelines taking ITSD into account are missing (Roberts, 2005). Hence, back then and also today, therapists need to be their own clients and help themselves regarding the usage of TSD and develop coping strategies with potential upcoming defensive reactions. To support a confidently TSD usage in the following existing TSD guidelines will be presented and discussed along with suggestions based on the conducted interviews and additional empirical research. Finally, the applicability of these suggestions for ITSD will be examined in order to enhance the competence to talk about social inequalities existing outside and inside the therapy room.

HELPFUL GUIDANCE FOR IMPLEMENTING TSD

From research and case vignettes the reflection of the following interfacing topics arise to be helpful for a supportive usage of TSD focussing single therapies. Those guiding topics need to be interpretated as literally guiding as they need to be adapted to specifications of each therapeutic orientation, related concepts and setting. Still, as in Germany the psychotherapeutic law is in force for all therapeutic orientations, I argue that despite being challenging, attempts for TSD guidelines across therapeutic orientations are beneficial to both therapists who often use concepts from several orientations and to clients who often don't know the specifics of therapeutic orientations.

CLIENT-CENTRED TSD

Focussing clients' feelings and needs is required for all therapeutic techniques and especially for TSD (Knox & Hill, 2003; Miller & McNaught, 2018; Roberts, 2005) being illustrated by my interviews. Therapist Penis highlighted clients' focus for general TSD: 'It mustn't be about the therapist. Focus should always be helping the human, the patient' and for disclosing intersectional social belongings: 'Mention it for sure if it is related to patient's difficulty'. Regarding ITSD also Ela formulated impulses from clients as premising:

> I am learning to partly leave abstinence if clients give impulses. [...] Sometimes I am asked 'Where are you from?' or I get my language corrected. [...] I make it transparent if asked. I am not forcing it but create contact through it.

A client centred approach of TSD also considers clients' boundaries shown by recent studies (Knox & Hill, 2003; Miller & McNaught, 2018) and replicated by my interviews. Penis stated: 'Generally, specific boundaries need to be maintained' and R: 'Maintaining a professional distance signalising here is a safe space with trust without coming to close if not wished'. Focussing clients' needs, ITSD might also be inappropriate sometimes as Xx explained:

> If I see persons having parents from several countries, which are not German, without having the need to dispute this. I can think 'it could be important for you, for me it was a gain. [...]' but maybe it isn't relevant for this person at all and I need to accept it and I do accept it.

Acceptance is also demanded regarding diverse clients' reactions to TSD without making clients feel to comfort you (Roberts, 2005) having special importance for ITSD highlighting therapeutic neutrality to several responses to disclosed discrimination experiences without expecting solidarity or empathy. Facing unsupportive reactions to TSD, defensive reactions need to be avoided. This might particularly be challenging when therapists and clients share communities where allyship outside the therapy room already exists or is common ground.

A client centred approach of TSD moves beyond focussing actual feelings and thoughts of clients centring overall therapy outcome and therapeutic methods along the way and can be catalysed through reflecting questions as given by Roberts (2005).

INVITATIONAL AND EVALUATIVE TSD

Considering different needs regarding TSD among clients, invitational and evaluative TSD supports staying client-focused. Before actual TSD usage it could be introduced first as a concept (Watts-Jones, 2010). Moreover, before each TSD it could be asked if a short TSD is wished and perceived as helpful which could be evaluated through short feedback afterwards. Regular overall therapy evaluation with open questions not focussing TSD might avoid social desirability (Roberts, 2005).

CONSIDERING HETEROGENEITY IN PUTATIVE HOMOGENEITY BEFORE USING TSD

Some clients take therapy decisions based on social positionings and assumed experiences of social inequalities. In line with case vignettes from Roberts (2005), Xx described 'Regarding putative homogeneity. Many say "I would only go to a Black therapist or to someone who shares experiences of oppression"'. Hence, ITSD can help clients finding the desired therapeutic constellation but putative similarity of experiences asks for reflection for not overlooking differences or mistaking own experiences for client's perspectives (Plitt, 2019; Watts-Jones, 2010). Focussing heterogeneity in experiences of similar perceived group discrimination is given as a client-centred strategy to this dilemma by therapist Xx: 'It became natural to say I share a similar experience but I want to understand even more the experience of the other person, what is different for this person'.

COMFORT AND EMOTIONAL STABILITY FOR USING TSD

In line with existing TSD recommendations (Knox & Hill, 2003; Watts-Jones, 2010) feeling comfortable and confident with TSD was an important factor for the interviewed therapists replicating existing findings (Miller & McNaught, 2018) while also extending them as especially those therapists who experienced discrimination named personal comfort as an important factor for TSD decision-making. Despite experienced discrimination insufficient TSD training can lead to vulnerability and discomfort regarding TSD usage (Hill et al., 1988) which is important as my interviews and Burkard et al. (2006) indicate that minimal or no TSD training in included in therapeutic training. Thus, emotional stability regarding the mood of the day and the specific TSD topic is important to check before, while and after the usage of TSD (Roberts, 2005). Especially if the topic was never disclosed before or still present such as a new diagnosed disease, TSD should be reconsidered only disclosing resolved issues (Knox & Hill, 2003). As intersectional experiences of structural discrimination are not a timely limited problem which can be easily resolved, regarding ITSD Roberts' (2005) suggestion of not sharing many particulars helps building joining without getting emotionally too involved. Thus, intense reflection about own emotional stability and well-functioning coping strategies are needed when own experiences of discrimination are involved. Prof. David Becker brought to my mind the complex example of a Jewish therapist and a Jewish client directly after both survived Holocaust illustrating the multilayered difficulties of avoiding own re-traumatisation while focussing client's needs especially when intergenerational structural violence is involved. In my interviews this sensitive issue was indirectly addressed through choosing a Jewish Museum as place of interview and through a comment by Penis:

'For my fellow trainee with Russian-Jewish background it was a topic in self-experience'. ITSD considerations will get even more complex when imagining a Palestinian therapist or client in this constellation. Sadly, genocides happened all over the world and therefore (in)direct involvement and intergenerational trauma enter the therapy room (Sue & Sue, 2008) asking for sensitivity and emotional stability.

Considering intersectionality, my interviews indicate in line with minority stress model (Meyer, 2003) and recent findings (Moore & Jenkins, 2012; Roberts, 2005) that therapists' social positionings influence vulnerability when using ITSD. Explicitly asked about conditions for disclosing own social positionings Penis who didn't experienced discrimination just answered: 'I would be relatively open for this' while interviewees with several discrimination experiences highlighted own vulnerability and conditions for ITSD use. Fahimi made feeling understood conditional to her otherwise self-positioning ITSD habit: 'I wouldn't [come out] with any random person [...]. I did in the beginning. But having for example a 60-year-old heterosexual man I don't want to say "I am queer" because he will say "What does this mean?"'. Good relationship and privileges as resources were ITSD conditions for R to minimise vulnerability:

> I only [disclose private things] sometimes and with joy if I feel it fits, if a good relationship exists and the patient himself is not crossing boundaries. [...] it is much easier for me as I am self-confident. I know my competencies. Even if my self-disclosure would be negatively judged it couldn't hurt or devalue me through a carrier I am proud of and other attributes. An academic career is a form of protection and is a privilege I have.

Higher vulnerability and a wish for ITSD training were described by Xx not only while using ITSD but also while thinking on ITSD regarding shared experiences of discrimination: 'First it paralysed me. [...] I was so touched I couldn't relate. [...] This is important for me [knowing] how to handle being triggered or when I disclose because I am sitting there all the time'. Vulnerability was also described by Ela especially to unintended ITSD: 'I don't always like being asked where I am from. I am German, yes, I have a German passport. [...] But I notice I get angry over that question sometimes'. Ela also offered supportive mechanisms regarding unwished ITSD like examination of client's intention: 'The difference makes emphasising [...] it is not generally wrong to ask me. It depends on the intention of the question due to fine nuances' and thankfulness for new perspectives: 'Sometimes I get my language corrected and then I think 'oh yes, this is important, thank you very much, I have something learnt from you'. Moreover, Ela shared a helpful strategy for intentional ITSD to feel less vulnerable: 'A shared experience or at least any experience of discrimination is important to me to feel better understood'. Fahimi shared additional intersectional-informed therapeutic training as an overall strategy to gain comfort regarding ITSD:

> The self-experience of the [additional queer therapeutic training] enabled talking about own feelings in relation [to clients]. How may I differently be affected having a queer identity if talking to other queers or trans persons or hetero persons? How is my coming out influenced? How does living and working in the same community feel?

These found therapists' emotional safety needs for ITSD usage specify findings that TSD is not felt obligatory if personal boundaries are transgressed even if it would be in client's interest (Miller & McNaught, 2018).

STEPWISE AND REFLECTIVE TSD

Stepwise TSD is not only a possibility to evaluate clients' reaction regarding helpfulness and sufficiency of TSD (Knox & Hill, 2003; Roberts, 2005) but also a possibility to check in with your own emotions and agenda as well as reducing perceived vulnerability. Thus, continual reflection is recommended starting before introducing TSD to examine how perceived similarities and differences might limit or benefit therapy (Roberts, 2005; Watts-Jones, 2010). Referring to case vignettes from R and Fahimi stating privileges as resources I suggest that demanded therapists' self-awareness can be catalysed for ITSD through privilege awareness as one resource-oriented way to gain intersectional self-awareness. Existing recommendations to reflect and name own single social identity dimensions such as cisgender privilege and related biases (Chang et al., 2018) need to be intersectionally extended. In line with Roberts (2005), findings from Miller and McNaught (2018) indicated that decision-making on TSD needs to stay a reflective process considering interacting client, therapist, situational factors and growing TSD experience. The process of stepwise and reflective TSD was well illustrated by R:

> I try to involve my whole personality not pretending to be a blank slate. This happens often at first when getting to know the person checking if I can work together. The more you come acquainted with each other the more I can involve my whole personality, being ironic or witty.

TSD AS POTENTIAL ROLE MODEL

Deciding to present TSD as a successful role model or an open dilemma without giving advices requests reflection of current situation and client's state. In line with recent research (Hill & Knox, 2001) and behavioural theory of Bandura (1986), my interviewees proposed therapists as role models for successful behaviour indicating that coping strategies and associated thoughts and feelings should be part of TSD. Regarding ITSD Penis highlighted role modelling when having made shared experiences facing discrimination:

> If I experienced discrimination [...] I could share this. I have a colleague whose dad is [Central African], thus she can tell you a thing or two about racist experiences. It would be ridiculous not to use it, if important for therapy [...] Could also be sexual orientation. [...] I have a fellow trainee who is open gay, very open gay. He has also [some] patients who were coming out having difficulties with it. Thus, he is a good model because of his open handling and understanding of the situation.

When asked if he talks about his sexuality or sexual orientation himself in therapy, Penis' stated role modelling challenging when being privileged:

> Yes no. Once it played a role due to his male-female-issue. Thus, I disclosed I am heterosexual. I think it is different because as a heterosexual you experience less typical experiences of discrimination than a homosexual. Thus, I don't need to proclaim: 'I'm a hetty, take me as an idol'.

From an intersectional perspective Penis' quote is interesting as it discusses own privilege as hindering for role modelling but shared discrimination as a useful privilege for role modelling due to deeper situated knowledge indicating a double load for therapists with experiences of discrimination. This double load moves also beyond the therapy room as illustrated by R:

> I feel if therapists are afflicted they are more engaged in this topic such as giving lectures for different ethnic background to enlighten own blind spots. We had this for Muslim background and related religiosity, spirituality with big heterogeneity among practicing people. Also, about interesting laws and rules similar to let's say the ten amendments in Christianity. This was very good to know. Sometimes I have the feeling you are afflicted yourself wanting to share it with colleagues, I also feel like it.

R's comparison from Islam to Christianity reminds us that religion as a social experience and life reality is a social dimension which becomes only a privileged or discriminated experience through the context we live. Considering intersectional privilege as only one perspective of a specific social dimension might reduce Penis' insecurity of being a role model despite privileged sexual orientation opening possible antidiscriminative or allied role modelling. Moreover, ITSD training might reduce this insecurity as Göth and Ralph Kohn (2014) illuminate in a diversity-based therapy guide that also heterosexual therapists may support queer clients for example to make correcting experiences of relationships.

For decision-making on role modelling of ITSD, therapists need to reflect similarities and differences with clients in social positionings and related privileging and discrimination. Considering intersectionality, similar perceived experiences might differ through privileges resulting in demotivating unreachable role models for clients. Thus, instead of role modelling, Roberts suggested to present TSD as a dilemma without concrete solutions (2005) to avoid putative homogeneity and overseen heterogeneity. Presenting TSD in a multilayered way supports client's capacity building through offering diverse perspectives enabling connecting to the topic but reflecting own needs and possibilities for problem solving. However, from an intersectional perspective the understanding of therapists as tools for self-help aid is a western view (Tseng & Streltzer, 2001). Hence, decision-making on TSD might differ when clients with other understandings are involved.

TSD REFLECTING THERAPY ENVIRONMENT

Therapy environment contains several intentional and unintentional personal markers having impacts for TSD. In my case vignettes, after questioned about TSD therapist R described pinkish personal accessories from his university office as marker for unintended TSD supporting the client and the therapeutic relationship:

> I offer therapy here in my office. Thus, some things happen automatically. [...] When asking her about [her created skill box] [...] she said 'It is a nice shoe box, pinkish, where she started collecting'. I answered 'Amazing this sounds like a reminder of the therapy room'. She liked the idea. I have the feeling understanding, acceptance and mutual affection happen through small things.

This experience might be different in own therapy offices, community clinics, university outpatient care, schools, orphanages, prisons, home offices or client's homes due to different milieu, ambiance, degree of personal shaping and hiding and normative expectations regarding disclosure, boundaries and boundary crossings (Roberts, 2005). TSD in totally deprived environments such as penal institutions where one interviewee offered therapy needs to be further investigated.

Environment is especially an important factor for unintentional TSD if the town or community is very small due to known neighbourhoods, to shared groups such as anonymous alcoholics or shared communities such as a queer community resulting in decreased anonymity especially when only few therapists exist. Fahimi mentioned earlier the importance of reflecting how to live and work in the same community addressing handling seeing clients in free time and creating boundaries.

INTERSECTIONAL TSD

Despite general suggestions of TSD usage with intersectional implications I suggest intersectionality as a self-sufficient TSD guideline as both therapists and clients have complex social identities with privileging and discrimination entering the therapy room.

In line with self-positioning TSD (Roberts, 2005) and location of self (Watts-Jones, 2010), Fahimi usually discloses social positionings in therapy: 'in the beginning of therapy, I always directly say 'hello my name is, my pronoun is she, I am cis and I define myself as queer'. This helps people totally. At least this is the feedback I get'. To move ITSD beyond self-positioned TSD, therapist-client-constellation regarding intersectional social positionings and related experiences need to be considered. Fahimi's habit of self-positioning changed when working with an older, cis, hetero client:

> But having for example a 60-year-old heterosexual man I don't want to say, 'I am queer' because he will say 'What does this mean?' and it is also not relevant for him regarding therapy. He is coming because of an anxiety disorder and just wants his 25 hours and move on. But with most of my clients it is different where those topics matter.

Especially age differences in therapy and their impact were discussed by my interviewees indicating that ITSD about age happens automatically. Fahimi highlighted their role for (counter)transference processes of ITSD of age: 'Age is very interesting because it effects transference and countertransference. 'You remind me on my strict mother' can be said also by a 60-year-old being independent from my biological age'. Also Penis reflected age relations intersectionally:

> ...oh yes, age is very important like most [social categories] [...] for therapy process reflecting where am I positioned in life in relation to the other but also what are the age-typic development tasks. Is it someone in the early twenties doing a vocational training with the need of learning autonomy being away from home or is it someone in the autumn of his life with the need of adapting to rising social and physical restrictions [...] Not to forget interactions. How does is it make a difference that I in this specific age work with someone. Which is important for all here mentioned [social categories]. Which effects on [therapy and client] are found through me as a 35-year-old, cis-hetero, cis man, hetero, *white*, what did I miss? I don't know. Ah, educated middle-class with immense career-prestige.

Unintended ITSD about age was specifically an important issue for Ela who works with young girls who experienced sexual violence making her appearance as an adult a potential threat:

> I also would say age, because I adapt my way of talking to it [...] My youngest patient, a 3,8-year-old girl. To reflect how I come in contact with the child without her feeling threatened [...] She brought a puppet and I tried to create dialogue through it. This was very good [...] and helpful [...].

Different therapist-client-constellations regarding social positionings often reveal fluid experiences of discrimination and privileging. My interviews suggest resource-oriented talking about social hierarchies both existing inside and outside therapy while focussing both privileged and de-privileged positions. Fahimi highlighted unintended ITSD of privileges through inherent hierarchies in therapeutic relationships:

> Some privileges are visible. Because me sitting on this chair and they sitting on the other chair, a power difference is inherent which is ok but needs visibility. To discuss in dialogue how is it in their position and also for me in my position.

To equalise the therapeutic relationship, Penis suggested disclosure of privileged self-positionings and preknowledge regarding expected clients' life realities:

> If I have clients with different sexual orientation, I say indeed 'okay, I am a hetty but if I understood correctly it was for you like this.' I can say that I don't share the same experience but I know people who experienced this but please tell me more. Thus, they know who they are working with.

Fahimi highlighted privileges as resources: 'Privileges could be called resources. Thus, having a relevance [for therapy]. [...] Taking depression as simple example, to look 'everything is shitty because of depression but what is there? Despite discrimination experience what access to community exists?' This easing connection between access to community and depression is consistent with findings from Reisen et al. (2013) and social identity theory (Taifel & Turner, 1979) describing group identification as a possibility, or as Fahimi called it a privilege and resource, to preserve a positive sense of self when facing negative reactions regarding belonged social groups. Thus, for ITSD I suggest focussing privileges might be supportive and affirmative as clients might be inspired to think about self-positionings and their potentials as resources in different situations and contexts.

Finally, taking recommendations of affirmative therapy when working with marginalised clients into account, ITSD is suggested to show visibility of marginalised identities and allyship. In line with this, Fahimi deepened her earlier stated habit of ITSD usage at the beginning of each therapy through general advocation for more open queer therapists as a call of solidarity:

> In my opinion change only comes if we become part of the system. Thus, lesbian, trans, inter, queer, whatever psychotherapists are needed [...] In my regard it is difficult to escape societal power positions. I think only when taking societal power positions you can make a difference.

CONCLUSION

As culture shapes society, individuals and therefore also therapy through norms, expectations, attitudes and beliefs leading to potential social injustices also entering the therapy room (Sue & Sue, 2008), a cultural perspective framed as perceived, performed and discussed social positionings supports therapeutic interventions preventing reproductions of oppression. Especially awareness of intersectional privileging and discrimination is internationally used to address social injustices. For applying intersectionality to therapy, this article has shown the promising role of ITSD aiming at equalising the therapeutic relationship, acknowledging social injustices, affirming identities and life realities, and increasing collaboration and agency of clients without violating therapeutic abstinence. Thus, I advocate for the concept of ITSD and its usage.

Despite the ambivalence character of constructed and deconstructed social identity categories, addressing intersectional social positionings and awareness of social inequalities through ITSD was shown to increase trust, decrease cultural mistrust, strengthen and equalising the therapeutic relationship as well as support clients' disclosure about experiences of social injustice and beyond. As these positive effects of ITSD depend on many factors and as therapists receive only little to non ITSD training recommendations from western and nonwestern perspectives from literature and conducted interviews were offered. However, ITSD training is suggested to be included in therapeutic training as practice and routine enhance comfort in talking about identities and related privileging and discrimination (Watts-Jones, 2010).

The recommended ITSD guidance focussing single therapy across therapeutic orientations needs adaptation to couple, poly, family or group therapies as well as specifications for each therapeutic orientation and related concepts. All ITSD usage requires intersectional cultural competence. Possible content of ITSD contains sharing of social positionings, intersectional experiences of privileging and discrimination, solidary statements regarding social inequalities and thoughts on how these might affect therapeutic specification, theory, methods and relationship as well as how social positionings of therapist and client intersect having potential benefits or limits for therapy. ITSD can be intentional or nonintentional, verbal or nonverbal as also therapy environment and personal accessories reveal personal information, perceived identities and social positionings. Therapists need to reflect their ITSD intention, social positionings and related experiences of social injustices, emotional stability as well as heterogeneity of similar perceived experiences before, during and after ITSD usage to ensure client-centred approach, avoiding defensive reactions and inappropriate usage. Thus, invitational, evaluative, stepwise and reflective ITSD supports monitoring own and clients' thoughts and feelings. As also therapists may have experienced discrimination for ITSD usage good emotional coping strategies are needed as therapist need to be present for the whole session even when triggered or partly retraumatised. Moreover, there is no need to self-disclose even if benefitting the client. Depending on homogeneity of experiences and client's general views regarding help services as self-help aid, authority or advice giver, ITSD might be presented as role model or open dilemma. Finally, ITSD is recommended to be affirmative, resource-oriented and solidary.

Until now, regarding TSD promising but insufficient research is found and researchers are especially encouraged by an APA task force to examine the effectiveness of TSD as part of therapist relationship behaviour (Norcross & Lambert, 2018). With the given overview about TSD and ITSD I hope to motivate not only further intersectional reflection of therapists, therapeutic trainers and supervisors but also researchers. In sum, only few studies examining TSD explicitly capture social identities focussing intersectionality of both clients and therapists. Thus, the slowly rising international research field of ITSD considering both differences and similarities in the therapeutic relationship needs to be further consolidated especially with empirical research deepening existing anecdotical research based on case vignettes. Similar to general TSD research, research regarding ITSD is challenged to standardise a definition for comparability and to creatively explore the concept at the same time such as TSDO for the disclosure of sexual orientation by Moore and Jenkins (2012).

This article aimed at motivating ITSD usage and research for addressing social injustices, diversifying perceptions of therapists, decreasing rigid hierarchies as well as improving the therapeutic alliance, process and outcome. More ITSD usage and research might foster privilege awareness and responsibility of therapists and counselling research regarding motivated blindness and herd invisibility in order to let western psychotherapy fall out of happyland developing strategies against oppression inside and outside therapy and the discipline of psychotherapy. ITSD potentially shapes not only therapeutic relationships but through role modelling also how we live together. Therefore, culture not only influences therapy but also the other way round.

NOTES

1. While in gender studies mainly labeled as social categories of difference e.g. regarding race, gender or sexual orientation, I highlight inherent similarities to prevent essentialism.
2. Italics to unmask *white*ness as an invisible norm (see Eggers et al., 2009).
3. **Ela**: a 39-year-old, female, heterosexual therapist in training (analytic child and adolescent psychotherapy), offering therapy to children who experienced sexualized violence and also therapy to adults; stated discrimination experiences in life through migration background (East European) and interwoven class background due to no access to governmental financial support of studying; with only 3 month work permit and no creditworthiness; stated privileging experiences in life through being an academic doing a PhD

even though hard worked for, inner stability and geo-political-historical context (being a woman in Germany in these times).

Xx: a 34-year-old; Black female heterosexual novice therapist (systemic family therapy), offering systemic therapy, stated discrimination experiences in life through ethnic (North African) and religious belonging, stated privileging experiences in life through having no physical limitations, socio-economic status, education.

Penis: a 35-year-old, *white*, male heterosexual novice therapist (cognitive behavioral therapy), offering therapy in penal system), stated no discrimination experiences in life, stated privileging experiences in life through being male, *white* and part of educated middle-class.

R: a 32-year-old, *white*, male, genderfluid, homosexual novice therapist (cognitive behavioral therapy), offering behavioral therapy; stated discrimination experiences in life through homosexual orientation, stated privileging experiences in life through being male, *white*, Christian.

Fahimi: a 36-year-old, *white*, female, queer novice therapist (cognitive behavioral therapy), offering queer-sensible therapy, stated discrimination experiences in life through queer sexual orientation, working class background, kinky sexual preference, stated privileging experiences in life through being *white* and an academic.

4. Obsolete diagnose stigmatizing women who didn't fit gender norms which was intersectionally expanded to stigmatize all gender of Jewish people by Nazi regime.
5. Obsolete diagnose stigmatizing Black Slaves who tried to free themselves.
6. depathologized not before 1973 (DSM) and 1989 (ICD). However, in Germany only since 2020 conversion therapy is forbidden.
7. The suggested concept of motivated blindness (Phillips & Lowery, 2018) is using ableist language which (unwillingly) imply both a kind of negative nuance of blindness as well as an exclusion of physically blind people in this study regarding motivated blindness due to being already blind. All language is full of discriminating metaphors that call for reflection.

REFERENCES

Bandura, A. (1986). *Social foundations of thought and action: A social cognitive theory*. Prentice Hall.

Berg, H., Antonsen, P., & Binder, P.-E. (2017). Sincerely speaking: Why do psychotherapists self-disclose in therapy? - A qualitative hermeneutic phenomenological study. *Nordic Psychology*, *69*(3), 143–159. https://doi.org/10.1080/19012276.2016.1198272

Bishop, A. (2015). *Becoming an ally – Breaking the cycle of oppression in people* (3rd ed.). Fernwood Publishing.

BPtK (Bundes Psychotherapeuten Kammer). (2025). *Muster-Berufsordnung für die Psychologischen Psychotherapeutinnen und Psychotherapeuten und Kinder- und Jugendlichenpsychotherapeutinnen und Kinder- und Jugendlichenpsychotherapeuten*. BPtK. https://api.bptk.de/uploads/Muster_Berufsordnung_der_B_Pt_K_412a6bcb36.pdf

Bühler, K. (1934). *Sprachtheorie. Die Darstellungsfunktion der Sprache*. Fischer.

Burkard, A. W., Knox, S., Groen, M., Perez, M., & Hess, S. A. (2006). European American therapist self-disclosure in cross-cultural counseling. *Journal of Counseling Psychology, 53*(1), 15–25.

Butler, J. (1990). *Gender trouble.* Routledge.

Chang, S. C., Singh, A. A., & Dickey, L. M. (2018). *A clinician's guide to gender-affirming care: Working with transgender and gender nonconforming clients.* New Harbinger Publications.

Combahee River Collective. (1977). *The Combahee River collective statement.* History is a Weapon. http://historyisaweapon.com/defcon1/combrivercoll.html//historyisaweapon.com/defcon1/combrivercoll.html

Crenshaw, K. W. (1989). Demarginalizing the intersection of race and sex: A Black feminist critique of antidiscrimination doctrine, *Feminist Theory and Antiracist Politics. University of Chicago Legal Forum, 1989*(1), 139-167.

David, E. J. R. (2013). *Internalized oppression - The psychology of marginalized groups.* Springer Publishing Company.

Decker, O. (Ed.). (2018). *Sozialpsychologie und Sozialtheorie. Band 2: Forschungs- und Praxisfelder.* Springer VS.

Du Bois, W. E. B. (1935). *Black reconstruction: An essay toward a history of the part which Black folk played in the attempt to reconstruct democracy in America, 1860-1880.* Harcourt, Brace and Company.

Eggers, M. M., Kilomba, G., Piesche, P., & Arndt, S. (Eds.). (2009). *Mythen, Masken und Subjekte. Kritische Weißseinsforschung.* Unrast.

Farber, B. A. (2006). *Self-disclosure in psychotherapy.* Guilford Press.

Festinger, L. (1957). *A theory of cognitive dissonance.* Stanford University Press.

Foucault, M. (1993). *Wahnsinn und Gesellschaft.* Suhrkamp.

Goldfried, M. R., Burckell, L. A., & Eubanks-Carter, C. (2003). Therapist self-disclosure in cognitive-behavior therapy. *Journal of Clinical Psychology, 59*(5), 555–568. https://doi.org/10.1002/jclp.10159

Göth, M., & Ralph Kohn, R. (2014). *Sexuelle Orientierung in Psychotherapie und Beratung.* SpringerMedizin.

Greenspan, M. (1986). Should therapists be personal? Self-disclosure and therapeutic distance in feminist therapy. *Women & Therapy, 5,* 5–17.

Haraway, D. (1988). Situated knowledges: The science question in feminism and the privilege of partial perspective. *Feminist Studies, 14*(3), 575–599.

Hilgers, M. (2010). Verelendung psychotherapeutischer Rahmenbedingungen. Rolle von Armut und Reichtum in der therapeutischen Beziehung. *Psychotherapeut, 55,* 515–524.

Hill, C. E., Helms, J. E., Tichenor, V., Spiegel, S. B., O'Grady, K. E., & Perry, E. S. (1988). Effects of therapist response modes in brief psychotherapy. *Journal of Counseling Psychology, 35,* 222–233.

Hill, C. E., & Knox, S. (2001). Self-disclosure. *Psychotherapy, 38*(4), 413–417. https://doi.org/10.1037/0033-3204.38.4.413

Hill, C. E., Knox, S., & Pinto-Coelho, K. G. (2018). Therapist self-disclosure and immediacy: A qualitative meta-analysis. *Psychotherapy, 55*(4), 445–460.

Knox, S., Hess, S. A., Petersen, D. A., & Hill, C. E. (1997). A qualitative analysis of client perceptions of the effects of helpful therapist self-disclosure in long-term therapy. *Journal of Counseling Psychology, 44*(3), 274–283.

Knox, S., & Hill, C. E. (2003). Therapist self-disclosure: Research-based suggestions for practitioners. *Journal of Clinical Psychology, 59*(5), 529–539. https://doi.org/10.1002/jclp.10157

Kontny, L., Stuhler, H., Schleu, A., & Strauß, B. (2019). Komplexität doppelter Beziehungsangebote – Inhaltsanalytische Untersuchung sozialer Grenzverletzungen in der Psychotherapie. *Psychotherapeut, 64*, 463–469. https://doi.org/10.1007/s00278-019-00384-y

Mader, E. (2015). Psychopathologisierung und Rassismus in Deutschland. Eine feministische Perspektive. In C. Schmechel, F. Dion, K. Dudek, & M. Roßmöller (Eds.), *Gegendiagnose – Beiträge zur radikalen Kritik an Psychiatrie und Psychologie* (pp. 47–75). Edition Assemblage.

Mahalik, J. R., van Ormer, E. A., & Simi, N. L. (2000). Ethical issues in using self-disclosure in feminist therapy. In M. M. Brabeck (Ed.), *Practicing feminist ethics in psychology* (pp. 189–201). American Psychological Association.

McIntosh, P. (1988). *White privilege and male privilege: A personal account of coming to see correspondences through work in women's studies.* Wellesley Centers for Women.

Meyer, I. H. (2003). Prejudice, social stress, and mental health in lesbian, gay and bisexual populations: Conceptual issues and research evidence. *Psychological Bulletin, 129*(5), 674–697. https://doi.org/10.1037/0033-2909.129.5.674

Miller (nee Johnston), E., & McNaught, A. (2018). Exploring decision making around therapist self-disclosure in cognitive behavioural therapy. *Australian Psychologist, 53*(1), 33–39. https://doi.org/10.1111/ap.12260

Moore, J., & Jenkins, P. (2012). 'Coming out' in therapy? Perceived risks and benefits of self-disclosure of sexual orientation by gay and lesbian therapists to straight clients. *Counselling and Psychotherapy Research, 12*(4), 308–315.

Norcross, J. C., & Lambert, M. J. (2018). Psychotherapy relationships that work III. *Psychotherapy, 55*(4), 303–315. https://doi.org/10.1037/pst0000193

Ogette, T. (2019). *Exit RACISM: Rassismuskritisch denken lernen.* Unrast.

Pearlman, S. F. (1996). Lesbian clients/lesbian therapists: Necessary conversations. In N. D. Davis, E. Cole, & E. D. Rothblum (Eds.), *Lesbian therapists and their therapy: From both sides of the couch* (pp. 71–80). Haworth Press.

Phillips, L. T., & Lowery, B. (2018). Herd invisibility: The psychology of racial privilege. *Current Directions in Psychological Science, 27*(3), 1–7.

Plitt, H. (2019). Ein Plädoyer für Anthentizität: A plea for authenticity. *Musiktherapeutische Umschau, 40*(4), 375–382. https://doi.org/10.13109/muum.2019.40.4.375

Reisen, C. A., Brooks, K. D., Zea, M. C., Poppen, P. J., & Bianchi, F. T. (2013). Can additive measures add to an intersectional understanding? Experiences of gay and ethnic discrimination among HIV-positive Latino gay men. *Cultural Diversity and Ethnic Minority Psychology, 19*(2), 208–217. https://doi.org/10.1037/a0031906

Roberts, J. (2005). Transparency and self-disclosure in family therapy: Dangers and possibilities. *Family Process, 44*(1), 45–63.

Saase, S. (2019a). *Pilotstudie – Zur Bedeutung von Mehrfachdiskriminierungen in der Psychotherapieausbildung.* Unpublished manuscript.

Saase, S. (2019b). Augen auf! – Zur historischen Ver(antw)ortung intersektional zu denken. In E. Mader, C. Schmechel, A. Steinweg, & K. Kawalska (Eds.), *Get well soon - Gegendiagnose 2. Beiträge zur radikalen Kritik an Psychologie und Psychiatrie* (S. 201–213). Edition Assemblage.

Saase, S. (2020a). Intersectional Privilege awareness traveling into psychology - An unsafe travel or a potential for social justice? In E. Gerbsch, L. Junker, F. Nastold, M. Hawel, J. Schmidt, S. Seefelder, F. Werner, & C. Wimmer (Eds.), *Work in progress – Work on progress* (pp. 181–194). VSA Verlag.

Saase, S. (2020b). Privilegien 5.0 - Cyborgs und Psyborgs mit intersektionalem Privilegienbewusstsein? In K.-J. Bruder, C. Bialluch, J. Günther, B. Nielsen, & R. Zimmering (Eds.), *"Digitalisierung" - Sirenengesänge oder Schlachtruf einer kannibalistischen Weltordnung* (pp. 221–234). Westend.

Saase, S. (2025). Intersektionalitätsinformierte Kompetenzen für Therapie und Coaching: Vorteile, Erkenntnisse und ein konkretes Kompetenzmodell. *Organisationsberatung, Supervision Coaching, 32*, 403–417. https://doi.org/10.1007/s11613-025-00925-2

Saase, S., Kreß, L., & Kauffeld, S. (2024a). *Psychotherapy as an evolving field of HRD: A qualitative study of intersectional psychotherapist competence development.* Manuscript submitted for publication.

Schulten, A. (2020). Sekundäre Traumatisierung als Berufsrisiko: Prävention – Schutz – Heilung. In F. Riffer, M. Sprung, E. Kaiser, & L. Streibl (Eds.), *Therapeutische Beziehungen. Aktuelle Kontexte der Behandlung psychisch kranker Menschen* (pp. 169–191). Springer.

Schulz von Thun, F. (1981). *Miteinander Reden: 1. Störungen und Klärungen - Allgemeine Psychologie der Kommunikation* (57th ed.). Rowohlt.

Soto, A., Smith, T. B., Griner, D., Rodríguez, M. D., & Bernal, G. (2018). Cultural adaptations and therapist multicultural competence: Two meta-analytic reviews. *Journal of Clinical Psychology, 74*, 1907–1923.

Sue, D. W., & Sue, D. (2008). *Counseling the culturally diverse – Theory and practice* (5th ed.). Wiley.

Taifel, H., & Turner, J. C. (1979). An integrative theory of intergroup conflict. In W. G. Austin & S. Worchel (Eds.), *The social psychology of intergroup relations* (pp. 33–47). Brooks/Cole.

Thibaut, J. W., & Kelley, H. H. (1959). *The social psychology of groups.* John Wiley.

Tißberger, M. (2013). *Dark Continents und das UnBehagen in der weißen Kultur. Rassismus, Gender und Psychoanalyse aus einer Critical Whiteness-Perspektive.* Unrast.

Tseng, W.-S., & Streltzer, J. (Eds.). (2001). *Culture and psychotherapy - A guide to clinical practice.* American Psychiatric Press.

Vill, B. (2019). Schlussfolgerungen für den therapeutischen Prozess. In B. Vill (Ed.), *Vom Preis der Sesshaftigkeit. Eine psychodynamische Betrachtung der Immobilie* (pp. 73–97). Springer.

Watts-Jones, T. D. (2010). Location of self: Opening the door to dialogue on intersectionality in the therapy process. *Family Process, 49*(3), 405–420.

Wolf, G. (2014). *Psychopathologisierungsprozesse von LSBT*I-Lebensweisen in DSM-V und ICD 10, Kapitel F.* VLSP. https://www.vlsp.de/files/pdf/diagnosemanuale_1404.pdf

Ziemba, S. (2001). Therapy with families in poverty: Application of feminist family therapy principles. *Journal of Feminist Family Therapy, 12*(4), 205–237.

CHAPTER 8

UNCONSCIOUS (GUILTY) CONFESSIONS: A DISCOURSE ANALYSIS ON THE REACTIONS TO A WHITE WOMAN'S SOCIAL MEDIA POST ABOUT HER EYE-OPENING ENCOUNTER WITH A BLACK MAN IN THE USA

Audrey S. Namdiero-Walsh
Independent Scholar and Researcher, Germany

ABSTRACT

This paper reviews the reactions to a post made on Facebook by a White woman about her first-time conversation with a Black man on the topic of racism, in the background of the Black Lives Matter protests in the USA. Discourse analysis was used to analyse the reactions from this post that were triggered. Four main reaction types were identified: (1) I commend you. Keep up the good work! (2) Yes, we are responsible; (3) Yes, this is happening.

Cultural Psychology in Clinical Research and Practices, pages 155–177

Published under exclusive licence by Emerald Publishing Limited
doi:10.1108/978-1-83742-213-520261008

But we are not responsible; (4) Yes, this is happening. But do you not see your involvement? The focus of the analysis was on the fourth reaction, which illuminated the unconscious biases and strategies that the author of the post may not have been aware of, but which act to maintain and reinforce these biases (blind spots). The analysis identified dynamics such as guilt reduction, denial, white privilege, power positions, identity formation, and social positioning. These dynamics were discussed to highlight how discourses and activities around white privilege and racism can still be permeated with unconscious biases that continue to enforce the same prejudices and discrimination they are intended to address.

Keywords: Racism; social media; privilege; prejudice; discrimination; discourse analysis

INTRODUCTION

Since the founding of America, systemic racism remains to be the most pertinent issue in the country to this date. Some consider slavery to be America's 'original sin'. The hateful acts of slavery were not solved by those who framed its constitution and neither was it resolved through America's civil war. Even the election of America's first black president, Barack Obama, did little to change America's legacy, and the hateful remnants of slavery persists today in the form of systemic racism; permeating nearly every aspect of America's society and its people. The reality of this history was on stark display when the death of George Floyd on the 25th of May 2020 saw hundreds of protests in America against untold acts of racism against African Americans that take place every day across America. These protests in turn sparked a wave of activism against structural racism and inequality in societies around the world, even in the midst of the Covid 19 pandemic.

The notion that the struggles with racism are related to the ideas about race having a social reality and its embodiment in texts and symbols of various kinds and in the practices of social life, support the argument that race is a social construct (Carter, 2000). This means that the concept and ideas around race refer to it as a product sociocultural interaction engendered by social actors, thereby making it an element of a cultural system (Carter, 2000). Just like culture evolves through a meaning construction process, so does the notions around race. Furthermore, these notions can be publicly expressed and have real observable social effects, such as what we see in today's mainstream media and public discourses about the unjust treatment of Black people, immigrants and other minority groups (Carter, 2000; Vala & Pereira, 2012).

This chapter identifies racial biases and strategies that reinforce and/or perpetuate them in a social media discourse. Reactions to a Facebook post on White woman's conversation with a Black man about racism in America will be the focus of the study. Using elements of discourse analysis, this study seeks to answer the following research questions: (1) what kind of reactions does a post on social media by a White woman about a conversation with a black man in the context of the Black lives Matter movement trigger, and; (2) how can these reactions help identify the blind spots the author of the post might have; that if addressed, would help her to identify discrimination maintaining mechanisms that she is involved in.

RACE: A SOCIAL CONSTRUCT OR BIOLOGICAL REALITY?

While there lacks a single definition of race today, it is generally viewed as a social construct that is primarily recognized phenotypically, or by physical appearance (Fluehr-Lobban, 2018). It is an unstable concept that

> [...] operates in the space of intersections, at the crossroads where social structure and experience meet. It is socially constructed and historically fluid. It is continuingly being made and remade in everyday life. Race is continually in formation. (Omi & Winant, 2014, p. x)

The concept of race could therefore be described as a multifaceted working model that incorporates what race is actually understood as (how it distinguishes an individual or race from another), how it operates, and why it matters (Morning, 2011).

From a historical point of view, anthropological studies reveal that the idea of race emerged as a 'biological category, a natural phenomenon unaffected by social forces' (Barkan, 1992, p. 2). It was through Europe's expansion in the 16th and 19th century that the central position of race as a physical descriptor unfolded, where physical attributes such as skin colour, hair texture, cranial measurements and even language were used to demarcate differences amongst human beings (Du Bois, 1897; Henry, 2004). Moreover, 'one's race conferred unalterable characteristics and qualities that, precisely because of their biological provenance, were not prone to melioration' (Carter, 2000, p. 2). This point of view saw Western scientists classify and rank human beings according to inferior and superior groups, a classification framework which was subsequently used to: defend slavery, colonisation and even genocide; deny the franchising of women and working-class groups; and deny education to races that were considered expendable, among other things (Carter, 2000; Fluehr-Lobban, 2018; Henry, 2004).

During the early 20th century, the traditional scientific classification of human beings according to biologically discrete races begun to be criticised from its lack of an epistemological foundation (Barkan, 1992; Carter,

2000). This method of categorising human differences appeared to be merely 'skin deep' as the following concerns were raised:

> For example, a popular anthropological method for delineating races was the measurement of skulls and other bodily features. Despite visible exterior physical differences among, say, Orientals, Whites, Blacks, and Ameri-indians, it become apparent to anthropologists that racial typology was incapable of any consistent demarcations, and the classification quandary made formal taxonomy impossible. Furthermore, numerous distinct populations did not conform to accepted categories, and any classification became hopelessly entangled with themes of ethnicity and nationality, encouraging many scholars to deny the possibility of a 'science of race'. (Barkan, 1992, p. 3)

Although the meanings of race have since changed, the historically based notions of race which form the basis of the racial thinking and the reproduction of racism today are still sustained (Barkan, 1992; Golash-Boza, 2016). In her book *Race and Racism: A Critical Approach*, Golash-Boza (2016) argues that the concepts of race and racism should be studied together under one analytical framework, as one cannot separate the construction of race from the reproductions of racism. She therefore defines racism as.

> [...] both (1) the *ideology* that races are populations of people whose physical differences are linked to significant cultural and social differences and that these innate hierarchical differences can be measures and judged, and (2) the micro- and macro-level practices that subordinate races believed to be inferior. (Golash-Boza, 2016, p. 9)

So how is race socially constructed? One of the underlying processes in racial formation and the reproduction of racism is in the construction of the 'self' and the 'other' concepts. This process involves the use of language (meaning it is a discursive process) to constitute and understand one's identity and thereby constructing the other in relation to hierarchical social differences (Jensen, 2011). Inherent in identity formation is the assignment of specific subject positions, where the self assumes a position of power, while the other is offered a subordinate or inferior position in discourse (Jensen, 2011). This discursive process affirms the 'legitimacy and superiority of the powerful and condition identity formation among the subordinate' (Jensen, 2011, p. 65). This is the process by which race is discursively construed and infused within culture which ultimately determines racial ideologies (and beliefs) and actions (racism) that are 'explicitly based upon, justified or motivated by, ideas about race' (Carter, 2000, p. 4). Therefore, racism first operates at a societal micro-level, where notions and ideas around race are developed by social actors in the course of everyday interactions (Carter, 2000; van Dijk, 1992). The micro-level racial ideologies form that society's symbolic resources and traditions which become available for use by ensuing social actors, who then implement 'structures and processes of dominance and inequality at the meso- and macro-levels of groups, social formations, neighbourhoods, institutions, organizations and even nations and whole world regions' (van Dijk, 1992, p. 88).

In summary, race and racism are conceptually about the division of people through the construction of difference and assignment of value to these differences (Henry, 2004; Thompson, 2006). Racism is a dialectical process where beliefs about certain individuals (e.g., their societal position, interests and aims, identity, etc) are shared, internalized, and enforced through social interaction. Race ideologies carry a long history of devastating consequences for people and remain to be a powerful and problematic force today, as seen through pejorative stereotypes, prejudicial and racial behaviour, and racist practices embedded in societal structures (Orrù, 2014; Thompson, 2006).

RACISM AND INDIVIDUAL PREJUDICE

Racism is often used interchangeably with 'prejudice (biased feelings or affect), stereotyping (biased thoughts and beliefs, flawed generalizations), discrimination (different treatment or the absence of equal treatment), and bigotry (intolerance or hatred)' (Salter et al., 2018, p. 150). Moreover, it is often conceptualised as a social-psychological phenomenon stemming from an individual's biased attitudes, beliefs and behaviours (Salter et al., 2018). Racism is, however, not limited to the biased individual, but it also permeates all levels of society through 'the advantages and disadvantages imprinted in cultural artefacts, ideological discourse, and institutional realities that work together with individual biases' (Salter et al., 2018, p. 150).

For Salter et al. (2018) racism should be understood in terms of a 'dynamic relationship between the psychological manifestations of racism in the mind and psychological manifestations of racism in the world' (p. 151). That is: one's sociocultural environment shapes their mind (culture shapes how we should view and be in the world) just as their mind shapes their sociocultural environment (we form and maintain features of our social context through everyday action). This understanding of racism is crucial to appreciating attitudes (whether in favour or disfavour of a group) and overgeneralised and erroneous beliefs and how they (attitudes and beliefs) work together to produce different types of negative actions (Allport, 1979).

In his classic, *The Nature of Prejudice*, Gordon Allport (1979) explains that prejudiced statements may sometimes bear an attitudinal factor or a belief factor. For example, in the statements below, the first sentence expresses an attitude and the second a belief (Allport, 1979, p. 13):

I can't abide Negroes.

Negroes are smelly.

I wouldn't live in an apartment house with Jews.

There are a few exceptions, but in general all Jews are pretty much alike.

Although prejudiced attitudes and beliefs often coexist in prejudiced thinking, Allport (1979) found that while belief systems could, to some extent, be altered, attitudes were problematic because through the process of rationalisation, generalised belief systems tend to accommodate themselves in antagonistic attitudes, thereby justifying the more enduring attitude. The following dialogue illustrates this point:

Mr X: The trouble with the Jews is that they only take care of their own group.
Mr Y: But the record of the Community Chest campaign shows that they give more generously, in proportion to their numbers, to the general charities of the community than do nonJews.
Mr X: That shows they are always trying to buy favour and intrude into Christian affairs. They think of nothing but money; that is why there are so many Jewish bankers.
Mr Y: But a recent study shows that the percentage of Jews in the banking business is negligible, far smaller than the percentage of nonJews.
Mr X: That's just it; they don't go for respectable business; they are only in the movie business or run night clubs. (Allport, 1979, pp. 13–14)

Elizabeth Paluck's (2009) study on the use of media in the reduction of prejudice found that contemporary social cognition research also supports Allport's findings about the relative stability of prejudiced attitudes compared to personal belief systems. Understanding this relationship between beliefs and attitudes helps us appreciate the complexity of racism, and why certain programs targeting racist acts, behaviours, and systems, may alter beliefs about a group or individuals from a certain group, without being able to shift attitudes (in favour or against) this group.

The Social Consequences of Racism

It is important to mention that while prejudiced attitudes and beliefs tend to express themselves in action, they do not always lead to discriminatory behaviour. Allport (1979) explains that the expression of negative attitudes is dependent on the intensity of the attitude, which subsequently also determines the intensity of the resulting hostile actions. Additionally, he distinguished the following five levels of negative social consequences in increasing order of intensity (Allport, 1979):

i. *Antilocution* – pertains to having an awareness of prejudiced attitudes and beliefs and even freely speaking freely about it. Prejudiced thinking, however, does not go beyond everyday talk.

ii. *Avoidance* – a more intense prejudiced, where an individual actively avoids the disliked group or individuals from a disliked group, even when the avoidance bears a heavy inconvenience cost to them. The individual does not inflict harm directly on the disliked people.
iii. *Discrimination* – prejudiced thinking translates to detrimental actions such as: excluding the disliked group from certain employment, financial, or educational opportunities; unequal distribution of economic, political, and social resources; negative representation of a group in media; denying access to social privileges (e.g., freedom of worship, voting and other political rights), and other practices, procedures or policies that directly or indirectly promote disadvantages for certain groups while sustaining advantages for another group (Henry, 2004).
iv. *Physical attack* – relates to instrumental use of violence against a disliked group or individual from that group. Examples include forcibly ejecting an unwanted member of the disliked group from a neighbourhood, gang warfare, and desecration of monumental cultural symbols.
v. *Extermination* – the ultimate degree of expression of prejudiced attitudes and beliefs. It includes genocides, terrorism, massacres, war, and other atrocities that involve snuffing life out of the disliked group or members of that group.

Allport (1979) points out that while many people would generally not progress from one level to the next, say antilocution to avoidance, being at one level makes the progression to a higher level of discrimination much easier:

> It was Hitler's antilocution that led Germans to avoid their Jewish neighbours and erstwhile friends. This preparation made it easier to enact the Nünberg laws of discrimination which, in turn, made the subsequent burning of synagogues and street attacks upon Jews seem natural. The final step in the macabre progression was the ovens at Auschwitz. (p. 15)

It is this progression from seemingly harmless prejudiced banter to horrific acts of violence, that is of growing concern today. The perpetual racism, in its myriad of forms, birthed socio-political movements such as Black Lives Matter, a global cry against prevailing and endemic racial injustices.

Confronting Racial Prejudices

People often strive to be egalitarian because they personally value its principles and the virtue in pursuing egalitarianism (Czopp & Monteith, 2003; Legault & Green-Demers, 2012; Monteith et al., 1996). Czopp and colleague (2003) further propose that because of their commitment to egalitarianism, people 'experience self-dissatisfaction when confronted with aspects of the self that are inconsistent with such ideals (i.e., their prejudicial tendencies)' (p. 532). This sense of self-dissatisfaction acts as a motivating factor for the individual to change their prejudiced belief systems, thereby realigning themselves with egalitarian values and self-concepts (Czopp & Monteith, 2003). It entails a process of self-regulation using goal-directed behaviour, that serves to bring the individual back to a state of emotional equilibrium (see Monteith, 1993).

Confronting racial prejudice and discriminatory behaviour could therefore be beneficial for both the target and perpetrator of these biases. Confrontation as used in everyday speech is synonymous with affectively charged terms such as 'argument, altercations, and conflict' (Ashburn-Nardo et al., 2008, p. 2008). Confronting here is defined as a 'verbally or nonverbally expressing one's dissatisfaction with prejudicial and discriminatory treatment to the person who is responsible for the remark or behaviour' (Shelton et al., 2006, p. 67). For the target, confronting has been linked to greater feelings of empowerment and decreased feelings of anger, guilt, and regret (Good et al., 2012). For the perpetrator, awareness of the discrepancy between their discriminatory behaviour and their egalitarian self-concept can activate the affect self-regulation mechanism to reduce or rid of the feelings of self-dissatisfaction, which reduces subsequent discriminatory responding (Good et al., 2012).

Interpersonal confrontations can therefore be effective in reducing prejudiced behaviour. For example, in Czopp et al.s' (2006) study on the effectiveness of interpersonal confrontations in decreasing stereotypic responses, they found that when participants were confronted about their prejudice, they not only experienced negative affect directed towards themselves (e.g., guilt and self-criticism) but also towards the person confronting them (e.g., irritation and anger). The level of these negative reactions was, however, influenced by the tone of the confrontation. That is, low-threat confrontations elicited more accepting response and less feelings of anger and irritation than high-threat confrontations. They also found that interpersonal confrontations appeared to be effective in curbing stereotypic responding. Chaney and Sanchez's (2017) study on the longevity of the effectiveness of interpersonal confrontation on prejudice supported Czopp and colleagues' 2006 study findings and suggest that interpersonal confrontations on racial stereotype reduction could have enduring effects (see Chaney & Sanchez, 2017).

While interpersonal confrontation can have beneficial consequences for both the target of discrimination and the confronted perpetrator, only a few targets of discrimination actually confront those discriminating experiences due to the perceived interpersonal costs (Ashburn-Nardo et al., 2008;

Good et al., 2012; Rasinski et al., 2013). The perceived costs include being disliked, labelled as a complainer or seen as overreacting, and even receiving retaliation (Ashburn-Nardo et al., 2008; Nicole & Stewart, 2004; Rasinski et al., 2013).

STUDY PROCEDURE

The data in this analysis is drawn from comments/responses to a story posted by a Facebook user on 01 June 2020. The post and the comments used for this study were reviewed on 15 June 2020. At the time of this study, the post had received 2,800 comments and had been shared 16,000 times (Kenney, 2020). Facebook account privacy settings however made it difficult to determine exact descriptive factors (gender, age, and race) of the Facebook users who responded to this post. The researcher, however, used the names and where available, profile pictures, to determine that a majority of the comments were made by White Facebook users. The focus on the analysis was done on the comments that criticised the post, from which the researcher observed were primarily made by African American Facebook users. To put the study in a context, a brief summary of the conversation is provided below, followed by the steps taken to analyse the data (the post's comments).

The Facebook Post

The story is about a conversation between a 45-year-old White female and a middle aged African American male. The storyteller is a White female named Caroline Crockett Brock (hence forth referred to as Caroline). Ernest, an African American male, is an appliance repairman and successful business owner who has been hired by Caroline. In the context of the public outcry on police violence targeting the African American population in America, Caroline invited Ernest to share his feelings and experiences, to which she described his responses as being enlightening. The invitation was offered on Ernest's second visit to Caroline's house, after she felt that a friendly rapport had been established. Caroline shares that this was the first time she ever spoke frankly about racism with an African American, and states that she was enlightened by this experience.

To Caroline's question 'What's it like for you on a day-to-day basis as a black man? Do cops ever give you any trouble?' (Kenney, 2020), Ernest goes one to describe that: (1) he is often stopped by the police without probable cause; (2) he does not offer his services after dark for fear of his personal safety; (3) he perceives that most White people fear him and is often asked by them to provide proof of his expertise; and (4) he has no hope that racism will ever end. For Ernest the most offencive term used to address him is 'boy', where when he tried to address the problem of its use at his former work place, he got fired. Regarding his thoughts on Black Bike Week,[1] which Caroline described as an event 'where thousands of black people come with bullet bikes and trash our town' (Kenney, 2020), he claimed that 'it hurts black people' (Kenney, 2020) and shared his dislike for working during this event.

Caroline highly recommends Ernest and his services; and with his permission, shares a picture of him and his contact details. In her concluding remarks, Caroline states that she could now begin addressing issues of racism in America by speaking with and listening to other African Americans, and by promoting their businesses.

Data Review Process

The review begun by identifying the types of reactions that emanated from the post. The reactions ranged from: (1) positive and supportive responses; (2) disbelief and distrust in Caroline's intentions; (3) allocation of blame to other agencies or social practices; and (4) criticism to Caroline's approach to self-awareness about racial injustice and her intended future actions to help bridge the racial divide in America. The responses were then allocated to four broad categories for the data review process using a discourse analysis approach. These broad categories were named as follows:

Category 1: I Commend You. Keep Up the Good Work!

This category describes positive acknowledgements of Caroline's story. They included thanks, acknowledgements of Caroline's actions and Ernest's pain, and well wishes to both Caroline and Ernest. These responses were general comments and did not refer to the commentator's intention or other's actions similar or in addition to Caroline's intended actions (i.e. engaging in dialogue with African Americans and supporting black owned businesses). For example:

Response 1:	What a beautiful man. My heart breaks to hear how he has to modify his life to be sage. God Bless you Ernest. God bless us all.
Response 2:	Amen to your efforts to make a difference in that man's life. Kudos. But really sad.
Response 3:	Please pass him on good wishes & thanks & for you too.
Response 4:	Thank you. I am hopeful that more conversations like yours will bring change!

Category 2: Yes, We Are Responsible

While positively acknowledging Caroline's efforts, these responses also included ongoing or recommended actions that could alleviate racial bias at different levels of society. Examples include:

Response 5:	I would never have imagined that a black person has to be afraid as this man is in 2020. Shame on me for not noticing. Thank you for inspiring me to listen to my black friends in a different way.
Response 6:	We need change. Black lives matter. The change needs to come from the top. Trump is not helping anything. Please everyone VOTE for change. My heart breaks for this man that he has to be afraid to work after dark because of his skin colours.
Response 7:	This is an awesome idea!!! We have started having conversations in trainings through our district pertaining to this same topic...we need to ask [questions], listen and stand together!!!
Response 8:	These are conversations white people need to have. We have no clue how much privilege is conveyed to us simply by the colour of our skin- by the 'luck' of being white. We have no idea about the racism that exists, in big and small ways, in our country.

Category 3: Yes, This Is Happening. But We Are Not Responsible

This category represents responses that acknowledged the presence of racism and pointed to its sources in American society. For example:

Response 9:	Poor man this is what life in America is under the orange face orangutan called Trump.
Response 10:	Hi(s) story is heart breaking. I do understand that because there is so much black crime in poverty-stricken states [and] cities that police tend to think all of the race is part of it. The black community should think about crime reform in their own community and social groups to prevent anymore prejudices that connect them with police. The whole system is in need of healing.
Response 11:	I just want to mention a quote. 'His dad taught him it's a white man's world'. It is put in black children's head when they are young. Stop it. This is where the racism starts. Teach your children that you are just as good as the next person.
Response 12:	Good for Ernest and those like him. It's a pity that lazy entitled sh*ts create such a poor, dangerous community reputation that law enforcement are bound to pursue due diligence. Change begins at home with good parenting.

Category 4: Yes, This Is Happening. But Do You Not See Your Involvement?

The responses under this category criticise Caroline and offer their perspectives on the shortcomings in her story. For example:

Response 13:	Thanks! I'm sharing this as how not to have a conversation with a POC[2]! Don't expect POC to teach you how not to be racist. This is perhaps the most racist ting I've read all day (but it's only 8:30a.m. so there's still time).

The analysis focuses on responses under Category 4 to address the research questions:

1. What kind of reactions does a post on social media by a White woman about a conversation with a Black man in the context of the Black Lives Matter movement trigger?
2. How can these reactions help identify the blind spots the author of the post might have; that if addressed, would help them identify discrimination maintaining mechanisms that they are involved in?

Under this category, a sample of responses to Caroline's post which also created other dialogs (e.g., criticising the response), were collected for deeper analysis. The analysis identified the inter and intrapersonal dynamics that emanated from the dialogue between Caroline and Ernest, and that were also pointed out by some readers about this exchange.

ANALYSIS

In contrast to the accolades that Caroline's story attracted, critics shared their concerns about the gaps and flaws in the story. A review of the criticism identified three main concerns: (1) a 45-year-old American should be aware of racism in the country; (2) Ernest was not in a position to be completely open; (3) this was not an appropriate way to approach the subject (of racism). Each will now be addressed in turn.

A 45-Year Old American Should Be Aware of Racism in the Country

Under this perspective, critics rejected Caroline's position that she was unaware of the challenges African Americans face due to racism. Under Extracts 1 (lines 2, 4, and 5) and 2 below, the term 'ignorance' is used in relation to Caroline's unawareness. Under Extract 1, TB and FUS associate the term 'to ignore' with a conscious level activity- 'willfully decided' (line 2) and 'conscious decisions' (lines 4 & 5). These references could be a display of Caroline's lack of critical historical knowledge, which would then explain an underlying denial and acknowledgement of systemic racism in America (Bonam et al., 2019). In Extracts 1 and 2, TB and MC use sarcasm in mocking response to Caroline.

Extract 1:

TB:	Oh what a mighty high horse you sit on to corner this black man and interrogate him on something you wilfully decided to ignore for all of the many years you been on this planet.
FUS:	She's 45. That is not a mistake. She has made thousands of conscious decisions to ignore Black pain.

Extract 2:

MC:	Amazing how ignorant 45 year old White Women in the South are.

One Facebook user also appears to respond with disbelief (Extract 3) to Caroline's seeming awakening to the reality of African American experiences with racism. ELM's use of uppercase for 'only now' (Extract 3, line 1), brings to our attention to the specific time period when Caroline's awareness is born relative to her age, geographical location, and its history with racism.

In Extract 4, RJ seems to question the genuineness of Caroline's intention to understand the plight of African Americans and her alleged positioning as an agent of change. RJ refers to Caroline's engagement with Ernest as being emotionally exploitive. The reference to Caroline's use of emotional exploitation could be perceived as the simultaneous expression of guilt and the reduction of this guilt through the act of expression itself. In the context of the state-wide and global Black Lives Matter protests, Caroline's guilt may stem from her realizing that social and cultural standards that have promoted and enforced prejudice and discrimination against the African Americans, have now come under question. And this questioning is not only by community members who bear the brunt of racial injustices (African Americans), but also by those members belonging to the society group (White Americans) that have been the source of oppression.

Extract 3:

ELM:	I mean OK cute and all but 45 yo in the South and she is ONLY NOW realizing that black folds might be treated differently and get shit from the police? Seriously?

Extract 4:

RJ:	So… You want ally cookies just because you made a disgustingly exploitative post about draining the emotional labour from a Black man for the first time ever in your 45 musty years living on this earth. Did I get that right??? You are such a trash for that.

Posts on Caroline's story also attracted criticism towards those Facebook users who applauded Caroline (Extracts 5 & 6 below). MBD (Extract 5) appears to place Caroline's applauders into one group that is characterised by: (1) choosing ignorance (lines 6 & 7, informs them that they should be in a position of 'knowing' rather than the position of 'not-knowing' that they have assumed in this discourse); (2) living in denial (line 8's reference to wilful blindness); and, (3) having the privilege of not having to endure racial injustices in America (lines 8 & 9, where reference to societal positions of 'comfort' and 'elitism' are made). JB responding to MBD (Extract 5, lines 10–12) points to accessible information sources that can aid shift Caroline and her applauders' position from one of 'not-knowing' to 'knowing'. In a way, JB appears to refer to how these actors can wilfully regain their own agency. MM shares similar sentiments in her address to MW, where she links the 'not-knowing' position with a choice that individuals have (Extract 6, line 25).

Extract 5:

MBD:	Crazy that [people] are saying thank you for POC daily report. Ya shoulda knew his experience. Ya shoulda knew my experience my sons experience. This isn't new. Either many of you are too blind and comfortable in your world and if so how elitist of you.
JB:	MBD there is no excuse for them not knowing everyone has access to some type of media holding so its out there they just have to open their ignorant eyes.

Extract 6:

MM:	I can't believe y'all are thanking her for interrogating this man while he's working just to make herself feel better. You don't have to corner a stranger and question them. READ. Look around you. You see this stuff everyday you just ignore it because it doesn't affect you. She should be ashamed for waiting half a century to be concerned about other people.
MW:	MM Maybe she was clueless as to how the black community has been treated. Give her a thumbs up because talking about and awareness are the first steps to change.
MM:	MW you guys are good at giving yourselves participation trophies. How can anyone in the world, least of all Americans, claim not to know the plight of Black people? Who do you think build America? Not your ancestors. White privilege only exists with Black oppression to balance it. You all CHOOSE not to know. Just like you choose to act like you're not contributing to by making Black people educate you on how what you're doing to us affects us.

Ernest Was Not in a Position to Be Completely Open

Under this category of responses, critics point out to the context or setting and dynamics within Caroline and Ernest's interaction took place that seem to predict the way Ernest would respond. For example, Facebook users described the different positions Ernest and Caroline occupied within their interaction, which were also unequal in power. Ernest took the position of a service provider, while Caroline of a paying customer. KN explains that Caroline is in a position of higher power (Extract 7, line 1) because she is the one who is paying Ernest for his services. Furthermore, KN points out to Caroline's use of her position to elicit additional emotional labour (Extract 7 line 2 & 3), to educate her on the plight of African Americans; an additional service that may not to have been part of the contract between the two parties. AA (Extract 8, lines 2 & 3) also observes that Ernest's position in this interaction comes with certain behavioural expectations – needing to be polite and friendly at all times, regardless of the other person's behaviour. DD (Extract 9, lines 2 & 3) mirrors KN's and AA's sentiments, and cautions Caroline against taking Ernest's responses as being 'the whole truth'. This could imply that the conversation was rather sanitised and cordial and did not allow for Ernest to fully express himself, thereby little opportunity for the emergence of the full array of latent content.

Extract 7

KN:	He's providing you a service. You are in a position of power as you drain his emotional and physical labour, twice drained this man so I hope you paid him twice.

Extract 8

AA:	The most patronising essay I have ever read. Typical Karen response. There's nothing beautiful about this dialogue because he had to be nice because he was providing a service you idiot. And then you had the audacity to bring 'black bike week.' Just to imply…not all blacks are deserving of basic humanity. Have a conversation with a black person that's not providing you a service, and this conversation would look totally different. You probably wouldn't post it.

Extract 9

DD:	*Edit* I am willing to answer questions for a fee There is a lot wrong. Namely, that man will never tell you the whole truth because he needs your money and you ambushed him. Now you've out it online for cookies when you've done nothing actually good. Did you tip him extra for the labour of teaching you? Things you could've learnt online and in books or those not in a forced position? This is so awful for him and you people always do this to us. When Black people teach you, pay them. They've worked for free and significantly reduced wages (as reflected in his story) for over 400 years. Pay Black people. Put your money where your mouth is. Donate. Call for reparations. Dismantle this damn system.

Because Caroline was not present to answer directly to questions raised about her post, Facebook users also sought to answer them amongst themselves. For example, under Extract 10, AB enquires about the background to Caroline's question about black bike week. AB and the other Facebook users engage in a meaning construction process, with the aim to understand Caroline's internal world. For example, AB refers to Caroline attempts to self-soothe (line 7), possibly as a result of guilt. AB also refers to Caroline's underlying prejudice (line 8) which appears to cause her feelings of self-negative affect. In order to reinstate an affective balance, Facebook users appear to determine that Caroline therefore solicits Ernest help by asking if he agrees with her opinion about black bike week. Ernest's agreement with her feelings about the event thereby acts to reduce her anxieties (line 9). This groups' analysis not only illuminates possible mechanisms that act to enforce and re-enforce racial prejudice but also supports the depth hermeneutic position that psychic and external reality exist in relation with each other and these realities are produced by and through social interactions.

Extract 10.

AB:	Imagine thinking this was such a hot take. So why did you ask him about black bike week?
HM:	Because she wanted to put a Black person in an awkward position to justify her own racism.
AB:	Bingo!
PY:	Yeah, I thought the same thing.
AB:	She needed to soothe herself. She needed to make sure her Prejudice was valid.
ABG:	AB if the black man agrees with her then she must be right, not racist.

This Was Not an Appropriate Way to Approach the Subject

Some Facebook users not only criticised Caroline, but also offered recommendations on other more 'appropriate' means of gaining insight into racial injustices in America as well as ways she could actively support efforts against such injustices. Facebook user TK below (Extract 11) below reflected a majority of these recommendations. While acknowledging good intentions, TK warns that Caroline's approach was not a good example of how to address racial injustices in America (line 1). This approach, an example of a low-threat confrontation, acknowledges the other party's well-meaning intentions, thereby presenting an opportunity for a meaningful dialogue while diminishing the likelihood of defensiveness.

TK then addresses the underlying expectation that African Americans should assume the position of spoke persons for all racial issues in America (lines 10 & 11). This questions the perceived responsibility bearer and forges a shift of responsibility to White Americans for their own awareness around the racially based prejudice and discrimination in American society. By recommending alternative sources of knowledge (lines 3 & 4), TK not only shifts the role and responsibility of an 'educator' from African Americans to individuals seeking to be educated, but it also seems to create a sense of agency for the education seekers themselves, by showing them available (nonthreatening) options within their reach. By linking Caroline's actions to socially or culturally relevant examples (see lines 11–16 & 19–23), TK appears to create resonance with Caroline's audience on why Caroline's approach was not appropriate. TK's post adds support to the notion that good intentions are not always received as such, nor do they necessarily lead to the best outcomes. Furthermore, without appropriate action relevant to a specific context, they (good intentions) alone are insufficient.

Extract 11.

TK:		White allies: PLEASE DON'T DO THIS. Even if it's well meaning. Here's why:
	1.	POC are constantly expected to educate for free. If you truly want to learn, it is better to do your own research, or to *pay* someone for their labour, rather than expecting it to just be a given. If you knew someone who was a plumber, would you just expect them to do all your plumbing for free? Would you approach a stranger in a plumbing uniform and ask them to teach you plumbing skills? POC are constantly expected to educate whenever a white person feels like learning, which is unfair and racially loaded.
	2.	Why is it racially loaded? Because the implicit expectation is that all POC are spokespeople on all racial issues. This is not true, or fair. How would you feel if you were constantly approached and asked to speak on the experience of all women? Or everyone living in your city? You might justifiably not feel comfortable doing so for many reasons. Yet POC are constantly expected to be available to white folks to educate about subjects that they might not feel comfortable speaking on.
	3.	The repairman's job is not to educate on racial issues. He may not be qualified to do so, or even interested in doing so. What he wants to do is his job, which is to repair appliances. By forcing him into a situation where he must take on extra labour, the questionner is being disrespectful of their time and purpose. If you were getting your hair done, would you ask your stylist if they could bake you a cake at the same time? Of course not, that's not their job. And even if they were able to do it, it would be ridiculous to ask because your interaction was not based on cake making at all. In the same way, POC should be able to do their jobs without the expectation of also having to educate curious folks about racial issues. They should be able to choose when to do that labour, and if they choose to do it, they deserve to be paid if they so ask. The repairman was not in a position where he could have asked you for compensation for his emotional labour, even if he wanted to. And it is clear that you also did not volunteer compensation for this work.

		Anyways, I hope this explanation helps. I think it's easy to overlook these things from an outside view, but keep in mind that POC are asked to be educators EVERY DAY by well-meaning white folks. We understand it's well meaning but that doesn't make it OK. If a white person genuinely wants to learn, there are so many resources and paid educators out there that they can consult. By constantly asking any POC in your vicinity to do that work, it subtly reinforces the power dynamics of white supremacy, which constantly relegate POC into a servile role under white folks.

DISCUSSION AND CONCLUSION

This study assessed how racial biases and strategies that reinforce and/or perpetuate them are identified, using a social media discourse. Two research questions were posed: (a) What kind of reactions would a social media post by a white woman about a conversation with a black man in the context of the Black Lives Matter movement trigger?; (b) How could these reactions support identify blind spots that the author of the post might have, that if addressed, would help her identify discrimination maintaining mechanisms she is involved in? For the first question, the study analysed the negative reactions and three main groups of commentaries were identified. The first group of comments (*a 45-year old American should be aware of racism in the country*) mainly challenged the genuineness of Caroline's confessions and intentions. Critics here referred to Caroline's maturity in the backdrop of her socio-political context - America's racial legacy that continues to haunt the country to the present day-as to why they doubted her. Some even pointed out to her actions as being an affect self-regulatory mechanism that is intended to balance the dissonance that the growing Black Lives Matter movement might have elicited within her.

The second group of comments (*Ernest was not in a position to be completely open*) shared concern about Ernest's ability to be completely honest given that they assumed different positions in their interactions; positions that assume a power hierarchy and come with expectations on how to behave and act. This power imbalance therefore did not allow for a truly enlightening dialogue between the two. Additionally, some critics in this group also felt that Caroline used her position of power in that exchange for self-serving purposes (affect self-regulation)- similar to what some critics in the first group mentioned. The third group of comments (*this was not an appropriate way to approach the subject*) not only criticised Caroline, but challenged her approach and offered recommendations for addressing racial prejudice and discrimination. Using low-level confrontational styles, alternative approaches that would facilitate her engagement with local efforts against racial injustices were recommended.

Before proceeding with the discussion, it is important to note that this study coincided with the increasing global protests against George Floyd's death (25 May 2020) at the knee of White police in America. For people of colour especially, as is the researcher (but non-American), this period was emotionally charged and many were reminded of traumas from racial prejudice and discrimination. While I, as the researcher tried to remain objective, through peer reflection and feedback, some loss of objectivity cannot be ruled out. Insights into the my own reactions to Caroline's post have therefore been included here.

These main findings also resonated with my impressions of Caroline's post. Upon reading the post the first time, I found it to be genuine, but a sense of disbelief lingered on which prompted further exploration. With knowledge of America's racial history, I found Caroline's confession of being unaware incredulous, given her mature age. This impression resonated with comments from the first group. I also reflected on the context and setting of the interaction and found myself assuming Ernest's position (in terms of racial background) and felt that the interaction assumed a more intimate or personal nature which did not resonate with typical professional encounters. I inferred that the interaction must have felt like an ambush which forced Ernest to act cordially. This sense also resonated with responses from the second group. Caroline's concluding remarks about the steps she will take moving forward to address issues of racism in America reminded me of the rhetoric of the 'white saviour' often associated with socially privileged individuals who decide to take up social actions alongside marginalised people. Not only does this maintain white privilege but also upholds systems of oppression (Willer, 2019).

Although we were not able to see Caroline engage with those who responded to her text, the dialogue that continued and existed between other Facebook uses in response to her post provided useful insights into the mechanisms through which racial prejudice and its associated meanings are constructed, transmitted, received and understood through discourse (see also Carney, 2016). The study findings can therefore be useful and relevant for clinical practice. For example, psychotherapists and other clinical practitioners are not immune to racial discrimination stemming from their values, assumptions, and beliefs about groups of people who are different from them (Bermúdez, 1997). In this study, a number of Facebook users pointed out that it was not the role of African American to educate white America about the racism in the country. Using this example in the clinical setting, the question as to whether the client is expected to educate the therapist about their racial biases arises. Should the client confront the therapist about their racial biases? For White therapists with clients from different cultural and racial backgrounds, a continuous assessment of their own racial biases and white privilege is highly recommended.

The perception of underlying white privilege in Caroline's post was also an important finding with regard to ongoing racial discourses as well as in clinical practice. Some Facebook users pointed out to the different positions of power that were accorded to Caroline and Ernest in the dialogue. This supports the understanding that white privilege, an expression of power, is maintained and reinforced by culturally constructed symbols and protocols which come to be adopted as societal norms (Neville et al., 2001). Furthermore, it calls for a training on white privilege for students in mental health services. It is also important to note that white privilege awareness training has also been shown to come with psychological costs as well as negative consequences for White students (Neville et al., 2001). Psychological costs include feelings of guilt, shame, and fear and loss associated with relinquishing unearned privileges (Neville et al., 2001). White people who have challenged racial hierarchy through social activism or establishing meaningful relations with people of colour have been known to suffer negative social costs differing in their level of brutality (Neville et al., 2001). On the lower side, social costs include loss of friends, censorship in the workplace, negative evaluations and impediments to career advancements (Neville et al., 2001). On the higher side, social costs include ostracisation, social isolation and even physical harm has been observed (Neville et al., 2001). Nonetheless, with an increasingly globalised world, the assessment and challenging of white privilege is still recommended, and should be incorporated into the training curriculum of training therapists, doctors, social workers, and any other public service provider.

Limitations of this study were also observed. First, as the researcher is a person of colour and conducted the study during a time of high social and political racial tensions, complete exclusion of subjectivity in different aspects of the research process cannot be ruled out. On the other hand, a researcher's subjectivity can never be eliminated and is instrumental for allowing a connection with the latent contents of study material. This allows a generation of understanding that goes beyond common-sense level of interpretation. Another possible limitation could be that Caroline's own response are lacking, therefore the observation of the meaning making process may be considered incomplete. This presents an opportunity for future follow up research. Future research could involve an in-depth interview with Caroline to gain additional historical background to her knowledge about racial issues in America, and her view from the summary findings in this study.

In conclusion, with the evolution of information and communication technology and social media, the meaning making process that emerges from discourse these days occurs within a wider public sphere, thereby making it both an agent and product of the social and political change shaping process (Orrù, 2014). Social media now allows psychologists to observe new and rare psychological phenomena and conduct research more efficiently (Kraut et al., 2004). When using social media sources, researchers however need to be aware about the challenges that may be presented such as issues around data quality and generalisability and ethical concerns around human subjects (Kraut et al., 2004).

NOTES

1. Black Bike Week is an annual motorcycle rally hosted at the city of Atlantic Beach (South Carolina) and is largely comprised of African American motorcyclist. It was founded in the 1980s, in response to African American motorcyclists being turned away from the annual Harley Davidson Week in the 1960s and 1970s, a time of heightened race segregation. This popular event draws hundreds of thousands of people each year. Further details of the history of this event can be found here – https://bikeweek.com/myrtle-beach-bike-week/black-bike-week-history/.
2. POC is a commonly used acronym for 'people of colour'.

REFERENCES

Allport, G. W. (1979). *The nature of prejudice* (25th Anniversary Ed.). Addison-Wesley Publishing Company.

Ashburn-Nardo, L., Morris, K. A., & Goodwin, S. A. (2008). The Confronting Prejudiced Responses (CPR) model: Applying CPR in organizations. *The Academy of Management Learning and Education*, *7*(3), 332–342.

Barkan, E. (1992). *The retreat of scientific racism: Changing concepts of race in Britain and the United States between the world wars.* Cambridge University Press. https://books.google.de/books?hl=en&lr=&id=-c8aSO-gnwMC&oi=fnd&pg=PP13&ots=9ETx7j9n-x&sig=Aqqpo0CaeP077Wgj2murkrz0lXo&redir_esc=y#v=onepage&q&f=false

Bermúdez, J. M. (1997). Experiential tasks and therapist bias awareness. *Contemporary Family Therapy*, *19*(2), 253–267. https://doi.org/10.1023/A:1026123303796

Bonam, C. M., Nair Das, V., & Coleman, B. R. (2019). Ignoring history, denying racism: Mounting evidence for the Marley Hypothesis and epistemologies of ignorance. *Social Psychological and Personality Science, 10*(2), 257–265. https://doi.org/10.1177/1948550617751583

Carney, N. (2016). All lives matter, but so does race: Black lives matter and the evolving role of social media. *Humanity & Society, 40*(2), 1–20. https://doi.org/10.1177/0160597616643868

Carter, B. (2000). *Realism and racism: Concepts of race in sociological research.* Routledge. https://books.google.de/books?hl=en&lr=&id=lzSCAgAAQBAJ&oi=fnd&pg=PP8&dq=definitions+of+the+concepts+of+race+and+racism&ots=DeQtXhvk_y&sig=Wxd2lF8UG9Dy5a4ueEPJrx8llRk&redir_esc=y#v=onepage&q=definitions%20of%20the%20concepts%20of%20race%20and%20racism&f=false

Chaney, K. E., & Sanchez, D. T. (2017). The endurance of interpersonal confrontations as a prejudice reduction strategy. *Personality and Social Psychology Bulletin, 44*(3), 418–429. https://doi.org/10.1177/0146167217741344

Czopp, A. M., & Monteith, M. J. (2003). Confronting prejudice (literally): Reactions to confrontations of racial and gender bias. *Personality and Social Psychology Bulletin, 29*(4), 532–544. https://doi.org/10.1177/0146167202250923

Czopp, A. M., Monteith, M. J., & Mark, A. Y. (2006). Standing up for a change: Reducing bias through interpersonal confrontation. *Journal of Personality and Social Psychology, 90*(5), 784–803. https://doi.org/10.1037/0022-3514.90.5.784

Du Bois, W. E. B. (1897). *The conservation of races*. American Negro Academy. http://public-library.uk/ebooks/23/70.pdf

Fluehr-Lobban, C. (2018). *Race and racism: An introduction* (2nd ed.). Bloomsbury Publishing. https://books.google.de/books?id=WYtSDwAAQBAJ

Golash-Boza, T. (2016). *Race and racisms: A critical approach*. Oxford University Press.

Good, J. J., Moss-Racusin, C. A., & Sanchez, D. T. (2012). When do we confront? Perceptions of costs and benefits predict confronting discrimination on behalf of the self and others. *Psychology of Women Quarterly, 36*(2), 210–226. https://doi.org/10.1177/0361684312440958

Henry, F. (2004). Concepts of race and racism and implications for OHRC policy. *Canadian Diversity, 3*(3), 4–6. https://acs-metropolis.ca/wp-content/uploads/2021/11/canadiandiversity-vol3-no3-2004-538bt.pdf#page=6

Jensen, S. Q. (2011). Othering, identity formation and agency. *Qualitative Studies, 2*(2), 63–78.

Kenney, M. C. (2020, June 1). *Caroline Crockett Brock*. Status Update. Facebook. https://www.facebook.com/marycarolfigurativeartist/

Kraut, R., Olson, J., Banaji, M., Bruckman, A., Cohen, J., & Couper, M. (2004). Psychological research online: Report of board of scientific affairs' advisory group on the conduct of research on the internet. *American Psychologist, 59*(2), 105–117. https://doi.org/10.1037/0003-066X.59.2.105

Legault, L., & Green-Demers, I. (2012). The protective role of self-determined prejudice regulation in the relationship between intergroup threat and prejudice. *Motivation and Emotion, 36*(2), 143–158. https://doi.org/10.1007/s11031-011-9242-9

Monteith, M. J. (1993). Self-regulation of prejudiced responses: Implications for progress in prejudice-reduction efforts. *Journal of Personality and Social Psychology, 65*(3), 469–485. https://doi.org/10.1037/0022-3514.65.3.469

Monteith, M. J., Deneen, N. E., & Tooman, G. D. (1996). The effect of social norm activation on the expression of opinions concerning gay men and blacks. *Basic and Applied Social Psychology, 18*(3), 267–288. https://doi.org/10.1207/s15324834basp1803_2

Morning, A. (2011). *The nature of race: How scientists think and teach about human difference*. University of California Press.

Neville, H. A., Worthington, R. L., & Spanierman, L. B. (2001). Race, power, and multicultural counseling psychology: Understanding white privilege and color-blind racial attitudes. In J. G. Ponterotto, J. M. Casas, L. A. Suzuki, & C. M. Alexander (Eds.), *Handbook of multicultural counseling* (pp. 257–288). Sage Publications, Inc. https://www.researchgate.net/profile/Lisa_Spanierman/publication/232553783_Race_power_and_multicultural_counseling_psychology_Understanding_white_privilege_and_color-blind_racial_attitudes/links/0deec5366bd15191f3000000.pdf

Nicole, S. J., & Stewart, R. E. (2004). Confronting perpetrators of prejudice: The inhibitory effects of social costs. *Psychology of Women Quarterly, 28*(3), 215–223. https://doi.org/10.1111/j.1471-6402.2004.00138.x

Omi, M., & Winant, H. (2014). *Racial formation in the United States* (3rd ed.). Routledge.

Orrù, P. (2014). Racist Discourse on social networks: A discourse analysis of Facebook posts in Italy. *Journal of Linguistics, Philology and Literature, 5*(1), 113–133.

Paluck, E. L. (2009). Reducing intergroup prejudice and conflict using the media: A field experiment in Rwanda. *Journal of Personality and Social Psychology, 96*(3), 574–587. https://doi.org/10.1037/a0011989

Rasinski, H. M., Geers, A. L., & Czopp, A. M. (2013). "I guess what he said wasn't that bad": Dissonance in nonconfronting targets of prejudice. *Personality and Social Psychology Bulletin, 39*(7), 856–869. https://doi.org/10.1177/0146167213484769

Salter, P. S., Adams, G., & Perez, M. J. (2018). Racism in the structure of everyday worlds: A cultural-psychological perspective. *Current Directions in Psychological Science, 27*(3), 150–155. https://doi.org/10.1177/0963721417724239

Shelton, J. N., Richeson, J. A., Salvatore, J., & Hill, D. M. (2006). Silence is not golden: The intrapersonal consequences of not confronting prejudice. In S. Levin & C. Van Laar (Eds.), *Stigma and group inequality: Social psychological perspectives.* Lawrence Erlbaum Associates.

Thompson, E. C. (2006). The problem of 'race as a social construct. *Anthropology News, 47*(2), 6–7.

Vala, J., & Pereira, C. (2012). Racism: An evolving virus. *Proceedings of the British Academy, 179,* 49–70.

van Dijk, T. A. (1992). Discourse and the denial of racism. *Discourse & Society, 3*(1), 87–118. https://doi.org/10.1177/0957926592003001005

Willer, J. (2019). *Working through the smog: How white individuals develop critical consiousness of white saviorism* [Merrimack College]. https://scholarworks.merrimack.edu/soe_student_ce/29

CHAPTER 9

PSYCHOLINGUISTIC PHENOMENON IN COUNSELLING ENCOUNTERS WITH BILINGUAL INDIVIDUALS

Lan-Sze Pang
Hong Kong Shue Yan University, Hong Kong

ABSTRACT

This chapter examines the psycholinguistic phenomenon in counseling encounters with bilingual individuals, emphasizing how language choice shapes emotional expression, identity, and therapeutic process and outcome. Opening with a clinical vignette of a Chinese international student mistaken as potentially psychotic breakdown due to monolingual bias, which demonstrates how symptoms such as slow speech and flat affect in English disappeared when the student conversed in Mandarin, his first language. Drawing on qualitative research with Chinese international students in the United States, three key dimensions of bilingual experience were discussed: code-switching for contextualizing emotions, code-switching for emotional detachment and intimacy, and the experience of dual selves across languages. Participants consistently switched from Mandarin to English when labelling mental health conditions like depression and anxiety in post-arrival narratives. Conversely, they preferred English for taboo topics and curse words, experiencing it as emotionally lighter

Cultural Psychology in Clinical Research and Practices, pages 179–195

doi:10.1108/978-1-83742-213-520261009

and more detached than their first language. Participants also expressed feeling a different self when speaking each of their respective language, describing Mandarin as reserved and English as more open and direct. The chapter challenges monolingual assumptions in psychological practice, arguing that exact language matching between therapist and client is not essential. Instead, it advocates for linguistically-sensitive counseling that incorporates psycholinguistic histories into psychological assessment and strategically uses code-switching as a therapeutic tool. Clinical examples illustrate how inviting bilingual clients to express feelings in their first language can unlock deeper emotional processing and facilitate therapeutic breakthrough, even when therapists do not speak the clients' first language.

Keywords: Bilingual counselling; code-switching; psycholinguistics; linguistically-sensitive counselling; psychotherapy research; counselling international students

A referral call was received from a faculty member expressing concern about an international student from mainland China during a meeting regarding his unsatisfactory academic performance. The faculty member reported that the student might be showing signs of early psychosis, including depressive mood, disorganized and slow speech, flat affect, and lack of eye contact. The student was sent over for a walk-in triage session, and I prepared to conduct a thorough screening for psychosis, and possibly, a suicide risk assessment.

The student was somewhat nervous and reserved when he came into my office. With my accented Mandarin, I invited him to use Mandarin, and within a few seconds, the student showed a more relaxed posture and began to share in Mandarin his difficulties adjusting to the academic and cultural environment in the United States during his first semester. Throughout the triage session, his speech was clear and coherent, and his eye contact was solid. He raised his tone and showed more facial expression when expressing his frustration about his studies and communicating with teachers. He then told me at a somewhat fast pace that the meeting with the faculty member was anxiety-provoking because he was struggling to articulate himself and comprehend what was being said in his second language (L2), English. He described needing to pause and translate in his head before speaking, with his eyes looking upward. As he gazed at the ground, he expressed feeling inept and ashamed in front of the faculty member.

MONOLINGUAL BIAS: THE OBVIOUS IS OBLIVIOUS

Language is a primary vehicle for negotiating emotions, thoughts, identities, traditions, values, and beliefs (Betancourt & Lopez, 1993; Hamers & Blanc, 1989; Wierzbicka, 1995). In psychological assessment, diagnosis, and counseling, how clients express their mental, emotional, psychological, and physiological realities is crucial (Altarriba & Santiago-Rivera, 1994). Despite over half of the global population using more than one language (Grosjean, 2021, 2024), the role of language in shaping bilingual clients' experiences within mental health services remains underexplored. While multicultural counseling research often focuses on cultural factors like ethnic identity, cultural values, and acculturation (Atkinson et al., 1993; Cokley, 2005; He et al., 2026; Smith & Silva, 2011; Wang et al., 2019), language itself is largely overlooked in counseling encounters.

The real-life triage scenario introduced earlier mirrors findings from a study on Spanish-English bilinguals, which revealed that participants showed greater symptoms of schizophrenia – such as slow speech, frequent pauses, emotional withdrawal, and anxiety – when interviewed in English compared to Spanish (Marcos et al., 1973). This study underscores a monolingual bias in psychological assessment, where English is treated as the *lingua franca*, and deviations from this norm are often perceived as pathological or deficient (Okazaki & Sue, 1995; Padilla, 2001). This bias raises ethical concerns about the misdiagnosis and mistreatment of bilingual clients, as their linguistic realities are often ignored or misunderstood in psychotherapeutic contexts (Altarriba & Morier, 2004; ; Guttfreund, 1990). As a result, the mental health needs of bilingual individuals are not accurately reflected in mainstream psychological services (Esposito, 2001).

Further complicating the issue, contemporary research often treats the languages of bilingual individuals as isolated, overlooking the fluid nature of their communication. For instance, in cued recall studies, bilingual participants are often restricted from switching between languages (e.g., Marian & Kaushanskaya, 2004; Marian & Neisser, 2000). However, studies on bilingual speakers and writers demonstrate that code-switching – the practice of alternating between languages within a conversation – is a common and natural communication strategy among bilinguals (Besemeres, 2004; Chung, 2006; Grosjean, 1982, 2024; Poplack, 1980).

A study on code-switching among college students in Hong Kong and Taiwan further illustrates this. They were asked to avoid using English during their conversation for a day, while documenting their feelings in journals and sharing their experiences in focus groups. These participants expressed discomfort and frustration when they couldn't switch languages for specific words (Li et al., 2010). This emphasizes how monolingual research frameworks marginalize bilingual realities by treating languages as distinct and rigidly separate.

In the following sections, I will draw on my previous study, which explored the code-switching phenomenon among mainland Chinese international students in the US as they shared autobiographical stories (Pang, 2009). Autobiographical stories, as core therapeutic material in counseling, encapsulate the cultural, mental, psychological, emotional, and linguistic dimensions relevant to clients. In semi-structured interviews simulating counseling encounters, these students were encouraged to use both Mandarin and English in sharing their experiences before and after arriving in the United States. This approach reflects the intertwined nature of language and culture in bilingual lives and emphasizes the importance of considering both languages in understanding their realities.

CODE-SWITCHING FOR CONTEXTUALIZING EMOTIONS

In the study, mainland Chinese students predominantly shared their pre-arrival and post-arrival stories in Mandarin. However, all participants, regardless of their length of stay in the United States (ranging from one to six years), engaged in code-switching. Notably, those who had been in the US for only one year switched languages as frequently as those who had been there longer. Mandarin-to-English intrasentential switching was especially common when labeling emotions in their post-arrival narratives.

For example, one male participant, Jie, switches to English to label his depressive state while narrating his language struggles after a year in the United States.

1 Jie: 自己知道英语不是一下两下
Zi Ji Zhi Dao Ying Yu Bu Shi Yi Xia Liang Xia
'[I] know for me English is not one time [or] two times'

2 Jie: 交流也不是一下两下就来的了的
Jiao Liu Ye Bu Shi Yi Xia Liang Xia Jiu Lai De Liao De
'Communication is also not "one time [or] two times" for it to come'

3 Jie: 所以有时候也是觉得很 (.) 很 *depressed*
Suo Yi You Shi Hou Ye Shi Jue De He (.) Hen *depressed*
'So, sometimes [I] also feel very, very depressed'

4 Jie: *Depressed* 的时候
Depressed De Shi Hou
'When [feeling] depressed'

5 Jie: 就感觉沉 (.) 沉进去这种*depressed* 的这种状态
Jiu Gan Jue Chen (.) Chen Jin Qu Zhe Zhong *depressed* De Zhe Zhong Zhuang Tai
'[I] feel like sinking, sinking into this depressed state'

6 Jie: 跳不出去了
Tiao Bu Chu Qu Le
'Not able to jump out [of it] [particle]'

7 Jie: 自己觉得好 *depressed*
Zi Ji Jue De Hao *depressed*
'I feel so depressed'

In Jie's pre-arrival stories, he describes feeling 'Ya Yi' (压抑) to convey the stress of preparing for the TOEFL and GRE while working full-time in mainland China. The term 'Ya Yi' (压抑), which combines the concepts of suppression and restraint, is commonly used in mainland China to describe a state similar to, but not exactly the same as, depression. Jie's figurative description of his depressive feelings in Mandarin aligns with the meaning of 'Ya Yi' (压抑) – a sense of being suppressed (sinking) and restrained (unable to escape).

Similarly, another female participant, Meifang, switches from Mandarin to English to label her depressive feeling when sharing her post-arrival experiences.

1 Meifang: 觉得 (.) 啊我一个人来这边
Jue De (.) A Wo Yi Ge Ren Lai Zhe Bian
'[I] feel, oh, I came here alone'
2 Meifang: 天高地远的
Tian Gao Di Yuan De
'Heaven [is] high [and] earth [is] distant [particle]'
3 Meifang: 就有一种很 *depressing* 的感觉
Jiu You Yi Zhong Hen *depressing* De Gan Jue
'Then having a very depressing feeling'

Like Jie, Meifang's entire narrative is in Mandarin until she switches to English for the word 'depressing'. Another male participant, Guohua, also switches to English only to describe feelings such as 'anxious' and 'concerned'. In the following excerpt, Guohua reflects on his first six months in the United States. He initially arrived on an F-2 (dependent) visa, which prevented him from attending school or working.

1 Guohua: 那个时候心情是变化比较大
Na Ge Shi Hou Xin Qing Shi Bian Hua Bi Jiao Da
'At that time, [my] mood fluctuates quite huge'
2 Guohua: 主要是对 (.) 是对将来的话呢
Zhu Yao Shi Dui (.) Shi Dui Jiang Lai De Hua Ne
'Mainly is to.. is to the future [particle]'
3 Guohua: 就是 (.) Um (.) 比较(.) 比较
Jiu Shi (.) Um (.) Bi Jiao (.) Bi Jiao
'That is..Um..somewhat..somewhat'
4 Guohua: 就是说(*concern*) 或者是 *anxious*
Jiu Shi Shuo (*concern*) Huo Zhe Shi *anxious*
'That is to say, concern[ed] or anxious'

5 Guohua: 不知道就是之后是什么境况
Bu Zhi Dao Jiu Shi Zhi Hou Shi Shen Me Jing Kuang
'[I] don't know, that is, what will be the situation afterwards'

These excerpts from Jie, Meifang, and Guohua demonstrate that code-switching occurs primarily with feeling words in their post-arrival narratives, and this switch is performed consistently from Mandarin to English.

The concept of mental health was largely foreign in mainland China until the Opening and Reform policy. The feeling word 'Ya Yi' (压抑), rich with cultural connotations unique to Chinese people, is used by Jie only in his pre-arrival stories. However, when describing a similar emotional state in his post-arrival experiences, Jie switches to English. The use of English feeling words like 'depression' and 'anxiety' by Meifang and Guohua further reflects how these terms, commonly discussed in US society, have influenced their emotional narratives and prompted the switch from Mandarin to English in the context of their post-arrival stories.

CODE-SWITCHING FOR EMOTIONAL DETACHMENT AND INTIMACY

Most students in the study preferred using English when cursing or discussing socially taboo topics, as they felt English carried less emotional weight than Mandarin. In the following excerpt, Guohua explains why he perceives cursing in English as more elegant and less offensive than in Mandarin.

1 Guohua: 英文比较文雅一点嘛
Ying Wen Bi Jiao Wen Ya Yi Dian Ma
'English is somewhat elegant [particle]'

2 Guohua: 比如骂人 *son of a bitch*
Bi Ru Ma Ren *son of a bitch*
'For example, scolding someone son of a bitch'

3 Guohua: 这种东西
Zhe Zhong Dong Xi
'this kind of thing

4 Guohua: 可能对他们会很过
Ke Neng Dui Ta Men Hui Hen Guo
'Maybe to them [Americans] is too much'

5 Guohua: 但是相对中国的程度来讲的话
Dan Shi Xiang Dui Zhong Guo De Cheng Du Lai Jiang De Hua
'But, contrasting to the Chinese level'

6 Guohua: 中文的程度来讲 <chuckles>
Zhong Wen De Cheng Du Lai Jiang <chuckles>
'Chinese level, [relatively] speaking'

7 Guohua: 比较轻松很多
Bi Jiao Qing Song Hen Duo
'A lot lighter in weight'

Guohua's perception may stem from the notion that English is often seen as a high-prestige language (Grosjean, 1982; Zentella, 1990).

Similarly, Meifang preferred using English when sharing her feelings about a crush.

1 Meifang: 我觉得用中文讲就会觉得有些 (.) 第一个觉得说不出口
Wo Jue De Yong Zhong Wen Jiang Jiu Hui Jue De You Xie (.) Di Yi Ge Jue De Shuo Bu Chu Kou
'I feel that using Chinese would [make me] feel a little... first [I] could not get myself saying it'

2 Meifang: 因为中文的词太重了
Yin Wei Zhong Wen De Ci Tai Zhong Le
'Because the Chinese words are too heavy [particle]'

3 Meifang: 中文就是（.）跟一个男孩子的感觉就好像
Zhong Wen Jiu Shi (.) Gen Yi Ge Na Hai Zi De Gan Jue Jiu Hao Xiang
'In Chinese language [it is [like]..about a feeling toward a guy, just like'

4 Meifang: 我很喜欢他
Wo Hen Xi Huan Ta
'I like him much'

5 Meifang: 或者我对他很有好感
Huo Zhe Wo Dui Ta Hen You Hao Gan
'Or I have a favourable impression about him'

6 Meifang: 但是 (.) 其实我对那些人的感觉没有到这么深
Dan Shi (.) Qi Shi Wo Dui Na Xie Ren De Gan Jue Mei You Dao Zhe Me Shen
'But...actually my feeling about them is not yet that deep'

7 Meifang: 我总觉得用中文说出来有时候 (.) 很正式的感觉
Wo Zong Jue De Yong Zhong Wen Shuo Chu Lai You Shi Hou (.) Hen Zheng Shi De Gan Jue
'I always feel that using Chinese to express... [giving] a very formal feeling'

8 Meifang: 但你用英文说—
Dan Ni Yong Ying Wen Shuo—
'But [when] you use English to say'

9 Researcher: 你会用英文说 (.) 你会怎么说呢?
Ni Hui Yong Ying Wen Shuo (.) Ni Hui Zen Me Shuo Nei?
[If] you use English to say, [then] how would you said it [particle]?'

10 Meifang: 就说 (.) *I think he's cute*
Jiu Shuo (.) *I think he's cute*
'Just say...I think he's cute'

11 Meifang: (.) 我知道这样子说一个人
(.) Wo Zhi Dao Zhe Yang Zi Shuo Yi Ge Ren
'I know that to say such a way about a person'

12 Meifang: 就是说—
Jiu Shi Shuo—
'That is to say'

13 Researcher: [有兴趣—
[You Xing Qu—
'having interest'

14 Meifang: [有兴趣—
[You Xing Qu—
'having interest'

15 Researcher: 但是又未至于好感 (.) 喜欢—
Dan Shi you Wei Zhi Yu Hao Gan (.) Xi Huan—
'But [it is] not to the point of having a favourable impression, or liking'

16 Meifang: 也没有那么严重啦
Ye Mei You Na Me Yan Zhong La
'Not even that serious [particle]'

17 Meifang: 就说 (.) 大家一起玩玩 (.) 蛮好的
Jiu Shuo (.) Da Jia Yi Qi Wan Wan (.) Man Hao De
'That is to say, having fun together, quite nice [particle]'

18 Meifang: 就说 (.) 但是也没有什么很近
Jiu Shuo (.) Dan Shi Ye Mei You Shen Me Hen Jin
'That is to say...but it's not even that close'

19 Meifang: 还没有很近一步发展
Hai Mei You Hen Jin Yi Bu Fa Zhang
'Not yet a step forward to develop [a relationship]'

In her later conversation with the researcher, Meifang elaborated that saying 'I love you' in Mandarin – 'Wo Ai Ni' (我爱你) – feels like a commitment, making it sound more serious, whereas in English, the phrase feels less weighty.

Tianyun, another female participant, preferred using English when discussing topics related to sex. She noted that Chinese people do not put sex 'on the table' and often shy away from the topic. Using English terms, however, made the conversation less embarrassing. She provided an example of how she would approach a sex-related conversation with Chinese people, demonstrating how language use can impact emotional comfort around sensitive subjects.

1	Tianyun:	Um:: (.) 这种(.) 具体的我也不好讲(..) Um:: (.) Zhe Zhong (.) Ju Ti De Wo Ye Bu Hao Jiang (..) 'Um::..this kind..it hard for me to talk about it in concrete..'
2	Tianyun:	就比如说 (.) 你说 *have sex* Jiu Bi Ru Shuo (.) Ni Shuo *have sex* 'for instance..you said "have sex"'
3	Tianyun:	那我可能不会用中文说 Na Wo Ke Neng Bu Hui Yong Zhong Wen Shuo 'Then I probably would not use Chinese to say'
4	Tianyun:	哎呀 (.) 去跟人上床(.) 我不会这么讲 Ai Ya (.) Qu Gen Ren Shang Chuang (.) Wo Bu Hui Zhe Me Jiang 'Aiya..going to bed with someone..I would not say like that'
5	Tianyun:	我会 (.) 譬如跟朋友谈到这个 Wo Hui (.) Pi Ru Gen Peng You Tan Dao Zhe Ge 'I would..for example, talking about it with friends'
6	Tianyun:	就是说 *have sex with—* Jiu Shi Shuo *have sex with—* 'That is to say, have sex with—'

The reflections of Meifang and Tianyun highlight how emotional association with and expression of taboo topics are shaped by cultural values tied to each language. This illustrates how language and culture work together to influence a bilingual's self-expression.

Tianyun further shared her thoughts on why cursing in English (e.g., 'shit') felt more acceptable than cursing in Mandarin.

1	Tianyun:	可能是 (.) 英语是第二种语言— Ke Neng Shi (.) Ying Yu Shi Di Er Zhong Yu Yan— 'Perhaps..English is the second language'
2	Tianyun:	你不觉得这个字很坏或是很脏 Ni Bu Jue De Zhe Ge Zi Hen Huai Huo Shi Hen Zhang 'You won't feel that the word is very bad or very dirty'
3	Tianyun:	但我不知道他们对这个字的理解是怎么样 Dan Wo Bu Zhi Dao Ta Men Dui Zhe Ge Zi De Li Jie Shi Zen Me Yang 'But I don't know how they understand this word'

4 Researcher: 但对你来说—

Dan Dui Ni Lai Shuo—

'But to you—'

5 Tianyun: 就是说我想可能还是说隔了一层去看这个

Jiu Shi Shuo Wo Xiang Ke Neng Hai Shi Shuo Ge Le Yi Ceng Qu Kan Zhe Ge

'That is to say I think maybe still yet, through a screen layer to look at'

6 Tianyun: 去理解这个字

Qu Li Jie Zhe Ge Zi

'To understand this word'

Tianyun likened cursing in English to placing a 'layer of screen', suggesting a detachment from the emotional weight of the curse word. As a result, she found cursing in her second language (English) less 'bad' or 'dirty' than in her first language (Mandarin). This aligns with previous studies showing that using a second language creates emotional detachment (Marcos, 1976; Perez Foster, 1998), which serves as a defense mechanism when addressing taboo topics or emotions (Bond & Lai, 1986; Dewaele, 2004; Harris et al., 2006; Javier, 1989; Pavlenko, 2005).

Many bilinguals have described perceiving their first and second languages differently in terms of emotional and personal significance (Besemeres, 2004). The first language is often referred to as the 'language of the heart' or the 'language of the senses', evoking feelings of intimacy, belonging, and seriousness (Novakovich & Shapard, 2000, pp. 161 & 218). In contrast, the second language is seen as the 'language of the head', evoking a sense of distance, as if 'being you but in someone else's house' (Pavlenko, 2006, p. 19).

EXPERIENCE AND PRESENTATION OF DUAL SELF

Most mainland Chinese students in the study expressed that speaking English feels distinct from speaking Mandarin. Some noted that they become more polite and formal in English, while others felt more open when using it compared to Mandarin.

Yi, a female student majoring in English Education (英语教育) in mainland China, has been in the United States for about six years. She shared that she feels more direct when giving affective feedback in English than in Mandarin.

1 Yi: 我好像更容易抒发自己的感受

Wo Hao Xiang Geng Ron Yi Shu Fa Zi Ji De Gan Shou

'I feel that it's easier for me to express feelings'

2 Yi: 然后讲一些赞美的词语呀
Ran Hou Jiang Yi Xie Zan me De Ci Yu Ya
'And then say some praising words [particle]'
3 Yi: 我不知道是不是因为受美国的影响
Wo Bu Zhi Dao Shi Bu Shi Yin Wei Shou Mei Guo De Ying Xiang
'I don't know if it is because of the U.S. influence'
4 Yi: *Oh (.) you are so nice!*
'*Oh..you are so nice!*'
5 Yi: 中国人就不會說 (.) 哎(.) 妳這么好啊!
Zhong Guo Ren Jiu Bu Hui Shuo (.) Ai (.) Ni Zhe Me Hao Ya!
'Chinese people would not say, Oh, you are nice [particle]!'
6 Yi: 中国人是靠心來体会的
Zhong Guo Ren Shi Gao Xin Lai Ti Hui De
'Chinese people use [their] heart to appreciate'

Jie, a male participant majoring in computer science, had been in the US for one year. He used a programming analogy to illustrate his internal state in both languages.

1 Jie: 讲中文的话
Jiang Zhong Wen De Hua
'Speaking Chinese'
2 Jie: 可能还是处于一个「闭包」儿* 的状态
Ke Neng Hai Shi Chu Yu Yi Ge 'Bi Baoer*' De Zhuang Tai
'perhaps [I am] still in The condition of a 'Closure'
3 Jie: 若果是讲英文的话
Ruo Guo Shi Jiang Ying Wen De Hua
'If speaking in English'
4 Jie: 能够让我把这个「闭包」儿* 的状态能够打开
Neng Guo Rang Wo Ba Zhe Ge 'Bi Baoer*' De Zhuang Tai Neng Gou Da Kai
'[It] can allow me to open up the status of this "Closure"'
5 Jie: 所以呢我觉得
Suo Yi Ne Wo Jue De
'So [particle] I feel that'
7 Jie: 就是说这个讲英文的话
Jiu Shi Shuo Zhe Ge Jiang Ying Wen De Hua
'That is to say, speaking in English'
8 Jie: 能够把我释放出來
Neng Gou Ba Wo Shi Fang Chu Lai
'can release me from [the "Closure"]'

Jie compared speaking Mandarin to the concept of Closure ('Bi Bao' 闭包) in JavaScript, a reserved and closed-off structure, reflecting the Chinese cultural emphasis on 'Nei Lian' (内斂) – modesty and restraint. In contrast, he felt liberated when speaking English, equating it to the opening of 'Closure', associating English with greater openness in American culture.

These excerpts highlight how speaking a language involves internalizing its associated cultural values and beliefs, which shapes the presentation of self (Ervin-Tripp, 1964; Pavlenko, 2006). And switching between languages can feel like shifting between different versions of the self (Burck, 2004; Fouad & Tang, 1997).

LINGUISTICALLY-SENSITIVE COUNSELLING

Although pioneers of the multicultural counseling movement have emphasized the importance of assessing and matching language between therapist and client (Sue et al., 1992), an exact language match is not necessarily required. Perez Foster (1998), a bilingual psychodynamic therapist, challenged the monolingual assumption in clinical practice by asking therapists to critically reflect on a key question when working with bilingual clients who are proficient in English as a second language: *Do we assume that their presentation in English fully reflects their internal experience?*

Incorporating Psycholinguistic History Into Assessment

Perez Foster (1998) advocates for integrating a psycholinguistic history into the clinical assessment of clients who use more than one language. This approach helps therapists understand how each language shapes a client's construction of reality and identity. During the assessment, therapists are recommended to explore:

- The client's psycho-development of language acquisition (e.g., age and context of each language acquisition, learning experiences of each language).
- The client's current language use (e.g., contexts of usage, language preference, and attitudes toward code-switching).
- The client's proficiency of his/her respective languages and psycholinguistic experience in the host country, particularly for intentional students, immigrants, refugees.

Bilingual clients may express emotions differently depending on the language they use. Both monolingual and bilingual therapists can explore the linguistic meanings of psychological symptoms with their bilingual clients, as well as how mental health issues are perceived and treated in the client's country of origin (Perez Foster, 1998). This culturally congruent approach allows therapists to contextualize psychological concerns in alignment with clients' ethnolinguistic values and beliefs.

Early Roots of Code-Switching in Psychoanalytic Practice

Psychoanalysts have long recognized the interplay between language, emotional expression, and early memories in bilingual clients (e.g., Clauss, 1998; Guttfreund, 1990; Javier, 1989; Marcos & Urcuyo, 1979; Perez Foster, 1998; Rozensky & Gomez, 1983). For example, Buxbaum (1949) and Greenson (1950), both German psychoanalysts practicing in the US, observed that their German-English bilingual clients accessed deeply emotional childhood experiences when speaking German (their first language). One of Greenson's clients described the contrast between her bilingual selves:

> In German, I am a scared, dirty child; in English, I am a nervous, refined woman. (Greenson, 1950, p. 19)

Aragno and Schlachet (1996) further illustrate this dynamic through a case study of a Spanish-English bilingual client. A Puerto Rican college student sought therapy for anxiety and lack of purpose. During one session, he described a dream in which a bear threatened his girlfriend, and he intervened to protect her. The therapist asked, 'What's the word for 'bear' in Spanish?' The client responded in shock:

> Orso! That used to be my nickname for my father when I was a kid!

The revelation unlocked an unconscious association – the bear symbolized his abusive father. The Spanish word, *Orso,* unveiled the core of his anxiety in a way that the English word *bear* could not.

Such cases highlight code-switching in counselling can facilitate therapeutic breakthroughs and reveal psychological truths that remain inaccessible in a second language.

A Clinical Illustration of Strategic Code-Switching

Informed by both research and clinical experience, I intentionally integrate psycholinguistic elements into my work with bilingual clients. Rather than viewing language differences as barriers, I see them as strengths – bilingual clients have a broader emotional repertoire and an additional linguistic resource to express themselves (Pang, 2009).

For instance, I worked with a Hispanic male client fluent in both Spanish and English who presented with moderate suicidal risk. While sharing traumatic childhood experiences in English, his affect remained flat, and his tone was subdued. Noting this, I asked, 'How would you describe your feeling at that time in Spanish?'

He uttered a single Spanish word – and immediately broke into tears. In a gentle tone, I asked him what the word meant. He explained that no English equivalent fully captured it; it was a blend of two emotions. This word encapsulated the core feeling that had driven his lifelong struggles with suicidality.

The invitation to code-switch in the counseling process is more than a linguistic shift. Some feelings only exist fully in the language they were first felt in.

CONCLUSION

Linguistically-sensitive counseling recognizes that language is more than a communication tool. It is woven into how we feel, think, and understand ourselves. Bilingual clients do not simply translate between languages; they carry within them different cultural worlds, each with its own emotional textures and meaning-making frameworks. Effective counselling honors this complexity. Moving beyond the notion of language matching, the therapeutic use of code-switching can unlock dimensions of a client's inner world that would otherwise remain out of reach.

APPENDIX: TRANSCRIPTION CONVENTION

(.)	A ½ to 1-second pause within or between utterances
(..)	A 2-second or longer pause within or between utterances
:	Prolonged sound
::	2-second or longer prolonged sound
—	An abrupt end of a speech
[	An onset of an overlapping conversation
[word]	Additional grammatical description of the translation
english	Code-switched to English
(*english*)	A mispronunciation of an English word
zi*	A Mandarin enunciated reduction
<tone>	A sigh or chuckles within an utterance
!/?	An exclamatory intonation

REFERENCES

Altarriba, J., & Morier, R. G. (2004). Bilingualism: Language, emotion, and mental health. In T. K. Bhatia & W. C. Ritchie (Eds.), *The handbook of bilingualism* (pp. 250–275). Blackwell Publishers Limited.

Altarriba, J., & Santiago-Rivera, A. (1994). Current perspectives on using linguistic and cultural factors in counseling the Hispanic client. *Professional Psychology: Research and Practice, 25*, 388–397.

Aragno, A., & Schlachet, P. J. (1996). Accessibility of early experience through the language of origin: A theoretical integration. *Psychoanalytic Psychology, 13*(1), 23–34.

Atkinson, D. R., Morten, G., & Sue, D. W. (1993). A minority identity developmental model. In *Counseling American minorities* (4th ed., pp. 25–39). William C. Dubuque, IA.

Besemeres, M. (2004). Different languages, different emotions? Perspectives from autobiographical literature. *Journal of Multilingual and Multicultural Development, 25*(2&3), 140–158.

Betancourt, H., & Lopez, S. R. (1993). The study of culture, ethnicity, and race in American psychology. *American Psychologist, 48*, 629–637.

Bond, M. H., & Lai, T. M. (1986). Embarrassment and code-switching in to a second language. *The Journal of Social Psychology, 126*(2), 179–186.

Burck, C. (2004). Living in several languages: Implications for therapy. *Journal of Family Therapy, 26*, 314–339.

Buxbaum, E. (1949). The role of second language in the formation of ego and superego. *Psychoanalytic Quarterly, 18*, 279–289.

Chung, H. H. (2006). Code switching as a communicative strategy: A case study of Korean-English bilinguals. *Bilingual Research Journal, 30*(2), 293–307.

Clauss, C. S. (1998). Language: The unspoken variable in psychotherapy practice. *Psychotherapy, 35*(2), 188–196.

Cokley, K. O. (2005). Racial(ized) identity, ethnic identity, and Afrocentric values: Conceptual and methodological challenges in understanding African American identity. *Journal of Counseling Psychology, 52*(4), 517–526. https://doi.org/10.1037/0022-0167.52.4.517

Dewaele, J.-M. (2004). The emotional force of swearwords and taboo words in the speech of multilinguals. *Journal of Multilingual and Multicultural Development, 25*(2&3), 204–222.

Ervin-Tripp, S. M. (1964). Language and TAT content in bilinguals. *Journal of Abnormal and Social Psychology, 68*, 500–507.

Esposito, N. (2001). From meaning to meaning: The influence of translation techniques on non-English focus group research. *Qualitative Health Research, 11*(4), 568–579.

Fouad, N. A., & Tang, M. (1997). Caught in two worlds: Jessica Chang from a cross-cultural perspective. *The Career Development Quarterly, 46*, 155–160.

Greenson, R. (1950). The mother tongue and the mother. *International Journal of Psycho-Analysis, 31*, 18-23.

Grosjean, F. (1982). *Life with two languages: An introduction to bilingualism.* Harvard University Press.

Grosjean, F. (2021). *Life as a bilingual: Knowing and using two or more languages*. Cambridge University Press.

Grosjean, F. (2024). *On bilinguals and bilingualism: Fifty years in the field. Fifteen Eighty four blog*. Cambridge University Press.

Guttfreund, D. C. (1990). Effects of language usage on the emotional experience of Spanish-English and English-Spanish bilinguals. *Journal of Consulting and Clinical Psychology, 58*, 604–607.

Hamers, J. F., & Blanc, M. H. A. (1989). *Bilinguality and bilingualism*. Cambridge University Press.

Harris, C. L., Gleason, J. B., & Ayçiçeği, A. (2006). When is a first language more emotional? Psychophysiological evidence from bilingual speakers. In A. Pavlenko (Ed.), *Bilingual Minds: Emotional experience, expression and representation* (pp. 257–283). Multilingual Matters.

He, K., Gamst, G., Kernes, J. L., & Der-Karabetian, A. (2026). The relationship among cultural variables and mental health for Chinese international students in the U.S. *International Journal of Advanced Counselling, 48*(6), 1–30. https://doi.org/10.1007/s10447-025-09630-2

Javier, R. A. (1989). Linguistic considerations in the treatment of bilinguals. *Psychoanalytic Psychology, 6*, 87–96.

Li, D. C. S., Chen, S.-C., & Tsao, F.-F. (2010). Self-reported code-switching motivations of educated Chinese speakers in Hong Kong and Taiwan: An experimental study. In M. Jodłowiec & J. Lesniewska (Eds.), *Ambiguity and the search for meaning: English and American studies at the beginning of the 21st century* (Vol. 2, pp. 107–122). Jagiellonian University Press.

Marcos, L. R. (1976). Linguistic dimensions in the bilingual patient. *The American Journal of Psychoanalysis, 36*(4), 347–354.

Marcos, L. R., & Urcuyo, L. (1979). Dynamic psychotherapy with the bilingual patient. *American Journal of Psychotherapy, 33*(3), 331–338.

Marcos, L. R., Urcuyo, L., Kesselman, M., & Alpert, M. (1973). The language barrier in evaluating Spanish-American patients. *Archives of General Psychiatry, 29*(5), 655–659. https://doi.org/10.1001/archpsyc.1973.04200050064011

Marian, V., & Kaushanskaya, M. (2004). Self-construal and emotion in bicultural bilinguals. *Journal of Memory and Language, 51*, 190–201.

Marian, V., & Neisser, U. (2000). Language-dependent recall of autobiographical memories. *Journal of Experimental Psychology: General, 129*(3), 361–368.

Novakovich, J., & Shapard, R. (2000). *Stories in the stepmother tongue*. Buffalo: White Pine Press.

Okazaki, S., & Sue, S. (1995). Methodological issues in assessment research with ethnic minorities. *Psychological Assessment*, 7(3), 367–375. https://doi.org/10.1037/1040-3590.7.3.367

Padilla, A. M. (2001). Issues in culturally appropriate assessment. In L. A. Suzuki, J. G. Ponterotto, & P. J. Meller (Eds.), *Handbook of multicultural assessment: Clinical, psychological, and educational applications* (2nd ed., pp. 5–28). Jossey-Bass.

Pang, L. S. (2009). *The role of code-switching in emotional expression and autobiographical memory recall: Implications for bilingual counseling*. (Publication No. ED532682) [Doctoral dissertation. Southern Illinois University at Carbondale]. ProQuest Dissertations and Theses Global.

Pavlenko, A. (2005). *Emotions and multilingualism.* Cambridge University Press.
Pavlenko, A. (2006). Bilingual selves. In A. Pavlenko (Ed.), *Bilingual minds: Emotional experience, expression and representation* (pp. 1–33). Multilingual Matters.
Perez Foster, R. (1998). *The power of language in the clinical process.* Jason Aronson.
Poplack, S. (1980). Sometimes I'll start a sentence in Spanish Y TERMINO EN ESPAÑOL: Toward a typology of code-switching. *Linguistics, 18,* 581–618.
Rozensky, R. H., & Gomez, M. Y. (1983). Language switching in psychotherapy with bilinguals: Two problems, two models, and case examples. *Psychotherapy, 20,* 152–260.
Smith, T. B., & Silva, L. (2011). Ethnic identity and personal well-being of people of color: A meta-analysis. *Journal of Counseling Psychology, 58*(1), 42–60. https://doi.org/10.1037/a0021528
Sue, D. W., Arredondo, P., & McDavis, R. J. (1992). Multicultural counseling competencies and standards: A call to the profession. *Journal of Multicultural Counseling and Development, 20,* 64–88.
Wang, L., Bordon, J. J., Wang, K. T., & Yeung, J. G. (2019). Acculturation, enculturation, perceived discrimination, and well-being: A comparison between U.S.-raised and non–U.S.-raised Asian students. *Asian American Journal of Psychology, 10*(1), 22–32. https://doi.org/10.1037/aap0000117
Wierzbicka, A. (1995). Everyday conceptions of emotion: A semantic perspective. In J. Russell, J. Fernandez-Dolz, A. Manstead, & J. Wellenkamp (Eds.), *Everyday conceptions of emotion: An introduction to the psychology, anthropology, and linguistics of emotion* (pp. 117–147). Kluwer Academic.
Zentella, A. C. (1990). Returned migration, language, and identity: Puerto Rican bilinguals in dos worlds/two mundos. *International Journal of the Sociology of Language, 84,* 81–100.

CHAPTER 10

(NON)-VERBAL COMMON GROUND NEGOTIATIONS: A MICROANALYTIC STUDY OF INITIAL PSYCHOTHERAPY SESSIONS IN ENGLISH AS LINGUA FRANCA

Michal Blau
Arbeitsgemeinschaft für Psychoanalyse und Psychotherapie Berlin, Germany

Jasmin Spiegel
The Hebrew University of Jerusalem, Israel

ABSTRACT

In this study, the cultural components of language as expressed in a psychotherapeutic dialogue meet the phenomenon of nonverbal communication. The meeting takes place in moments of common ground creation in three videotaped transcultural consecutive psychotherapeutic sessions. The analysis of nonverbal communication is often minimised in conversation analytical studies, thus the analysis of the nonverbal communication accompanying such common ground offerings is yet to be examined. Furthermore, the phenomenon of nonverbal communication is brought into a multicultural

Cultural Psychology in Clinical Research and Practices, pages 197–221

doi:10.1108/978-1-83742-213-520261010

context, as the dyad in the videotaped sessions has different cultural origins, therefore, using English as a lingua franca. The objective of this study is to identify occurrences of common ground related actions through conversation analysis, by defining and locating them according to their definition, as well as extracting those which relate to the lingua franca communication. The inclusion of the communicative function of (non)-resonant nonverbal behaviour as described in reference to two observer-based methods (NEUROGES, 3RS Manual) in moments of common ground offerings, is discussed as a facilitator of the clinical understanding of establishing a working alliance in a culturally diverse psychotherapeutic setting. Clinical implications of the connection between language and culture in moments of common ground creation are discussed, leading to a better understanding and openness for trans- and cross-cultural psychotherapy.

Keywords: Common ground offerings; conversation analysis; nonverbal communication; multicultural communication; English as lingua franca; therapeutic dyad

BODY LANGUAGE AND MUTUALITY IN MULTICULTURAL INTERACTION

Today, a scientific as well as clinical interest has recurred in what Freud defined in 1923 as the 'body-ego' (p. 27) in 'The Ego and the Id'. The concept of *embodiment* includes a broad spectrum of meanings and it became common sense that the body is involved in all psychic processes (Barsalou, 2008; Caruana & Gallese, 2012; Damasio, 1999; Scorolli, 2019). This is especially relevant for psychotherapeutic interactions with the goal of exploring the psyche, where intersubjective conscious as well as unconscious processes – for example in forming an interactional memory while interacting – play a vital role in creating the feeling of *inhabiting the same mental landscape in an intersubjective matrix* (Stern, 2004). It is the intersectionality between two subjective individuals that forms this matrix (Benjamin, 1990). Affects in this matrix can be understood through an analysis of nonverbal behaviour (Benecke et al., 2005). An appropriate methodological approach to assess this matrix is to focus on what happens between two interlocutors on a microanalytical level in the concrete psychotherapeutic situation; i.e. what happens when they are *Doing-We*, as Buchholz (2022) proposed as a way to describe common ground relevant activity. More specifically,

> pointing to interactive events is an attempt to focus joint attention to unknown aspects of unknown things. If Doing-We succeeds not only a 'problem' is solved, but new objects of conversation are also created. [...] Both participants

do not only cooperate by sharing attention and pointing to common objects, but for moments they share a common form of being which to make talkable, then, is the next task. (2022).

Valsiner (1999) noted the potential addition to in noticing interlocutors' use of *integration*, e.g. using *we*, or *differentiation*, e.g. using *I*, in psychotherapeutic interaction, as well as its relationship to the social aspect of an individual. He maintained that society is a source of tools an individual possesses, which one may put into use when encountering excitations of different kinds; similar tools could be created and utilised in the therapeutic situation by the therapeutic dyad. Moreover, he explained that in the therapeutic situation there is a meeting of experts. Each participant is an expert to their own self (including cultural components). Their interaction potentially entails influences from both 'fields of expertise', and therefore co-construction in multicultural psychotherapy has the potential of entailing particles of both cultures, and of encompassing moments of meeting between them.

Currently, English as lingua franca (ELF) is the most common means of cross-cultural communication (Melitz, 2018), conclusions regarding which have the potential to be generalised to other forms of transcultural interaction (Baker, 2018). This is the first study to assess verbal and nonverbal interaction in the psychotherapeutic setting while interacting in ELF. Research undertaken so far has focused on differences between the use of ELF in comparison to the use of foreign language, intercultural communication or the communication between native speakers (Mauranen, 2018). One method of researching such interactions, which will be used in the current research, is conversation analysis (CA), according to which the act of spoken interaction is referred to as doing talk-in-interaction (Heritage & Clayman, 2011). CA is an interdisciplinary field, relying on the understanding of a multiplicity of constructs such as social constructions, culture, gestures, gaze and many others (Stivers & Sidnell, 2013). In talk-in-interaction non- and misunderstandings are often followed by repair activities (Schegloff, 1987), which will be shortly sketched in the following.

Different strategies are found to occur in multicultural communication in ELF in relation to repair and the maintenance of understanding while doing talk-in-interaction; for example, the *let-it-pass strategy* – ignoring an utterance which was not understood (Firth, 1996); *echoing* – verbatim repetition of an utterance, often used to flag it as potentially tricky (Pietikäinen, 2018), this act is thought of as going beyond cultural origin and lingual capabilities; *accommodation strategies* – the use of convergence, maintenance or divergence of one's own uttering in response to that of an interlocutor's (Cogo, 2009); as well as *code-switching* – a tool supporting self-clarification, which makes use of a language other than the agreed upon interactional language or lingua franca (Cogo, 2009; Pietikäinen, 2018). The latter three phenomena are especially relevant for the current study. However, these activities are conversational ones; the nonverbal and bodily levels of interaction are often overlooked in the examination of ELF interactions. This fact is often protested, as it seems that one could learn much more when taking these into consideration (Block, 2014). Code-switching, therefore, becomes very relevant, yet not from the common perspective of switching between different spoken languages, but rather from the point of view designating nonverbal communication as a lingua franca by itself. This helps one consider the interplay between verbal and nonverbal utterances, as well as in how far these can help maintain and evolve common ground despite non- and misunderstandings. In sum, such repair activities in multicultural communication may be considered a collaborative work on common ground.

In our study, the therapeutic dyad under investigation is interacting in a multicultural scenario as they originate in different cultures with different native languages. When we are speaking to someone foreign to us, there is a need to engage with one's whole personality, not just parts of it, unlike when we are talking to someone from the same in-group, indicating the same cultural background. As known from early social psychological findings, various outgroup biases – concerning people from different backgrounds – can occur and shape one's (un)-conscious perceptions and evaluations of the other foreign person (Tajfel & Turner, 1986). It can thus be assumed that the intersubjective interplay between body and language in creating mutuality is expanded and possibly impeded by the need to make sense of the other person's behaviour, emotions and thoughts not only from an individual perspective but from a social one as well, as compared to a same-cultural setting. In order to address this issue, a macro-as well as microanalytic view is applied. First, from a metaperspective, culture is understood as a context hypothesis in psychotherapy in terms of understanding a patient from his/her biography and psychodynamics as well from his/her cultural context. Such a context model is 'pointing towards a more nuanced model of emotion perception in which culture and language are key to constructing emotional perceptions' (Gendron et al., 2014, p. 252).

Second, the creation of a mutual therapeutic experience is an ongoing microanalytic construction process. When it succeeds, it enables an understanding process in terms of a sense giving fiction of the patient's psychic problems and creation of a collective therapeutic unity. This intersubjective perspective on psychotherapy corresponds with an intersubjective understanding of cultural psychology by Valsiner (2014), who proposed to understand culture as an ongoing co-constructed process (not as an outer structure) and localised it on an internalized microanalytic level, as a tool within a person. Thus, our research question combines these perspectives by exploring whether culture's manifestations can be traced back to the very specific therapeutic (non)-verbal interaction, and if so, how they do manifest themselves concretely in the interaction.

We hypothesise that common ground activity on a micro-level can be seen as a counteracting phenomenon to exclusionary phenomena, as reported above on a macro-level. It is to be found in the centre of every relationship, while it supports the relationship being perceived as meaningful by the people it includes (Buchholz, 2016). Common ground refers to that which is presupposed to be mutually noticed and accepted by interlocutors in interaction (Stalnaker, 2002), and it entails common beliefs, expectations, knowledge, information etc., which is shared by a number of people, and could be later referred to or presumed to be known by all who share it (Enfield, 2006). It could relate to the relationship with an interaction partner, the context one originates in, their education and understanding of society and its rules, etc. (Enfield, 2006). Common ground is established by the process of grounding; it is most commonly performed as interlocutors direct their attention to one specific object, while acknowledging this mutual direction of attention (Enfield, 2006). When an object is not properly grounded, yet assumed by an interlocutor to be common ground, it may either result in breaks in the progressivity of interaction (Albert & De Ruiter, 2018), or rather in the *presupposition accommodation* – an interlocutor accepting the presupposed common ground to be so, although in fact it was not grounded (Stalnaker, 2002). Common ground is invaluable in the context of psychotherapy, as it relates to the establishment of the working alliance succeeding the initial psychotherapy sessions, common ground is constantly established in every relationship (Buchholz, 2016). The working alliance between patient and therapist has been demonstrated to be one of the most important indicators for the quality of the psychotherapeutic treatment (Flückiger et al., 2012) and is defined as working and connecting with each other emotionally (Horvath & Luborsky, 1993). Thus, a close interactional study of the therapeutic relationship and its components, such as common ground, is crucial for the better understanding of the psychotherapeutic process.

THE PRESENT STUDY

Sample

The sample included three consecutive initial psychotherapeutic sessions with a senior female therapist from Israel and a female patient in her 30s from East Europe, communicating in ELF. The patient consulted the therapist due to mild depressive symptoms and challenges of adapting to the new culture in the town she had recently moved to. The sessions were recorded at the therapist's private clinic and, thereafter, transcribed following the Gesprächsanalytisches Transkriptionssystem (GAT; translation: conversation analytical transcription system) (Selting et al., 2011). Therapist and patient consented to the recordings as well as to the use of the analysed data for research purposes in a written informed consent beforehand.

Methods

CA is a growing field of investigation using an analysis method, stemming from the work of Sacks et al. (1978). It refers to the understanding of talk-in-interaction, following a turn-by-turn organisation, where each turn consists of one or more Turn Constructional Units (TCUs), which are the the basic units of speech (could be a sentence, word, clause etc.), allowing interlocutors to predict when a turn in interaction is reaching its completion (Schegloff, 2007). CA recommends the use of a detailed transcript in order to follow and analyse this organisation (Mondada, 2013). Its use with regard to interaction in psychotherapy has rapidly developed in recent years, while attempting to 'fill in the gaps' in the theories psychotherapy relies upon (Stiles, 2008, p. 1). CA is applied onto recordings of naturally occurring interactions, which are transcribed in detail and, thereafter, analysed (Mondada, 2013). The transcription method followed the revised version of the GAT transcription system, on the level of a basic transcript (Selting et al., 2011). A complementing transcription key is supplemented in the results section of the paper.

In order to analyse the nonverbal expressions in addition to the verbal content, two observer-based methodological approach were chosen. It included, on the one hand, the application of NEUROGES (NEUROpsychological GESTure system; Lausberg & Sloetjes, 2015) module 1 (consisting of the categories Activation, Structure and Focus). Here, the nonverbal analysis is analysed separately from the verbal content. The first module identifies body gestures as unconscious, self-regulative coping mechanisms to deal with psychological stress. It consists of three categories: 1. Activation (general impression of the individual's motor activity and arousal); 2. Structure (mental states in movements, either based on conceptual levels or more associated with routine, primitive concepts such as repetitive or irregular movements independent of the interaction); and 3. Focus (ranging from an internal focus of within-body movements to an external in-space focus without counterpart movements). For all categories, the body is segmented into left and right upper limbs (hands, arms, shoulders, elbows).

On the other hand, nonverbal rupture markers were taken from the Rupture Resolution Rating System 3RS (Eubanks et al., 2015, 2018), where ruptures are mainly understood as a deterioration in the therapeutic alliance, 'manifested by a lack of collaboration between patient and therapist on tasks or goals, or a strain in the emotional bond' (Eubanks et al., 2015, p. 2). Although the manual focusses on verbal ruptures as coded from the analysis of the written transcript of the session, it still describes complementary nonverbal impressions, for example by instructing to code a withdrawal marker when the 'patient slumps down, sinks into his/her chair, avoids eye contact' (3RS Manual, p. 11).

The latter approach was chosen in order to empirically enhance the nonverbal concept of ruptures as an opposing concept to common ground action. Those markers were, until now, not sufficiently empirically assessed and are therefore of exploratory nature in this study. Subsequently, an identification of the two subtypes of ruptures (Harper, 1989a, 1989b; Horney, 1950) as either *confrontation ruptures* – patients moving towards the therapist such as being overly compliant[1] or *withdrawal* ruptures – patients moving away from the therapist such as experiencing a loss of contact or nonresponse to interventions[2] will be identified. This classification is supplemented by the distinction between either *active* or *passive* rupture-markers, i.e. indirect handling via the physical appearance or the intonation in which a patient speaks, moving away or forward physically (Harper, 1989a, 1989b; Samstag et al., 2004). It is important to note that although the vocabulary of the two methods was made use of, there was no full execution of all intended methodological steps, e.g., the calculation of an interrater reliability, since the focus was on examining the extracted segments as a complement to the conversation analytic method, rather than providing a full motion analysis of the videos.

Design and Goals

The three initial sessions were video-recorded during a time frame of five weeks and, thereafter, transcribed. First, following a longitudinal CA of the three session's transcripts, moments which entailed common ground related activities were selected. According to this analysis, a typology of common ground related actions was brought forth. Second, those moments and their different types were re-examined nonverbally by means of module 1 NEUROGES analysis and the nonverbal rupture markers of the 3RS Rating Manual. Both verbal as well as nonverbal analyses will be presented in the results section on the basis of five excerpts of the anonymised transcripts of the sessions. Third, a synthesis between the verbal and the nonverbal results, as well as an interpretation of the temporal development throughout the three sessions, will follow.

When approaching this study, we considered that the expression of common ground related actions does not receive much academic attention, on neither the verbal nor the nonverbal levels of communication. Therefore, we set as our first goal to identify a typology of common ground related acts as manifested through the verbal transcript of the sessions. This goal serves the initiative of better recognising such actions in future research. Our second goal was to examine the manifestation of such common ground related actions of the nonverbal level of interaction. This goal serves two incentives. First, to encourage the future empirical research of verbal and nonverbal interaction side by side. Second, to find nonverbal markers of interaction regarding common ground in multicultural interaction and add the nonverbal manifestation of each type of these to the verbal one.

Nonverbal communication in a multicultural setting was expected to serve as a dominant facilitator for common ground offerings as a way of using a helping 'second language' as described in the context of code-switching on top of ELF. Moreover, concrete common ground offerings were expected to be connected to synchronous turn-taking of gestures, as previous studies (Bleimling, 2021) have shown, empirically assessing nonverbal expressions in *moments of meeting* (Boston Change Process Study Group, 2018; Stern, 2004).

RESULTS – A VERBAL AND NONVERBAL VIEW OF COMMON GROUND IN PSYCHOTHERAPY IN ELF

In the following, five examples from the transcripts of the videotaped sessions will be described. Three different types of common ground related activities were found in the data, namely *belongingness offerings, knowledge offerings* and *vocabulary offerings,* as well as some subtypes of these actions (see Fig. 10.1). Initially, they will be individually exemplified from the perspective of CA, then supplemented with nonverbal observations of each presented excerpt according to NEUROGES as well as from the 3RS Manual. Following these analyses of the verbal and nonverbal levels of communication between therapist and patient, a synopsis of temporal developments within and between the three sessions will be shared. The patient will be described as P and the therapist as T.

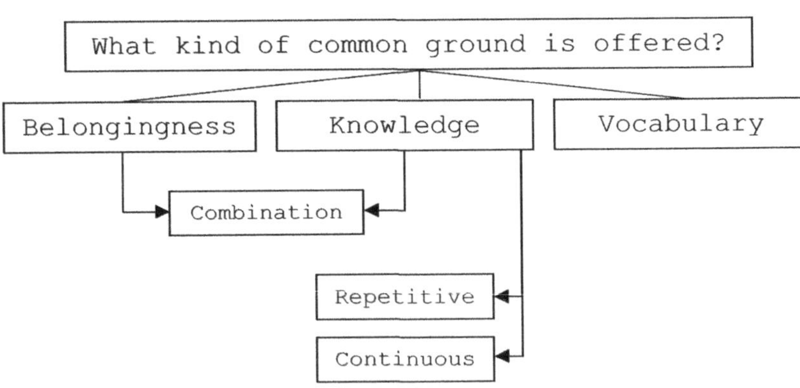

Fig. 10.1 Types of Common Ground Related Actions Which Were Found in the Data.

Transcription Key

The transcription key follows the GAT 2 transcription conventions as described by Selting et al. (2011).

°h / h°	breathing in/out for 0.2-0.5 seconds
[ ]	speech overlap/simultaneous speech
(.)	pause of up to 0.2 seconds
(-)	pause of 0.2-0.5 seconds
(--)	pause of 0.5-0.8 seconds
(---)	pause of 0.8-1.0 seconds
(1.4)	pause of 1.4 seconds
((laughs))	audible actions with scope indication
:	extension of 0.2-0.5 seconds
cApital	focus accent
WORD	emphasized in speech
?	intonation rising to high
,	intonation rising to mid
-	level intonation
;	intonation falling to mid
.	intonation falling to low
→	relevant to argument

Belongingness Offerings

One type of common ground related activity was the offering of belongingness to one group. People belonging to the same group, e.g., a social group, could deduce common ground from this belongingness. Interaction in ELF is one example of such group belonging, from which common ground could be deduced or presupposed. In the following example, Excerpt 1 (Patient, personal communication, 08 September 2020), we see an offering of belongingness to a group of people who share tendencies and behave in a similar manner:

Excerpt 1 – We Tend to Project (Session 1, 39:20–40:12)

```
01 P:   i am gOOd i am hEAlthy i m: i (.) some people
        aren't; °h
02      h° does that make sense?
03 T:   mhm m:
04    → yeaH: we tend so often to projEct OUr nEEdiness,
05    → Our wIshes, ah our hm desires, to OTHER pEople and to,
```

```
06        satisfy try to satisfy THEIR needs and wishes like,
07     →  we are taking care about OURselves-
08     →  it's Difficult to take care about ourselves it's
09        eAsier to take care about OTHER people;
10 P:→    yeah i feel good when i'm helping someone i feel good
11        about myself that today i did something good and this
12        is it.
13 T:     mhm
```

Conversation Analysis

In line 01, the patient addressed her subjectivity by repeating the subjective pronoun, i, four times in one turn; she then compared this subjectivity with others - `some people`. She followed this TCU with a comprehension check in line 02 – `does that make sense?` In return to the comprehension check, the therapist offered common ground by suggesting that she and the patient belong to the same group, and attempting to unite them, rather than emphasise their separateness (such as manifested by the patient's repetitive uttering of `i`). This was done, through her offering of her understanding of the patient's TCU from line 01, and an addition of information to it, while addressing the patient and herself with the plural pronouns `we` and `Our`. By doing so, the therapist offered common ground of a shared tendency – `we tend so often to projEct OUr nEEdiness, our wIshes, ah our hm desires`. She offered the patient's similar characteristics to those she herself possesses and, as they both tend to behave in the same manner (`projEct OUr nEEdiness, our wIshes, ah our hm desires`), and they now know that they share this behaviour, it will be part of their common ground if the patient accepts it, or merely does not negate it.

In the end of the extract, in lines 10–13, the patient accepted the therapist's common ground offering. The acceptance was marked with a token of understanding in the opening of the turn in line 10 - `yeah`, which was followed by the patient's paraphrasing of the therapist's previous turn. The patient then made a reference to a part of the therapist's offering, i.e. `take care about OTHER people`, as she paraphrased it into, `helping someone`. This reference emphasised the addition and acceptance of the therapist's suggestion to the dyad's common ground.

Nonverbal Communication Analysis

As CA pointed out, the patient started by repeating the pronoun, i, four times. In doing so, she showed high movement activity, using broad, open, repetitive in-space gestures directed towards the ceiling, a movement pattern she used the majority of the time in the first session, laughing charmingly when asking, `does that make sense?`

In comparison, the therapist showed low movement activity (analogue to her low verbal activity) throughout the whole first session as well as in the beginning of this sequence. The first psychotherapeutic intervention in this session, was followed by the therapist stating that, `we tend so often to projEct OUr nEEdiness, Our wIshes, ah our hm desires, to OTHER pEople`. This interpretation was accompanied by subtle, repetitive round foot movements as well as emphasised repetitive in space movements with the right hand. These were directed at the patient (when talking about helping others) as well as to herself (by saying it is easier than helping ourselves), marking projections as a universal topic, belonging to both their inner worlds.

The patient responded to this interpretation nonverbally by performing hand movements on her body directed towards herself, indicating a shift in the movement pattern which preceded this one, accepting the location of projections as an inner process. Neither confrontation or withdrawal nor active vs. passive rupture markers could be observed in this sequence, further indicating that no miscommunication was perceived and common ground was accepted.

Common Knowledge Offerings

Common knowledge is also a source of common ground. Sharing knowledge, language for example, is a commonality people can share and deduce other commonalities from Enfield (2006). Two manifestations of knowledge offerings were found in the data. The first was one interlocutor's *repetitive offering of common knowledge* and the second was *continuous offering of common knowledge.*

Repetitive Offering of Common Knowledge

This kind of action is done by a single interlocutor, a self-repair, which is common among ELF interlocutors (Cogo, 2009) and could, therefore, be considered as a self-repetition. Self-repetition relates to making oneself understood by another, with regard to making an utterance easier for the other to follow and understand precisely (Mauranen, 2006) or rather with regard to making the utterance as clear as possible (Pietikäinen, 2018). In the context of common ground offerings, it could relate to an attempt to clarify the piece of information or knowledge, which is suggested as common ground, making it clear to the other, while emphasising its importance to the utterer of it. One can observe the manifestation of this action in Excerpt 2 below (Patient, personal communication, 08 September 2020):

Excerpt 2 – Erase Your Stuff (Session 1, 41:11–41:49)

```
01 P:→i don't know if forgIveness works in yourself;
02    →LIKE because you knOw you have the dAta.
03     a:nd:- (-)
04     you knOw what hAppened,
05     you knOw why you did what you dId,
06     you knOw why you took this decision,
07     but even though all that-
08     i personally can't forgive myself for something that i
09     have done
10 T:→yeah you can't erase your stuff from your internet
11     hehe
12 P:→um: Exactly exactly you cannot delEte your mEmory,
13    →you cannot forget what HAPPENED and
14 T:  mhm
```

Conversation Analysis

In line 01, we find a repairable uttered by the patient – `i don't know if forgIveness works in yourself`, which was followed by a self-clarification in line 02, `LIKE because you knOw you have the dAta`. Lines 04 to 06, which were a few more TCUs of the same turn, were used to continue the self-clarification. This turn of self-clarification involved the self-repetition of the phrase, `you know`, four times and the use of self-repair of different kinds, which is common among ELF interlocutors. The self-repetition of the specific term, you knOw, emphasised that the patient's goal in this turn was to offer common knowledge, i.e. that she knows what the therapist knows. Moreover, she repeatedly self-clarified this knowledge so it would be grounded with high precision by both interlocutors.

It seems that while the patient had put much effort into repetitively self-clarifying, the therapist had understood quite well. In order to manifest her understanding, the therapist responded to this multiple TCU turn with a token of understanding – yeah (line 10) – and an attempt at paraphrasing it – `yeah you can't erase your stuff from your internet`.

Two considerations regarding this paraphrasing are relevant. Firstly, the paraphrasing signals to the patient, that the hard work she invested in making herself clear was rewarded by the therapist's precise understanding as hoped for. This precise understanding is manifested by the therapist's ability to clearly paraphrase the patient's repetitive self-clarification and suggestion of common knowledge. Secondly, the therapist paraphrased the patient's utterance using a metaphor, which seems to be an attempt of convergence of her vocabulary and world of associations to that of the patient. With this metaphor, the therapist referred to the patient's previous utterance, `you have the DATA`, while referencing the comparison introduced between mental processes and computer data, as she said, `you can't erase your stuff from your internet`.

This paraphrasing was accepted by the patient as a sign of understanding, which was signalled in line 12 with a token of acceptance – `Exactly exactly`. However, as the therapist used a metaphor in the paraphrase, the patient re-paraphrased the paraphrase twice more and without a metaphor, making it undoubtedly understood in the same manner by both interlocutors: once in line 12 – `you cannot delEte your mEmory` – and once in line 13 – `you cannot forget what HAPPENED`. The re-paraphrasing also introduced multiple utterances referring to the same piece of knowledge the patient wished to introduce as common ground.

Nonverbal Communication Analysis

In this sequence, which follows shortly after the one which preceded it, the patient was approaching the therapist by shifting her sitting position to mirror the position of the therapist. She also took in the therapist's hand pose (both hands touching each other in the lap), while performing no hand gestures, and showing lower movement activity than in the first sequence.

As the patient repetitively used the pronoun, `you`, to explain herself, she was performing repetitive in space movements with her hand directed to the therapist. This connected to the intersubjective space between them, trying to reach out to the therapist, who verbally picked up the patient's metaphor of `dAta` (and a cycle of paraphrasing starts, as CA points out). The therapist was shaking her head and making subtle repetitive whipping actions with her feet. Although this low movement activity could be rated as a passive withdrawal nonverbal rupture marker, the smiling at the patient displays an ambivalent nonverbal message. The patient answers rhythmical – `Exactly exactly` – accompanied by repetitive in space movements with her hand directed to the ceiling, while the therapist is repetitively nodding her head, confirming the common knowledge. In sum, the implicit communication could hint at a rewarding understanding of each other.

Echoed Offering of Common Knowledge

Yet another subtype of offering of common knowledge with the use of the utterance 'you know' was found in the data – the echoed kind. The echoing of an utterance is often a reference for the need of said utterance to be further clarified (Pietikäinen, 2018), or rather the need of clarification of what that utterance refers to. Another suggestion is that echoing could be an attempt of making one's speech resemble the speech of another, as a form of accommodation (Cogo, 2009). An example of the echoing of an offering of common ground in the form of 'you know' is in Excerpt 3 below (Patient, personal communication, 09 October 2020):

Excerpt 3 – Your Psyche Knows Better (Session 2, 01:35–02:40)

```
01 P: and um: it is nice to have someone to tAlk about some.
02   → things that you know,
03     don't usually come up in conversAtions.
04 T:  mhm-
05 P:  i'm not having thAt deep conversations with my
06     friends for example;
07     it doesn't hAppen. ((laughs))
08 T:  yeah it's some specIfic situation created for SUCH
09     topics; ((laughs))
10 P:→ um: it's the fAct that you know that you can TALK
11     about everything and there will be no judgement and
12   → there will be advising instead of you knOw whatever
13     else there can be-
14 T:  hm hm-
15   → yeah so even not advIsing you know because your
16     psyche knows better than (.) ME.
17     we just need to ask your psyche;
18 P:→ um: you know you're an external observator so,
19     sometimes you cannot see things that are just in front
20     of you just because they are happening to you-
21     and sometimes maybe just talking to another person
22     about it gives you another perspective;
23 T:  mhm-
24   → yeah we all have a need to be obsErved you know,
25 P:  m: true (.) true.
26 T:  mhm mhm-
```

Conversation Analysis

This extract started with the patient's answer to the therapist's question of how she felt in therapy thus far. This initiated a negotiation of meaning sequence, as the patient suggested another (fourth) paraphrase of the previous utterances (01–03, 05–07, 08–09). The therapist continued negotiating meaning in line 15, however, she accepted the patient's attempt to focus the interaction on communication and actions in psychotherapy rather than the psychotherapeutic situation. She attempted to repair the patient's utterance from lines 10–13, by negating her expressed wish to be advised - `not advising`.

The first common ground offering to be found in this sequence is in line 02 by the patient, as she offered a, `you know`, to the therapist. Later in the sequence a, `you know`, was offered by the therapist (line 15) with which the therapist suggested that she knew what the patient knew. With this offering, the therapist changed the topic under negotiation, emphasising that the patient was not the only one trying to clarify at the moment, but the therapist was as well. This, `you know`, was further echoed by the patient in line 18, and then again by the therapist in line 24.

The negotiation came to an end when the therapist accepted the patient's last paraphrase from lines 18–22 with a token of understanding – `yeah` (line 24) – and added yet another paraphrasing in line 24 – `we all have a need to be observed` – introducing a 'we,' which hinted that the patient and therapist both `have a need to be observed`, which was also offered as part of their common ground. This was followed by another common ground reference – `you know`. This action was there to secure understanding and conclude the negotiation cycle, as the first TCU of the utterance accepted the previous turn; the second suggested an utterance which could be accepted by both interlocutors, and the third referred to closing the negotiation cycle by echoing yet another – `you know`. The patient acknowledged this termination of the negotiation in line 35 with a token of acceptance which she repeated twice – `true true`. Finally, the therapist signalled that progressivity could be resumed in line 26 with an, `mhm mhm`, which also included a self-repetition, as the patient did in her last turn.

The echoed uttering of, `you know`, receives more meaning in a negotiation of meaning. As a negotiation is by its definition an argument aimed at agreement (Cogo & Dewey, 2006), the echoing of a common ground offering may be an emphasis of the mutuality of the interlocutors. As they are aiming at agreement in the end of the debate, they keep reminding themselves and each other that they already have common ground, which they aim to elaborate as a result of the negotiation they are engaged in.

Nonverbal Communication Analysis

This sequence can be understood as *cycles of negotiation* of common ground as pointed out by the CA. The content of this sequence was both about a misunderstanding (that the patient thinks therapy is about advising, though the therapist points out that it is not), as well as about a common ground offering by the patient, i.e. `you know`.

The patient was performing repetitive rolling hand movements on her legs while talking. As her conversational-turn was over, she showed irregular face stroking movements. The therapist was restrained, almost still in her movements, slightly nodding with her head. An interrelational interaction could be observed by the use of an inviting smile of the patient, which was answered by the therapist.

The therapist's nonverbal behaviour in the first part of the sequence can be interpreted as an approaching behaviour (smiling, nodding with the head); therefore, as the hypotheses suggested, it acted as a helping 'second' language to clarify the miscommunication and to concentrate on creating a common ground, verbally accompanied by repeating the words, `you know`. Further, as the therapist clarified the miscommunication verbally – `yeah so even not advIsing you know` – she was performing a single eruptive self-deictic gesture pointing towards her heart centre as she says, `your psyche knows better than (.) ME`, which could be interpreted as a noninclusive gesture, withdrawing from the common ground negotiation.

Synchronously, the patient's next speech-turn gestures were directed to her heart centre. The self-directed gestures in space could be observed as a following-up of the therapist's withdrawal activity from the common ground and, instead, focussing on the individual horizons of experience. The single different gesture was performed by the patient as she was talking about `perspective`, where her right hand was moving open in space and changing its direction, from being directed from herself towards the therapist, as if inviting the therapist to speak.

In the last part of this sequence, which could be described as the conclusion of the common ground negotiation cycles, the therapist stated that, `we all have a need to be observed`. This can be understood as a rescue maneuver of the common ground by explicitly stating that both she and the patient have the same need. Nonverbally, the therapist and patient showed almost no movement activity in this part, although again, a mutual smiling behaviour, as well as head nodding, could be observed, which is analogue to the rhythmical, `true (.) true` and `mhm mhm`, emphasising confirmation of this shared knowledge.

A Combination of Offerings – Common Knowledge and Belongingness

As understood from the last part of Excerpt 3 – Your Psyche Knows Better – in some cases we see common knowledge and common belongingness offerings intertwined in one turn or one sequence. While in the previous example, the offerings were mostly about common knowledge and minimally (only one) about belongingness. In the following sequence, we see an example below in which the two types are constantly intertwined in Excerpt 4 (Patient, personal communication, 09 October 2020):

Excerpt 4 – Think Before Forget (Session 2, 03:07–04:04)

```
P:   °h i'm not sure i have a feeling that (-)
       if you don't talk about it and try to forget it it
       will remain there though and it will kind of create a
       problem; (-)
   → but i'm not sure if talking about it you know makes
       it more important, (-)
       °h instead of forgetting about it; (-)
   → what do you think- (.)
T: → i think that sometimes we need to think carefully
       before forget
   → you know it's not possible to forget if we don't
       understand everything clearly;
       m: wha what is all about this our experience.
   → so we need to get some meaning of this- (-)
P:   true i agree. (.)
T:   mh[m]
```

Conversation Analysis

In this case, the patient attempted to address a personal uncertainty. Firstly, she attempted to clarify her uncertainty in lines 01–04. In the next TCU, the patient offered knowledge to the therapist – `you know makes it more important` (in line 05); however, another activity is noticed thereafter, i.e. a direct question – `what do you think`. This direct question signalled that the patient, although offering knowledge, was uncertain and wished to hear the therapist's opinion.

The therapist replied with a belongingness offering in line 09–10, suggesting that she and the patient both, `need to think carefully before forget`. She followed this belongingness offering with a combination of knowledge offering (`you know it's not possible to forget`) and belongingness offering (`we don't understand everything clearly`) in the next TCU in line 11–12. The, `you know`, from line 11 could also be seen as an echo of the patient's uttering of it in line 05. It seems that the direct request for an offering from the therapist, encouraged her to make yet two more belongingness offerings in the same turn: one in line 13 – `our experience` – and another in line 14 – `we need to get some meaning of this`.

Therefore, although the patient was the first to offer common ground in this sequence, the therapist seems to be the one who did most of the practical offering in this sequence. The patient accepted the therapist's offerings with a token of acceptance and agreement in line 15 – `true i agree` – which was followed by the therapist's suggestion that progressivity may be resumed in line 16.

Nonverbal Communication Analysis

Patient and therapist were sitting in a crossed-leg mirrored sitting position. The patient was gesticulating calmly, compared to her general baseline of movement, forming, dominantly with her right hand, repetitive in space movements close to her body centre. The first common ground activity came from the patient by asking her for help, i.e., `what do you think`, showing hands that opened themselves in space, forming an open question pantomime, and thereafter taking in a pose position with the left hand resting on the right. The therapist was in line with her regular low movement activity and was almost not moving while answering the patient, as she proposed that, `we need to think carefully`, and to focus on, `our experience`, she was nonverbally withdrawing from the patient with her shoulders shrugging back in space, away from the patient, who was – again – stroking her own head repetitively. Still, the question raised by CA, whether common ground activity continues to be bargained for, could be answered positively by having a look at the very end of the sequence, which consisted of a small mutual silent pause and, again, a resolving mutual smile.

Vocabulary Offerings

This kind of action was mentioned in the context of Excerpt 2 and will be here further elaborated. The suggestion of paraphrasing and re-paraphrasing in that excerpt could be considered as a suggestion of an elaboration of the mutually understood ELF vocabulary: the dyad was, thereafter, well aware that multiple utterance relate to one specific piece of knowledge which they share with one another. This kind of vocabulary offering could also directly relate to the psychotherapeutic endeavour or present itself as a metaphor, as shown in the Excerpt 5 (Patient, personal communication, 16 October 2020) below:

Excerpt 5 – Small Baby (Session 3, 45:10–45:35)

```
01 P: and i hAte being ignored. (1.12)
02    i i'd a: g:- (--)
03    i'm saying the word hAte with a: its all (.) all of
04    its pOwer; (--)
05    i hAte being ignored (.) i cannot hAndle this. (1.09)
06    and thIs is where Usually i put ultimatums because i
07    cannot be ignOred (---)
08 T: f: (.) that's: a: (--)you're like a small (-) baby
09    ((giggling) you know[)]
10 P:                    [i] know (.) i know it's: a: and
11    it's okAy i feel that way- (-)
12 T: yEs,
```

Conversation Analysis

The excerpt began with the patient's description of her own behaviour in lines 01–07. The patient self-clarified several times and self-repeated the word, `hAte`, as well as the word, `ignored`. This multiple TCU turn was reacted to by the therapist's paraphrasing of the patient's description of herself into a metaphor – `you're like a small (-) baby`, comparing the patient's behaviour to that of a baby. This comparison is followed by – `you know` – an offer of this metaphor as a common ground fact for the approval of the patient. The therapist also suggested that the behaviour the patient was trying to clarify could be later referred to again as a baby's behaviour, and thus save repetitive self-clarifications and self-repetitions.

It is worth mentioning here that the therapist might have also used a formulation as a psychotherapeutic intervention in this case, which she then followed with a – `you know` – in order to 'soften' the confrontation with the patient about how others perceive her behaviour, and remind her that she shares common ground with the therapist, as well as working on it constantly and avoiding resistance from the patient.

The patient responded to the paraphrasing with an acceptance of the offering, while referring to it directly with an echoing of it in the first tense, as well as a self-repetition – `[i] know (.) i know`. Both these self-actions were presumably aimed at a clear acceptance of the therapist's offering of common ground.

Nonverbal Communication Analysis

In this short excerpt taken from the end of the third and last session, the patient and the therapist showed neither confrontation nor withdrawal markers. They were sitting towards each other in a relaxed mirrored sitting position, with low muscle tension, both with crossed arms and legs. They were, further, both performing irregular fidgeting behaviour with their hands, i.e. irregular hand on hand movements that were located in the middle of their laps. Throughout this short 25 second interaction, their gaze stayed directed openly towards each other, mutually smiling. The patient rocked with her hand, the therapist nodded, and both smiled broader as they agreed at the end of the sequence that they both know that, `you're like a small (-) baby`.

AN OVERALL CONSIDERATION OF THE THREE SESSIONS

It seems that in the first session the common ground offerings were more focused and easier to define as belonging to one category or the other, while their acceptance or rejection seemed also clear to interpret. Yet, as the sessions advanced, the types of common ground offerings seemed to not only intertwine with one another, but also intertwine with other conversational acts as well as psychotherapeutic interventions.

The general baseline of the therapist's movement activity can be described as low, and she performed few hand gestures. Instead, she showed emotional expressiveness through the mimics of her face in terms of inviting smiles, head shaking and nodding. The patient, on the other hand, showed a high general movement activity, expressed in broad in-space gestures. Her frequent laughter was remarkable, especially in connection with pain-associated topics, which was mostly not accompanied by the therapist.

Considering the nonverbal interaction between the therapist and the patient, the movement baselines of patient and therapist turn around throughout the sessions. In the beginning, the patient displayed broad in-space gestures, while the therapist was gesticulating very little and if so, close to her body. At the end of session three, the therapist was less restricted in her movements, while the patient was less outwardly expressive than in the beginning. This finding could be interpreted as a mutual approach and possible synchronization of each other's movement basic activity. Another noteworthy nonverbal finding was that withdrawal and confrontation markers occurred rarely and solely as there were miscommunications; they did not occur during the establishment of common ground, which was possibly so due to the time spent with the negotiation of common ground.

DISCUSSION

The results of the verbal and nonverbal analysis of the data, within as well as across the sessions, will be discussed. While some points of discussion relate to the relationship between verbal and nonverbal interaction, others relate to one of the two or to the ELF interaction.

First of all, limiting factors in the design of our study need to be mentioned critically. Moments of common ground offerings were selected subjectively; no neutral scenes served as comparisons for common ground scenes and the chosen excerpts vary in their length and time position in the sessions, making it hard to compare them.

Second, the setting, consisting of initial multicultural sessions with the purpose of establishing an emotional connection stable enough to start a psychotherapeutic treatment, in itself encourages common ground activity. Our results hint at a temporal development from a rather one-dimensional offering of common ground from the side of the therapist and either accepting or rejecting (of the patient) in the beginning of the sessions to a more differentiated negotiation of common ground between the dyad at the end. Future conceptual research needs to be undertaken to better distinguish between the concepts of common ground, working alliance and intersubjective theories (e.g., Stern's moments of meeting), as well as empirical research on how to operationalise common ground activity.

Moreover, the act of offering common ground could be perceived as a risk; therefore, it makes sense that in the second session, in which the patient was more active with regard to offering common ground, she was also repetitively engaged in nonverbal activities such as synchronizing herself to the low body movement activity of the therapist or a recurring stroking of the head; thus, this irregular self-touching behaviour supported regulation of intensive feelings, as some kind of preparation for rejection or nonacceptance of her suggested common ground. This may relate to the therapeutic endeavour, as the patient may be aware that in psychotherapy, due to its asymmetric nature and abstinence, unlike in other daily interactions, common ground may be more closely examined before accepted.

Although smiling behaviour, being part of facial movement behaviour, was not initially designed as a methodological focus of this study, it turned out to be an important indicator for the negotiation of common ground with this psychotherapeutic couple. In the first two sessions, the patient is smiling and laughing significantly more than the therapist, especially when she is talking about conflictual topics; the therapist, on the other hand, mostly does not resonate with her smile in those moments and stays abstinent. Thus, smiling and laughing could be interpreted as a defence mechanism of the patient in the first two sessions to cope with painful emotions and avoid their exploration (Bänninger-Huber et al., 2016; Bänninger-Huber & Huber, 2017). In the third session, patient and therapist gaze and smile more mutually towards each other than before, which has been described as *successful prototypical affective microsequences* (Benecke et al., 2005) and implies here the success of common ground offerings.

The mutual approach of the level of bodily activity brings up another consideration in relation to verbal accommodation. While the patient's level of body activity became lower as the sessions moved forward, the therapist's became higher. This could result from an attempt to accommodate on the bodily level and finding a level of common ground nonverbal interaction. Further, as the sessions grow in their emotional intensity, the amount of self-touching irregular on-body behaviour also increased for both of them. In the third session, the amount of irregular on-body self-touching behaviour as well as shielding behaviour (i.e. restless nibbling and fumbling hands) was higher compared to the first and second sessions. The dyad was presumably converging to their interaction partner's level of bodily movements, until they reached a comfortable middle ground for their interaction. The use of accommodation strategies among ELF interlocutors on the verbal level (Cogo, 2009), as well as synchrony on the nonverbal level are known as indicators for a positive therapeutic alliance (Ramseyer & Tschacher, 2011). Thus, we suggest that nonverbal accommodation can be seen as a characteristic of multicultural interaction in a third, implicit common language. This microanalytic accommodation progress can be seen as one answer to the question posed at the beginning in how far cultural 'foreignness' is negotiated in the interaction.

The categorisation of the findings into belongingness offerings, knowledge offerings and vocabulary offerings is a first step in the direction of utilising both common ground and references to it in interaction, for the better understanding of ELF interaction and psychotherapy. Vocabulary offerings, for example, seem to relate quite intuitively to ELF interaction. They involve language, as well as its use and perception, and they connect it to common ground, as it manifests ELF interlocutors' method of developing a common ground vocabulary as well as integrating each other's language abilities and proficiency into their common ground and mutuality. When interlocutors paraphrase, for example, they suggest more levels of understanding to their mutuality, while agreeing that certain words have similar meanings and can be used with regard to certain topics. In addition, vocabulary offerings relate to psychotherapy. As seen in Excerpt 5, paraphrasing was used as a psychotherapeutic interpretation and it was perceived, simultaneously, as a common ground offering. Moreover, the move between what Valsiner (1999) called integration and differentiation, which corresponds to subjectivity and intersubjectivity, may entail an attempt to reconstruct the other: to perceive another as an equal to the self, or alternatively to perceive oneself as equal to the other. When considered in a multicultural situation, this could be understood as attempts to either maintain or overcome difference.

The relationship of these constructs leads to reflections on the similarity of functions between psychotherapeutic interventions, conversational acts relating to ELF interaction and common ground offerings. When we considered negotiation of meaning (Excerpt 3), for example, the common ground offerings seemed to have multiple functions in the interaction and establishing common ground was only one of these. As common ground could be presupposed in ELF interactions, it may make the therapist's opportunities to interpret and confront a patient possible earlier in the dyad's relationship than conventional in psychotherapy and, as indicated, by psychotherapeutic theory. This also emphasises the importance of investigating verbal and nonverbal common ground offerings in more advanced sessions of psychotherapy. If they are to be found there as well, they could be seen as potential markers of successful psychotherapeutic interventions. Moreover, it makes the relationship of common ground and the working alliance clearer, as common ground offerings may be utilised by therapists to establish a working alliance, e.g. joint meaning making and setting norms for working together.

Lastly, the manifestation of common ground related actions as the dyad's relationship developed, in comparison to its beginning, brings up a relevant consideration. The common ground offerings were more intuitively categorised in the first session, while they were more intertwined with other acts in the second and third session; this fact may relate to the developing working alliance. This change might actually be the manifestation of the beginning of a working alliance, built on established common ground. With this regard, it would be interesting in future research to examine how long it takes for a dyad to establish enough common ground in order to start building a working alliance in psychotherapy, and whether this process takes the same amount of time among mother tongue speakers and ELF interlocutors or other forms of multicultural interactions. As ELF interlocutors in psychotherapy start their interaction with more presupposed common ground than mother tongue speakers, such as being immigrants (common experience), speaking a foreign language daily (common experience and common language) etc., they may be able to trust their mutuality earlier and count on it in order to develop a working alliance.

NOTES

1. Coding Example: Patient: I can see I'm not gonna get anything useful out of you (3 RS Manual, p. 18).
2. Coding Example: Therapist: You look upset – Patient: I'll be fine. Don't worry about me (3 RS Manual, p. 10).

REFERENCES

Albert, S., & De Ruiter, J. P. (2018). Repair: The interface between interaction and cognition. *Topics in Cognitive Science, 10*(2), 279–313.

Baker, W. (2018). English as a lingua franca and intercultural communication. In J. Jenkins, W. Baker, & M. Dewey (Eds.), *The Routledge handbook of English as a lingua franca* (pp. 25–36). Routledge.

Bänninger-Huber, E., Ahrends, L., Hofer, M., Huber, E., Gillmann, J., Kainz, G., & Wolski, V. (2016). Prototypische mikrosequenzen und spezifische lachepisoden in einer psychoanalytischen psychotherapie. In E. Bänninger-Huber & S. Monsberger (Eds.), *Prozesse der Emotionsregulierung in psycho-analytischen Langzeittherapien* (pp. 91–99). Innsbruck University Press.

Bänninger-Huber, E., & Huber, E. (2017). Nonverbal processes in psychotherapeutic interaction. *Journal of Psychology and Psychotherapy Research, 4*(1), 1–8. https://doi.org/10.12974/2313-1047.2017.04.01.1

Barsalou, L. L. (2008). Grounded cognition. *Annual Review of Psychology, 59,* 617–645.

Benecke, C., Peham, D., & Bänninger-Huber, E. (2005). Nonverbal relationship regulation in psychotherapy. *Psychotherapy Research, 15*(1–2), 81–90.

Benjamin, J. (1990). An outline of intersubjectivity: The development of recognition. *Psychoanalytic Psychology,* (7), 33–46.

Bleimling, J. (2021). Nonverbal moments of meeting–An analysis of three psychodynamic therapy sessions. *Body, Movement and Dance in Psychotherapy,* 1–16.

Block, D. (2014). Moving beyond “lingualism”: Multilingual embodiment and multimodality in SLA. In S. May (Ed.), *The multilingual turn: Implications for SLA, TESOL, and bilingual education* (pp. 54–77). Routledge.

Boston Change Process Study Group. (2018). Moving through and being moved by: Embodiment in development and in the therapeutic relationship. *Contemporary Psychoanalysis, 54*(2), 299–321. https://doi.org/10.1080/00107530.2018.1456841

Buchholz, M. B. (2016). Conversational errors and common ground activities in psychotherapy: Insights from conversation analysis. *International Journal of Psychological Studies, 3,* 134–153.

Buchholz, M. B. (2022). Doing we – Working alliance in psychotherapeutic relationships: A recursive model. In C. Scarvaglieri, E.-M. Graf, & T. Spranz-Fogasy (Eds.), *Relationships in organized helping* (pp. 51–78). John Benjamins Publishing Company.

Caruana, F., & Gallese, V. (2012). Overcoming the emotion experience/expression dichotomy. *Behavioral and Brain Sciences, 35*(3), 145–146.

Cogo, A. (2009). Accommodating difference in ELF conversations: A study of pragmatic strategies. In *English as a lingua franca: Studies and findings* (pp. 254–273).

Cogo, A., & Dewey, M. (2006). Efficiency in ELF communication: From pragmatic motives to lexico-grammatical innovation. *Nordic Journal of English Studies, 5*(2), 59–93.

Damasio, A. (1999). *The feeling of what happens: Body, emotion and the making of consciousness.* Heinemann.

Enfield, N. J. (2006). Social consequences of common ground. In N. J. Enfield & S. C. Levinson (Eds.), *Roots of human sociality. Culture, cognition and interaction* (pp. 399–430). Berg Publishers.

Eubanks, C. F., Lubitz, J., Muran, C., & Safran, J. (2018). Rupture resolution rating system (3RS): Development and validation. *Psychotherapy Research, 29*(3), 1–13. https://doi.org/10.1080/10503307.2018.1552034

Eubanks, C. F., Muran, J. C., & Safran, J. B. (2015). *Rupture resolution rating system (3RS): Manual* Unpublished manuscript. Mount Sinai-Beth Israel Medical Center.

Firth, A. (1996). The discursive accomplishment of normality: On 'lingua franca' English and conversation analysis. *Journal of Pragmatics, 26*(2), 237–259.

Flückiger, C., Del Re, A., Wampold, B. E., Symonds, D., & Horvath, A. O. (2012). How central is the alliance in psychotherapy? A multilevel longitudinal meta-analysis. *Journal of Counseling Psychology, 59*(1), 10–17.

Freud, S. (1923). The ego and the id. In J. Strachey (Ed.), *The standard edition of the complete psychological works of Sigmund Freud, volume XIX (1923–1925): The ego and the id and other works* (pp. 1–308). The Hogarth Press and the Institute of Psychoanalysis.

Gendron, M., Roberson, D., van der Vyver, J. M., & Barrett, L. F. (2014). Receptions of emotion from facial expressions are not culturally universal: Evidence from a remote culture. *Emotion, 14,* 251–262.

Harper, H. (1989a). *Coding guide I: Identification of confrontation challenges in exploratory therapy.* University of Sheffield.

Harper, H. (1989b). *Coding guide II: Identification of withdrawal challenges in exploratory therapy.* University of Sheffield.

Heritage, J., & Clayman, S. (2011). *Talk in action: Interactions, identities, and institutions* (Vol. *44*). John Wiley & Sons.

Horney, K. (1950). *Neurosis and human growth.* W.W. Norton & Co.

Horvath, A. O., & Luborsky, L. (1993). The role of the therapeutic alliance in psychotherapy. *Journal of Consulting and Clinical Psychology, 61*(4), 561–573.

Lausberg, H., & Sloetjes, H. (2015). The revised NEUROGES-ELAN system: An objective and reliable interdisciplinary analysis tool for nonverbal behavior and gesture. *Behavior Research Methods, 48,* 1–21.

Mauranen, A. (2006). Signaling and preventing misunderstanding in English as lingua franca communication. *International Journal of the Sociology of Language, 177,* 123–150.

Mauranen, A. (2018). Conceptualising ELF. In J. Jenkins, W. Baker, & M. Dewey (Eds.), *The Routledge handbook of English as a lingua franca* (pp. 7–24). Routledge.

Melitz, J. (2018). English as a lingua franca: Facts, benefits and costs. *The World Economy, 41*(7), 1–25.

Mondada, L. (2013). The conversation analytic approach to data collection. In J. Sidnell, T. Stivers, & D. G. Mouton (Eds.), *The handbook of conversation analysis* (pp. 218–226). John Wiley & Sons.

Pietikäinen, K. S. (2018). Misunderstandings and ensuring understanding in private ELF talk. *Applied Linguistics, 39*(2), 188–212.

Ramseyer, F., & Tschacher, W. (2011). Nonverbal synchrony in psychotherapy: Coordinated body movement reflects relationship quality and outcome. *Journal of Consulting and Clinical Psychology, 79*(3), 284–295.

Sacks, H., Schegloff, E. A., & Jefferson, G. (1978). A simplest systematics for the organization of turn taking for conversation. In *Studies in the organization of conversational interaction* (pp. 7–55).

Samstag, L. W., Muran, J. C., & Safran, J. D. (2004). Defining and identifying alliance ruptures. In D. Charman (Ed.), *Core concepts in brief dynamic psychotherapy* (pp. 187–214). Erlbaum.

Schegloff, E. A. (1987). Some sources of misunderstanding in talk-in-interaction. *Linguistics, 25*(1), 201–218.

Schegloff, E. A. (2007). *Sequence organization in interaction: A primer in conversation analysis I* (Vol. *1*). Cambridge University Press.

Scorolli, C. (2019). Re-enacting the bodily self on stage: Embodied cognition meets psychoanalysis. *Frontiers in Psychology, 10,* 1–18.

Selting, M., Auer, P., Barth-Weingarten, D., Bergmann, J., Bergmann, P., Birkner, K., Couper-Kuhlen, E., Deppermann, A., Gilles, P., Günthner, S., Hartung, M., Kern, F., Mertzlufft, C., Meyer, C., Morek, M., Oberzaucher, F., Peters, J., Quasthoff, U., Schütter, W., Stukenbrock, A., & Uhmann, S. (2011). A system for transcribing talk-in-interaction: GAT 2 translated and adapted for English by Elizabeth Couper-Kuhlen and Dagmar Barth-Weingarten. *Online-Zeitschrift zur verbalen Interaktion,* (12), 1–51.

Stalnaker, R. (2002). Common ground. *Linguistics and Philosophy, 25*(5/6), 701–721.

Stern, D. N. (2004). *The present moment in psychotherapy and everyday life.* W. W. Norton & Co.

Stiles, W. B. (2008). Filling the gaps. In A. Peräkylä, C. Antaki, S. Vehviläinen, & I. Leudar (Eds.), *Conversation analysis and psychotherapy* (pp. 1–4). Cambridge University Press.

Stivers, T., & Sidnell, J. (2013). Introduction. In J. Sidnell & T. Stivers (Eds.), *The handbook of conversation analysis* (pp. 1–8). John Wiley & Sons.

Tajfel, H., & Turner, J. C. (1986). The social identity theory of intergroup behavior. In S. Worchel & W. G. Austin (Eds.), *Psychology of intergroup relations* (pp. 7–24). Nelson Hall.

Valsiner, J. (1999). I create you to control me: A glimpse into basic processes of semiotic mediation. *Human Development, 42*(1), 26–30.

Valsiner, J. (2014). *An invitation to cultural psychology.* Sage Publications.

CHAPTER 11

GENDER IDENTITY CONSTRUCTION FROM A SEMIOTIC CULTURAL PSYCHOLOGY PERSPECTIVE: CLINICAL IMPLICATIONS

Leonardo Rafael Leite da Rocha[†]
Universidade Federal da Bahia, Brazil

Cristiana Kaipper Dias[‡]
Universidade Federal da Bahia, Brazil

Giuseppina Marsico[§]
Univerity of Salerno, Italy

ABSTRACT

This chapter explores gender identity construction and its clinical implications through the lens of Cultural Psychology. Drawing on Valsiner's semiotic approach, the authors conceptualize human development as a dynamic process of meaning-making mediated by cultural signs. Integrating Cultural Psychology with Clinical Psychology, the chapter examines how semiotic

†https://orcid.org/0000-0002-6951-4363
‡https://orcid.org/0000-0003-3669-9653
§https://orcid.org/0000-0002-8683-2814

Cultural Psychology in Clinical Research and Practices, pages 223–240

Published under exclusive licence by Emerald Publishing Limited
doi:10.1108/978-1-83742-213-520261011

processes – such as internalization, externalization, semiotic hierarchies, and symbolic mediation – shape subjectivity, particularly in the experiences of transgender individuals. Building on Queer Theory and feminist perspectives, the text situates gender as a socio-discursive construct, emphasizing how cisheteronormative norms restrict personal development and self-expression. A clinical case study of a transgender woman ('Mayara') illustrates how conflicts between internalized cultural meanings can produce psychological suffering and how therapeutic interventions grounded in semiotic principles – such as awareness of hypergeneralized signs (Sign with infinite Borders), construction of Demolishing Signs (D-Signs), and symbolic removal – can foster self-understanding and empowerment. The authors propose a semiotic-cultural clinical model based on awareness and change, aiming to restore individuals' capacity for meaning-making and self-coherence. The therapeutic relationship is viewed as a dialogical and co-constructive process essential for personal transformation. Ultimately, the chapter advocates for a psychology that integrates personal, social, and political dimensions of human experience, contributing to the well-being and emancipation of gender-dissident individuals.

Keywords: Cultural psychology of semiotic dynamics; gender identity; transgender experience; meaning-making; clinical psychology; empowerment

Culture is a fundamental human phenomenon, and many psychology theories have explored the intricate relationship between cultural and psychological processes. One such perspectives is Cultural Psychology of Semiotic Dynamics (Valsiner, 2007), which conceptualises culture as a human semiotic regulation system. Subjectivity develops within social relationship within a cultural setting and through processes of internalisation and externalisation. Meaning making permeates all psychological processes. In every interaction, humans construct meanings about the world and themselves.

The Cultural Psychology of Semiotic Dynamics (also known as Semiotic Cultural Psychology – hereafter referred to as CPSD) is a recent theoretical perspective in psychology. Initially proposed by Valsiner (2007), CPSD has emerged as an important framework, especially, though and not exclusively, in developmental and educational psychology (Marsico & Tateo, 2018; Marsico et al., 2015; Valsiner, 2007, 2012). While strongly committed to basic research, theoretical development, and reflections on epistemology and research methodology (Valsiner, 2007, 2014, 2017), its practical application in clinical settings remains relatively underdeveloped.

Our background and professional practice as psychologists are primarily rooted in clinical psychology, though we are currently conducting research in educational psychology based on the CPSD framewoek. As clinicians studying CPSD, we are exploring the potential for dialogue between CPSD and Clinical Psychology. While CPSD has only few tentative approaches clinical intervention, we believe its concepts offer significant theorertical potential that could eventually inform clinical practice. Therefore, we aim to connect key CPSD concepts to relevant clinical phenomena.

As researchers interested in gender identity and the psychological experience of transgender people, we are exploring how the psychological processes described by CPSD relate to gender identity development, a fundamental aspect of human subjectivity. Just as individuals exercise agency, they also an internalise culturally constructed meanings of gender, which are subsequently externalised through gender expression.

According to Butler (1999), gender is constructed through performative acts, suggesting that it's more a *doing* than an essence or intrinsic characteristic. Furthermore, gender identity can be understood as developing through semiotic processes, as Valsiner (2014) proposes that our bodies are culturally constructed through signs. From a Cultural Psychology Semiotic perspective, both body and mind are co-constructed through interactions between the individual, the world, and meaning-making processes. Thus, the body becomes a vehicle for gender expression, extending far beyond simple genital differentiation.

This chapter explores some clinical implications of this complex gender identity development process and the semiotic processes involved. We also discuss the suffering produced from the social treatment of sexual and gender minorities, and how clinical intervention based on semiotic cultural principles might be implemented.

Our clinical experience has shown that issues related to gender and sexuality can be a source of suffering and related symptoms for individuals who, for various reasons, do not conform to socially established gender and sexualitynotrms-what is termed cisheteronormativity[1] (Warner, 1999). This is a recurring theme in clinical psychology, and we therefore, consider it an important issue to address in academic publications. Considering the complexity and variety of gender identities and human sexualities, we will refer to those who do not fit the normative standards as 'dissidents of the sex-gender system' (Butler, 1999; Rubin, 1989).

Social normativity exerts considerable social and cultural pressure to conform to gender norms. These values are common in Western Judeo-Christian cultures and their institutions, especially those responsible for the education and development of children and adolescents. From an early age, expectations around gender and sexuality embedded with the values that guide the human developoment. These expectations permeate much of an individual's trajectory, influencing children's interests, their games, behaviour, speech, and the objects or people they value or disregard. When any of these aspects deviate from gender expectations, pressure ensue, often immediately, from peers, and school, and/or family. This pressure can range from provocations about behaviors, interests or habits, to physical violence (Jesus, 2013).

Therefore, gender issues are related to the socialisation of individuals from a very early age, and works to ensure that all individuals grow and develop within prescribed and expected gender standards-that is the 'gender police' (Preciado, 2020). Once the child begins to express themselves through words, gestures and games, they are led to adapt to behavior expected from the gender assigned to them at birth (Jesus, 2013).

> The child is a biopolitical artifact that guarantees the normalization of the adult. The gender police supervise the cradle of the living beings about to be born, to transform them into heretosexual children. The norm patrols tender bodies. [...] The gender police requires different characteristics from the little boy and the little girl. It shapes bodies in order to map our complementary sexual organs. (Preciado, 2020, p. 47)

While some children navigate this process without major turmoil, to some extent, all experience a form of 'violence' when they must relinquish certain modes of expression deemed inappropriate for their gender. For those children who strongly identify with activities and objects considered inappropriate for the assigned gender, 'dissent from the sex-gender system' becomes even more distressing and painful (Jesus, 2013).

Over the course of development, these restrictions can impose limitations on their self-expression. Moreover, the internalisation of these prohibitions often leadws to anxiety, diminished motivation, and lower self-esteem, effects that tends to intensify over time-especially for transgender children. Jaqueline de Jesus (2013) explains that:

> Transgender children exist, that the experiences of concealment, suppression, stigmatization, fear, isolation, doubt and repression that they suffer can 'affect their lives as adults', and that need to be analyzed beyond the therapeutic scope, considering social and cultural issues involved. (p. 3, free translation[2])

As transgender children grow older, some express their gender identity through their feelings and behaviours. These expressions may deviate from the ciseteronormative expectations, exposing them to social stigma and discrimination. On the other hand, individuals, despite expressing their inner conflict, conform to societal gender norms but later face psychological suffering as a result. In both cases, pressure to confomr, can lead to self-destructive behaviours, depression, or other psychopathologies - and sometimes even suicide (Arán, 2006). A similar process occurs in relation to sexuality, though with specific nuances. Adolescents who experience desires and sexualities that diverge from societal norms, have often already encountered gender-based violence in childhood (Dias et al., 2019).

Furthermore, living out affective and sexual stories in a dissident way has other implications. Acceptance, or lack thereof, by oneself, family, friends, and society plays a critical role in shaping these experiences (Nascimento & Scorsolini-Comin, 2018). Many individuals initials keep these relationships secret, later decising whether to disclose their sexual orientation publicly or continue to be living in secrecy. This is often 'in line with the historically created expectations that these relationships should remain invisible in public space and restricted to the private life of those involved' (Miskolci, 2013, p. 303, free translation[3]). These processes are typically fraught with tension and emotional suffering, with significant implications for mental health.

For these reasons, it is crucial that psychologists, and society at large, are equipped to deal these challenges. By fostering greater awareness and providing appropriate psychological support, we can better assist those in need and contribute to a more inclusive and supportive environment.

THEORIES AND CONCEPTS ABOUT GENDER, SEXUALITY AND IDENTITY

The 20th century witnessed significant waves of questioning, struggles, and transformations related to gender and sexuality, beginning with feminist movements and, continuing, towards the end of the century, with LGBTQIA+ movements.

At first, feminists challenged the great social disparities between men and women regarding rights and power. Early feminists took to the streets to fight for political rights, with an emphasis on the right to vote, as in the case of suffragettes (Monteiro & Grubba, 2017).

Later, the second wave of feminism, marked by Beauvoir's publication 'The Second Sex' (1949/1961), introduced the concept of gender as a social construction, distinct from sex, which was considered a biological condition. In this sense, most of the efforts was on demonstrating that 'becoming a woman' is a cultural process, not a natural given. Consequently, activities traditionally considered feminine and justified as naturally predetermined began to be questioned. According to Martins (2015):

> New guidelines and demands emerged from the publication of 'The second sex', by Simone de Beauvoir, in 1949. Responsible for the re-articulation of European feminism after the Second World War, the text explains how women constituted themselves as the 'other' in relation to man, without this relationship resulting in reciprocity. Thus, even when it extends the visibility of women in the public sphere - and gain political and socialrights, the man remains the measure of all things, the power holders and creators of culture, keeping themselves as the universal category. (p. 233, free translation[4])

These criticisms were instrumental in demonstrating the political and epistemological roots of the inequality of power between men and women in modern society.

Finally, the third wave of feminism began to question the very concept 'woman', as an essentialist and universal category, moving towards a post-gender, postidentity world. It recognises the vast diversity among women, making it difficult to define 'woman' in a universal and totalizing way. This wave highlights the embracing of 'intersectionality' (Crenshaw, 2002), and how other categories such as race and class profoundly shape the different experiences of womanhood (Martins, 2015). Black, Chicana, community and decolonial feminisms, among others, have significantly contributed to these discussions and reconfiguration of feminism as a heterogeneous, critical, and political movement. (Collins, 2000; Curiel, 2010; Davis, 2013; Gonzalez, 1988; hooks, 1995; Lugones, 2008; 2014; Miñoso, 2009; Oyěwùmí, 2004; Spivak, 2010). These authors critically examined the 'subject of feminism', arguing that, as previouisly presented, it only represented white, middle-class, heterosexual Euro-American women.

Within this context, Queer Theory (Butler, 1999; Preciado, 2020; Rubin, 1989) emerged and gained prominense, shaping subsequent debates on sex and gender. Butler (1999) argues that both sex and gender are cultural constructs, emanating from the poststructuralist notion that there was no prediscursive truth. Inspired by Austin's (1965) theory of speech acts, she argues that discourse does not simply describe a preexisting objective and external reality; rather, the act of naming constitutes that reality. Thus, the body and the sex are discursively constructed, and not objective data from nature.

Considering sex and gender as discursive constructs positions gender as a performative act, constantly being constructed in an individual's relationship with the world. Consequently, the notion of a fixed identity is questioned, as it implies an essential, stable, and coherent truth, within the individual that dictates how gender should be organized (Butler, 1999). We subsequently saw the decline of fixed identities that supported society's discourses and the emergence of new identities and forms of identification. The postmodern subject is formed from a procedural matrix, which is not fixed. Identity becomes a mobile celebration, being continuously built in everyday life (Ferreira, 2018).

> The fully unified, completed, secure, and coherent identity is a fantasy. Instead, as the systems of meaning and cultural representation multiply, we are confronted by a bewildering, fleeting multiplicity of possible identities, any of which we could identify with - at least temporarily. (Hall, 1992, p. 277)

Since identities were the fixed structure from which sexualities were organized, sexuality is also seen as a fluctuating construct that responds to the interactions of the environment, which is not anchored in any specific bodily or gender reality. The binary and stable gender was, therefore, the condition for which Foucault (1977) denounced the sexuality dispostion, and argued that sex was social construct used to regulate behaviour. According to Foucault (1977), the feminine and the masculine as biological facts are a production of medical and scientific discourses of the 19th century. In this context, heterosexuality becomes the norm, and all other sexualities are pathologized.

The creation of these abjected subjects served the purposes of political and cultural domination, defining who would be entitled to the rights and duties of the welfare state and who would fall outside the norm and subsequently occupy subordinate positions. For Foucault (1977), sexuality is centeral to the modern process of subjectivation, necessitating submission to cisheteronormativity for social acceptance.

Based on this criticism, the feminist and LGBTQIA+ movements have been organised to demand political and civil rights, and generally advocating for greater freedom and diversity in values, practices, and laws. While many of these movements are based on Queer Theory,[5] the identity categories have proliferated.

Recognising sexuality and gender as complex, fluid, and diverse, individuals have formed groups around specific guidelines, to advocate for their specific needs (Jesus, 2012). These group are often differentiated based on:

- Sexual orientation (e.g., homosexual, bisexual, pansexual and asexual);
- Gender identity (e.g., transgender, transvestite, transsexual);
- Gender expression (e.g. drag queens and kings, crossdressers);
- Bodily characteristics (e.g, intersex).

This demonstrates the complexity of human experience and the different needs of grouping based on sexual and gender identities. In many countries, the dissidents of the sex-gender system are often encompassed by the acronym LGBT (lesbian, gay, bisexual, transgender).[6]

These are socially subordinated groups often do not have state policies that support their needs. For example, homosexual marriage is not legalized in several countries, and, in others, legalization is not accompanied by all rights. For example, where homosexual marriage is legalized, adtoption by these individuals is not possible (Bastos et al., 2017).

Finally, the letter 'T' represents an 'umbrella category' for transgender people, which encompasses transsexual, transvestite, and nonbinary identities. There is, however, no general consensus on this umbrella classification. By definition, transgender people do not identify, totally or partially, with the gender assigned to them at birth (Jesus, 2012).

Transgender individuals, in general, experience the most prejudice and difficulty in chieving social acceptance. They face exclusion from school and the formal labor market, as well as high rates of violence. This group perhaps bears the brunt of prejudice and violence in society (Queiroga, 2018). Therefore, this chapter focuses on transgender individuals to understand how gender issues and the prevailing ciseteronormative context affect their development and psychologival wellbeing.

Having explored key questions about Queer Theory and the issues related to gender and sexuality, we will now examine the role of cultural signs, aiming to illumniate psychological processes that complement the sociopolitical issues highlighted by Queer Theory.

CULTURAL SEMIOTIC PERSPECTIVE ON GENDER AND SEXUALITY

According to Valsiner (2007), Cultural Psychology aims to understand how culture influences human psychological processes. This approach focuses on mental functions featuring higher levels of complexity and require meaning making to fully operate. This is the basic premise of CPSD about human nature: Homo Sapiens needs to build and assign meanings for absolutely everything around them, whatever it may be. It's a basic psychological need (Valsiner, 2007).

Meaning making processes are possible within a cultural context. Under CPSD perspective, culture is understood as a semiosphere - a set of signs built and shared by individuals. These set of signs works as a semiotic system of regulation by building, organising, and developing the psyche, through processes of internalisation and externalisation (Valsiner, 2007).

Internalisation and externalisation describe individuals incorporate signs from their semiospheres. This internalisation process involves several ongoing internal dialogues and negotiations between the individual and the system of collectively shared signs. This intrapsychological process leads to the individual developinh a unique and personal interpretation of the collective meanings present in their shared culture. This subjective version of culture, present within each individual, is called personal culture, while the system of collectively built and shared signs is referred to as collective culture (Valsiner, 2014).

These psychological processes unfold across irreversible time, a central tenet of CPSD. This premise states that psychological phenomena cannot be fully understood from a single temporal perspective (past, present or future). Because they are irreversible, psychological phenomena are never identical and can never be precisely replicated. A past thought, even if similar in content to a current thought, is distinct from it. Therefore, analysing psychological processes exclusively by their history (past) or describing only their characteristics (present) provides an incomplete analysis.

A direct implication of the irreversible temporal perspective is that CPSD emphasises the processual and developmental nature of its phenomena of interest. As human beings are prospective (i.e., future-oriented), internalisation processes have a cognitive and affective function of building a meaningful future for individuals. Psychology research and intervention, through this viewpoint, must consider the entire developmental process of a phenomenon. Rather than simply describing and modifying individual behaviors and characteristics, CPSD focuses on understanding 'becoming' processes, and it is through this lens that a possible Semiotic-Cultural clinical practice should be approached.

Individuals are not passive recipients in the internalisation process. Rather they actively select and modify elements that shape their personal culture. Before being expressed, these elements undergo modification through the process of externalisation. These active cycles of internalisation and externalisation cycles position individuals as agents in their own development, a process that both consucts culture and is shaped by it (Valsiner, 2007, 2014).

Higher mental functions operate through signs. A key characteristic of signs, according to Valsiner (2007), is their inherent complexity and ambiguity. From a semiotic-cultural perpective, the ambiguity is essential for development, as it generates tension that drive the construction of new meanings to navigate life's uncertainties. This ongoing creation and reinterpretation of meaning is essential for human development (Valsiner, 2007). Human beings constantly create and use signs to make sense of the world (Valsiner, 2007), a process Valsiner (2007) terms semiotic mediation: every human act of meaning making is mediated by signs.

Social suggestions and orientations, which are abundant in culture, are a prime example of semiotic mediation that fosters development. From an early age, individuals are guided towards certain development paths while others are discouraged. These suggestions may or may not be followed, as individuals actively internalize and negotiate them, creating a personal synthesis (Valsiner, 2012).

Many social suggestions influence the formation of the self throughout development. The construction of the self is also understood as a semiotic process, involving the internalisation and externalisation of signs, strongly influenced by intersubjective relations. A substantial part of an individual's self-concept derives from relationships with significant others (Valsiner, 2005, 2012). Therefore, the construction of the self is intrinsically linked to socialisation. From this premise of semiotic mediation emerges a core concept of CPSD: the notion of semiotic hierarchy.

According to Valsiner (2014), hierarchies exist in nature as a way to organise and ensure the survival of individual organisms and maintain natural order. Similarly, the human mind is organised through a hierarchy of signs (a semiotic hierarchy). The main feature of semiotic hierarchies, according to Valsiner (2014), is their intransitivity. This means they are open to changes in the positions of signs over time, as well as the emergence of novelty and/or changes in the meanings of existing elements. This is evident in the shifting meanings attributed to the same thing – for example, in a broken relationship, a once significant partner may become less meaningful after a certain time or series of experiences that change the meaning of that former partner. This illustrates the changing meaning of an element within a given semiotic hierarchy (Valsiner, 2014).

Two important concepts from the notion of semiotic hierarchy are the Sign with infinite Borders (SWIBs) and the Demolishing Sign (D-Sign). We will discuss these concepts along with symbolic removal and the semiotic notion of *self*, before analysing a fictional case study. We believe these four concepts can illumniate the psychological suffering associated with gender identity issues.

A SWIB, as described by Valsiner (2014), is a hypergeneralised sign that transcends the limits of human verbalisation. Its main feature is its ability to catalyse changes of meanings that 'are rapid and directed towards the complete takeover of the person's *psyche*' (Valsiner, 2014, p. 123). Many psychological phenomena emerge through SWIBs, such as sublime and aesthetic feelings, mood swings and panic attacks. These phenomena are characterised by their rapid onset and disappearance, and dominate and individual's mind, at least temporarily.

Conflict can arise when different signs within a semiotic hierarchy, especially those with opposing meanings, clash. Such psychological conflicts are common in human experience. These conflicts persist until a D-Sign intervenes. A D-Sing possesses the power to resolve a psychological conflict, thereby demolishing, rebuilding, and reorganising one's semiotic hierarchy, leading to new meaning-making and form a psychic homeostasis (Valsiner, 2014). The idea of a D-Sign resonates with the concept of 'insight' in various psychotherapeutic approaches, where a new understanding or interpretation can dramatically shift an individual's perspective and emotional state. However, the semiotic framework of the D-Sign offers a specific mechanism for how this change occurs, focusing on the restructuring of meaning within the semiotic hierarchy.

Symbolic removal is another important concept derived from this framework. According to Valsiner (2014), this semiotic process involves replacing a symbol within a semiotic hierarchy with another, or modifying its existing meaning. This often happens when an individual needs to reinterpret certain meanings to make sense of their life. Symbolic removeal can be observed in various clinical phenomena. For example, consider a male client with depression trigerred by marital problems. Other aspects of life, onece important, such his children, friendships, family relations, leisure activities, and work, may also become negatively affected. Those can be viewed aws sumpbos that initially held positive meanings for the client. However, through symbolic removal, their meanings have shifted, becoming sources of suffering. While symbolic removal can contribute to clinical problems, it can also be a part of the solution. A clinician can facilitate further symbolic removal processes through verbal interventions. This concept has similarities with the psychoanalytic notion of 'working through,' where individuals re-evaluate and reinterpret past experiences and relationships. However, symbolic removal emphasizes the semiotic nature of this process, focusing on the changing meanings of symbols within the individual's semiotic hierarchy.

Having discussed these concepts (SWIB, D-Sign, and symbolic removal), we will now explore their application in a fictional case of a Brazilian transgender woman.

PSYCHOLOGICAL SUFFERING RELATED TO GENDER TRANSITION: A CULTURAL SEMIOTIC PERSPECTIVE

Mayara (a fictional name), a 19 years-old Japanese Brazilian woman identifies as transgender woman. Unemployed, she lives with her parentes in a middle-class neighborhood in São Paulo. Her therapist, Joana, is a 35 years-old white, cisgender, heterosexual woman who has provided psychotherapy to Mayara for the last 3 years. At the beginning of the therapy, Mayara reported internal conflicts about openly expressing her sexuality. At that time, she identified as a gay man and had come out to her parentes at the age of 15 year, approximately one year before starting psychotherapy.

According to Mayara, her parentes were accepting and she describes them as being liberal. Despite this supportive family environment, Mayara feel uncomfortable engaging in relationships with men, fearing social judgment from the neighbours, schoolmates, friends, or others. She also reported feeling ashamed to be seen publicly in a homosexual relationship and guilty from being aware of society's disapproval of homosexuality.

Through therapy, Mayara began to discuss her sexuality more openly, increasingly affirming it as normal and acceptable. This was part of psychological interventions aimed at promoting self-acceptance. Moreover, Mayara's growing acceptance of her sexuality also had a socio-political dimension: as she became more comfortable and open about her sexuality, and as her identity strengthened, she felt empowered-a therapeutic goal in itself. As this process unfolded, Mayara began to address gender identity issues as well. She told her therapist that since childhood, she had enjoyed playing with 'girl stuff' and was interesterested in 'feminine' things, such as makeup and women's clothing, including women's underwear and wearing her mom's shoes, often secretly. Mayara also reported that frequently imagining herself as a woman and that, given a choice, she would choose to become female. She had always been curious about 'sex reassignment' surgery. Discomforts with her own genitalia was also common in Mayara's experience, although she often ignored them, claiming that she 'though it was normal for 'bottom' gay men dislike their own penis'. Although she was curious about 'sex reassignment' procedures, she also expressed fear of them.

Mayara's therapist explored her curiosity about the 'feminine world', as well as her discomfort with her genitalia. Over time, Mayara began to understand herself not as a gay man, but as a transgender woman. She realised that her dissatisfaction with her body and her long-held curiosities deeply reflected how she always had, albeit unknowingly, understood herself: as a woman, even if she had previously rejected this identity. After this process of self-understanding and acceptance as a transgender woman, Mayara started hormone therapy and is now in the legal process of name change. Despite these personal advances, Mayara still shares concerns with Joana: fear to presenting herself publicly with a body in transition; doubts and psychological conflicts about whether or not to have sex reassignment surgery; and fear of socialising and being verbally or physically assaulted. As a result of these fears, Mayara has adopted a strategy of self-isolation.

Mayara reports experiencing intense anxiety and fear about going out in public, leading her to stay at home. She explains that hormone therapy has given her body some feminine characteristics, so it is no longer completely masculine, yet it is not fully 'feminine' either. Thus, Mayara atributes meanings of ambiguity and indeterminacy to her body, which she struggles to reconcile. She describes experiencing anxiety symptoms (e.g., tachycardia, sweating, shortness of breath) even when stepping onot her house's terrace, and fears having a panic attack if she ventures out onto the street. She is afraid of potential judgments and negative reactions from people in her neighborhood.

In cultural semiotic terms, Mayara's anxiety symptoms (similar to agoraphobia) can be understood as a manifestation of semiotic dynamics involving SWIBs. Her symptoms emerge suddenly in ordinary daily situations, such as going onto the terrace, and persist, occupying her entire mental landscape, until she returns to the context of domestic isolation and exclusive contact with her parentes-a context that favours the emergence of signs other than the anxiety-related SWIBs. Because SWIBs are difficult to define due to their inherently undefined nature, an importante part of the clinical process can involve helping Mayara name this feeling and its associated meanings. Attributing meaning to these situations can help Mayara develop self-awareness and better manage them.

Mayara's doubts and internal conflict about whether or not to have surgeries can be understood through the lens of semiotic hierarchy. Valsiner (2014) argues that semiotic hierarchies are typically characterized by the coexistence of signs that, while present, can come into conflict. In Mayara's case, 'I WANT the surgery' can be seen as a sign promoting future action. However, her semiotic hierarchy may also be influenced by an inhibitor sign, such as 'I SHOULD NOT have the surgery; it will hurt, I'm afraid, I will be judged and it's irreversible-what if I regret it?'.

A crucial part of Mayara's therapy involves exploring, describing, and deeply analysing both the favorable (promoter signs) and unfavorable (inhibitor signs) factors related to the surgery. It is important to emphasise that a semiotically oriented clinical process should not simply describe these factors; to do so would fall short of CPSD's primary goal: understanding the processes of meaning-making in whicht human beings engage. Therefore, beyond mere description, the therapeutic approach should focus on meanings associated with each favorable and unfavorable factor, creating a space for the externalisation of these meanings and their related affects.

The clinical management of Mayara's semiotic hierarchy can benefit from a dialogue between CPSD and cognitive therapy, as both perspectives are concerned with higher mental functions. Linehan (1993) proposed a dialectical model of cognitive therapy, based in two fundamental axes: acceptance –psychological skills of openness to unpleasant feelings and thoughts – and change – engagement in daily actions aimed at building a meaningful life based on the client's values. Linehan's (1993) method inovles developing both acceptance and change skills in each client and, importantly, establishing a dialectical balance between the two.

Similar to Linehan's (1993) proposal, we suggest that a cultural-semiotic clinical process can also be structured around two axes: awareness and change. The awareness axis involves helping Mayara recognise and understand the promoter and inhibitor signs, their effects on her psychological dynamics, their meanings, and how they have developed throughout her life. The change axis focuses on collaboratively constructing, between therapist and client, D-Signs *t* that can help Mayara manage this conflict and catalyse a decision, if making such a decision is important for her. From this perspective, the clinical process acts as a cataclyst for these signs.

This conflict between 'I WANT' and 'I SHOULD NOT' may persist until a sufficiently powerful D-Sign emerges, resolving the conflict and reorganising the semiotic hierarchy. Examples of such D-Signs in Mayara's case could be: 'I WON'T MIND the judgments', 'my life IS MINE and it's nobody's business', 'I DECIDE what is the best for me', living with a penis HAS NOT BEEN WORKING for me', and 'I WILL TAKE care of myself, pre and postsurger'. It is important to acknowledge that such conflict arises not only from individual psychology, but also, and perhaps primarily, from the broader social context in which transgender people exist.

Mayara's final concern is the fear of living openly as a transgender woman and facing potential verbal or physical assault. Regarding the fear of physical assault, intervention should focus on developing strategies for protection and self-care, including providing relevant information and resources. While not necessarily unique to a cultural-semiotic approache, this is standard practice in any therapeutic context involving potential victims of violence.

The fear of verbal violence falls within the symbolic realm of words, their meanings, and affective charges. Here, the concept of symbolic removal can be of great value. A common derogatory slang y used in Brazil to insult transgender people is 'traveco', a corruption of 'travesti', a term for one type of transgender identity in Brazilian culture. Terms also used against gay men are often directed at transgender women.

In this regard, it would be beneficial for Mayara to engage in a process of symbolic removal (i.e., meaning transformation) of these potentially offensive words. Symbolic removal can help her attribute meanings beyond the intended insult and contextualize the terms. Joining a transgender community could be helpful, as these communities sometimes reclaim such terms, using them humorously or affectionately among members. Thus, a new context and its intersubjective relations can catalyse symbolic removal. While some of this process can and should occur in a clinical setting, it is also important to support Mayara in building these interpersonal networks that can facilitate this reframing.

CONCLUDING REMARKS

The semiotic processes here – awareness of SWIBs and promoter/inhibitor signs, the construction of D-Signs, and symbolic removal – are all processes that a cultural-semiotic clinical intervention must catalyse. However, we argue that such catalysis is unlikely without a fundamental process: strengthening Mayara's sense of self. Mayara is in a transition, not only physically but also in her self-concept, gradually constructing and exploring a transgender identity. Because the self, as CPSD posits, is built through socialisation and influenced by the voices of others, the therapist-client relationship becomes a social relationship in itself, with the therapist's voice contributing to the reframing and strengthening of Mayara's self.

Therefore, the therapeutic relationship can be used to foster new self positionings that Mayara needs to navigate her life within her lived social reality. The importance of the therapeutic relationship is emphasised by authors representing other clinical Psychology approaches, given the strong evidence that a positive bond between therapist and client promotes change. This notion can be found, for example, in Functional Analytic Psychotherapy (Tsai et al., 2009) and in Psychoanalysis, which emphasise relational concepts like transference and countertransference (Freud, 1912).

This chapter aimed to disucss theoretical and analytical aspects, not to provide a comprehensive guide to cultural-semiotic intervention for gender identity issues. It is important to clarify that the suggested interventions in Mayara's case are, at this stage, an attempt to apply CPSD's theoretical notions to an empirical example. These suggestions should be understood as exploratory approaches resulting from theoretical effort. We emphasize this point because CPSD currently lacks a well-developed technical arsenal for intervention. We have the theory and its potential (and plausible) applications. Developing specific interventive techniques is a crucial area for future research. For now, we believe in the plausibility of the analysis presented and the potential of CPSD to inform clinical interventions aimed at reducing the psychological suffering of transgender individuals.

As clinical psychologists studying CPSD, we believe that, from a cultural-semiotic perspective, clinical work should focus on facilitating the client's personal culture building. The therapist acts as a facilitator, enabling the individual to create a personal synthesis of cultural elements and constantly validateing their unique interpretation of collective culture. The clinical process must promote autonomy and empowerment – particularly for individuals belonging to marginalised social groups, such as transgender people. Given CPSD's fundamental axiom that human beings are active meaning-makers, constantly creating meanings from their experiences, psychological suffering can be understood as a difficulty in creating new meaning, leading to persistent psychological states that generate distress.

Therefore, the role of the clinical psychologist, from this viewpoint, is to restore this capacity and help the client construct new meanings, which in turn can promote wellbeing, development, and autonomy. Lastly, we believe in the fundamental principle that the individual well-being is deeply intertwined with social environment. Thus, clinical support should extend beyond individual aspects of psychological suffering, encompassing socio-political factors. Clinicians should also promote processes of political empowerment as an integral part of psychological care.

NOTES

1. 'Cisheteronormativity: a set of power relations that normalises, regulates, idealises and institutionalises gender, sex and sexuality along a strictly horizontal line – and identifies some individuals who present specificities under different social, political and moral' (Morera & Padilha, 2017, *free translation*).

'Conceito que faz referência a um conjunto de relações de poder que normaliza, regulamenta, idealiza e institucionaliza o gênero, sexo e a sexualidade em uma linha ilógica e estritamente horizontal (1) – e identifica alguns indivíduos que apresentam especificidades sob diversos marcos discursivos sociais, políticos e morais' (Morera & Padilha, 2017).

2. 'Crianças trans existem, que as experiências de ocultação, supressão, estigmatização, medo, isolamento, dúvida e repressão que sofrem podem 'afetar suas vidas quando adultos', e que precisam ser analisadas para além do âmbito terapêutico, considerando as pressões sociais e culturais envolvidas' (Jesus, 2013, p. 3).
3. 'Conformando-o a expectativas historicamente criadas de que essas relações deveriam permanecer invisíveis no espaço público e restritas à vida privada dos envolvidos' (Miskolci, 2013, p. 303).
4. 'Novas pautas e demandas surgiram a partir da publicação de "O segundo sexo", de Simone de Beauvoir, em 1949. Responsável pela rearticulação do feminismo europeu após a Segunda Guerra Mundial, o texto explicita de que forma a mulher se constituiu como a "outra" em relação ao homem, sem que desta relação resultasse reciprocidade. Desse modo, mesmo quando se amplia a visibilidade das mulheres na esfera pública – e se conquistam direitos políticos e sociais, o homem permanece como a medida de todas as coisas, detentores do poder e criadores da cultura, mantendo-se como categoria universal' (Martins, 2015, p. 233).
5. The Queer Theory is antiidentity, since it argues that there is no stability of sex, gender sexuality to justify an identity.
6. Currently, we commonly find the acronym LGBTQIA+ (lesbian, gay, bisexual, transgender, queer, intersex, asexual, and other possibilities not listed), which may vary with other elements, dependending on the group which uses that and the defended arguments.

REFERENCES

Arán, M. (2006). A transexualidade e a gramática normativa do sistema sexo-gênero. *Ágora: Estudos em Teoria Psicanalítica, 9*(1), 49–63. https://doi.org/10.1590/S1516-14982006000100004

Austin, J. (1965). *How to do things with words.* Press.

Bastos, G. G., Garcia, D. A. e S., & Abrahão, L. M. (2017). A homofobia em discurso: Direitos Humanos em circulação. *Linguagem em (Dis)curso [online], 17*(01), 11–24. Disponível em. https://doi.org/10.1590/1982-4017-170101-0416

Beavoir, S. (1961). *O segundo sexo.* Difusão Europeia do Livro.

Butler, J. (1999). *Problemas de gênero. Feminismo e subversão da identidade* (Trad.de Renato Aguiar). Civilização Brasileira.

Collins, P. H. (2000). *Black feminist thought: Knowledge, consciousness and politics of empowermente* (Vol. 2). Routledge.

Crenshaw, K. (2002). Documento para o encontro de especialistas em aspectos da discriminação racial relativos ao gênero. *Florianópolis, 10*(1), 171–188.

Curiel, O. (2010). Hacia la construcción de un feminismo descolonizado. In Y. E. Miñoso (Ed.), Coord *Aproximaciones críticas a las prácticas teórico-políticas del feminismo latino-americano.* En la Frontera.

Davis, A. (2013). *Mulher, raça e classe* Tradução livre. Plataforma Gueto.

Dias, A., Rios, P., & Brazão, P. (2019). As brincadeiras denunciavam que eu era uma criança viada. *Revista Educação em Questão. Natal, 54*(57), 01–21.

Ferreira, D. (2018). *Construção da Identidade de Gênero: reflexões em contexto escolar. Traballho de Conclusão de Curso pela Pontifícia.* Universidade Católica.

Foucault, M. (1977). *História da Sexualidade I: vontade de saber.* EdiçõesGraal.

Freud, S. (1912). *The dynamics of the transference* (Vol. *II*). Coll. Papers.

Gonzalez, L. (1988). *A categoria político-cultural de amefricanidade* (pp. 69–82). Tempo Brasileiro. 92/93 (jan/jun.).

Hall, S. (1992). The question of cultural identity. In S. Hall & T. McGrew (Eds.), *Modernity and its futures* (p. 277). Polity Press.

hooks, bell. (1995). Intelectuais negras. *Porto Alegre: Revista Estudos Feministas, Porto Alegre, 3*(2), 464–478.

Jesus, J. (2012). *Orientações Sobre Identidade de Gênero: conceitos e termos. 2a edição – revista e ampliada.* Brasília. https://repositorio.ifsp.edu.br/items/880972a4-8394-4043-b7ef-161557712054

Jesus, J. (2013). Crianças Trans: Memórias e desafios teóricos. In *III seminário internacional enlaçando sexualidades. Salvador, Bahia.* Recovered from. https://www.researchgate.net/publication/250305355_Criancas_Trans_Memorias_e_Desafios_Teoricos

Linehan, M. M. (1993). *Skills training manual for treating borderline personality disorder.* Guilford press.

Lugones, M. (2008). *Colonialidade e gênero.* Tabula Rsa. (Vol. *9*, pp. 73–101). jul-dez.

Lugones, M. (2014). Rumo a um feminismo descolonial. *Revista Estudos Feministas, 22*(3), 935–952. https://doi.org/10.1590/S0104-026X2014000300013

Marsico, G., Dazzani, V., Ristum, M., & Bastos, A. (2015). *Educational contexts and Borders through a cultural Lens: Looking inside, viewing outside.* Springer.

Marsico, G., & Tateo, L. (2018). *The emergence of self in educational contexts: Theoretical and empirical explorations.* Springer.

Martins, A. (2015). O Sujeito "nas ondas" do Feminismo e o lugar do corpo na Contemporaneidade. *Revista Café Com Sociologia, 1*(4), 231–245.

Miñoso, Y. E. (2009). Etnocentrismo y colonialidad en los feminismos latinoamericanos: Complicidades y consolidación de las hegemonías feministas en el espacio transnacional. *Revista Venezolana de Estudios de la Mujer, Caracas, 14*(33), 37–54.

Miskolci, R. (2013). *Machos e brothers*: Uma etnografia sobre o armário em relações homoeróticas masculinas criadas *on-line. Revista Estudos Feministas, 21*(1), 301–324. https://doi.org/10.1590/S0104-026X2013000100016

Monteiro, K., & Grubba, L. (2017). A luta das mulheres pelo espaço público na primeira onda do feminismo: De suffragettes às sufragistas. *Direito e Desenvolvimento, 2*(8), 261–278.

Morera, J., & Padilha, M. (2017). Representações sociais do sexo e gênero entre pessoas trans. *Revista Brasileira de Enfermagem, 70*(6), 1235–1243. https://doi.org/10.1590/0034-7167-2016-0581

Nascimento, G., & Scorsolini-Comin, F. (2018). A Revelação da Homossexualidade na Família: Revisão Integrativa da Literatura Científica. *Trends in Psychology, 26*(3), 1527–1541. https://doi.org/10.9788/tp2018.3-14pt

Oyěwùmí, O. (2004). Conceptualizing Gender: E Eurocentric Foundations of Feminist Concepts and the challenge of African Epistemologies. In *African gender scholarship: Concepts, methodologies and paradigms* (Vol. *1*, pp. 1–8). CODESRIA Gender Series. Dakar, CODESRIA.

Preciado, P. (2020). *An apartment on Uranus: Chronicles of the crossing.* MIT Press.

Queiroga, L. (2018, Novembro 14). *Brasil segue no primeiro lugar do ranking de assassinatos de transexuais.* O Globo. Editora Globo. https://oglobo.globo.com/sociedade/brasil-segue-no-primeiro-lugar-do-ranking-de-assassinatos-de-transexuais-23234780. Accessed on September 19, 2021

Rubin, G. (1989). Reflexionando sobre el sexo: Notas para uma teoria radical de la sexualidade. Trad. Julio Velasco e Maria Angeles Toda). In C. s. Vance (Ed.), *Placer y peligro: explorando la sexualidadefeminina.* TalasaEdiciones. (Comp.).

Spivak, G. C. (2010). *Pode o subalterno falar?* Trad. Sandra Regina Goulart Almeida, Marcos Pereira Feitosa e André Pereira Feitosa. EDUFMG.

Tsai, M., Kohlenberg, R. J., Kanter, J. W., Kohlenberg, B., Follette, W. C., & Callaghan, G. M. (2009). *A guide to functional analytic psychotherapy. Awareness, courage, love and behaviorism.* Springer.

Valsiner, J. (2005). Scaffolding within the structure of dialogical self: Hierarchical dynamics of semiotic mediation. *New Ideas in Psychology, 23*(3), 197–206.

Valsiner, J. (2007). *Culture in minds and societies: Foundations of cultural psychology.* Sage.

Valsiner, J. (2012). *The Oxford handbook of culture and psychology.* Oxford University Press.

Valsiner, J. (2014). *An invitation to cultural psychology.* Sage.

Valsiner, J. (2017). *From methodology to methods in human psychology.* Springer.

Warner, M. (1999). *The trouble with normal: Sex, politics, and ethics of queer life.* Free Press.

CHAPTER 12

'MY UNBEARABLE WIFE GAVE ME A BRAIN TUMOR:' SUBJECTIVE THEORIES OF ILLNESS AND RECOVERY IN ROBERT MILLER'S YOGA-CENTERED HEALING NARRATIVE

Josephine Kirschner
Clinical Psychologist, Germany

ABSTRACT

Subjective theories of illness are considered essential for the integrative processing of diseases. This chapter therefore investigates the importance of subjective theories of recovery following a brain tumor. The aim is to develop a grounded and improved understanding of the needs and supporting mechanisms for holistic recovery from serious physical illness. Using a research-based adaptation of positioning analysis, the narrative interview of a recovered brain tumor patient was analyzed in the interpretative logic of a single-case study. The analysis revealed that the belief in one's own influence on the course of illness or recovery, in conjunction with supportive therapy, is key to

Cultural Psychology in Clinical Research and Practices, pages 241–262

Published under exclusive licence by Emerald Publishing Limited
doi:10.1108/978-1-83742-213-520261012

successful coping with illness. These findings provide clear guidance for all therapeutic professions supporting individuals with serious illnesses.

Keywords: Cultural psychology; subjective theories of illness; recovery; supportive therapy; yoga; brain tumor

INTRODUCTION

Bright eyes, a youthful smile and palpable drive. The participant of this study is a retired man, father and grandfather, who bears a scar above his left temple, visible only upon close inspection. A year prior, a brain tumor the size of a mandarin, as he describes, was completely removed in the surgery department of a Berlin hospital – a medical success with far-reaching personal consequences.

The tumor was benign – not infiltrative or metastatic. Thus, it does not belong to the cancers that account for the most common causes of death worldwide (Robert Koch Institute, 2019). Proliferative tissue caused by faulty cell division is initially classified neutrally as a tumor. According to the WHO, benign tumors (grade 1) are distinguished histologically from malignant tumors from grade 3 onwards (Louis et al., 2016).

The prognosis for lethality in benign brain tumors is significantly lower compared to malignant brain tumors. However, in the brain, which has limited capacity for abnormal tissue, displacement of structures and functional areas can lead to psychological changes and physical limitations, which may become life-threatening. If damage to surrounding tissue is feared, surgical resection remains the (conventional) medical treatment of choice.

Despite intensive research, little is still known about the precise background and risk factors for brain tumors (Robert Koch Institut & Gesellschaft der epidemiologischen Krebsregister in Deutschland e. V., 2023). According to the Deutsches Krebsforschungszentrum (2017), ancient theories about a melancholic cancer personality are now largely rejected, while 'emotional problems and stress' are predominantly considered causative, despite scant scientific evidence. A study by Förster (2003) found that cancer patients themselves most commonly attribute tumors to fate, stress, and environmental pollution, whereas God's will and character are mentioned less frequently. Over the course of the illness, attributions relating to heredity and one's own behavior tend to increase.

Adjustment and trauma-related disorders are discussed as a result of overcoming tumor illnesses (Mehnert et al., 2013). The ongoing objective of psycho-oncological interventions is to facilitate the formation or re-establishment of identity (Pindl, 2015).

A cancer diagnosis can be viewed as a critical life event that requires immediate adjustment and influences everyday life, one's biographical trajectory, as well as one's dreams and goals. After successful treatment, a person becomes a 'survivor'. They then face the challenge of integrating this critical life event into their life story and identity. This chapter therefore explicitly addresses the question of how an individual constructs personal theories about the origin of the tumor and the recovery process one year after a medically successful procedure.

A HOLISTIC UNDERSTANDING OF ILLNESS AND RECOVERY

In order to investigate subjective theories about illness and recovery, and the state of health towards which these theories lead, it is first necessary to clarify the current scientific and societal understanding of these constructs. The study presented in this chapter touches on interdisciplinary topics, the scientific and theoretical foundations of which partly lie in the distant past. In this inductive study, however, the theoretical considerations were derived from the specific context and insights of the material.

Various models of illness development have been proposed in the literature, with the integrative *biopsychosocial* model of von Uexküll and Wesiack (1986) having established itself as the most popular across medical disciplines. This model provides a theoretical basis for a holistic perspective on the development and maintenance of states that we describe as 'ill' or 'healthy'. According to the model's logic, individual factors interact and are mutually dependent. Through this interplay, illness can be viewed as a consequence of irritation, while health can be seen as a state of harmony. The model addresses the limitations of reductionist and objectifying medicine at the organic level, which is inadequate for treating and supporting unhealthy individuals in their unique realities.

A Societal Understanding of Illness and Recovery

As this chapter focuses on a German-language study, it is worth examining the socially shared understanding of the concepts of illness and recovery in this language area. The Duden dictionary is the most authoritative German dictionary, similar to the Oxford English Dictionary. It can be seen as a reflection of what is expressed in the German language and is thus a relevant guide for social attributions of meaning, mirroring the spectrum of what can be constructed linguistically.

On the one hand, the Dudenredaktion (n.d.a) defines *Gesundheit* (health) as a normative 'state or certain degree of physical, psychological or mental well-being', addressing the various areas of human experience to which this modifiable condition can potentially apply. At the same time, a sense of relativity is implied, as in a 'more or less' thereof. Additionally, health is defined negatively as the 'absence of illness' (Dudenredaktion, n.d.a), which distinguishes it from illness.

On the other hand, *Krankheit* (illness) is defined as a 'physical, mental or psychological disorder' (Dudenredaktion, n.d.b). In the sense of a normative deviation, it refers to the same areas of life that can be impaired or experienced as healthy. Furthermore, the term is understood to mean 'a period of being ill' (Dudenredaktion, n.d.b), which defines it as a *limited* deviation from a normal state.

Recovery from illness arises from the verb 'genesen' (to recover), meaning to 'become healthy again,' describing the process of transition from illness to health. The verb 'heilen' (to heal) shares this passive definition but also includes the active form of 'making someone healthy through appropriate medical, medicinal, etc. treatment', thus implying a clinical monopoly on healing.

An Individual Understanding of Illness and Recovery

While these definitions are consistently explained as expressions of the German language, Petrie and Weinman (1997) argue that subjective theories of illness are complex cognitive structures relating to a person's individual relationship with and engagement with their illness. Accessing these theories is considered essential for the integrative processing of the illness. Recognition of these theories enables self-determined and self-effective engagement, as it allows the individual's illness-associated experience to be meaningfully explained within a continuous sense of self. It is only then that ideas about prognosis and individual decisions.

Each subjective theory of illness arises in direct relation to a specific illness and is shaped by the following individual domains of experience and corresponding approaches to coping:

- Physical experience of symptoms
- Biographical experiences
- Communicated knowledge (from those affected/experts)
- Media-transmitted information
- Observation of other affected individuals

These aspects are further moderated by individual assumptions and expectations, resulting in the model's profound subjective complexity:

- Expected symptoms: by linking symptoms and medical terminology
- Short- and long-term consequences
- Course of the illness
- Treatability and curability
- Causes of the illness
- Controllability
- Meaningfulness in the biography

These theories are particularly relevant in clinical psychology as they facilitate constructive, process-accompanying communication with those affected. This allows their individual needs and personal stages of engagement to be recognized and supported, which is essential for healing. According to Faller (1990), from the moment a symptom is perceived, an intrapsychic discourse is formed, with dynamic shifts in attention towards the experience of threat (fear) or away from it (denial).

In the psychoanalytic tradition, these demanding mental processes can provoke unconscious defense mechanisms that protect the individual from fear, shame, or a loss of self-esteem. Alternatively, they can lead to partially conscious adaptation processes that reduce and process existing or anticipated stress at cognitive, emotional, or behavioral levels (Folkman & Lazarus, 1984). The goal-oriented adaptation processes described in stress research can also be observed when processing a threatening illness. According to Flath (2017), expected strategies in tumor-associated illnesses include denial, distraction, optimism, seeking information, making meaning and religiosity.

A Gender-Based Understanding of Illness and Recovery

In examining the subjective theories concerning the origins and recovery from illness of a male patient following the successful removal of his brain tumor, it is worth noting that research indicates gender-specific variations in health behavior and morbidity (Sieverding, 2010). Due to societal norms in ongoing production and reproduction (Rose, 2015), gender categories demonstrate significant differences in health behavior and risk of illness between women and men (see, for example, Kolip & Hurrelmann, 2016; Sieverding, 2010). Women tend to suffer more from chronic conditions, especially psychosomatic ones, or are diagnosed with them more often, whereas men are more likely to perceive acute, life-threatening illnesses as a threat. However, higher-risk behavior among men mitigates these gender differences in health-related behavior, favoring women (Sieverding, 2010) – possibly because women are better protected by their stronger social networks (Gamper et al., 2020).

Gender-specific attributions are also evident in relation to health. For example, women are often considered to be more caring and health-conscious, whereas men tend to try to deal with health issues independently in order to maintain a sense of control (Kolip & Hurrelmann, 2016). However, other studies have questioned the general assumption that men use healthcare less frequently (Kuhlmann, 2016).

An Identity-Based Understanding of Illness and Recovery

The necessity of subjective theories of illness for the integrative processing of health threats appears to be gender-neutral (see Section 'An Individual Understanding of Illness and Recovery'). These theories underpin the ability to perceive oneself as a coherent individual despite biographical disruption, and to distinguish oneself from the (social) environment. In this sense, psycho-oncological interventions primarily support the formation or re-formation of identity (Pindl, 2015).

Confrontation with a potentially life-threatening illness can present challenges that are similar to the processual identity types of *diffuse* (and less critical) identity, as described in Marcia's (1980) identity model for adolescence. Depending on the stage of life, an illness can shake a formerly *achieved* identity, forcing those affected to re-explore their values and self-esteem in the context of the 'crisis' and, if necessary, reconstruct them. The crucial question that threatens the consistent ego experience across different situations, contexts and time (Erikson, 1994) is how the affected person perceives themselves in relation to their illness, its symptoms and prognosis compared to their previous healthy self.

A particularly significant challenge is achieving coherence between personal and social identity. According to sociological identity research (Ohlbrecht, 2006), there are four dimensions that may be significant for adolescents' development when affected by (chronic) illness: (1) transformation and change; (2) restoration and repair; (3) continuity and maintenance; and (4) loss and damage to identity. The author emphasizes that it is learned coping behavior and social resources, rather than the severity of the illness, that moderate these dimensions.

In their research on psychosocial coping with multiple sclerosis, Ziegeler and Friedrich (2002) describe how patients can experience the loss of physical integrity and limitations on self-determination when faced with a threatening and invasive illness. For patients with brain tumors, whose tumors invade the functional structures of the brain, whether benign or not, the challenge is also to develop a new sense of coherence. According to Antonovsky's (1997) salutogenesis model, this forms the basis for constructive coping and the continual regaining of healing and health, complementing the illness-based model of *pathogenesis*.

However, the way in which individuals cope with illness depends significantly on the stage of life they are at, their psychosocial identity development and their social opportunities for success (Ohlbrecht, 2006). Various theories on experiencing and dealing with illness share the protective construct of self-efficacy expectation (Lippke & Renneberg, 2006). Consequently, this chapter's study includes the phenomenon of *agency*, referring to an individual's ability to act (see Section 'The Interview – An Enlightening Story'), and its implications for subjective theories of illness and recovery.

In the case of life-threatening illnesses, individuals are confronted with their vulnerability and mortality. Depending on the prognosis, they may experience some or all of Kübler-Ross's (1977) five stages of dying: (1) *denial*, a refusal to accept the reality of the diagnosis; (2) *anger*, feelings of frustration or unfairness about their situation; (3) *bargaining*, attempts to negotiate for more time or a different outcome; (4) *depression*, a deep sense of sadness or despair in response to the impending loss; and (5) *acceptance*, an eventual coming to terms with the situation and finding peace with it.

For patients with diagnosed brain tumors, an additional burden may lie in the fact that proliferative tissue – even if benign – displaces functional areas of the brain. These areas are attributed as the center of our self (consciousness) and, more broadly, the foundation of our identity. This special case of brain tumor, involving an invasion of identity, likely places different demands on coping strategies than operatively treated benign prostate enlargement, for example.

UNDERSTANDING AN INDIVIDUAL COMPLEX CASE

As subjective theories of illness have been shown to be crucial for the integrative processing of disease, this chapter will examine subjective theories of recovery from tumor illnesses, investigating their protective and integrative significance. Specifically, it examines how a brain tumor survivor narrates his experience of illness and recovery, with a focus on his sense of agency during this period. To capture these aspects, a former brain tumor patient was interviewed using a narrative approach.

The case will be examined from a cultural-psychological perspective, considering the formation and management of personal theories of illness and recovery as a cultural act that fulfils a fundamental human desire for meaning and significance. Language is key to understanding this practice, as the individual structuring of the self and self-understanding occurs through (linguistic) interaction with the (social) environment. Therefore, the spoken word provides access to the analysis of specific attributions of meaning and linguistic patterns.

The positioning analysis method, as described by Lucius-Hoene and Deppermann (2002, 2004), was adapted and developed to meet the requirements of this study, with the aim of analyzing the linguistic utterances of the interviewee. The research process involves a *triple distillation* of meaning and relevance, achieved through targeted data collection, evaluation and analysis. The circular process of collection and analysis is detailed below in accordance with research ethics. To reduce individual bias and encourage diverse discussion of the results, this chapter underwent double peer review.

The Interviewee – Introducing Robert Millner[1]

A trained locksmith, Robert was in his late 60s and retired at the time of the interview. By then, he had lived with his wife on and off for about 15 years, most recently separated. He has two daughters, a granddaughter and a grandson. Two years prior to the interview, Robert underwent surgery for benign prostate enlargement, which was complication-free. Against the backdrop of his brother dying from a brain tumor at 50 and one of his two sisters dying from breast cancer at 65, Robert was diagnosed with a 'mandarin-sized' benign brain tumor (meningioma) a year before the interview. The tumor was completely removed through neurosurgery. Due to displaced prefrontal brain structures and the invasive nature of the procedure in the left frontal lobe, he experienced significant changes in emotional regulation, describing himself as 'thin-skinned, sensitive and not very resilient', and experiencing distress due to emotional incontinence. Due to the proximity of the tumor to the optic nerve, he now struggles with double vision and balance disorders. He also suffers from walking, standing and posture problems accompanied by painful movement limitations, as well as impaired concentration, thinking and memory, and orientation problems.

About eight years before his dramatic diagnosis, he began a yoga course at his sister's urging. Four years later, he visited a leading yoga teacher and physician for the first time, having been prompted by herniated discs, chronic back pain, restricted movement and psychological stress due to recurring conflicts with his wife. The same doctor oversaw his recovery after surgery with a yoga therapy program focusing on eye and vision exercises, movement therapy, breathing therapy, and relaxation techniques, as well as visualization and meditation.

By the time of the interview, all of the aforementioned symptoms had either largely or completely disappeared, and Robert claimed that he had regained his preillness functional level. He was invited to take part in this study specifically because of his remarkable recovery process. As an expert on his illness and recovery, particularly with regard to protective and preventive measures, as well as anchor points for supporting clinically ill patients therapeutically, Robert's personal experiences of illness and recovery, and the dynamics and sense of agency involved, are of interest.

The Interview – An Enlightening Story

The interview was conducted on a Friday afternoon during the first COVID-19 lockdown in Germany, following hygiene measures and distancing in the familiar practice room of the yoga-therapeutic doctor in Berlin. Through the 'pressures of narrating' (Schütze, 1983), the interviewee is prompted to intuitively mark those contents that are subjectively meaningful to him ('setting relevance'), while presenting them within a reasonable amount of narrative time ('condensation') and with sufficient and socially comprehensible 'detail'. The process assumes an intuitive need for 'closure of form', i.e., a logical framework that spans a comprehensible arc from beginning to end (Mey & Mruck, 2020). On the basis of these theoretical considerations, a hint at Robert's wish for structure through questions was taken up with concern.

Robert and the study's author met for the first time at the interview appointment. The session lasted about two hours, with the interview taking up about 90 minutes. Robert was very punctual, appeared curious and energetic, he seemed younger than expected. Despite a careful look, the surgical scar above his left forehead was not immediately noticeable, and there were no signs of frailty or limitations. Contrary to fears of a forced question-and-answer setting, the interview began with a relaxed conversation starter, followed by a prompt for a complete narration of Robert's life story. This led to a free flow of speech that required little encouragement. The atmosphere became very relaxed, and Robert's sometimes entertaining remarks repeatedly made both the interviewer and the interviewee laugh.

The interview was recorded with Robert's consent for later transcription using the Conversation Analytic Transcription System 2 (GAT-2) by Selting et al. (2009). Robert's breathing-related language, already noticeable during the interview and even more so in the transcription process, became a key guide for subsequent analysis and is described in the following section.

The Analysis – Encoding the Secret of Breathing

The Analysis arose organically from the material and its resonance. Through a cultural-psychological lens, the addressed phenomena naturally stood out from the interview content. The analysis was genuinely guided by traces of depth in terms of intense subjective meaning. Both linguistic and stylistic features, such as word repetitions, interruptions or pauses, played a role. In Robert's case, his noticeably breathing-related language was evident during the interview and especially in the transcription process, as displayed in Table 12.1. 'Laughter' is transcribed in over 100 places; only selected research-relevant references are documented. For all other markers, transcript positions relevant to the analyzed excerpts are highlighted in bold.

This material-inherent clues proved a valuable guide for analysis. If this inherent meaning is understood as central to answering the research questions, it opens up a special way for the material to explain itself. In this sense, a tailored methodology was developed to investigate the subjective representations of the phenomena of illness and recovery that were of interest. The fundamental understanding of the material is based on the positioning analysis proposed by Lucius-Hoene and Deppermann (2002, 2004), whose linguistic research framework conceives of the interview as an interaction between two participating communication partners (Deppermann, 2013) and builds on early developments of positioning theory in social psychology (Harré & van Langenhove, 1999; Hollway, 1984).

In an adaptation of positioning analysis, an inductive procedure informed by the research questions was used to examine and identify (I) how Robert assigns positionings related to illness and recovery in his narrative and (II) whether and how he develops capacities for experiencing agency in this process. The act of positioning refers to the discursive practice through

TABLE 12.1 References to Breath-Related Positionings of Illness and Recovery Within the Transcript.

Breath-Related Positionings of Illness	Breath-Related Positionings of Recovery
Out of breath *(Line 443)*	Giggling *(Lines 22, 29, **104**, 397, 471)*
Drawing in breath (tight/constricted) *(Lines 319, **326f**, 375, 379, 394, 498, 512, 534, 538, 546, 656, 666, 883, 927, 1036, 1086)*	Deep inhalation *(Lines 26, 246, 247, 251, 388, 418, 451, **566**, 663, 850, 851, 852, 949)*
Choked *(Lines **334**, 1114)*	Drawing in breath (freer/unobstructed) *(Lines **101**, 559, 575, 577, 658, 1036, 1170)*
Sighing, groaning *(Lines **129**, 139, 142, **326**, 379, 444, 482, 666)*	*Laughing* *(Lines 104, 380, 548, 561, 638, 966, 1116)*
Panting *(Lines 387, 447, 721)*	Sighing *(Lines 172, 420, 523, 633, 663)*
Content-related *(Lines 913f)*	Content-related *(Lines 193f, 247, 385f, 849f)*

which individuals present themselves and others as persons within linguistic interaction (Lucius-Hoene & Deppermann, 2004). This renders their narrative constructions methodologically accessible. In this study, the attribution of external positions does not refer to other people but specifically to the phenomena of illness and recovery as outlined at the beginning. The theoretical origins of this approach in linguistic identity research proved particularly suitable for investigating subjective theories of illness and recovery, as tumor- and therapy-induced identity crises appeared possible (see Section 'An Identity-Based Understanding of Illness and Recovery').

According to Cornelia Helfferich (2011), the concept of agency refers to cognitive representations of individual capacity for action and efficacy. In positioning analysis (Lucius-Hoene & Deppermann, 2002, 2004), it is further defined as the capacity to act autonomously (rather than heteronomously), opening up spaces between conforming and oppositional behavior in light of societal expectations and discourses. In a sociological model, agency, particularly within individual lifestyles, also functions as health-relevant behavior and, together with the social environment and individual psychological dispositions, moderates health- and illness-related opportunities and risks (Sperlich, 2016).

The inductive approach helps answer questions about the subjective meanings of experiences and associated processing by attempting to grasp and expand their complexity, in contrast to (quantitatively) flattening approaches. This resulted in the following six-stage analysis process:

1. Identifying all positionings related to research priorities (I) and (II)
2. Condensation guided by meaning regarding content overlaps and repetitions
3. Marking the categorical dyad of self (internal) and other (external) attributions to answer the question of who is in control
4. Analysis of nonverbal markers: breathing-associated markers as guide (*laughter, gasping for air, breathing, sighing, giggling, panting*)
5. Breath-supported selection of quotes
6. Analysis of implicit dynamics of the positionings of illness and recovery

In a permanently dynamic process with the material, findings were continually adjusted, expanded or discarded, so that the findings presented below emerged gradually and with dense reference to the material. The analysis was fundamentally guided by sincere interest in the participant's personal experience. Relevant excerpts are presented below to illustrate the individual significance of Robert's internal representations of his brain tumor and subsequent recovery process.

NOW, WHAT DO WE KNOW?

Engagement with the material revealed an inherent logic of positionings in self- and externally-attributed meanings, which are presented in the following chapters in tabular form. Both Robert's positioning activities and exemplary transcript excerpts provide clues to his construction of agency and its significance in the illness and recovery process.

Positioning the Illness

All relevant positionings were first summarized into 18 initial categories and then condensed into the nine presented in Table 12.2. For example, positionings of illness as a negative thought spiral, as affect- and pain-associated, and as limitation of motor functionality were combined under *limitation of physical and psychological functionality*. These, in turn, are causally linked to *opportunity for self-development*, as they provoke the loss of basic and identity-constructing abilities such as 'walking', 'cycling' and 'driving', which ultimately motivate Robert to empowered, stepwise, recovery-associated coping with this critical identity vacuum. In this

TABLE 12.2 Illness Positionings Differentiated by Self-Referenced and Other-Referenced Attributions.

Attributions in Reference to Self (Internally)	Attributions in Reference to Others (Externally)
Illness as...	Illness as...
Activeley modulatable *(Lines 22f, 88f, 100f, 118f, 244f, 449f, 470f, 522, 564, 609f, 747f, 876f, 1143, 1214f)*	Medical-technological dependency *(Lines 70f, 128, 346, 1214)*
Disturbance of sense of coherence and joy of life *(lines 54f, 138, 195f, 1110)*	not (entirely) controllable *(Lines 70f, 113f, 334, 509f, 739, 900f)*
Limitation of physical and psychological functionality *(lines 70f, 108, 124f, 179, 372, 479f, 511, 1112)*	Socially reactive *(Lines 133, 196, 321f, 692f, 1133 f, 1177f)*
Noticeable continuum *(Lines 70f, 139, 325)*	
Bogeyman of related cases/source of (death) anxiety *(Lines 329, 350f, 439, 498, 509, 855, 891)*	
Opportunity for self-development *(Lines 683, 966)*	

destabilization lies potential for agency, which Robert repeatedly addresses by positioning illness as *actively modulatable*. More internally attributed than externally attributed positionings are evident, the latter including *disruption of coherence and joy of life*, which at least contains reactive potential for seizing agency.

In externally-attributed positioning of illness as *not (entirely) controllable*, it becomes clear that there is an uncontrollable component, pointing to a fate-attributed aspect of the 'unpredictable', 'unforeseeable' and 'merciless' disease, as well as the associated loss of control. Closely related is a feeling of *medical-technical dependence*, which, given limited personal expertise about the tumor, requires an ability to 'trust' therapeutic expertise, while Robert initially feels at the mercy of recurrent symptoms due to a purely symptomatic therapy concept. These 'limits of conventional medicine', exemplified in transcript excerpt (1), are lamented by Robert with a sigh as a recurring *limitation of his psychological functionality*.

Excerpt (1): 'Limits of Conventional Medicine' (lines 124f).

```
01  I was in SUCH bad shape (.) that like (-) for da:ys NOTHING
02  (-) wo:rked anymore (--) nothing worked anymore (--) of
    co:urse I we:nt
03  to ne:urologists and eve:rywhere (.) (I) went to
    orthopedists (.) a:nd
04  no one could (.) thE ne:urologist could ta:ke the pa:in
05  away a bit (--) ye:s (.) [sighing] he gave me inje:ctions
06  (.) then a C:T (.) and oh [...] u:h (.) ye:s (.) he also
07  he:lped me a LO:t (.) I must say (-) bu:t it
08  came back regularly (.)
```

The positioning of illness as *socially reactive* includes both illness-related social discomfort about the (in)visibility of the disease and its consequences, as well as newly acquired access to social closeness and support. Complementing this, however, is a category that includes a chronically destructive conflict in Robert's marriage, positioned as causative for the illness.

The narrative also reveals uncertainty about a dualistic or continuous understanding of illness and recovery. While Robert repeatedly describes the *physiological* symptoms of the tumor, he, for example, discusses his experience of (death) anxiety based on *family projection* mainly elsewhere. This medically dichotomous view of the two concepts was color coded in the author's analysis memo. In contrast to this dichotomous view, Robert's explicitly healing-oriented, holistic, and dynamically continuous understanding of the two concepts is – with implications for diagnosis and therapy (see paragraph 'Positioning the Recovery') – possibly reflected implicitly in his balanced narrative of illness and recovery.

Exemplary excerpt (2): 'The Genetic Template' (lines 326f).

01 it a:lso happens [sighs] (.) th:at (.) [inhales] my
02 br:other (-) ha:d a si:milar thing (.) which he did not
03 survive (--) […] (.) ye:s (.) so I CO:uld a:lso not
04 so:me- I couldn't- desp- WIth yo:g:a a:nd no:thing
05 (.) I (.) th- that MO:vie you can somehow
06 (-) switch off with it (.) flip the switch (.) for a short
07 ti:me (.) bu:t sti:ll (.) a:lways a:gain the
08 tho:ught was there (.) […] (--) a:nd [choked voice]
no:w YOU
09 a:re ne:xt (-)

This excerpt 2 belongs to the *bogeyman* category, capturing the existential fear experienced by Robert – a fear fueled by witnessing the fatal course of his brother's brain tumor and turning it into a vivid template for a genetic attribution. His increasingly breathless account makes the confrontation with his own mortality, and the accompanying loss of agency, directly palpable.

Positioning the Recovery

In this analysis process as well, 18 initial categories first emerged, which were then consolidated into the 12 categories presented in Table 12.3. In this case, for example, positionings of healing as life joy, passion, hope, dreams, and visions – partly induced by (medical) supportive others (lines 27, 615, 699, 963, 1007, 1036, 1115) – were incorporated into the positioning of healing as a vibrant and potentially contagious *healthy spirit* (lines 883, 1036). As with the illness positionings, the positionings of healing likewise show a stronger prevalence of self-attributed ascriptions.

A striking contradiction is constructed between positions of recovery as an externally-attributed *miracle* and Robert's self-attributed understanding of recovery as *actively modulatable*.

Excerpt (3): 'The Self-Made Miracle' (lines 561f).

01 a:nd th:ere I of co:urse sa:w the misalignment (--) a:nd
02 the:N I (.) rea:lly di:d those e:xercises rEE:gulaarly
03 (-) but not no:w (.) th:At HAS to ge:T be:TTer
04 (-) but ra:ther re:ally i:N co:ACtion again (.) with all
05 the o:ther yO:gA e:xercises (---) [breathes in deeply]
(-) A:ND su:ddenLY
06 (.) it was li:ke a MI:racle (--) oHH (.) th:e MISali:gnment
07 is no lo:nger so- is (.) is no longer je:rky (--) unti:l
08 the images a:re on top of each other (.)

TABLE 12.3 Recovery Positionings Differentiated by Self-Referenced and Other-Referenced Attributions.

Attributions in Reference to Self (Internally)	Attributions in Reference to Others (Externally)
Recovery as...	Recovery as...
Actively modulatable *(Complementary to illness-positionings, See Table 12.2)*	Social and professional support *(Lines 16f, 166f, 364f, 398f, 547, 577, 632f, 1132f)*
Feeling of being loved and needed *(Lines 25f, 34f, 906, 956f)*	Miracle *(Lines 34, 401f, 428f, 564f, 870f)*
Healthy spirit *(Lines 27, 615, 699, 883, 963, 1007, 1036, 1115)*	Physiologically measurable and attestable *(Lines 75f, 97f, 400f, 423f, 750f)*
Tangible sense of coherence *(Lines 58, 62., 167f, 177, 180f, 196, 250f, 683, 1171f, 1220f)*	Object of a competition for competence *(Lines 110, 155, 337, 345, 498)*
Tangible functionality and quality of life *(Lines 103f, 178f, 183f, 524f, 629f, 637f, 966,* 1114f, 1220f)	not: symptom treatment/symptom suppression *(Lines 126f, 1213f)*
Individual overcoming *(Lines 155, 196, 345, 398f, 1164f, 1200)*	
Complex/holistic body–mind dyad *(Lines 194f, 523f, 558f, 1108f)*	

In excerpt (3), these complementary healing-positionings are linked 'in one breath,' and the passage exemplifies his internal mediating discourse about whether healing is a matter of autonomous choice or of miraculous intervention. Robert describes his patient and regular practice of the yoga-therapeutically prescribed exercises used to treat his postoperative visual disturbance. His deep inhalation then marks the transition to his portrayal of the successive yet distinct healing progress of his double vision, which he positions as miraculous. In relation to yoga, he describes here a core element of his self-attributed understanding of a healing process that is *actively modulatable.*

Robert associates further components of modulatability with 'nutrition' (e.g., lines 150, 853, 877, 1143), 'nature' in the form of forest and lake (e.g., lines 518, 851, 862), 'dynamic movement' (line 595), 'breathing' (e.g., lines 385, 849, 387), 'community' (e.g., lines 26, 265, 965), and repeatedly and explicitly with 'his yoga' (e.g., lines 101, 436f, 469, 1103). At one point, he reflects that 'the entire way of life is yoga' (line 150). Robert's positionings of 'his yoga' can thus be abstracted as actively modulatable insofar as he has found his personal method for shaping healing in an active way.

In this sense, yoga appears to function as a particular kind of tool for a healing (self-)experience of agency and its positive effects, perceived as a positive *sense of coherence.* This experience is further reinforced by the other-attributed positioning of healing as *physiologically measurable and attestable,* specifically in relation to the yoga-associated curative effects that were, for instance, recognized by clinical professionals (see Excerpt 4).

Excerpt (4): 'Curtain Up' (lines 97f).

```
01  fi:rst of a:ll a:gain he:re THI:s OXY:gen sa:turation
02  OR wha:tever that wa:s (.) a:nd they ha:d a RE:AL (.)
03  I sa:y a co:mPUt:er the:n (.) li:ke a move: (.) yeah
04  li:ke a mo:va:ble de:VICE [...] (-) [inhales] (-) a:nd
05  yea:h (.) she the:n (.) she (.) WHA' di:d YA GO and DO,
    then? (.)
06  she sa:id (.) I di:d (.) mY yo:gA
07  [giggles] (-) ye:ah (.) OH! I a:m sa:tisFIED wi:th yo:ur
08  va:lues, she the:n sAID (.)
```

The excerpt refers to a passage in the first section of the interview, in which Robert recounts an experience during a hospital stay. He describes how, during morning rounds, his oxygen levels were initially low, and he asked for the measurement to be repeated later. He becomes visibly excited and almost childishly delighted – slipping even into dialect – when the nurse, in disbelief, asks him about the cause of the marked improvement in his values.

Building on this experience as well, the other-attributed positioning of healing as the *object of a methodological competition for competence* between (alternative) medical approaches emerges as an expression of the wish to integrate these approaches within the curative field. In this regard, Robert repeatedly emphasized the other-attributed aspect of *social and professional support.* He stressed, above all, that the development of personal trust in treating authorities depends on their ability to listen to his questions, worries, and fears concerning the brain tumor, as well as on their competence in explaining complex medical matters in a comprehensible and accessible manner on the basis of a stable therapeutic relationship. These very qualities characterize the approach of supportive therapy (see Flath, 2017), which is why this finding can be understood as an instance of *appellative agency* – a call addressed to all members of the interdisciplinary treatment team to enact such forms of relational and communicative competence.

Key Findings

Analysis of Robert's positionings of illness and recovery, set clearly in a biopsychosocial context, provides implications for the theory development arising from this research.

Based on the core concept of subjective theory of illness (Petrie & Weinman, 1997), Robert's individual experiences and coping with the brain tumor and its consequences can be categorized as follows: During the progression of the tumor and following its surgical removal, Robert faced various psychological and physiological deficits. With regard to information from various doctors, he repeatedly emphasized the 'good experiences' with which he 'was lucky'. Regarding his previous urological surgery, he could draw on biographical experience of surgery and recovery, although the different locations of tissue changes, especially the brain as the seat of identity and self-concept, meant a new quality of burden and threat. Whether Robert drew on media information is unknown. What is certain is that, regarding his sister (who died of breast cancer) and especially his brother (who did not survive the same type of brain tumor he had), he had family models for identification and re-enactment that reinforced his existential fears. Robert's assumptions and expectations are accordingly aligned with the expected symptoms of his brain tumor, its prognosis, and short- and long-term consequences. Preoperatively, his hopes for treatability and curability were limited, given his brother's fatal course, while postoperatively, he flexibly positioned the tumor and its consequences as not (entirely) controllable. While the overarching coping strategy, the attribution of healing, and the postoperative construction of meaning are rooted in Robert's extensively described yoga practice and the sustainably improved health behavior derived from it, the sequence analysis of his causal attributions presents an unambiguous episode entitled *My unbearable wife gave me a brain tumor* (lines 294–326), which centers on his marriage, described as highly destructive and marked by intense conflict.

Although attempts to cope with this conflict also appear in the narrative, only the coping strategies initially proposed in connection with life-threatening illnesses (Flath, 2017) shall be briefly discussed at this point. While denial of the threat cannot be inferred from the underlying material, elements of distraction are evident in his intensive involvement with his grandchildren, and optimistic tendencies appear in his vivid understanding of healing as a 'healthy spirit'. His search for information is reflected in his exploration of suitable healing methods in nutrition, movement, breathing techniques in choral singing, and communal activities – elements that Robert ultimately finds and integrates for himself within yoga. Finally, he is certainly also supported by his Christian faith, which he sees symbolized in a hymnbook belonging to his 'mum', suggesting a form of spiritual triangulation involving mother, (holy) father, and yoga.

Regarding gender-related theoretical backgrounds to illness and recovery, only the (higher) risk of life-threatening illness is reflected in Robert (Kolip & Hurrelmann, 2016; Sieverding, 2010). Pronounced risk behavior, lack of social network (Gamper et al., 2020), or aversion to doctors (Kolip & Hurrelmann, 2016) are explicitly not observed in Robert's narrative.

Thus, his case cautiously supports Kuhlmann's (2016) critical perspective on strongly gendered inequalities in illness and recovery.

In adaptation of Marcia's identity model (1980), Robert positions his illness-related identity crisis in a self-esteem-protective way as an opportunity for personal growth. From an *identity diffusion* triggered by postoperative deficits, he develops – through a forced and resolutely undertaken *moratorium*, characterized by the ambitious, yoga-therapeutically supported coping process and the regaining of those bodily functions that were essential to his sense of identity but lost due to the surgery, especially 'cycling and driving' – toward an *achieved identity*.

In the sense of Ohlbrecht's (2006) identity-related challenges, this encompasses all four dimensions: (1) a transformation and shift toward a new and holistic health consciousness; (2) a restoration and repair with regard to the bodily functions he has worked to regain; (3) continuity and preservation in terms of his ongoing transgenerational sense of responsibility and obligation toward his 'little rays of sunshine' – his grandchildren; and (4) the loss or impairment of his self-understanding as a 'resilient man'. Taken together, this constructive integrative achievement points to a repertoire of adaptive coping behaviors as well as to stable social resources.

With regard to *agency*-associated self-efficacy expectations, which correlate positively with various health models and theories (Lippke & Renneberg, 2006), these can be demonstrated in particular in the empowering positionings related to *modulatability* and the ability to exert influence on both illness and healing (see paragraphs 'Positioning the Illness' and 'Positioning the Recovery'). Especially in the predominantly self-attributed positionings within the illness and healing process, one finds concrete or potential opportunities for protective experiences of agency. In this context, Robert possesses – with 'his yoga' in particular – a method for addressing actionable controllability, whose direct positive and healing effects can be perceived and attested to both by himself and by competent others.

Despite Robert's concrete engagement with his impending death, the stages of dying described by Kübler-Ross (1977) cannot be clearly assigned within the narrative. In stark contrast, however, stands Robert's distinctly breath-accentuated language, which runs through the entire interview like a symbolic elixir of life.

DISCUSSION

'I personally am still really into breathing' (lines 384f): Robert's guiding breath – or poetically, 'breath of life' – as an expression of pure vitality symbolizes his determined and integrative process of coping with the illness. He underscores his lively, alert demeanor with forward-looking fantasies and visions, while also expressing his existential fears, worries, anger and sadness in light of his own diagnosis and the loss of his brother to the illness he survived. In his inner engagement, palpable, visible and traceable in the meanings he constructs, vitality prevails. The breath, as a voluntary link to our autonomic nervous system, holds great potential: We can, on the one hand, (voluntarily) stimulate the sympathetic nervous system through simulated hyperventilation, and, on the other, by means of meditative abdominal breathing with the parasympathetic nervous system, consciously activate the state in which supportive 'self-healing' is possible (Schmid, 2011).

Similarly, breathing (*pranayama*) is a central concept in yoga practice, which Robert often references in his narrative. His positioning activities led to the hypothesis that Robert, above all, experienced agency and self-efficacy in his recovery process through the application of yoga as a method, attributing his practice to the 'miraculous' progress of his recovery. It offers a way to deal with the threatening, not always influenceable component of illness and recovery. By employing the tool that encompasses almost all the means of modulation Robert has identified for himself, his sense of individual influence – agency – is strengthened, while yoga as a method can indeed effect psychological and physical stabilization. Yoga, for Robert, has emerged as a holistic method, in contrast to the federal understanding of health.

To clarify this finding, further research on the health behavior of cured brain tumor patients is planned, using the methodological approach of informative contrast cases to shed more light on the significance of the yoga aspect.

The background of positionings, agency, and a holistic cultural-psychological understanding of a societal phenomenon as manifested within the individual proved particularly appropriate for the clinical context in this study. This is because it addresses a frequently – also in Robert's case – articulated deficit in the medical-clinical care of ill individuals. Viewing the patient's subjective experience opens possibilities for accompanying their healing process in a holistic manner and for becoming more finely attuned and responsive to individual risks, worries, and fears. In the principles of supportive therapy (Flath, 2017), which Robert attributes as concretely conducive to healing, an appellative assignment of agency to all members of the interdisciplinary treatment team is constructed. In order to further investigate and improve the management of life-threatening illnesses in the best interests of those affected, interdisciplinary collaboration between (clinical) therapeutic and therapy-scientific professions is indispensable.

Until then, in Robert's words, 'laughter is the best medicine'. For laughter is breath, and as long as we breathe, we live.

NOTE

1. The name is a pseudonym used to ensure anonymity.

REFERENCES

Antonovsky, A. (1997). *Salutogenese. Zur Entmystifizierung der Gesundheit* [*Salutogenesis: Toward a demystification of health*]. Deutsche Gesellschaft für Verhaltenstherapie.

Deppermann, A. (2013). Interview als text vs. interview als interaktion [Interview as text vs. interview as interaction]. *Forum Qualitative Sozialforschung, 14*(3), 13. Article. https://ids-pub.bsz-bw.de/frontdoor/deliver/index/docId/1398/file/Deppermann_Interview_als_Text_2013.pdf

Deutsches Krebsforschungszentrum. (2017). *Psychische Faktoren als Ursache für Krebs. Was hält die Bevölkerung von dieser Theorie?* [*Psychological factors as a cause of cancer: What does the public think of this theory?*]. https://www.dkfz.de/de/presse/pressemitteilungen/2017/dkfz-pm-17-43-Psychische-Faktoren-als-Ursache-fuer-Krebs.php

Dudenredaktion. (n.d.a). *Gesundheit*. Duden. https://www.duden.de/rechtschreibung/Gesundheit

Dudenredaktion. (n.d.b). *Krankheit*. Duden. https://www.duden.de/rechtschreibung/Gesundheit

Erikson, E. H. (1994). *Identity and the life cycle*. W. W. Norton & Company.

Faller, H. H. J. (1990). *Subjektive Krankheitstheorie und Krankheitsverarbeitung bei Herzinfarktrehabilitanden* [*Subjective illness theory and coping with illness among heart-attack rehabilitation patients*]. Dissertation. Europäische Hochschule.

Flath, B. (2017). Psychoonkologie und psychiatrische Störungen bei Krebskranken [Psycho-oncology and psychiatric disorders in cancer patients] In K. Possinger, A. C. Regierer, & J. Eucker (Eds.), *Facharztwissen Hämatologie Onkologie*. Fischer.

Folkman, S., & Lazarus, R. S. (1984). *Stress, appraisal, and coping*. Springer.

Förster, C. (2003). *Subjektive Krankheitstheorien von Tumorpatienten* [*Subjective illness theories of tumor patients*]. Dissertation. Freie Universität Berlin.

Gamper, M., Seidel, J., Kupfer, A., Keim-Klärner, S., & Klärner, A. (2020). Geschlecht und gesundheitliche Ungleichheiten – Soziale Netzwerke im Kontext von Gesundheit und Gesundheitsverhalten [Gender and health inequalities – Social networks in the context of health and health behavior]. In *Soziale Netzwerke und gesundheitliche Ungleichheiten* (pp. 273–307). Springer.

Harré, R., & van Langenhove, L. (1999). Positioning theory. In N. Bozatzis & T. Dragonas (Eds.), *The discursive turn in social psychology* (pp. 129–136). Taos Institute Publications.

Helfferich, C. (2011). *Die Qualität qualitativer Daten* [*The quality of qualitative data*]. Springer VS.

Hollway, W. (1984). Gender difference and the production of subjectivity. In J. Henriques, W. Hollway, C. Urwin, C. Venn, & V. Walkerdine (Eds.), *Changing the subject* (pp. 227–263). Methuen.

Kolip, P., & Hurrelmann, K. (2016). Geschlecht und Gesundheit: Eine Einführung [Gender and health: An introduction]. In *Handbuch Geschlecht und Gesundheit* (pp. 8–18). Hogrefe.

Kübler-Ross, E. (1977). *Interviews mit Sterbenden* [*Interviews with the dying*]. Herder.

Kuhlmann, E. (2016). Gendersensible Perspektiven auf Gesundheit und Gesundheitsversorgung [Gender-sensitive perspectives on health and health care]. In *Soziologie von Gesundheit und Krankheit* (pp. 183–196). Springer VS.

Lippke, S., & Renneberg, B. (2006). Theorien und Modelle des Gesundheitsverhaltens [Theories and models of health behavior]. In B. Renneberg & P. Hammelstein (Eds.), *Gesundheitspsychologie* (pp. 35–60). Springer.

Louis, D. N., Perry, A., Reifenberger, G., von Deimling, A., Figarella-Branger, D., Cavenee, W. K., Ohgaki, H., Wiestler, O. D., Kleihues, P., & Ellison, D. W. (2016). The 2016 World Health Organization classification of tumors of the central nervous system: A summary. *Acta Neuropathologica, 131*(6), 803–820.

Lucius-Hoene, G., & Deppermann, A. (2002). *Rekonstruktion narrativer Identität: Ein Arbeitsbuch zur Analyse narrativer Interviews* [*Reconstruction of narrative identity: A workbook for analyzing narrative interviews*]. Springer.

Lucius-Hoene, G., & Deppermann, A. (2004). Narrative Identität und Positionierung [Narrative identity and positioning]. *Gesprächsforschung, 5*(1), 166–183.

Marcia, J. E. (1980). Identity in adolescence. In J. Adelson (Ed.), *Handbook of adolescent psychology* (pp. 159–187). Wiley & Sons.

Mehnert, A., Vehling, S., Scheffold, K., Ladehoff, N., Schön, G., Wegscheider, K., Heckl, U., Weis, J., & Koch, U. (2013). Prävalenz von Anpassungsstörung, akuter und posttraumatischer Belastungsstörung sowie somatoformen Störungen bei Krebspatienten [Prevalence of adjustment disorder, acute and posttraumatic stress disorder, and somatoform disorders in cancer patients]. *Psychotherapie – Psychosomatik – Medizinische Psychologie, 63*(12), 466–472.

Mey, G., & Mruck, K. (2020). Qualitative interviews [Qualitative interviews]. In *Handbuch Qualitative Forschung in der Psychologie* (pp. 315–335). Springer.

Ohlbrecht, H. (2006). *Jugend, Identität und chronische Krankheit: Soziologische Fallrekonstruktionen* [*Youth, identity, and chronic illness: Sociological case reconstructions*]. Barbara Budrich.

Petrie, K. J., & Weinman, J. (1997). *Perceptions of health and illness: Current research and applications.* Harwood Academic Publishers.

Pindl, M. (2015). Krebspatienten und ihre Suche nach Identität [Cancer patients and their search for identity]. *URO News, 19*(3), 38–43.

Robert Koch Institut. (2019). *Neue Zahlen zu Krebs in Deutschland* [*New figures on cancer in Germany*]. https://edoc.rki.de/bitstream/handle/176904/6452/PM%20Krebs%20in%20Deutschland.pdf

Robert Koch Institut, & Gesellschaft der epidemiologischen Krebsregister in Deutschland e. V. (2023). *Krebs in Deutschland für 2019/2020* [*Cancer in Germany 2019/2020*]. https://edoc.rki.de/bitstream/handle/176904/11438/krebs_in_deutschland_2023-1.pdf

Rose, L. (2015). Geschlecht als soziale Unterscheidungskategorie in unserer Lebenswelt [Gender as a social category in our lifeworld]. In *Vielfalt und Differenz in der sozialen Arbeit* (pp. 63–73). Kohlhammer.

Schmid, G. B. (2011). *Selbstheilung durch Vorstellungskraft* [*Self-healing through imagination*]. Springer.

Schütze, F. (1983). Biographieforschung und narratives Interview [Biographical research and the narrative interview]. *Neue Praxis, 13*(3), 283–293.

Selting, M., Auer, P., Barth-Weingarten, D., Bergmann, J. R., Bergmann, P., Birkner, K., Couper-Kuhlen, E., Deppermann, A., Gilles, P., Günthner, S., Hartung, M., Kern, F., Mertzlufft, C., Meyer, C., Morek, M., Oberzaucher, F., Peters, J., Quasthoff, U., Schütte, W., Stukenbrock, A., & Uhmann, S. (2009).

Gesprächsanalytisches Transkriptionssystem 2 (GAT 2) [Conversation-analytic transcription system 2 (GAT2)]. *Gesprächsforschung, 10,* 353–402.

Sieverding, M. (2010). Gesundheitspsychologie [Health psychology]. In G. Steins (Ed.), *Handbuch Psychologie und Geschlechterforschung* (pp. 189–201). Springer VS.

Sperlich, S. (2016). Handlungsorientierte Perspektiven auf Gesundheit und Krankheit [Action-oriented perspectives on health and illness]. In *Soziologie von Gesundheit und Krankheit* (pp. 41–54). Springer VS.

von Uexküll, T., & Wesiack, W. (1986). Wissenschaftstheorie und Psychosomatische Medizin: Ein bio-psycho-soziales Modell [Theory of science and psychosomatic medicine: A bio-psycho-social model]. *Psychosomatische Medizin, 3,* 1–30.

Ziegeler, G., & Friedrich, H. (2002). *Multiple Sklerose – das einzig Sichere an ihr ist ihre Unzuverlässigkeit! [Multiple sclerosis – the only certain thing about it is its unreliability!] Eine Langzeitstudie über Formen der psychosozialen Bewältigung einer chronischen Krankheit* [*A long-term study on forms of psychosocial coping with chronic illness*]. VAS.

CHAPTER 13

LIMINAL BODIES IN PAIN: A CASE STUDY ON AN INDIVIDUAL'S EXPERIENCE WITH CHRONIC PAIN

Jovanna Ulmschneider
Clinical Pschologist, Germany

ABSTRACT

Liminal bodies in pain are transforming, moving bodies. This paper aims to adopt a critical, phenomenological perspective in order to explore ambivalences and movements around chronic pain experience in relation to discourse, to practitioners, researchers and relatives. The hypothesis shall be, that chronic pain is a liminal phenomenon. But how is this liminality experienced, approached and averted? Chronic pain experience appears to be negotiating change processes that concern around the question how to (re-) act, hot to move – always and inevitably in relation.

Keywords: Chronic pain experience; liminality theory; critical phenomenology; biopolitics; meaning making in chronic pain experience; the betwixt and between of bodies in chronic pain

Cultural Psychology in Clinical Research and Practices, pages 263–289

Published under exclusive licence by Emerald Publishing Limited
doi:10.1108/978-1-83742-213-520261013

INTRODUCTION

(…) 'pain will remain unseen due to its nature'. (Ojala, 2015, p. 69)

One of five persons experiences some sort of chronic pain (Breivik et al., 2006; Gatchel et al., 2007). Chronic Pain has many different facets, forms, masks and unmasked experiences. In discourse chronic pain is getting circumscribed as 'silent epidemic' (Sessle, 2012); a description which points to its ungraspable nature: its manner to resist the attempts to measure it, to make it visible, to detect, name and heal the wound that seems inevitably and questionably associated with its expression. And while seemingly 'imperfect bodies' rebelliously challenge familiar body-mind dualisms (Jackson, 2005), scratch at 'functioning' boundaries of medical, social and psychological working systems, what remains, is a person experiencing chronic pain while others witness it – or not.

In this study I want to consider myself as a witness of a relative's pain. Within the framework of qualitative, critical and phenomenological research, I want to approach the phenomenon and experience of chronic pain. Therefore, I will elaborate current definitions and perspectives on chronic pain. Furthermore, I will emphasize the *betwixt and between* (Turner, 1977) of bodies in (chronic) pain. I will outline current studies on this ambiguous experience, resulting assumptions, conclusions, inspirations and questions. Subsequently I will argue for an approach that puts the perspective of the person experiencing pain in relation to the discourse in the foreground of this research. Ultimately the focus shall be this case study: I will outline the analysis' insights: the meaning-making as well as movements and (trans)formations that surround this experience of chronic pain, the psychosocial, cultural, political around and especially relational negotiations within this interview. I want to close with ideas and hints for further research and multidisciplinary practice, examining the role of qualitative researchers as well as my specific role as a witness: Someone who approaches a close person's pain while still, it remains hers. 'Such an impossible hearing is only possible if we respond to a pain that we cannot claim as our own' (Ahmed, 2014, p. 35).

PERSPECTIVES ON, UPON AND AROUND (CHRONIC) PAIN

The International Association for the Study of Pain (IASP) argues that pain is an 'unpleasant sensory and emotional experience associated with, or resembling that associated with, actual or potential tissue damage' (IASP, 2020) and completes their previous definition with an emphasis on subjectivity. Pain is mostly connotated with negative meaning. In Christianity pain appears as punishment being described from the 'outside'

(Padfield, 2003, p. 8). Damage, disabilities, discomfort and distress are associated with and bound to the phenomenon. Pain seems to point to an injury, a trauma, a wound with its own history. We endure pain, passively. We experience pain, actively. As a subjective experience it appears as an essential and protective feature of the body. Out of the negative it paves the way towards relative action, towards self-defence and transformation of existing relationships, towards acceptance as well as its overcoming. Therefore, pain seems to be about survival, living, about tracing and experiencing borderland. Pain in the IASP's description appears as a subjective, emotional experience which is torn and built by various, multidimensional and interacting social, psychological, cultural and biological factors. So, pain is nothing private. But still, the unsharability of pain sensation and experience makes it so difficult to talk and act around it. While there is pain that appears as a congruent re-action towards an 'impression', chronic pain and its consistency leave us with a 'lack of physical evidence for pain' (Ojala, 2015, p. 21), with its 'invisibility' (Jackson, 2005) and uncertainty within its both silent and screaming persistency.

Susan Wendell's *The Rejected Body: Feminist Philosophical Reflections on Disability* (1997) takes a feminist perspective in which she argues the extent to which modern, Western scientific discourse produces body experiences. The question she asks, is whether and how chronic pain patient's coping is being helped by existing pain theories – or not. In her exploration of diseased body experiences, she explicitly turns towards bodies, while resisting control mechanisms and framing a concept of a discursive body. Which debates and *standpoints* (Harding, 1983) can we find in the recent discourse about (chronic) pain? Which cultural norms and their transgressions are tangled with (chronic) pain theories? It's about the way we talk about and silence with pain. In the following section I want to outline paradigms and perspectives with their body theories as models and pictures, that try to grasp the indefinite contingency of bodily experience. How do we[1] think about chronic pain in discourse?

Medical Perspectives

The majority of pain studies are drawn upon the medical perspective (Gatchel et al., 2007; Ojala, 2015; Steinhaug, 2007). In this perspective the roots refer to natural science. The diagnosis seems to be in the focus: questionnaires and anamneses detect symptoms, measure and classify them on their way towards healing. Pain appears as a trace of a search towards an underlaying tissue damage and cause that provides explanations. In its chronicity it transforms from a symptom itself to a disease: 'the chronicity of pain is the effect of changes in pain processing through transcription and transduction processes. Consequently, chronic pain is no longer simply a symptom but becomes itself a disease' (Trachsel & Cascella, 2020, paragraph 2). In the medical diagnosis chronic pain often appears as an abnormal system, a dysfunctional process in the light of an absent (tissue) damage.

Platon's *Intensity Theory* focusses on the intensity of sensations and stimulations. In the centre of this pain understanding there is a stimulus that is 'intense and lasting' (Trachsel & Cascella, 2020, paragraph 4) and a threshold that needs to get crossed to process pain experience. It's a perspective guided by the outside.

Dualistic Theories like Descartes' *Cartesian Dualistic Theory* are all about dualism: the physical and the psychological are strongly divided. The theory lacks explanations as to why there is an inter and intrapersonal incongruence between injury, damage and pain experience (e.g. in sense of intensity and timing) (Ojala, 2015; Trachsel & Cascella, 2020).

The *Gate Control Theory* presented a first theory where the dualism between body and the mind was shaken up by a perspective that acknowledged the influence and complex interactions between psychological and physical factors, between the multidimensionality of the cognitive, the emotional and the physical and therefore had a great influence in pain theory and research (Trachsel & Cascella, 2020). Ronald Melzcack's and Patrick Wall's theory opens up the relationship with the voice and acknowledgment of the patient: patients articulations and the individuality of their experiences were getting integrated in questionnaires (Scarry, 1985). Melzcack extended his theory towards a *Neuromatrix Model* and the Neurology of pain that puts the central nervous system and memory formations in focus (Melzack, 2001). Ojala (2015) states, that the present pain research concentrates on the brain (p. 19). Neuroimaging opens up new perspective on pain processing and appears to be opening up insight into the *black box* between input and sensory output. 'A major limitation in our ability to relieve the suffering of patients with chronic pain is an insufficient understanding of the role of meaning' (Fields, 2007, p. 36). Fields (2007) explores neural representations and projections and argues for a perspective that looks at pain being generated in the brain, obviously emphasizing that in this view the mental and the physical can be thought of together as if 'it becomes obvious that all pain is mental' (p. 43). While there is hope towards a shift that emphasizes a dysfunctional nervous system instead of a dysfunctional person (Jackson, 2005, p. 346), critiques get loud that the experience of pain is not getting visualized nor explained through brain imagining (Derbyshire, 2011; Ojala, 2015). With the *Biopsychosocial Model* appearing in the pain discourse, sociological factors get added into the equation. A lot of voices claim and aim for approaches that consider the *Biopsychosocial Model* as a promising philosophy that is able to path the way towards a more multidimensional and interdisciplinary understanding of individual chronic pain experience (Gatchel et al., 2007; IASP, 2020; Trachsel & Cascella, 2020). Ojala (2015) adds:

> It is incongruous that 60 years after Bonica's recommendations of multidisciplinary treatment of chronic pain and 40 years after Engel's publication of the Biopsychosocial Model, the Cartesian legacy still dominates in the treatment of chronic pain, which is seen as a symptom of an underlying disease and not as an experience. (p. 68)

At the same time Ojala (2015) formulates the blind spot of the biopsychosocial theory naming the lack of understanding the individual experience and the meaning making within the experience (p. 22).

Phenomenological Perspectives

Drawing upon the critique that the individual experience, the negotiations and meaning making in the experience of chronic pain is hardly considered in research and practice around chronic pain patients, phenomenological perspectives enter the discourse with a plea for holistic and subjective approaches that learn to include the actual embodied experience rather than focusing on effects and causes. Morris (1991) and many other voices enrich the debate with the state that there is a difference between *sensation* and *experience* of pain. A sensation, cut off from perceiving, means cutting off human interpretation, creativity and subjectivity. To accept a definition that includes the subjectivity of pain means to involve the actual experience of pain, the attribution of meaning and the complex interactions between 'aversive feelings' that interplay (Ahmed, 2014) in a multitude of relationships. A phenomenological perspective includes the historicity, the disproportionality, ambiguity, systemic and dynamic nature of pain. Instead of focusing on the aetiology and causality there are new questions being raised: 'what *does* pain do'? (Ahmed, 2014, p. 27); 'What does the pain mean to the person experiencing it?' (Ojala, 2015, p. 47).

As Lee and Tracey (2010) suggest: the search for evidence of pain sensation and experience needs to be based around the sufferer's report. It is the acknowledgment of the subjective experience, the relationship towards that experience and towards what is experienced in a certain context, that seem to enable a pathway that accepts the dynamic, invisible and immeasurable nature of pain. Also D. Morris (1991) is concerned about the meaning people make out of pain and discloses the gap between dualistic concretizations and constructions of pain narratives: 'Between these two different events we seem to imagine a gulf so wide and deep that it might as well be filled by a sea that is impossible to navigate' (Morris, 1991, p. 9). In his book he problematizes a culture in which chronic pain is being seen as a symptom, bound by an *either or* perspective. He seems to claim for a *both and* perspective and for the acknowledgement of a body – mind – culture interaction, that learn to integrate 'family, class, gender, ethnicity, time and place' (Graham, 1992) into pain literature and medicine.

In this perspective pain appears as an individual life experience; within and interaction with culture, society, economics, historic and political contexts. Drawing upon e.g. Franz Brentano, Jean-Paul Sartre and Maurice Merleau-Ponty, Phenomenology opens up a lens that holds up intersubjectivity, fluctuate intentionality and relations between person and world. Merleau-Ponty's (1962) *lived body* outlines the importance of the embodied experience. The *lived body* appears as a concept that transcendences the dualism between the physical and the mental through a focus on interactions that result in lived experience instead of an objectified body. The *lived body* seems to get noisy when there is pain. A point of view which reminds of Drew Leder's *The Absent Body*. Leder rocks Cartesianism with a phenomenological view on the paradoxical experience of corporeality: 'Insofar as the body tends to disappear when functioning unproblematically, it often seizes our attention most strongly at times of dysfunction' (Leder et al., 1990, p. 4). Leder describes a body that disappears while we try to perceive it. Therefore he is tracing the question why there is such a difficulty to understand and talk about the body and pain without dualistic and machinising acts and concepts. And leaves the reader with an awareness for pain action as spatiotemporal disruptions: 'As such, pain reorganizes our lived space and time, our relations with others and with ourselves' (p. 73).

Introducing the *Leib* as a body picture into (chronic) pain theory means a turn towards the lived experience in its interplay between presence and absence. Instead of measuring and categorizing pain, research and practice gets concerned about *understanding* the silent and vibrant relationships between the observer, the observed and their embeddedness. As a result, knowledge is understood as 'being a dynamic activity by which organisms guide and are guided by their transactions with the world' (Sullivan, 2001, p. 142). While the contingency of the body seems to open up a paradox in which the experiencer is the experienced at the same time (Merleau-Ponty, 1962), the ambiguous relationship between the two, the complex meaning making around it, moves into interest. The meaningful relationship between pain and the experiencing person within culturalized and socialized contexts (Ojala, 2015) opens up a debate of bodies that swing around passivity and activity, existence and transcendence, deficiency beings and healing stories. And with this a complex, interactional relationship of the person who suffers pain and the witness – the doctor, the interviewer, the relative. 'Whatever pain achieves, it achieves in part through its unsharability, and it ensures this unsharability through its resistance to language' (Scarry, 1985, p. 4). The contingency of pain, the difficulty to communicate about it, points to the nonexistence and loss of an object (of pain). In *Perceptions of Pain* Padfield (2003) thematizes the speechlessness, the silence out of which pain moves, the difficulty of chronic pain patients to feel believed while their suffering doesn't fit the recognizable patterns (p. 8). With the 'I' as the point of view she argues for pictorial representations that have successively helped with 'phantom limp' pain, calling those representations 'vivid testimonies' that open up a sharable space (p. 10): A photograph, a picture as 'a shared reference point from which patient and doctor can work together' (p. 20). A picture that learns to uphold uncertainty, contradictions instead of enforcing the danger to put patients at the mercy of the (doctor's) power to control and objectify the uncomfortable. She states: 'the age-old concept of sharing and talking about problems is increasingly denied in the high tech medical environment in which doctors practice' (p. 127). Connecting this thought with Dori Laub's *Bearing Witness or the Vicissitudes of Listening* (1992) allows to add living and processual relationships into research and practice. In his writings testimonies appear as a relational process, in which insecure listeners balance between their search for objective truth and their recognition of the silence, the 'gaping black hole' and recognition of their own vulnerability. And it is the expression of those resistant fragments that create knowledge, shared knowledge. In order to 'act about that which I cannot know, rather that act insofar as I know' (Ahmed, 2014, p. 31). The focus on meaning-making appears as an act, that, understood as modes of subjectification, informs how subjects move within (biopolitical) regimes of knowledge and power.

A Liminal Synthesis?

There are perspectives that try to *explain*, others focus on *understanding* the phenomenon. There are the ones who seem to enforce dualistic paradigms, others that try to 'make theories messy' (Sullivan, 2001, p. 156). Medical perspectives, phenomenological perspectives, feminist approaches, psychoanalytic and cognitive-behavioural lenses seem to enter into an ambiguous gap, a contradictory field that circles around chronic pain. Jackson (2005) thematizes the confusions around objectivity and subjectivity, causality and experience, the mind-body-dilemma, the fight between physical and psychological explanations, their difficulty to speak among themselves and the consequences of those debates for chronic pain patients (p. 337f). Neither a purely physiological or neurological approach, nor an exclusive focus on psychology or cognitive-behavioural patterns seem to enrich the discourse alone by themselves. The former struggles with the acceptance and integration of subjective and de-hegemonic experience. The latter provoke the depreciation of pain as being of imaginary origin (Jackson, 2005; Pesut & McDonald, 2007) while beginning to opposite 'real pain' from 'hypochondriac pain' unfolding a tendency towards neoliberal and positivist self-management and self-responsibility. Both result in an attitude that does not seem to listen. Dualism is obviously not an option. Additionally Sullivan (2001) states: 'The total elimination of distinctions between things is merely one half of the dualism of atomistic isolation and indistinguishable sameness and does not further an understanding of how things can be simultaneously related and different' (p. 14). The *Biopsychosocial Model* with its focus on multidimensional interactions sounds promising. Also a *Materialist Feminism* and its intersectional approaches seem to enrich the debate with pictures of bodies within the intersection of discourse and materiality (Kerschgens et al., 2013). What remains are people with chronic pain and their very different and incomparable forms of suffering and activism within their own and discursive history. What remains is a *stigmatization process* and sanctions that go with it. Jackson (2005) names a process that normatively marks chronic pain patients and their behaviour – with negative effects. Be it the disbelieve, that patients are confronted with, when failing the existing categories (Padfield, 2003, p. 8) or the guilt that is appearing while talking about psychological mechanisms that uphold the chronicity, be it the gap between pain experience and pain communication, be it the social disruptiveness (e.g. in not being able to be productive) (Jackson, 2005). Therefore Jackson (2005) calls chronic pain a *liminal phenomena*. Drawing upon liminality theory (Turner, 1969, 1977) she describes the *betwixt and between* and ambivalent nature of chronic pain. Due to its fluctuating nature culturally constructed logic and (moral, social) order gets threatened, rituals and anxiety-relieving and dichotomizing, dualistic categorizations, stigmatization and tabooisation are getting provoked: 'chronic pain mysteriously straddles the mind-body boundary – and the more a pain sufferer lacks a clear-cut diagnosis, the more he or she is ambiguous with respect to this boundary' (Jackson, 2005, p. 343). She unfolds chronic pain as a shifting nature not only between categories, but also between medical and therapeutic treatment, between sick and healthy, between different places and times (ebd., p. 344f).

TOWARDS RESEARCH

Research Direction and Questions

> Our experience of pain is therefore foundational to medicine. So is recognition of the immensly varied ways we express and communicate it: silently in

> shivers, gazes, winces, and in the stetching, twisting, writching movements of the body (…). (Padfield, 2003, p. 7)

Pain as a creator of the 'very impression of a bodily surface' (p. 5) appears in Sarah Ahmed's (2014) writings as an active mediator and as a recognition of transforming relationships between the inside and the outside. Ahmed's *Cultural Politics of Emotion* focusses on the labour and language of pain in between deep subjectivity and discourse; an in-between-ness where norm borders continuously and subversively are getting transgressed and newly established. Ahmed opens up a deeply critical perspective. She is writing about 'pain politics' which oscillate between normalizing, securitizing wound fetishization by cutting up historicity and movements of subaltern voices that try to remember and testify separation and loss (p. 32f). She designates 'overinvestments in the wound' (p. 32) that are contrary to movements that want to let go. But how does this 'work' look like? How does it feel like? How is it psychosocially negotiated and embedded discursively? How is its politics apparent in narratives and the relationship within an interview? Therefore it's the experiencing person's perspective that needs to be understood. This research wants to bring to the fore the (de-)structuralizing movements and voices of people who experience and live with chronic pain, who themselves live with cultures and politics that deal with chronic pain. As Ojala (2015) states, the phenomenon of chronic pain is still poorly understood (Apkarian et al., 2009; IASP, 2020; Sessle, 2012). In this analysis I want to focus on phenomenological and critical perspectives that integrate material-discursive interconnections within the research interest about pain experience. The hypothesis shall be, that chronic pain is a liminal phenomenon. But how is this seemingly liminality experienced, approached and averted? I will apply the suggested critical-phenomenological perspective in order to learn how to understand chronic pain from and in relation to the perspective of the person experiencing it – being aware of the discursive context the phenomenon is embedded in. I immersed into the field of interpretative social research and conducted an interview that follows Witzel's *Problemzentriertes Interview* (2000). I was driven by the following questions:

i. How is chronic pain individually experienced?
ii. What negotiations, dilemmas, strategies and narratives unfold within an interview and discussion with a person talking about his*her chronic pain?
iii. How is which meaning getting attributed, constructed and reflected? Which disruptive and reinforcing movements can be found?
iv. How is this linked with the surrounding cultural order; with class, gender and age?

Fields of Research

Before entering the field of chronic pain research, I would like to take this opportunity to list a glimpse of research that has already been done on chronic pain experience with a focus on phenomenological and critical perspectives.[2] There is Ojala's (2015) work, that enriches the phenomenon's understanding with his qualitative analysis of open interviews concerning the meaning of chronic pain throughout the perspective of the person experiencing it. He comes across 4 essential themes, that swing across the experience: (1) *Chronic pain affects the whole person,* (2) *Invisibility of chronic pain,* (3) *Negative meaning of chronic pain,* and (4) *Dominance of chronic pain.* The former extracts an inseparability of pain experience, loss of identity, 'a new identity needed to be reformed to redefine new normality with chronic pain' (p. 56), accompanied with psychological distress and uncontrollability and therefore dominance of chronic pain (4). The invisibility undermines the lack of visibility of physical evidence and the distressing outcomes (feelings of disbelieve and stigmatization) for the experiencing person (p. 57). The third theme describes how meaning making in sense of an acceptance of pain helps and emphasizes reflection, acceptation and the need for supporting and believing contexts (p. 58). Ojala concludes with an emphasis on psychosocial support on the way towards acceptance of chronic pain: 'In the analysis it was concluded that the most important issue in the management and acceptance of chronic pain was to believe in the participants' pain by their close ones and health care providers' (p. 64). He stresses multidisciplinary (and context (e.g. family) integrating) treating approaches and sends a call for further research and interaction on experiences as a connection points for help towards pain transformation. Broom et al. (2015) conducted a diary study on women living with chronic back pain. Considering back pain as a sociocultural, political and ambiguous phenomena they identified moral dilemmas between 'fighting' and 'listening' to bodies, between 'dominance' and 'passivity' (p. 720f), between 'perpetually' and 'silence' (p. 721), 'expression' and 'repression' (p. 723). Pain appears as an experience of 'entrapment', 'withdrawal', 'shame', 'guilt', 'stigma' and 'illegitimacy' (pp. 723–724) and there is pain as a 'relative experience' within social and gendered (caring) roles (p. 725). They close with the need to enforce social and cultural *recognition* as an alternative way out of self-management and individualistic self-improvement (p. 727f). Themes that come up again and again is the violence and danger of feelings of disbelief, the fights around legitimacy and illegitimacy, the lack of acceptance and empathy by other people and contexts, activity and structural constraints, and the dilemmas around the uncertainty of chronic pain (Breivik, 2015; Broom et al., 2015; Cohen et al., 2011; Dow et al., 2012; Lavie-Ajayi et al., 2012; Ojala, 2015; Osborn & Smith, 1998) – all studies seemingly with the aim to learn how to talk about chronic pain out of the perspective of the person who experiences it.

METHODOLOGY

Who Am *I* Talking With?

As an interviewee I chose a person in my close environment. She sees herself as and declares herself to be a person with chronic pain. She is 66 years old, a pensioner and lives with the experience of chronic pain since about 14 years. She lost her husband 2006 and lives alone in Southern Germany. Besides back pain this interview revolves around 'a burn' in her mouth that is accompanied by running up liquid and salivary flow. As a related person I followed her medical as well as her personal history closely. Thereby I take on a wide variety of roles: the co-sufferer, the observer, the advice-giver, the 'container', the rationalizer, the one she doesn't want to overwhelm, the one who doesn't want to be overburdened herself, of suffering, of sadness, of diffuseness. This complex relationship strengthens the importance to reflect and retractably explain the established relationship within the interview. Following Kühn's critical social research (2015) the subjectivity of the researcher is considered as a source of knowledge, consistently in interaction within a framework of acteur-centered and discourse-analytical perspectives onto the approached experience. Therefore it is important to reflect on the transmission processes and resonances between the researcher, the research field and the interviewee. I would like to learn to work with my insecurities and weaknesses, with my desires, with my bodily boundaries and resonances in the research process in the sense of Devereux (1984). The countertransferences and postreflections, that were written down directly after the interview, flow into this analysis.

Interview

I met the interviewee at her home during Christmas. The interview was postponed until the end of my visit and spontaneously inserted into the context of a joint breakfast. Pain is a normal topic of conversation between us, which finds expression in a wide variety of approaches. However, the emotionality is often overshadowed, overplayed, rationalized. The professional framework of the interview seemed to provide a sort of protection for me. A protection from the flood of emotion, the hurt. With this protection I approached the thematic always being able to distance myself in a 'professional role'. As the Interview should open up a sphere, where the interviewee talks about her pain history and experience, I decided to start the interview with the following open impulse: 'I am interested in and would like to understand how you experience your chronic pain. Tell me about your chronic pain and how it started, how you perceive it, how you deal with it, for yourself and with others'. The interviewee's narrative was in the focus. In addition, I have asked narrative-supporting follow-up questions and inquiries that I noted beforehand in relation to my research interest according to Schütze (1983) which weaved fluidly into the course of the conversation. In terms of Witzel's 'problem-centered interview' I followed an explorative logic, which should enable me to create a dialogical-open and process-oriented conversation situation on the one hand, and a problem-centered orientation framework on the other hand. The length of the interview was 50 min.

Analysis

The interview was recorded and transcribed using Bohnsack's (2014) transcription guidelines. Since the interview was conducted in German, I translated the paragraphs that are presented in this writing. Mayring's qualitative content analysis (Mayring, 2003) was intended to enable a detailed and exploratory view on the collected data in order to elaborate categories following an inductive-deductive dialectic and to provide a guideline that allows me to verbalize essential topics around the narratives. My aim was to fillet those categories (or rather: *moving themes*) close to the text that enter into dialogue with the research interest. In doing so, I have condensed mutually reinforcing and supporting expressions into overall categories in such a way that connections of meaning become recognizable in order to be able to map and trace their relationship and (contextualized) movement networks around chronic pain experience. Another marker that became central within this 'filtration' was my own countertransference. I focused on parts where I felt irritation, confusion and conflict in order to trace the ambiguous interplay and make visible tensions of unconscious, tabooed and stronger voices revolving around the experiences' subjectivity. In addition, I have extracted a dense and particularly ambivalent part of the interview in order to analyse it with Kiegelmann's Voice Centered Listening Method (Kiegelmann, 2000). I have woven this detail-interested look onto ambivalent, negotiating voices into the following presentation of the analysis' 'results'. After extracting essential and interwoven themes, an important part of my analysis was to get into dialogue with my interview partner, again. I added this step to be able to continue to hold up the research interest – the individual experience in relation – also within the analysis. In the spirit of participatory research, I cross-referenced the extracted themes with the interviewee. This followed a process logic and was repeated three times.

FINDINGS

Dynamics and Countertransferences

The narrative course of the interview is driven by the interviewee's dynamic towards an account of the course of the disease, physical developments, and encounters with physicians. She specifies the feeling of what it's like to live with *the burn*, how she deals with it, now and as it progresses. Increasingly, I become a conversation partner. Together we seem to seek to make the body and the experience of pain visible – or not. The question is whether this can be endured. And how. I try to be aware of my role to put her experience of pain at the centre of our conversation. Besides encircling the experience of pain, the dynamics of the interview also turn out to be a search for clues. The interviewee as well as I more and more tend to try to connect, analyse and understand the expressed symptoms, signs and expressions. Inevitably, the conversation is driven by the ambivalent nature of the pain experience toward a search for explanations, amplifications and hurdles on the way towards healing. Accompanied by rational distancing, I as the interviewer and analyser slip again and again into a role that implicitly wants to solve the 'problem'. I consider this counter-transference as a re-action to and interaction with the liminality of the phenomenon to be encircled, which longs for relaxation and unambiguity in the face of expressed tension. And alongside this there are narrative movements that seek to encircle the insolubility. At this point, it should not go unmentioned that it is equally noteworthy that I am writing this paper about the pain experience of a relative of mine. As Sarah Ahmed (2014) puts it elegantly: 'It is the ungraspability of her pain, in the face of the thereness of my own, that throws me into disbelief' (p. 30). This interview appears to be a secure-insecure framework, learning to approach vulnerability (in relation).

Movements

This subjective pain story is accompanied by ambivalent movement formations and negotiations, that lead toward the pain as well as point away from it as shown in the following illustration (Fig. 13.1). Those dilemmas are accompanied by and move along the encircled and the relation towards the 'object' of this case study: chronic pain. Linguistically supported by a variety of expressions such as 'on one side, on the other side' (e.g. ll. 194, 201, 502, 564) basic movements around chronic pain experience and its meaning-making appears to be negotiations about how to approach and deal, change and move around and with pain's liminality and therefore as well: how to refer to the own body as well as to the environment. In the following section I will outline and specify moving categories together with selected text passages for clarification, that are in resonance with this research interest and questions.

'Basic' Movements

Pain's Liminality

Within the storyline the diffusivity and indescribability of the pain experience was formulated in many places. The pain experience gets paraphrased as a 'grey area' (ll. 63), as a holistic 'sphere' (ll. 238f) without clear and objectifiable explanations and multiple interconnected factors that obscure the overview, accompanied by a 'weird rhythm' (ll. 175), appearing as a spatiotemporal irritation, 'somewhere':

> 'so somewhere they can't explain it' (ll. 25–26)
>
> 'And this burning is the inexplicable thing, (…) it is still somewhere in a grey area.' (ll. 63)
>
> 'Uh:; it is: just something diffuse; probably; and- less bad; that it is not somewhere in
>
> in- (takes a breath) in any values, ä::h to determine,' (ll. 87–89)
>
> 'these are all such diffuse things; they are not tangible things;' (ll. 262–263)

When expressing the difficulty, the diffusivity and the missing explanations around the pain experience, there are *doubting* movements: 'I sometimes feel like a hypochondriac' (ll. 264) and *trivializing* movements that

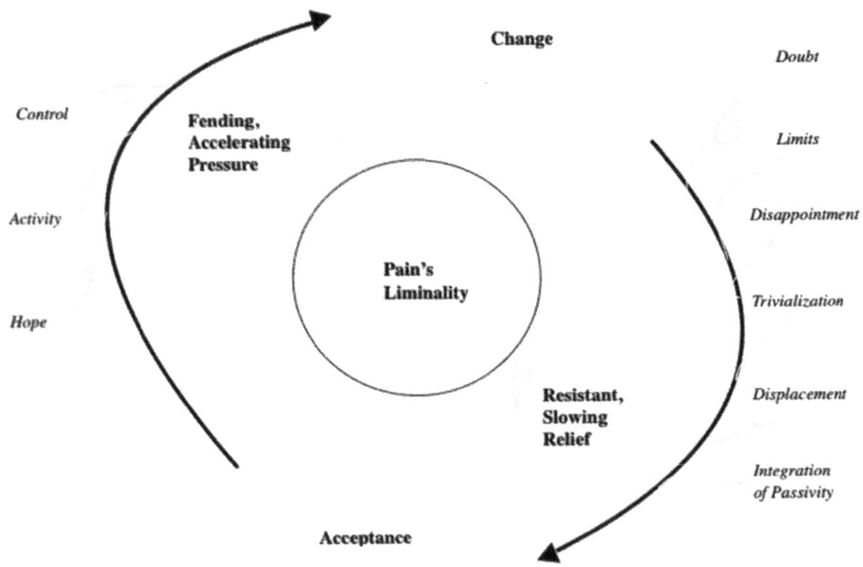

Fig. 13.1. Movements Around and With Pain's Liminality.

suddenly appear: It will pass (ll. 16), It's not that bad (ll. 36, 270), 'something less bad' (ll. 88).

Change – Acceptance

Around these descriptions of diffusivity there appears a *will to change*, which carries with it the following attributes: She describes movements that emphasize her 'fighting spirit' towards being healthy:

> 'I don't want to accept that for myself; I want to have it differently again. That's my fighting spirit then to say; I have to manage that; I have to try that.' (ll. 194–196)
>
> 'And that rhythm change; I need to work on that too. That I can do something else' (ll. 454–455)

There appears a strong will and wish for *quick* change, *activity* and associated practices that are eager to improve, to get better, to take over the lead, the *control*:

> 'I'd rather take 10 pills at once and be fine, or I'd rather run a marathon and be fine;' (ll. 410–412)
>
> 'yes i wish the whole thing went faster; if I initiate anything' (ll. 280)
>
> 'yes, Spo:rt; I moved more, and ä:h eating change tried; (...) yes for example 16 hours nothing to eat kept (...) although just as I said my weight does not go particularly down with it. Well, I've already lost a few kilos. But still too much, yes?' (ll. 138–142)

There is a search for solutions (doctors, investigations, medicaments, diets), for a physically evident and clear issue, a reason. There are movements being in search for a diagnosis bringing clear relief. These movements tend to split and fend off the experiences' ambiguity towards a clear, stabilizing changing movement:

> 'Now go to the ENT and let them check if it has anything to do with this sense of balance.' (ll. 260–262)
>
> 'I thought maybe there was a reason there somewhere;' (ll. 68)
>
> 'so you have to see that you find solutions in another areas there (takes a breath). And that's where I'm at' (ll. 271, 272)

There is *hope* that comes with these movements and the will to change, which after its expression is mostly replaced by *disappointment* naming *limits*. Emerging disappointment and limits are leading to a counter and accompanying movement that tends towards a sort of *acceptance*, being accompanied by the following attributes: This movement seems to integrate the experience's inaccessibility as well as *disappointment* with a reflective-clarified manner:

> 'I can still improve a bit; from: body tension and so on, but I won't be able to do it quite like I used to' (ll. 583–584)
>
> 'I have no other choice. Can examine everything possible, but (takes a breath) if somewhere a point is reached, just had to say okay.' (ll. 89–91)
>
> 'well now, what else do you want to do; now I just have to try to live with it' (ll. 78–79)

Thereby she emphasizes a *lengthiness* of the path in dealing with the chronic pain, the need for patience, seemingly in connection with the language of the body:

> 'but it will be a long time' (ll. 111)
>
> 'but the slow is also not mine; but I've learned that; I can't do it any other way; (…) I have to do what my body signals to me. And if that's it that one should not exaggerate; then that's just it.' (ll. 412–416)
>
> 'I have to be considerate and try to achieve something piece by piece.(…) Is very (takes a breath) annoying because it is very long and because I also have other things to do.' (ll. 425–427)

Fending Pressure – Resistant Relief

As already shown, these search movements are accompanied by *hope* and *disappointment* – and the designation of *limits*. These limits appear as too much change, as pressure that changes life for the worse and therefore tend towards a relieving resistance:

> I always try to think about what can be changed in this sphere, what I could do to improve it, to make it run more smoothly, and that's what I try to do; but only as far as it's possible for me without losing my mood without changing my life, without not liking anything in life anymore, without getting depressed, without limiting myself too much, I want to have my life already. And that's what I fight for (ll. 253–259)

As limits she further names her 'weaker self (Schweinehund)' (ll. 290), her need for recreation and rest (ll. 190, 218) her *passive* 'phlegma', her dizziness and the fatigue, that stands between her and her will to be active – as she subsequently reiterated in the debriefing of the interview. There are opening up movements that present themselves as a dilemma between an *accelerating, fending and tensing pressure* itself hoping for a clearing, as well as diffusivity-relieving solution – and a relieving defence of the current and not preserving state dressed as a pressure-opposing *resistance*. These different forms of tension and relief accompany and regulate the movements between change and acceptance in an amplifying or irreconcilably contradicting manner:

> 'The stress was just too high to also change anything possible.' (ll. 46)
>
> 'and maybe some overexertion with running, so that I am tired in the evening; can really go to bed; or fall asleep;' (ll. 199–200)

When asking her about the problems and issues she experiences with her pain, her narration often wanders after a few sentences toward a description of positive things. The *positivity* appears as a rescuing resource – seemingly rescuing from the overdominance of combats against the negativity of pain. She names it 'principle displacement' (ll. 463) expressing a *fear of negativity*. In many cases the negativity gets named 'depression' hindering existing relationships (ll. 249, 496). Therefore, the negativity appears as a counter-part one can position oneself on the opposite in order to move and fight towards active change, but also as a frightening counterforce that appears when too much change has been demanded. These dynamics have the appearance of an interplay between *remembering* and *forgetting*: fighting negative remembrance on the one hand, while letting go as a displacing forgetting, on the other[3]

> 'I always want beautiful things. That is displacement principle, principle displacement. But that's me, I can live with that, it just makes me feel better' (ll. 462–464)
>
> 'You see, I always see only the positive.' (ll. 484–485)
>
> 'I don't want to be constantly reminded of something that could make me feel negative;' (ll. 158–159)
>
> 'and maybe I wouldn't be able to enjoy it anymore if I fell into a depression like that. Everything is stupid; always this and there:: and it also pinches the back and the front and yes. I don't want that. I never want to become like that.' (ll. 248–259) +

Negotiating Spatiotemporal Normativities

And there are further influencing issues, conflicts and arenas with resources and forces as cultural experiences that are moving along and interacting with the individual experience and managing movements. These issues seem to feed and get fed by the dynamic. They appear as further stages of controversy – directly linked to society, economy and history, where agency-seeking positionings into normative places and times are getting negotiated. There are obviously appearing arenas that approach topics and conflicts such as *age, gender, class*. Being aware of the importance of their emphasize as a critical tool to be able to politicize supposedly individual experiences on the one hand, on the other hand I would like to stick with an analysis that puts the individually experienced dynamic of meaning-making in the foreground, also in order not to 'risk of fetishizing the race-class-gender-mantra without paying attention to what issues are rendered invisible and excluded' (Dhawan & Do Mar Castro Varela, 2016, p. 25). Therefore, I would like to emphasize and outline the complex interactions and movement formations – between diverse arenas, discourse, the individual experience's perspective, the body and therefore pain's liminality, that I would like to illustrate in the following graphic (Fig. 13.2).

Relations: Opening – Closing

Around the experience there are appearing *spatial* discussions about how and whether to open up to social bodies, to what extent spatial boundaries can be crossed, when it is time to close gates, to give space to self-reinforcing tendencies. These movements seem to search to re-formulate the experience of (social) relations, oscillating between Opening & Closing, Proximity & Distance. Movements appear that carry traces of dimensions concerning *Gender* with their dialectic between *Caring – Independence.* The narratives often present the interviewee as a person in *role of a carer.* There is a great responsibility to take over responsibility, to help others, to re-act upon others and there are *feelings of guilt* that are concerning around social relationships; especially those, that she doesn't react on (ll. 295, 525). While *trivializing* her own experience, she does not want to thematize her pain too much, neither talk about it with others: 'I don't want to talk about it so much. I want to deal with it myself; I want to see that I get a grip on it.' (ll. 156–158).[4] Throughout the thematic there are discussions unfolding

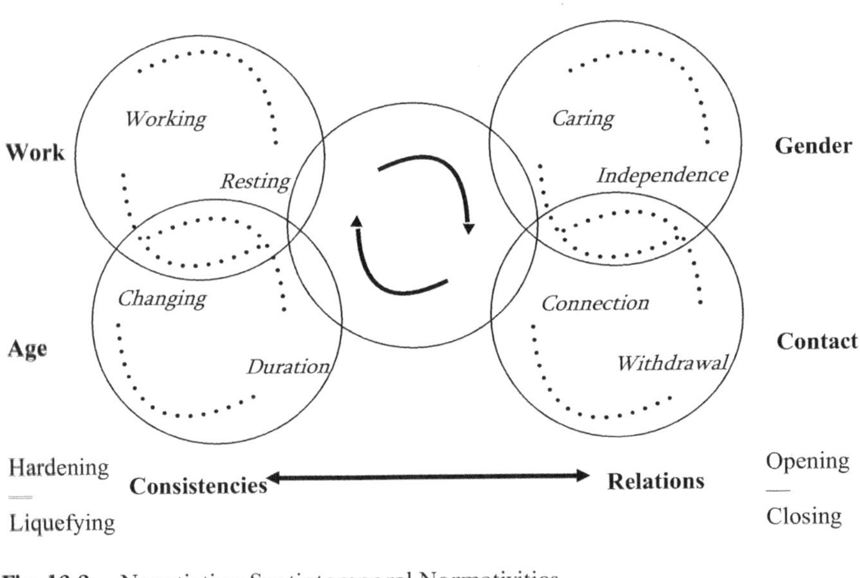

Fig. 13.2. Negotiating Spatiotemporal Normativities.

that negotiate (social) pressure, expectations and the need to maintain contacts, social constraints – and the counter-voice that emphasizes not to need to do that (ll. 302, 497): 'so that at Christmas I have to write to everyone; this compulsion: I do not like' (ll. 527). A dialectic unfolds between self- and external determination. A dialectic that moves back and forth between experiencing pressure from a seemingly established structure commanding to open and a resistance against it that wants to close the devoted nature with a proclamation of the right and claim to a space for herself. And there are arenas discussing *Connection – Withdrawal*. At many points in the interview, a desire for contact; inspiration and fascinating life stories (ll. 510–519, 545), feedback (ll. 146), resonance and mirroring (ll. 179–188), friendship (ll. 296–297): 'Seeing people on the road, having friends; it's all great.' (ll. 246–247) and partnership (ll. 300f), is being articulated. It's about contact, that accepts, strengthens, that is not advising (ll. 160–162). At the same time there is a *withdrawal* being formulated. A withdrawal, that seems to be a counter-movement against the force and pressure, against claims and expectations, to 'maintain contact' (ll. 525), to 'help' (ll. 503) and to 'fight around' (ll. 302) and therefore strongly interlinked with Gender-Normatives. There is securing and frightening distrust towards others (ll. 495f, 612) and there is the withdrawal that helps her to focus on herself: 'but I want to deal with myself' (ll. 617). She articulates a dilemma: her need to withdraw from experienced pressure, her insecurity and guilt about and contact-hindering effects of the withdrawal while as well and ambivalently her satisfaction about not being in contact.

> maybe what's not good (....) is uh that I actually, very quickly, think to be able to judge people and then, quite negatively,(...) and somewhere also try not to force the contact (...) I actually feel quite comfortable the way I live at the moment and I don't necessarily need to have a special new contact (ll. 494–510)

Consistencies: Hardening – Liquefying

Meanwhile there are other arenas that concern around how to structure within *temporal* order: how to structure within modern time's progressive linearity, hot to handle past and future, how to clock the rhythm, how fast to move (on), how to approach change and duration, transience and permanence. There is the ambivalent theme of W*orking – Resting*. Inevitably there is class and socioeconomic historicity being interlinked with this field, which at this point would go beyond the scope.[5] This issue concerns around controlling, completing and the pressure of 'being productive' (ll. 549): 'all the unwinding I still have to do on a business basis' (ll. 427). There is a need and a will to function in a self-regulating, *progressing* manner, but it is 'tight, tense, cramped and there are exhausting negotiations' (ll. 556) and it appears stuck, as a cold *constriction*, alone in rule-based compulsion that seemingly conserves a disappointed and hurt *remembrance*: 'Everything you delegate, what you let others do, you have to control. You have to see if it works the way you think; '(ll. 612). Accompanying the articulations of pressure and its unavoidable control requirements there is a 'bad conscience' when not reacting upon the pressure (ll. 551) and acts towards relieving the tense, to *forget*:

> Of course, it's good to have it done; (...) And it doesn't do me any good to push it like that; on the one hand, but on the other hand, it does good to me because it makes me feel better because I can forget about it. Because I can run over it. (ll. 559–565)

Progressive working shows itself in interaction with accelerating pressure experienced on the part of the struggling will for change. And there is a desire for support in the fields of work without social stress. There is a desire to recreation, air, *rest* for the body and enjoyment without struggle (ll. 190 217, 245f, 416) seemingly in interaction with the movements towards *slowing acceptance*. Night's rest appropriate to a rhythm is a central thematic. It's unfulfillability and irregularity gets expressed as an experience of suffering – either in case the 'rest' is not happening at all or when the tiredness appears at inappropriate and rhythm-incongruent times. Within this issue and distributed throughout the interview, *age* appears as an interacting factor, as moving between *Change & Duration*. It appears as a relieve, as a hope of not having to fight: 'every person who gets older lives with that;' (ll. 402); 'I'm not 20, am I? I do not have to be different' (ll. 581–582), of not having to work, as something that seems to take the pressure off, something that tends towards *acceptance* – and something that, again pressures, is not acceptable at all: 'I don't want to become such a grouchy old hunchbacked aunt in any case' (ll. 586–587). It appears, as well, as a dilemma:

> At a certain age, maybe something like that comes up; I'm not ready to accept that (...) But on the other hand, I don't want to accept this. (ll. 181–194)

And there is 'earlier' and 'today' getting mentioned, delimited from each other: 'I won't be able to do it quite like before' (ll. 584); 'I certainly don't have the lungs I used to have.' (ll. 224). Age is getting expressed in a way that nestles in the identity-forming, repeating negotiations between acceptance and the will to change, between a desire for an alleviation of tension and a fear to be stuck in restrictions of movement, between defending the outlook for progression and integrating the intangibility of transience. A dilemma that 'works' in-between times.

Movement-Network's Dialectic

While the first part of this chapter focuses on the individual formations of experience, the following one on the dynamic's accompanying socio-cultural arenas, this last part aims to test the linkage and interplay within and between the different experiencing perspectives in sense of a critical synthesis. Because it should not be a matter of psychologizing what is sociopolitical, nor of culturalizing what is psychological. It seems that these managing and searching wavy, or circling movements are directly interconnected within a relational and moving network. One can recognize how different approaches, re-actions, ways of dealing, associative impulses and expressive sensations are in negotiations with each other; a negotiation that curses around the question how to move with and against the experience of chronic pain, how to build structures, how to materialize and (trans)form around it – chronically repeating and acutely deregulating – both and.

With Pain's Liminality as starting point, or rather sphere, we discovered movements towards accelerating, pressuring change that seemingly fends of pain's liminality, as well as an opposing-amplifying movement towards slowing acceptance that is accompanied by disillusioned voices that more likely seem to be re-actions trying to somehow integrate the diffusivity that comes with the problem's articulations. A moving dialectic opens up, as can be seen in Fig. 13.3 above. The latter answers on the repeating, persistent nature of the pain utterances after tries and tries of analysis and interventions searching to structure. The latter suffers, displaces, relaxes, connects and integrates, while the former tries to retain and fight for the power to act within structural permanence, tries to concretize, to progress. Both are vital to survival. They seem to contradict as well as to be mutually dependent from another. It is not difficult to find a strong link to Turner's (1969) conception of the dialectic between 'structure' and 'communitas', that act within a liminal state-of-flux. There is opening up a (bio)political dilemma that is not unaffected by but rather necessarily bound to political circumstances that accompany them. Circumstances with very real arenas, that further create pressure, that let guilt formalize new sanctions, that urge to go beyond one's own limits, that built stages for resistant, rage-laden enactments, that itself deal with pain's liminality. Circumstances, that should listen to the movements's relations and consistencies in order to understand, to talk and negotiate together – but especially don't. So Turner (1969) states: 'Maximation of communities provokes maximization of structure' (p. 373) – and the other way around. The discourse's discussions seem rather dichotomizing, instead of dialoguing their interdependence while creating spaces and times that learn to recognize and witness a diversity of voices.

DISCUSSION

> Pain (…) as something that 'mediates' the relationship between internal or external, or inside and outside. (Ahmed, 2014, p. 24)

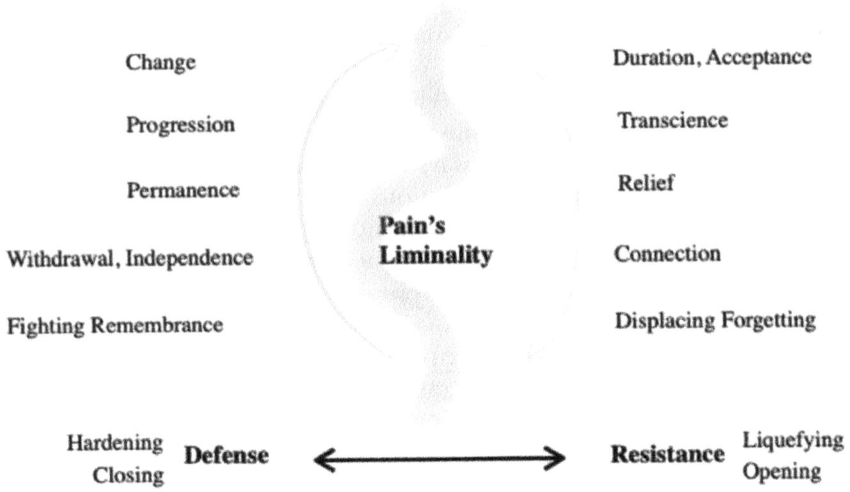

Fig. 13.3. Dialectics of Defense & Resistance.

The approach towards pain experience elaborated in this paper wants to show, how a wide variety of movements are in negotiation about how to move around chronic pain, how meaningful structures are established, re-established, dismantled and how existing relations are getting re-formed. This analysis wants to mark the importance to recognize liminality within the experience of chronic pain. Be it practitioners, mothers, theorists, societies, friends, economies, neighbours or daughters who are confronted with. Furthermore, to recognize that movements are relational, (bio)psychosocial, dialectical, political – resistant and vulnerable. Meaning, that those movements resonate and communicate with – practitioners', mothers', theorists', societies', friends', economies', neighbors' or daughters' 'both resistance and vulnerability' (Butler et al., 2016) within established and transforming contexts. Drawing upon a critical and phenomenological approach an aim is to learn to deal with the fact that science and its perspectives comes inevitably into connection with the movements that surround the phenomenon of chronic pain experience. Nevertheless, an increased concern of this research is to learn to understand the person's experience who lives with pain in his or her struggles. In the debriefing of the interview, the interviewee particularly made comments at points where she did not feel understood and testified to her desire to be understood. I would like to and hope I do take this seriously. In this analysis expressions of the 'grey sphere' of pain's liminality get accompanied by movements that oscillate between *fending change* – searching for an evidence and a controlling and *fast* activity against the expressed ambiguity – and *resistant acceptance,* that seeks to integrate processual slowness within its approach towards it. Accompanied by hope and disappointment, acceleration and slowness, guilt, tension and relaxation, (dis)connection, as well as (re-)formulations of boundaries and consistencies within spatiotemporal normativities there are different voices negotiating over the movement's agency and over different approaches towards diffusivity. I would like to explicitly emphasize the importance to be aware of the discursivity within these issues, as well as their dialectical and interconnected, driven and driving (trans)formations. Following this, to speak about *withdrawal* appears as just one side of a coin. If we do not recognize the complexity as well as political 'nature' of these biopsychosocial negotiations, their reinforcing and suppressing, tightening or relaxing interplay within diverse arenas, we would run the risk of essentializing and controlling movements, amplifying the dialectics' amplitude while ignoring integrative voices and needs. The same is true in reverse. Understanding and mapping meaning making processes and experiences should precisely not mean ultimately problematizing them, pathologizing them, individualizing them – as for example mobilizing resilience fantasies with individual's as active change-makers and fantasies that make acceptance and pain integration an individual task. This implicitly results in moralizing injunctions that would accelerate, further dichotomize and repeat, rather than engage with existing circuits of negotiation, as presented in this paper. It's a fine line. But when it is crossed, an initiative – originally intended to counter the over dominance of essentialism, functionalism and body's quantifications with actor-centred research – molds into research that seems to re-datafy and singularize while looking into the black box. And then, stigmatizing psychologizations are close at hand (Sontag, 2004). So it should not be about functionalistically improving algorithms of meaning making processes within the individual but to mirror the analysis' insights dialogically together with the person experiencing it – back and forth. And it's the person experiencing chronic pain who knows best which interpretations[6] are helpful fur him*her – in relation. Therefore, participative analysis can be understood as therapeutical work, not just for the person experiencing chronic pain.

As Ojala (2015) elaborated in his research within chronic pain experience there is normality being redefined within the formation of a new identity (p. 56). I want to stress that as well. There are boundaries getting crossed and established while (trans)formations taking place: between past and present, between public and private, between inside and outside… When Frigga Haug talks about 'Selbstveränderung und Veränderung der Umstände (Self-change and change of circumstances)' (2018) she draws a healing fantasy and conception of health that includes relation: the social, economic, political spheres with its inequalities. Which ones are the voices not being heard, systematically suppressed, systematically privileged? Where do political struggles repeat themselves? How can we empower communities? There needs to be more research and practice being done that integrate those intersections – concerning pain experience and concerning epidemiology in order to move toward health equity (e.g. Breilh, 2008; Krieger, 2001). And there is an obvious indication that complex and liminal phenomena are to be confronted with inter & transdisciplinary as well as dialogic-participatory, holistic and appreciative approaches to theory and practice in order to take empowerment within and with changing movements seriously. This means being aware of networks of interacting forces in its ambiguous complexity, so as not to merely proclaim imperatives for change to a minority of voices. In order to 'bridge communication chasms' within doctor-chronic-pain-patient interactions (Kenny, 2004) while acknowledging that there is a 'gulf' where it is difficult to navigate (Morris, 1991) and a 'gulf that cannot be overcome by empathy' (Ahmed, 2014, p. 37). In order to learn how to listen and testify, researchers and practitioners need to connect and grapple with their own vulnerability and resistance. In interaction with the phenomena and its liminality, inevitably you, as a witness, get confronted with your own vulnerability's uncertain ungrappability running the risk of trying to exlusively fend it off via objectivations, via 'western overcoming' (Ahmed, 2014), to 'separate, demarcate, purify and punish' (Jackson, 2005, p. 346) subversive voices. Or risking exclusively fantasizing about a world without violence, without normalizations, structure, sneaking towards acceptance as a both resilient and system adapting self-management technique that tends to ignore relational ebeddedness within power structures. I want to learn how to think along the dialectics of political dimensions of inevitably liminal pain experience. That is where educational work needs to be done. Starting with the multifaceted nature of models of pain and their body metaphors. And hopefully not in a moralizing way. But in a critical and an acknowledging way. So there is nothing 'wrong' with chronic pain experience. There is something wrong with and important about the relations and circumstances.

NOTES

1. Who are *we*? Who am *I*? As a White, European woman I mainly accessed 'western' philosophies and science in order to grasp the discourse surrounding my interviewee. Perhaps future research can already learn at this point to take up the diversity of forms of knowledge and learn to integrate them into the research process.
2. I would like to emphasize that this is a very small glimpse. I focus on presenting the research, that constructs the inspirational ground on which my own research wants to build up.
3. This dynamic reminds me of Judith Herman's *Trauma and Recovery* (1992) and how she speaks with victims who want to but cannot forget. Connecting

chronic pain research with trauma discourse, thinking about overwhelming, unintegrated memories, cycles of repetition, and lack of recognition by society and others seems meaningful and important to me at this and further points of this research field.

4. Trivalizing acts that tend towards self-responsibility and agency pressure (that Broom et al., 2015 put into discussion as the linked side-effect of emancipatory agency-strengthening measurements within (chronic) pain discourse as well as emphasizing chronic pain's liminality from where 'sociocultural expectations of individual agents potential' (p. 728) emerge) could be thematized as acts responding to a lost and violated (world) trust within a patriarchic society that doesn't acknowledge vulnerability nor is capable of listening to wounds as well as acts being driven by capitalistic imperatives as such as neoliberalistic self-regulation-pressure (see: following chapter).
5. Anyhow, class-evoked liberation- and generational economy-movements, modernity's stories of liberalism, Acceleration in accumulation pressure (Rosa, 2019), current neoliberal imperatives for change and self-responsibility, society's unmerciful drive to progress, that create very real work load that crushes bodies, people, communities, should be taken into account while approaching chronic pain experience's movements.
6. – and resources. Resource-network-formations as well as a historical perspective in terms of the genesis of transformations and negotiations of meaning could be interesting for future research.

REFERENCES

Ahmed, S. (2014). *The cultural politics of emotion.* Edinburgh University Press.

Apkarian, A. V., Baliki, M. N., & Geha, P. Y. (2009). Towards a theory of chronic pain. *Progress in Neurobiology, 87*(2), 81–97.

Bohnsack, R. (2014). *Rekonstruktive Sozialforschung. Einführung in qualitative Methoden.* Verlag Barbara Budrich.

Breilh, J. (2008). Latin American critical ('Social') epidemiology: New settings for an old dream. *International Journal of Epidemiology, 37*(4), 745–750.

Breivik, H. (2015). Invisible pain - Complications from too little or too much empathy among helpers of chronic pain patients. *Scand J Pain, 6*(1), 31–32.

Breivik, H., Collett, B., Ventafridda, V., Cohen, R., & Gallacher, D. (2006). Survey of chronic pain in Europe: Prevalence, impact on daily life, and treatment. *European Journal of Pain, 10*(4), 287–333.

Broom, A., Kirby, E., Adams, J., & Refshauge, K. (2015). On illegitimacy, suffering and recognition: A diary study of women living with chronic pain. *Sociology, 49*(4), 712–731.

Butler, J., Gambetti, Z., & Sabsay, L. (2016). *Vulnerability in resistance.* Duke University Press.

Coakley, S., & Shelemay, K. (2007). *Pain and its transformations: The interface of biology and culture.* Harvard University Press.

Cohen, M., Quintner, J., Buchanan, D., Nielsen, M., & Guy, L. (2011). Stigmatization of patients with chronic pain: The extinction of empathy. *Pain Medicine, 12*(11), 1637–1643.

Cohen, S., & Mao, J. (2014). Neuropathic pain: Mechanisms and their clinical implications. *BMJ British Medical Journal, 348.* https://www.jstor.org/stable/26513432. Accessed on January 8, 2021

Corbett, M., Foster, N. E., & Ong, B. N. (2007). Living with low back pain-stories of hope and despair. *Social Science & Medicine, 65*(8), 1584–1594.

Derbyshire, S. (2011). Can neural imaging explain pain?. *Psychiatric Clinic of North America, 34,* 595–604.

Devereux, G. (1984). *Angst und Methode in den Verhaltenswissenschaften.* Suhrkamp.

Dhawan, N., & Do Mar Castro Varela, M. (2016). What difference does difference make?: Diversity, intersectionality and transnational feminist politics. *Wagadu: A Journal of Transnational Women's and Gender Studies, 16,* 11–39.

Dow, C. M., Roche, P. A., & Ziebland, S. (2012). Talk of frustration in the narratives of people with chronic pain. *Chronic Illness, 8*(3), 176–191.

Fields, H. (2007). Setting the stage for pain: Allegorical tales from neuroscience. In S. Coakley & K. Shelemay (Eds.), *Pain and its transformations: The interface of biology and culture.* Harvard University Press.

Gatchel, R., Peng, Y., Fuchs, P., & Peters, M. & Turk, D. (2007). The biopsychosocial approach to chronic pain: Scientific advances and future directions. *Psychological Bulletin, 4,* 581–624.

Graham, P. W. (1992). Review of the book The Culture of Pain. *Literature and Medicine, 11*(2), 325–328.

Harding, S. (1983). *Discovering reality: Feminist perspectives on epistemology, metaphysics, methodology, and philosophy of science.* D. Reidel.

Haug, F. (2018). *Selbstveränderung und Veränderung der Umstände.* Argument Verlag.

Herman, J. L. (1992). *Trauma and recovery: The aftermath of violence - From domestic abuse to political power.* Basic Books.

Hill, R. (1986). Current perspectives on pain. *Science Progress, 70*(1 (277)), 95-107.

IASP. (2020). https://www.iasp-pain.org/Education/Content.aspx?ItemNumber=1698&navItemNumber=576

Jackson, J. (2005). Stigma, liminality, and chronic pain: Mind-body borderlands. *American Ethnologist, 32*(3), 332–353.

Kenny, D. T. (2004). Constructions of chronic pain in doctor-patient relationships: Bridging the communication chasm. *Patient Education and Counseling, 52*(3), 297–305.

Kerschgens, A. (2013). Geschlechtsentwürfe im Kontext von Geburt: Deutungsmuster und Bearbeitungsversuche werdender Väter. In H. Ehlers, G. Linke, N. Milewski, B. Rudolf, B. & H. Trappe (Hg.), *Körper — Geschlecht — Wahrnehmung.* LitVerlag.

Kiegelmann, M. (2000). Qualitativ-psychologische Forschung mit dem Voice-Ansatz. *Forum Qualitative Sozialforschung/Forum for Qualitative Social Research, 1*(2). Art. 13.

Kleinböhl, D. (2005). Schmerzgedächtnis und Sensibilisierung. *Psychoneuro, 31*(2), 84–91.

Krieger, N. (2001). Theories for social epidemiology in the 21st century: An ecosocial perspective. *International Journal of Epidemiology, 30*(4), 668–677.

Kühn, T. (2015). *Kritische Sozialpsychologie des modernen Alltags.* Springer.

Laub, D. (1992). Bearing witness, or the vicissitudes of listening. In D. Laub (Ed.), *Testimony.* Routledge.

Lavie-Ajayi, M., Almog, N., & Krumer-Nevo, M. (2012). Chronic pain as a narratological distress: A phenomenological study. *Chronic Illness, 8*(3), 192–200.

Leadley, R. M., Armstrong, N., Lee, Y. C., Allen, A., & Kleijnen, J. (2012). Chronic diseases in the European Union: The prevalence and health cost implications of chronic pain. *Journal of Pain & Palliative Care Pharmacotherapy, 26*(4), 310–325.

Leder, D. (1990). *The absent body*. University of Chicago Press.

Lee, M., & Tracey, I. (2010). Unravelling the mystery of pain, suffering, and relief with brain imaging. *Current Pain and Headache Reports, 14*, 124–131.

Makkreel, R. A. & Rodi, F. (Eds.). (2010). *Wilhelm dilthey: Selected works, volume Ii: Understanding the human world*. Princeton University Press.

Mayring, P. (2003). *Qualitative Inhaltsanalyse. Grundlagen und Techniken*. Beltz.

Melzack, R. (2001). Pain and the neuromatrix in the brain. *Journal of Dental Education, 65*(12), 1378–1382.

Merleau-Ponty, M. (1962). *Phenomenology of perception*. Routledge & Kegan Paul.

Morris, D. B. (1991). *The culture of pain*. University of California Press.

Ojala, T. (2015). *The essence of the experience of chronic pain - A phenomenological study*. University of Jyväskylä. [Doctoral dissertation, Wilmington University].

Osborn, M., & Smith, J. A. (1998). The personal experience of chronic benign lower back pain: An interpretative phenemological analysis. *British Journal of Health Psychology, 2*, 65–83.

Padfield, D. (2003). *Perceptions of pain*. EBS.

Pesut, B., & McDonald, H. (2007). Connecting philosophy and practice: Implications of two philosophical approaches to pain for nurses' expert clinical decision making. *Nursing Philosophy, 8*, 256–263.

Rosa, H. (2019). *Resonanz. Eine Soziologie der Weltbeziehung*. Suhrkamp.

Scarry, E. (1985). *The body in pain. The making and unmaking of the world*. Oxford University Press.

Schütze, F. (1983). Biographieforschung und narratives Interview. *Neue Praxis, 13*(3), 283–293.

Sessle, B. (2012). The pain crisis: What it is and what can be done. Review article. *Pain Research and Treatment, 12*.

Sontag, S. (2004). *Regarding the pain of others*. Penguin Books.

Steinhaug, S. (2007). Women's strategies for handling chronic muscle pain. A qualitative study. *Scandinavian Journal of Primary Health Care, 25*, 44–48.

Sullivan, S. (2001). *Living across and through skins. Transactional bodies, pragmatism, and feminism*. Indiana University Press.

Trachsel, L. A., & Cascella, M. (2020). *Pain theory*. Available from: https://www.ncbi.nlm.nih.gov/books/NBK545194/

Turner, V. (1969). Liminality and communitas. In *The ritual process: Structure and Anti- structure* (pp. 94–139). Cornell University Press.

Turner, V. (1977). Process, system, and symbol: A new anthropological synthesis. *Dædalus, 106*(3), 61–80.

Wendell, S. (1997). The rejected body: Feminist philosophical reflections on disability. *Hypatia, 12*(2), 219–223.

Witzel, A. (2000). Das problemzentrierte Interview. *Forum Qualitative Sozialforschung/Forum for Qualitative Social Research, 1*(1). Art. 22. http://nbn-%20resolving.de/urn:nbn:de:0114-fqs0001228

CHAPTER 14

A FIXED PERCEPTION AS A WAY OF KNOWING: DYNAMICS OF DELUSION AND REALITY

Caroline Skov Vestbjerg
Authorized Psychologist, Denmark

ABSTRACT

Truth is a dramatic judgment in which I attend to analyze the way we come to define something as *true* and to make it clearer how the abstract landscape of 'delusional' thinking can result in alternative interpretations of the perceived. The starting point of this investigation will be with the root of conviction led by the issue of the schizophrenic disorder with a focus of delusional perception. It will result in a discussion of the way of understanding diagnoses and the movement on the border from what was once normal to now being judged as pathological and vice versa. I apply a cultural angle to enlighten the differences between meaning-making systems in relation to idiosyncratic perception and psychopathology oriented towards patients in clinical practice and general perceptions in everyday life.

Keywords: Delusion and reality; meaning construction; reciprocity of person and environment; contextuality; perception; pathology and diagnosis

Cultural Psychology in Clinical Research and Practices, pages 291–313

Published under exclusive licence by Emerald Publishing Limited
doi:10.1108/978-1-83742-213-520261014

INTRODUCTION

Feeling 'this is true!' is a convenient fixation. It is easy to quickly fall into thinking in well-fixed patterns, get habits and live in one's own idiosyncratic world believing that my way is the common way. Everybody is constantly being influenced from outer sources and it comes to determine a way of understanding. The forms of influencers are many and all of them can be characterized as *culture*. Culture can be described as a tradition of knowledge and practice that is shared and keeps affecting throughout the lifespan (Zou et al., 2009). Any claim for *truth* is a cultural construction. My goal in this chapter is to investigate perception, more specifically the way we construct our knowledge and meaning in the world. The main focus will be regarding different ways of perceiving the same phenomenon and how one's position comes to define the way of constructing meaning hence a truth – for a given person *the* truth. I aim to present examples showing interpretation founded by different positions presenting how the conclusion of normal versus pathological may be determined through meaning-making and sign-regulated perception. I want to discuss the idea of a truth and a shared reality in relation to the normative society. To illustrate the important awareness that is necessary for this topic I will use concrete examples showing the movement across the border to or from pathology in psychiatric history. I intend to question phenomena that may be perceived differently in the future in relation to the changes that has already been from previous diagnoses that are now perceived differently in present day.

RECIPROCITY OF PERSON AND ENVIRONMENT

Cultural psychology perceives the environment and the individual fluently integrated in each other with reciprocal influence. Cultural psychology as a term is used to describe psychological systems of individuals where the culture belongs to the person in which culture is guided into the personal subjective world. Cultural psychology orients toward higher psychological functioning that entail the construction of meaning and take the environmental interactions into account. Through meaningful acting with the environment the person reconstructs it which can both be positive- or negative reconstruction. This process contains a constant negotiation between the inner and outer elements combining the personal deep inner feeling with the imagination and knowledge of the world out there. The human psyche is an open-systemic phenomenon that operates at the border of an intrasubjective as interexternal psychological world.

The way we construct meaning is individual and is led by past experiences and future ambitions. The mind works as a process and given the knowledge and experience one has, the process keeps being affected and impact the way of perceiving, concluding and handling surroundings. There will also constantly be influencers like feelings that come to regulate perception guided by the affective state. What we experience is mediated and the way each individual perceives will therefore be mediated. The signs we meet in our surroundings come to regulate the flow of presence as well as future actions. Signs can represent everything – a sign can be fixed like a label or a stereotype or signs can be something experienced as it can also be something one attribute something into (Valsiner, 2014). Signs can furthermore be mediated semiotically (Valsiner, 2021). Regulating signs toward each other is a dynamic process and they are changeable. He is criminal but not dangerous would be a regulation of signs. Signs are also embedded in time and place. Time is a strange concept grasping past, present and future. Irreversibility of time is a condition, and no actions, feelings or experiences can ever be the same again. This leads all perceptions and actions to be context-bound. The issue of irreversibility of time forces every individual to never be able to completely refer to 'what was' without integrating the ideas of 'what can be'. Meaning-construction, regulation of signs and time-aspects all lead to the instabilities of perception and meaning in the sense that meaning can override and still be controlled by past experiences, regulated in present actions and influence future goals. Meaning-making is hence happening inside one's mind influenced by affective state and guided by environment.

THE TURN TO SEMIOTIC MEDIATION: MULTILAYERED MEANING FIELDS FACING THE FUTURE

The focus becomes centralized to semiotic mediation in which the emphasis is on the subjective experiencing there is to all human beings. To this comes the relation between SELF <> OTHERS in which there is a constructing loop with the person relating with others through the shared creations of meaning (Valsiner, 2007, 2012). Likewise, the general inputs received from the outer world become internalized into personal knowledge in which information goes through a sequence of borders. This transforming process contains a selection which decides the level of internalization. The levels are divided on a spectrum from superficial chat to deep personal meaningfulness. Thus, the construction of meaning is both interpersonally related to people as to environment as it is subjective unique. How we interpret the immediate surrounding is founded by previous history and is influenced by the societal norms and agenda.

Psychiatric diagnoses are meanings of institutional use. The issue of diagnosing in western countries has been displayed and the growing focus on pathologizing human behaviour is a main concern. Diagnostic manuals are used to guide clinical practise and it is these that come to define when a certain behaviour or thinking pattern becomes maladaptive and is object to be pathologized. The way a practitioner interprets the elaborated symptoms of each diagnosis may vary and those interpretations may be guided by political and organizational differences in relation to the specific practise and institution. Furthermore, the ways of interpreting the diagnostical criteria might come to affect the perceptiveness made. The diagnostical manual: ICDs (International Classification of Diseases), is currently being updated and revised to the newest version being number 11. The changes from ICD-10 to ICD-11 may come to affect the way some diagnoses are interpreted which will influence the way it is perceived and understood in the future. It is not released yet so the changes are not definitive, but rumours have it that autism will change to become a spectrum diagnosis. One might wonder what the change from fixed ideas of a certain subtype to a spectrum disorder might come to mean in everyday practise and perception? The movement from 'fixed' to a 'continuum' may come to determine a new way of managing the term of autism. Whether other diagnoses will undergo the same change is still up for questioning and it will be interesting to see how a new formulation of judgement might come to determine a new perception of the same diagnosis.

The changes made in the diagnostical manuals will be with the foundation of above-mentioned criteria. The perception of a diagnosis (what-was to what-can-be), autism for example, will be guided by previous understandings in the attempt to differentiate the 'old and wrong' to the latest update of 'new and correct'. The movement is constant and the way we understand a diagnosis in present time is also guided by new understandings leading to reflections upon the ways it may be changed in the later edition of an ICD-12. The constant changeability, guided by the societal atmosphere, will be inevitable and what might be accepted to be the truth and correct perception will therefore be an endless discussion due to the constant movement.

PERCEIVING IN THE WORLD OF AS-IF: FUNCTIONAL NATURE OF FICTIONS

Hans Vaihinger (1924) described the phenomenon of acting in the world as subjective determent depending on the personal logic and rational based on the believe that the world is '*as-if*' what is individually perceived is right. Things perceived are not a correspondence to objective reality but based on the knowledge we have empirically leading the convictions we have to be 'as-if' they are the truth. He claims that things-in-themselves are not as relevant as what is made by the sensations that are attributed individually to them. *Fictions* is the term he uses to describe the self-made understanding of the world enabling one to understand and behave 'as-if' it is the reality.

Hypothesis is a second term used to describe the judgements made that are problematic given the assumption that it is possible A is B thinking that A is regarded '*as-if*' it is B – but in fact is not (Vaihinger, 1924).

Cases with issues on finding common ground to what is the truth hence the reality could be found more often when psychopathological issues are at stake especially concerning diagnoses that have a different fundamental understanding and perception as the root of their disease. When in clinical practise the psychologist or psychiatrist is trying to determine and distinguish an actual event with the personal construct of it, the ways of interpreting the irreality 'as-if' it is reality is important but may be very difficult. Delusional ideation is closely intertwined with regular perception and it is influenced by personal logic and comprehension. To draw a perfect line that separate the two would be impossible given the idea that not only one thing can be right. Some diagnoses contain a pathological picture of a distorted sense of reality in which the borders between reality and imagination are damaged and get blurred. Schizophrenia is a diagnosis with a disturbed sense of reality and a way of experiencing and perceiving that is often not relatable and, at times, not understandable to others (Simonsen & Møhl, 2017). This type of mental illness is marked by deranged contact and communication often accompanied by psychotic phenomena. Within the schizophrenic spectrum a multiplicity of symptoms and variety of forms appear and there are some typical for the disease as there are symptoms specific to the individual (Parnas, 2003).

INEVITABILITY OF DIFFERENCES IN MEANINGS: THE ORGANON MODEL

When working with people who try to express their inner life, the subjective experience explained and the transforming process from patient (messenger) to psychologist (receiver) becomes relevant. This interaction creates a room in which the principles for communication and reciprocal understanding and general meaning-construction becomes of big importance. In general, people operate with the consensus of common sense which can best be described as an ability to separate relevant and irrelevant information. The surrounding world is fluent and continuously changing and the common sense offers a way of sensing nuances and have a sense of situation in general. It creates a background for meaning as a kind of preunderstanding (Parnas, 2003). Karl Bühler (1934/1990) has created the Organon model (Fig. 14.1) as an instrument to comprehend human communication.

He sets up the conditions for the communication process and illustrates the framework through the expression, the appeal and the representation. The expression is made by the subjective messenger who wishes to construct a certain message. The transforming process, the appeal, is regarded as the

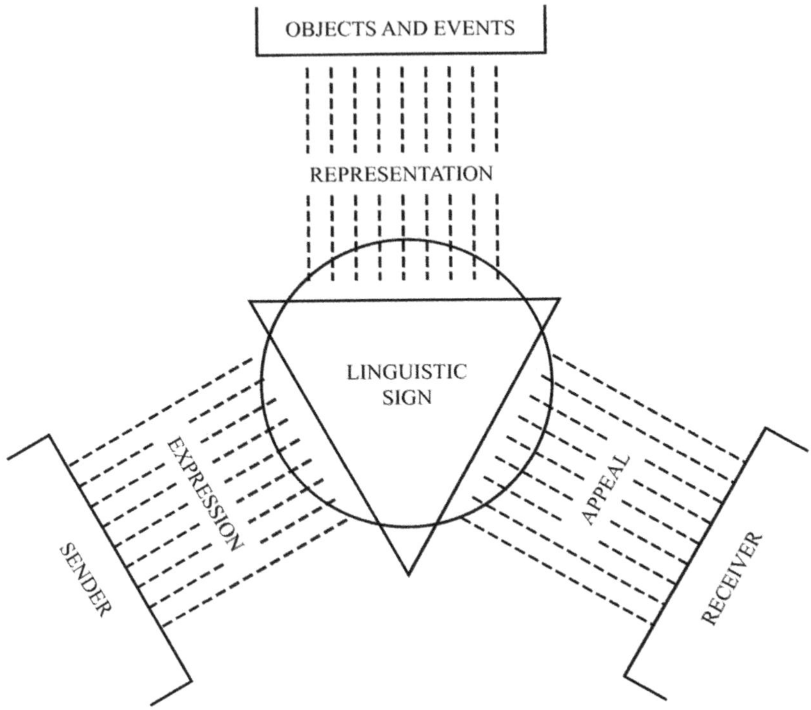

Fig. 14.1. Karl Buhler's Organon Model. *Source:* K. Bühler (1990). Theory of Language: The representational function of language.

impact it has on the receiver although the message is somewhat reconstructed. The representation symbolises the different standpoints making it impossible to send and receive a complete exact message. This is due to the transforming process where a reconstruction will happen in which some factors will influence both the intention with the points send in the message as to the receptive other part who constructs meanings based on personal evaluation.

THE RECONSTRUCTION OF A MESSAGE IN PSYCHIATRIC PRACTICE

Fixed perceptions can manifest and become tacit knowledge (Polanyi, 1962). Delusions may be based on falsified judgements due to pathology but is experienced as real. The separation from a fixed perception to a delusion may be difficult since they are both with a rooted conviction that it is the truth. A delusional person has come to live one's life 'as-if' the delusions are true, and a psychiatrist may practise toward a schizophrenic patient 'as-if' they are delusional. A psychiatrist may state that the content presented by a patient is delusional and this is the truth. The patient believes the psychiatrist is the one being delusional due to his fixed conviction because the patient himself do not believe he is and that is his truth. There may be changing perspectives on what the truth is and the position one has is guiding the given conviction. This dilemma may occur in psychiatric practise being disagreements toward the actual truth and fixations from both parties that may cause failure to see other aspects.

Fig. 14.2 represent the relevance of understanding the positional standpoint for comprehending the way of perceiving. The same statement can for one be interpreted to be pathological that for another can be concluded to be normal. Moreover, the contextual factors come to influence the perception hence the way of creating meaning and make relations to the immediate surrounding. A statement given by a schizophrenic patient in a psychiatric hospital may very well affect a biased way of interpreting. The same statement may be considered normal, or at least different – but not bizarre, by another person or in another contextual setting. Given the example of a patient describing religious connections to a God, this person might quickly be perceived to be delusional whereas a regular churchgoer sitting in a church feeling the same kind of special connection while praying may be perceived completely different. Factors that come to influence the way one attribute meaning to certain statements is related to the positional stance. Furthermore, the delusional content can be based on actual

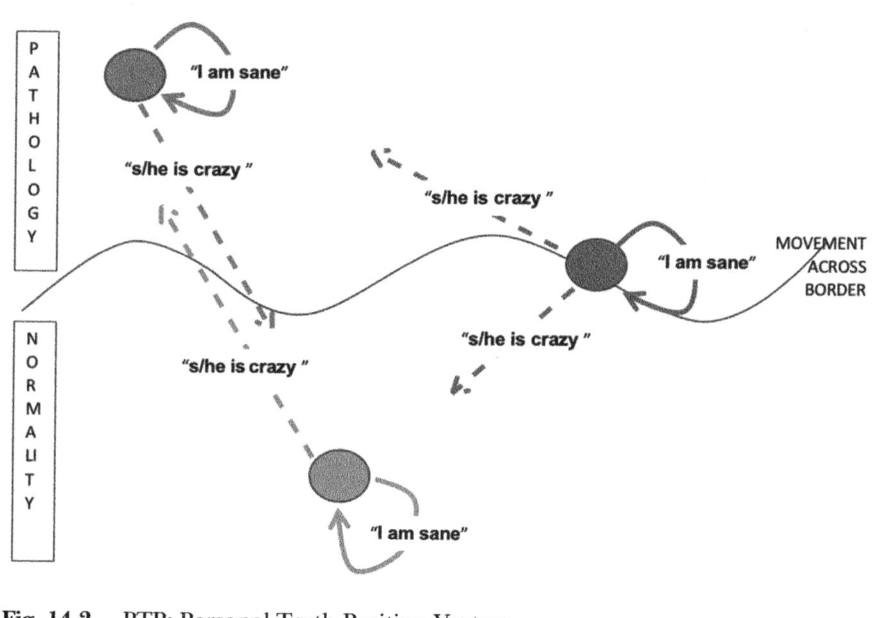

Fig. 14.2. PTP: Personal Truth Position Vectors.

facts for example concerns for the environment or a concern for being infected with Covid-19. The twist of the delusion lies within the extreme conviction and influence on behavior enough for it to be disturbed or decrease functionality. The delusion becomes bizarre when it contravenes what is socio-culturally accepted and does not belong to any other subtype of religious/political/subcultural group and when it is no longer based in accepted social norms and ideas.

Karl Jaspers has described the work with psychopathology and how all statements are always a secondary product when presented (Jaspers, 1997). The secondary product Jaspers refer to can also be conceptualized by the possibilities for reconstruction in the appeal process of the communication illustrated by Bühler. The expression of inner life undergoes a process of interpretation when presented to a second part. The expression will be loaded with feelings and the constructed meanings attached for the sender may be differently perceived by the receiver. The process presented by Bühler presents a formulation of a message that undergo a reconstruction before received by the receiver. The reconstructing process – the appeal – will by a professional be supplemented by an analysis based on theoretical knowledge and working experience that may influence the way the send message is perceived.

Schizophrenic disorder is usually marked by fundamental disturbances in the way of experiencing affect, thinking, perceiving and acting. Schizophrenic disorders can be given with different subtypes: F20.x-F29 (WHO, 1994). In the work with schizophrenic patients the practitioner can become familiar with different kinds of delusional content. As described previously, different symptoms can appear within the same diagnosis and the delusional content can take form differently. Some delusional content have already been categorized based on the subject matter. Examples could be:

Persecutory delusions that often take the character of the inflicted person to feel targeted in some way. It can often be experienced with a conviction of being harassed by someone either a person, an organization or something else (Roy, 2016).

Erotomanic delusions often take the character of believing someone is in love with the person or are in a relationship (Roy, 2016). This can often be with a conviction concerning having a relationship with a famous person.

Somatic delusions can often appear as a preoccupation with the appearance or function of the body. This could be delusions of body odour, believing one smell bad, or delusions about infestation, believing one is infested with parasites or having bodily sensations that aren't true (Roy, 2016).

There are many different types of delusional content and some a more regular than others. There are also other types of delusional content being: *Frégoli delusions* (conviction strangers are familiar being in disguise) (Langdon et al., 2014), *Capgras delusions* (conviction of a loved one being replaced by a stranger) (Capgras et al., 1923), or *religious delusions* (consisting of anomalous experiences that one communicates with a higher power) and many more.

These different delusions load into different convictions. How these convictions are made is what is important to discuss when grasping the extent and severity of the delusion. Delusion can generally be described as a: '… manifestation of knowledge and error in regard to the empirical reality…' (Jaspers, 1997, p. 108). Jaspers uses his terms: *believed-in-reality* where the facts conducted by the person is arising from the perceived reality and *delusion-proper* where the origin and idea of the delusion is vague and blurred. Jaspers emphasizes that the origin of the delusion is essential to correctly build an understanding of it. He elucidates the understanding of reality to be concerning a conceptual reality – the reality we experience. Senses can come to disturb even though they are rooted in the actual reality. He therefore distinguishes between immediate certainty of reality and reality-judgement. Delusions manifest themselves in judgements and will therefore be termed delusions when there are pathological falsified judgements included (Jaspers, 1997). The distinguishing between an extreme conviction and a delusion can therefore become difficult and the judgement of the pathological degree likewise.

The functionality of the delusion may be considered with regard to the content. A delusional conviction or a creation of meaning 'as-if' may serve to function as a coping strategy. Some delusional content may be created as a protective mechanism – protecting from the unbearable reality. The origin for the delusion might be of importance to understand the evolvement of it. Other kind of delusional experiences may be traceable to previous convictions or experiences that have resulted in the expansion of it. The functionality may be relevant to address for understanding the mechanisms of a delusion.

Fig. 14.3 serves to illustrate how something can be relative and move on a border between normal as pathological. The distinction can be difficult and the root for the conviction may create a different understanding that influence perception and meaning-construction. The pathological degree might be difficult and the reason for this may be because of the movement on the border. The same experience or situation might be perceived as

Fig. 14.3. Movement on the Border.

normal as it might be perceived as delusional and the judgement of it might change because of circumstances or due to new knowledge that is gained serving as an explanation. Hearing something from a schizophrenic patient may already be partly disregarded without paying attention to what is said because of the conviction that it will be delusional. A mentally ill patient may be symptomatic and express extreme delusional convictions now but may later, in an ordinary state, try to be humoristic and joke about topics relational to previous delusional content without actually showing signs of being delusional.

The known history for a particular patient comes to guide the interpretations made by the practitioner and may be info guiding a prejudiced perception. The initial position a practitioner has come to define the way statements and behavior is being construed and that may change over time while getting to know and understand the patient in question. What was once considered delusional is now considered as ordinary humor. The movement on the border between pathological and normal is not only guided by the statements of the patient himself but also by the position one has that is interpreting it. The pathological ideation can exist from mild to extreme. If the conviction seems unlikely but possible it can be placed on the end closets to mild – Fig. 14.4.

A humoristic comment can be interpreted as either slightly inappropriate or concerning depending on the messenger. A man joking about his x-wife by commenting 'I got rid of her' compared to a psychiatric patient using the same formulation joking about his love life 'I got rid of her' may create two different associations.

This subdivision and way of interpreting is guided by the person in hand. If a person in a psychiatric ward is expressing morbid humor one might be easier to judge it as real and may even create concerns rather than sharing a laugh. The interpretations of the movement are controlled by context, perception, time and place and more importantly the people present. Whether something is normal or pathological or whether it borders to be mildly pathological or just 'different' from the main norms and expectations is all an individual estimation.

Delusional or Ideal Concern?

Persecutory delusions may be somewhat regular with some schizophrenic patients who have a tendency toward paranoia. The persecutory content

Fig. 14.4. Spectrum of Pathological Degree.

can take a certain form and the origin of the delusion and the context may offer an explanation for the conviction. Different scenarios offer an illustration of the pathological degree and the chances for the persecutory delusional content to be true even though rarely seen. The illustrated examples beneath are inspired by delusional content of psychiatric patients and illustrates the levels of difficulty when assessing delusions that may or may not be true.

Taking the example of a schizophrenic patient who happens to be a gang member. It may be a part of the disease to feel threatened and to stay alert. The circumstances in this case offer foundation for questioning persecutory concerns in which it makes perfect sense that a gang member needs to be careful. Depending on the way one looks at it, it may be hard to define the pathological degree and whether the concerns are legitimate or imagined. This constellation of factors influences the ability to clinically separate delusional from real, and a wrongful judgement may be with bigger consequences than in other cases. If the schizophrenic patient is tried liquidated the persecutory content moves away from being solely pathological.

A different example, including a possible but less likely concern, may be a schizophrenic patient who believes that he is being monitored by the police, PET or other military forces. This patient may create a delusional idea that surveillance has been planted in his home. This may be true, but less likely if the person has no reason for being suspected for crimes that would result in this. If the patient happens to be known for associating with terrorism, the question of realness versus imagination becomes questioned. Now the possibility seems more likely due to contextual factors feeding into the possibility of realness.

A third scenario, offering an even less likely event to occur includes a schizophrenic patient who feels targeted, due to his delusions involving an idea of being captured and having his organs harvested by aliens. Some convictions may easily be placed on the spectrum to be undoubtedly bizarre hence pathological. The interesting aspects are the ones that move on the border between pathological and normal.

Delusional or Traumatised?

The origin of the delusional experience may offer some explanations for the way it has evolved and for the way it may inflict the personal life. Traumatic experiences can become the root for disturbed evaluations of the reality and the exact happenings in a given situation. Traumatic events can as a consequence lead to different psychological disorders like Posttraumatic stress disorder. The traumatic event can result in maladaptive reaction and become a long-term encumbrance and reduce social functioning. The symptoms appear initially as the person being in a state where one is fuddled with limited awareness and disorientation. Typical symptoms may appear as flashbacks, dissociation, nightmare and increased tension and irritability (WHO, 1994). Some of these symptoms may also move on the illustrated border above when the delusional content is rooted in memories or flash backs from real experiences.

Taking the example of a former soldier who has been captured and tortured by the enemy forces and later starts showing symptoms for stress and trauma. The torture during the capture has been inhumane and has resulted in severe posttraumatic stress. The flash backs experienced is filled with bad memories of the torture being electrocuted. When wakening up from a nightmare and still in the believe of being captured where are we then on the border? Some people can be traumatized due to experiences they have been victims of or due to their own actions. When reappearances of the previous experiences happen are they then delusional or only bad memories. Imagining that the trauma and several other factors had resulted in a delusional outbreak, one may be sure that the experience in present time is unreal but the root of the conviction is leading back to real happenings how should the delusional content then be approached and understood? Does it have a certain relevance that the delusions occurring are based on trauma. One might expect that the sense of reality becomes twisted in a torture situation even though it is real. It may be possible that the cruelty of the torture makes the reality unbelievable – a *reversed delusion* bordering to dissociation.

Being in a war one's perception changes and the idea of good and evil might change – even if just momentarily. The circumstances and contextual setting are crucial to understand the root of convictions and figuring out the source of the delusion which may create an understanding of what is behind and underlying. Having a patient experiencing radiation and believing people wants to electrocute him seems bizarre and definitely delusional. If the patient has these exact experiences from battle the bizarreness disappears. Having a patient in Denmark who fears to be electrocuted seems unlikely and therefore tend to be more bizarre. But could it be questioned if a patient in USA, fearing the same electrocution, would not be seen as bizarre because of the use of an electric chair as a death penalty in certain states. Bizarreness is evaluated in the immediate context and is judged by the ideas of the present time and place. What is a bizarre delusion for a Danish patient may not be a bizarre delusion for an American. And what is considered a bizarre religious delusion in Christianity may not be in Islam.

Delusional or Religious Conviction?

Religious experiences can become symbolic truths that has served human beings throughout centuries and the realness of them is hard to objectively decide. The religious convictions may have been incorporated as truths 'as-if' it is possible. One could come to question the differences when distinguishing religious experiences with religious delusions and the distinction may only be relevant to create if there is a necessary purpose. Christianity, Islam and Judaism all originates from some of the same stories and people. Although the origin may be similar the developments in each religion have evolved in very different ways. Islamic religion acknowledges the belief of Jinns [Djinns] – spirits. Some are believed to be evil and dangerous and some are believed to be good and helpful. The believe in spirits and supernatural creatures are for some real and for others imaginary bordering to delusional. In a society believing in Christianity the idea of spirits may seem delusional and the cultural differences might impact perceptiveness. Cultural and religious differences might create a gap between real and delusional and in the attempt to distinguish between the two the right judgement is made by peers when considering what borders to being pathological. Even mentally healthy individuals are able to make incorrect inferences from the external reality. There may come errors in reasoning and an ability to forming ideas based on 'shared truths' from what was happening in a given situation or by facts conducted personally. *Delusion-like beliefs* may be shared by some in the normal population for example the believe of telepathy, ghosts or have seen an UFO or other strange objects from the universe (Kleiger & Khadivi, 2015).

How we come to perceive certain people and how we construct meaning and create associations is important to bear in mind because it becomes tacit knowledge. If tacit knowledge becomes a part of the everyday assumption it might influence not only the way one perceives but also the way the surrounding environment come to act. Jaspers (1997) has argued that convictions made by the mass cannot be termed a delusion. Using this rationale, one might look at the believe of witches to understand a movement from nonpathological to pathological. Looking back historically, the existence of witches was a shared conviction and it led to mass-killings of mainly women being interpreted to be in accomplice with the devil or being 'different' in a way that did not fit the norm. At present day, only few share the conviction of witches and the mass believe has moved and made the believe of witches to border towards pathological.

FROM ORDINARY MEANINGS TO DIAGNOSTIC LABELS (AND BACK)

What we have experienced previously and the extent of our knowledge come to guide us in a world with abstract phenomena and different customs, norms and worldviews (Moscovici, 1981). Also, professionally, one becomes influenced by the textbooks, articles and research there has been made so far. These works as guidelines but must never become definite truths and this is the reason why: The truth keeps changing! What is right and true at the present moment may not be so in 1, 50 or 100 years from now or in present time in another community.

Diagnostic manuals: ICD and DSMs (Diagnostical and Statistical Manual of Mental Disorders) are kept being updated and revised on the basis of changed perspectives and due to new research and knowledge. Why these may only be used as guidelines is due to the level of update and with considerations on cultural differences. The perception of right and wrong changes and may be individual to different cultures and in different societies. In addition, the criteria for fulfilling the needed symptoms for a diagnosis can change as well. Having a diagnosis can help one to understand own behavior-patterns and to be educated in the pathology relevant for the disease.

On the downside, a diagnosis can also be an object for labelling and stigmatization and can wrongly be used as either an excuse or a misplaced explanation. In some countries, having a diagnosis can be relevant for being offered help both financially and in general. In other countries, a diagnosis can make it impossible to be seen as anything other than a limitation. Even the definition of what the diagnosis contains change depending on the way we understand the attributed symptoms. This may be influenced by especially the culture and the pathological picture that may come to influence the general perception of it.

'Diagnostic cultures' is a term that is used in some western societies. Diagnostic terms are in these applied in everyday practice more and more often and the purpose of the use between health professionals and lay people is different. Terms like stress, grief, OCD, ADHD, anxiety and depression to name a few. Besides the increased terminology, several new diagnoses have been suggested and the diagnostic manuals have increased the number of psychiatric diagnoses. The number of given diagnoses to people seem to increase concurrently (Brinkmann, 2016a, 2016b). Furthermore, there is a group of people who ought to be given a psychiatric diagnosis but do not have one. The difference between the ones who have and the ones who ought to have – the treatment gap – is relevant because of the societal context that usually give passage to treatment. Some that belong to the category of underdiagnosed may be there due to the idea of not feeling like having a psychiatric problem or because they do not wish to seek help for it. A phenomenological approach could be used to examine the way people experience being diagnosed or how they experience having the diagnosis (Shweder, 1990). Diagnoses affect the way a person interpret oneself and many discussions have been made on the topic of the issue of individualization of diagnoses (Brinkmann, 2016a, 2016b). The use of psychiatric language and the application of words within it – signs – are mediated through semiotic mediation and come to determine the way of thinking and acting upon them. This come together to constitute the practices of diagnoses.

The border between the normal and the pathological is transformed in the history of a society. An example could be the general phenomenon and feeling: grief. Grief is a human emotion and most likely an emotion everybody experiences. The expression can look different depending on the person or influenced by the culture. The way of experiencing mourning and expressing grief can be situated and people are sometimes subjected or subjugated by a certain narrative of grief. There may be expectations towards the appropriate way of expressing grief and even have rules or social expectations towards the way of handling and displaying it. If grief is not displayed in the right manner one might risk being labeled aberrant and judged by it. Grieving too long, at the wrong time or not grieving at all are all examples of a way grief can be interpreted to be wrong, different or in an inappropriate manner (Neimeyer et al., 2014a).

Grief is about to make its debut as a diagnostic category. It will become a diagnosis in ICD-11 with the name 'Prolonged Grief Disorder' and will be categorized as a pathological disease manifested with a series of certain symptoms (Jacobsen & Petersen, 2018). The way we perceive and evaluate an emotion in regard to a disease may change or be influenced through time and what was once normal may become pathologized. There are disagreements of whether an emotion like grief should be pathologized to the extreme of making it a diagnosis. Some of the concerns mentioned in the discussion of pathologizing grief is the issue of the tendency to make grief an individual psychological phenomenon. This means that it will be interpreted to be inside the person with individual symptoms hence individualizing it. The problem of individualizing it in regard to making it an intrapsychological phenomenon is the way one might perceive it as 'an assignment' that needs to be fixed or handled (Jacobsen & Petersen, 2018). This will implicate difficult feelings to become a part of the diagnostical culture.

Making grief a diagnosis may be problematic given the cultural expectations towards a 'right' way of experiencing and displaying it. The diagnosis will in some sense create a framework for abnormal grief and make the phenomenon sickened. Others will argue that the diagnosis will establish a way of separating pathological and normal grief. The argument is that normal grief will be reduced as a subject for treatment and with the diagnostical symptoms categorized for the pathological grief making sure that only that part will be treated. The continuing discussion will probably be whether the differentiation is that easy? The understanding and acceptance of death might influence the way of approaching the loss of a loved one. Grief is universal and biological but the way of handling a changed relationship to a deceased and come to accept it are personally narrated and socially shared and is complied in accordance to the societal rules (Neimeyer et al., 2014b). The way of handling grief is often connected to religious or normative traditions and different countries have different beliefs of the concept of death. Some believe in reincarnation, others believe that death is temporary and that they will be reunited once again. The belief and the traditional customs might also influence the way of perceiving death and the way of approaching grief and sorrow.

The narrative connected to grief and death and the customs and norms connected to the traditions when handling a passing might all be factors for creating a 'right' way of doing it. The issue of pathologizing grief might be that the general perception of what it is and how it is supposed to be felt and expressed might change. There might be movement on the border and the feeling, experience and expression of it may be controlled. This border can be discussed in the light of what is considered pathological by comparison to 'normal' – see Fig. 14.5. The difficult part is, that the idea of what is pathological depends (Vestbjerg, 2021).

As grief diagnosis comes – it takes an ordinary meaning and extends it to the institutional role of diagnosis. There may arise a problem when a phenomenon being an emotion, a way of thinking or whatever else becomes an object for being made maladaptive or sick. The example above is used with the emotion grief, but many things could take its place in the discussion of pathologizing general phenomena. The narration of grief may change. This may include the way we come to speak of it and the discourses and social constructions may come to influence the general perception. Once the general perception has moved on the border to be more likely to be considered maladaptive, other otherwise common phenomena may follow.

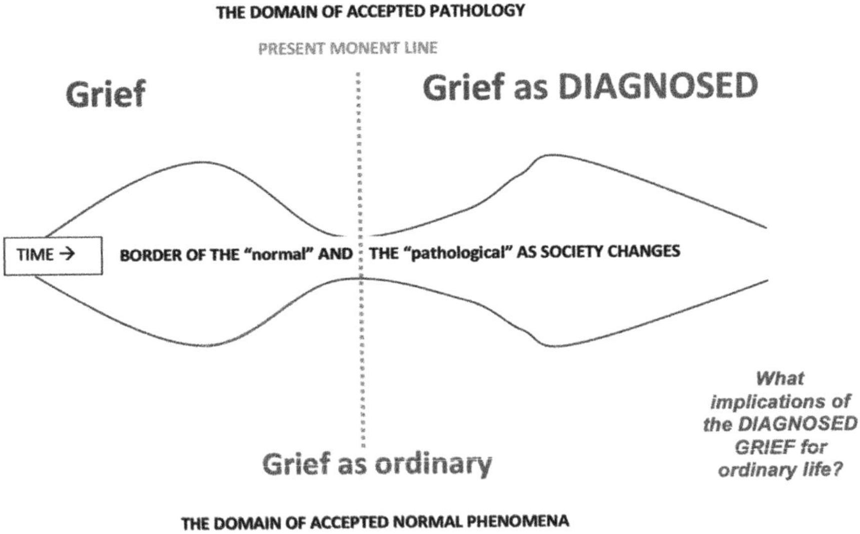

Fig. 14.5. Movement of the Phenomenon of GRIEF on the Border Toward Pathological.

In a similar vein – can we think of an emotion, state of mind or a certain kind of behavior that today is considered reasonable but may in the future be seen as a mental illness? Anger for example? May there be several phenomena that is now considered to be a condition to life, just like grief, will soon be considered to be made maladaptive if not expressed, felt or handled in a certain way accepted by the society?

Will the treatments applied for different diseases today be seen as catastrophic in the future? Will not only the idea of different diagnoses change, but the idea of how to handle such diagnoses follow the movement? Some treatment methods have been used prior in psychiatric history that we today could never imagine to even consider – for example lobotomy (prefrontal leucotomy). Could we come to reflect upon methods used in present day that will in the future be seen as the same kind of mistake that we today interpret a lobotomy surgery to be. Electroshock therapy (ECT), is today used to treat different diagnoses like depression (Cerletti & Bini, 2018). ECT is a method conducted by giving electric shock in the brain and one might wonder if that may be looked at very differently in the future? Do we have treatments either medically or psychologically that is considered decent in one's age but will be considered unimaginable in the future – will there be a similar kind of movement on the borderline separating normal and unimaginable.

MOVEMENT ON THE BORDER TOWARDS NORMAL

The discussion till now has been concerning the ability to pathologize different phenomena. It has mainly focused on the issue of making something sick or abnormal in regard to perceiving it as normal or reasonable explainable. The point of this discussion has been to offer a variety of versions that could function as explanations for the same act, experience etc. and how it may be interpreted. The idea has been to outline some of the main factors that come to influence a certain way of perceiving and the idea of a truth that can guide a way of understanding.

To make my point complete, I must also present cases that illustrate movement towards normalization. Pathologizing general as abnormal phenomena has not only been rising because some diagnoses have moved the opposite way on the border. Some of the latest developments in the perception of pathological toward normal has been the interpretation of gender – and sexual orientation.

The scope of sexual orientation has broadened and the idea of sexual orientation towards either opposite sex or same sex is changing. There even is a division between sexual orientation compared to sexual behavior and these two may not be equivalent with each other. It has been somewhat common to categorize, label and put orientations into boxes but the issue has been movement between those and some that may not fit at all. The numbers of categories are rising and it has moved from being either heterosexual or homosexual to contain several categories being: bisexual, pansexual, asexual and many more. Some will argue that the acceptance of the new categories has been difficult and that the understanding of these different orientations is still not shared by all. It was criminal to have sexual intercourse with someone of the same sex till the year of 1930. After 1930 homosexuality was considered to be a mental illness. Homosexuality was considered a mental illness up to 1981 in Denmark but it was not before the year of 1992 that it was removed from the lists of diagnoses of the World Health Organization (Lildal-Schrøder, 2020). Criminalizing and pathologizing homosexuality has influenced the way society perceives it. Even though it has moved away from being considered an illness in the diagnostic manuals, it is still in some countries frowned upon and it is still causing violence and death to homosexual people. Some people are still not able to express their true self and some are forced to hide their sexual orientation due to fear of being mistreated. This is the result of pathologizing a 'condition' or certain believe, feeling or behavior. Even though it has changed in the manuals to no longer being categorized as an illness the perception in society has not followed the movement in the same pace-illustrated in Fig. 14.6.

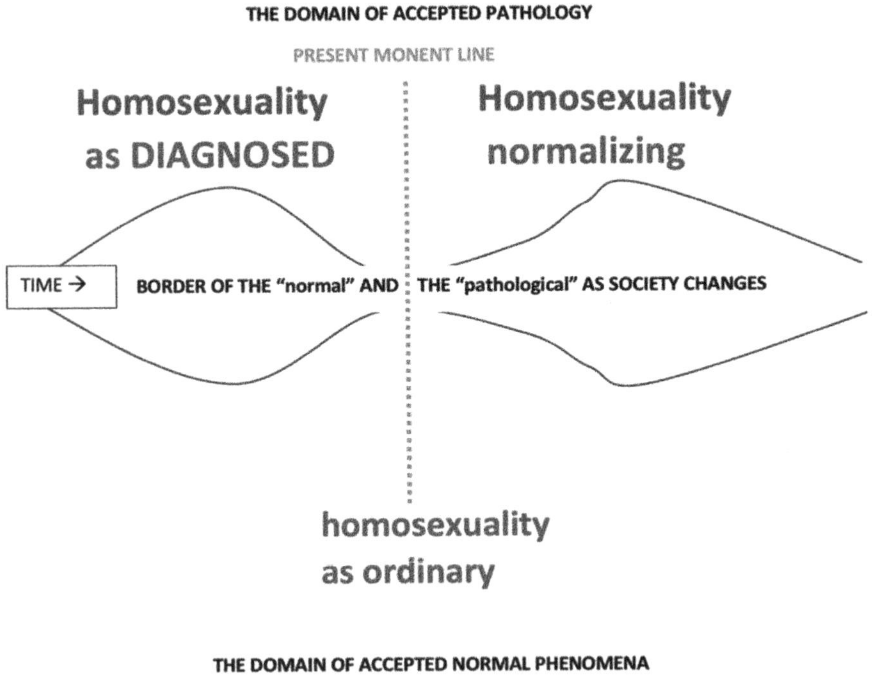

Fig. 14.6. Movement of the Phenomenon of HOMOSEXUALITY on the Border Toward Normal.

The word 'Queer' covers both a way of describing a person or an approach to gender and sexuality. It is a term used to describe opinions, forms of behavior and identities that are in opposition to heteronormative and cis-normative ideas and practices. It challenges the idea of making one orientation more normal than another. Transgender is a term describing a person whom does not identify oneself with the gender that was given at birth. Some people experience this by having a feeling of something being wrong or experiencing their body change in puberty that does not match the feelings inside. The movie 'The Danish Girl' about the first transgender getting a gender-changing operation in the world illustrates a way of understanding complex thoughts and behavior that is not yet a common phenomenon. The movie shows the issues of the personal crisis of feeling a stranger to one's own body and to have thoughts that does not match what is expected by the society or the assumed or common way of 'being'. The movie illustrates the difficulties connected with being 'different' from the normative society. There is a scene illustrating the main character visiting doctors in the attempt to be cured and while describing 'symptoms' the doctor note schizophrenia. Once a conviction is made, professionals may unknowingly submit to *confirmation bias.* Descriptions that are not yet known to be a common phenomenon and the symptoms described are associated with symptoms sounding alike other diseases. This may serve as an example to show that something brought into the field of psychiatry does not necessarily mean mental illness. It may just be something that is not yet described or accepted in the community. Transgender was considered a mental illness until the year of 2017 (Lildal-Schrøder, 2020).

Transgender is a second phenomenon (after homosexuality) that is now on the movement on the border from being pathologized to being normalized. But just as the issue with homosexuality, once something has been perceived to be sick, some people struggle with distancing themselves from the old truth. Diagnoses have been created to make people fit into categories making it easier to understand what is at stake in a given situation but the problem is the ability to accept new perspectives toward old understandings. There might be problematics connected to acceptance of the transition of previous diagnoses to being a common and normal phenomenon. The movement on the border makes it difficult to agree on right and wrong and the idea of what is true is changing – leaving a situation for people to debate and disagree influenced by historical, cultural and religious factors.

Homosexuality or being transgender may for some people never be accepted to be normal. Other movements like these are likely to occur and the changes in society may open up for new discussions leading people to change perceptions and ideas of what is true and not. What is currently being considered to be maladaptive at present time may be completely normal in the future. Some diagnoses historically classified under sections related to sexual orientation, gender identity, and gender incongruence have been revised or removed in newer diagnostic frameworks. Rather than being understood as mental illnesses, they are increasingly framed as part of natural variations in human sexuality and gender diversity.

Will our idea of pathological not only be connected certain diseases but also certain types of people or attributed based on stereotypes or gender roles? One might ask whether a certain perspective today is influenced by previous ideas of gender with regard to traits. Certain diagnoses can be argued to be labeled more often for a woman and others more often for a man. In everyday life, ADHD is often connected to the idea of a boy, more specifically, a boy in school who is not able to sit still. Other diagnoses are more known to be associated with women for example borderline. Stereotypes may occur in everyday perception which may come to influence the psychiatric assesment. It will be interesting to see if any kind of movement will influence the fixed ideas of certain 'types' fitting diagnoses – influenced by societal changes and a break with the typical gender roles.

Fig. 14.7 represents the two-way traffic across the border of Figure 14.3. The timeline illustrates the movement in society that affects the perception of different phenomena and the influence it has on the normalization or pathologizing of diagnoses. Grief is going to be a disease, in reverse to homosexuality, a natural phenomenon for loss now turned into pathology. In that context, truth in general is not determinable it will depend on the

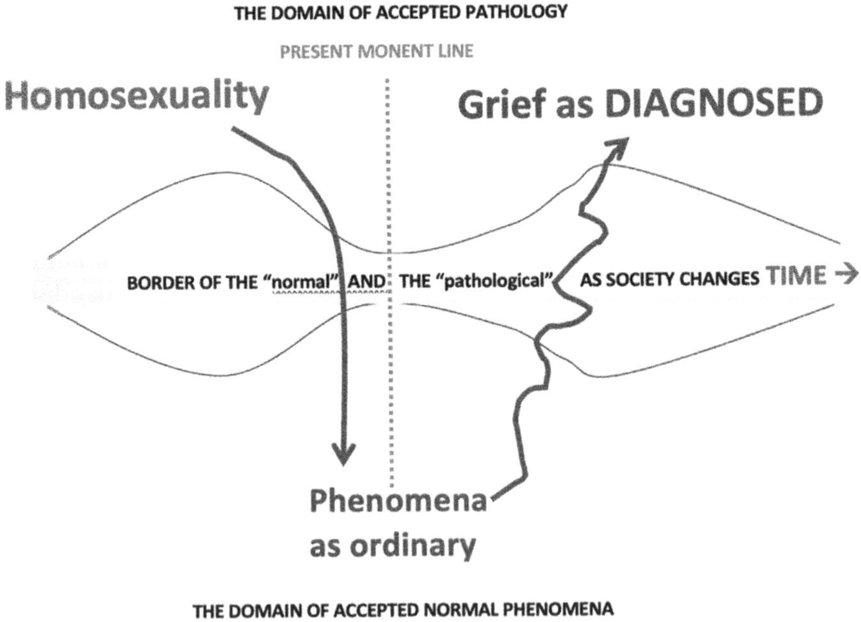

Fig. 14.7. Movement of Phenomena on the Border.

viewer's standpoints. Some phenomena are on a constant move on the border making it difficult to categorize as maladaptive behavior in regard to deviance from majority, societal expectations or political interests.

CONCLUSION: BEYOND DELUSIONS OF CLINICAL PSYCHOLOGICAL PRACTICES

Fundamentally we perceive the world preorganized for the way we come to think and act in it. Perception is linked to time and place and is guided by previous experiences and future goals. The known past is affecting the way we come to interpret the presence and the ideas and ambitions for the future.

The way we come to understand mental illness and the diagnoses we know of are categorized by the understanding of normal or maladaptive. There is a constant movement bordering between normal and pathological as I highlighted in this chapter. Where to place a phenomenon on the border, and deciding a pathological degree, come to be mediated by cultural factors. There is a fluctuation in the pathological <> normal contrasts in everyday life. The diagnostical changes concerning common emotions and an expected way of feeling and displaying them are changing in everyday life guided by pathological ideation.

My examples in this chapter came from the field of psychiatry, but the need to understand the implicit symbolic powers of turning ordinary meanings into diagnostic labels is even more important in ordinary practices of clinical psychology – in diagnostics and in therapy. In both, the lack of awareness of the cultural roots of the institutional meanings we honor as 'diagnostic' can in the end hurt the well-being of our patients, although this is a growing focus for example in ethnographic psychiatry. Cultural psychology offers an approach to stay aware of the personal meaning-construction of a person as it can also offer a more general notice on the way interactions with the environment and the people in it impacts. Emerging cultural psychological standpoints to the clinical practise is to create a science of human conduct looking at human relations to their social world. Human experience is deep and personal and the personal world is created through meaningful interaction with the immediate environment. Our cultural meaning systems are a part of our relating with the world and come of importance when trying to relate and create meaning with relevant others.

REFERENCES

Brinkmann, S. (2016a). Toward a cultural psychology of mental disorder: The case of attention deficit hyperactivity disorder. *Culture & Psychology, 22*(1), 80–93.

Brinkmann, S. (2016b). *Diagnostic cultures. A cultural approach to the pathologization of modern life.* Routledge.

Bühler, K. (1990). *Theory of language: The representational function of language.* John Benjamins.

Capgras, J., & Reboul-Lachaux, J. (1923). L'illusion des "sosies" dans un delire systematisé. *Bulletin de la Société de Médecine Mentale, 11,* 6–16. Translated by Ellis, H. D., Whitley, J., & Luauté, J-P. History of Psychiatry, 1994, pp. 134–137.

Cerletti, U., & Bini, L. (2018). Electroshock. *International Review of Psychiatry, 30,* 2. https://doi.org/10.1080/09540261.2018.1436662

Jacobsen, H. M., & Petersen, A. (2018). *Sorgens socialitet – en sociologisk kommentar til psykologiseringen og medikaliseringen af menneskelige følelser* (pp. 55–73). Psyke & Logos.

Jaspers, K. (1997). *General psychopathology – Vol. 1.* The John Hopkins University Press.

Kleiger, J. H., & Khadivi, A. (2015). *Assessing psychosis – A clinicians's guide.* Routledge, Taylor & Francis.

Langdon, R., Connaughton, C., & Coltheart, M. (2014). The Fregoli delusion: A disorder of person identification and tracking. *Cognitive Science.* https://doi.org/10.1111/tops.12108

Lildal-Schrøder, N. (2020). *Kort & Godt om LGBT+.* Dansk psykologisk forlag.

Moscovici, S. (1981). On social representations. In J. P. Forgas (Ed.), *Social cognition: Perspectives in everyday understanding* (pp. 181–209). Academic Press.

Neimeyer, R. A., Klass, D., & Dennis, M. R. (2014a). Mourning, meaning, and memory: Individual, communal, and cultural narration of grief. In *Meaning in positive and existential psychology* (pp. 325–346). Springer.

Neimeyer, R. A., Klass, D., & Dennis, M. R. (2014b). *A social constructionist account of grief: Loss and the narration of meaning* (Vol. *38*(8). pp. 485–498). Routledge, Taylor & Francis Group.

Parnas, J. (2003). Skizofreni, skizotypisk sindslidelse, paranoide psykoser, akutte forbigående psykoser samt skizoaffektive psykoser. In R. Hemmingsen, J. Parnas, A. Gjerris, N. Reisby, & P. Kragh-Sørensen, (Eds.), *Klinisk psykiatri* (Vol. 2. udg.).

Polanyi, M. (1962). *Personal knowledge – Toward a post-critical philosophy* (pp. 69–131). The University of Chicago Press.

Roy, M., (2016) Delusional disorders. In S. H. Fatemi, & P. J. Clayton, (Eds.), *The medical basis of psychiatry* (4.th edition). Springer. https://doi.org/10.1007/978-1-4939-2528-5

Shweder, R. A. (1990). Cultural psychology – What is it? In J. W. Stigler, R. A. Shweder, & G. Herdt, (Eds.), *Cultural psychology: Essays on comparative human development.* Cambridge University Press.

Simonsen, E., & Møhl, B. (2017). *Grundbog i psykiatri. 2* (pp. 325–346). udgave. Hans Reitzels Forlag.

Vaihinger, H. (1924). *The philosophy of 'as if' – A system of the theoretical, practical and religious fictions of mankind.* Routledge & Kegan Paul-.

Valsiner, J. (2007). *Culture in minds and societies. Foundations of cultural psychology* (pp. 19–72). Sage.

Valsiner, J. (2012). Culture in psychology: A renewed encounter of inquisitive minds. In J. Valsiner (Ed.), *The Oxford handbook of culture and psychology* (pp. 3–24). Oxford University Press.

Valsiner, J. (2014). *An invitation to cultural psychology*. Sage.

Valsiner, J. (2021). *Hyper-generalization by the human mind: The role of sign hierarchies.* Hans Kilian Preis Lecture. PsychoSozial Verlag. April 28, 2017.

Vestbjerg, C. S. (2021).The making of delusions: From imagination to irreality. *Integrative Psychological and Behavioral Science. 55,* p. 2. Springer. https://doi.org/10.1007/s12124-021-09614-y

World Health Organization. (1994). WHO ICD-10, Psykiske lidelser og adfærdsmæssige forstyrrelser, klassifikation og diagnostiske kriterier. In *F20-F29, Skizofreni, skizotypisk sindslidelse og psykoser* (pp. 65–79).

Zou, X., Tam, K., Morris, M., Lee, S., Lau, I., & Chiu, C. (2009). Culture as common sense: Perceived consensus versus personal beliefs as mechanisms of cultural influence. *Journal of Personality and Social Psychology, 97*(4), 579–597. https://doi.org/10.1037/a0016399

CHAPTER 15

CONCLUDING REFLECTIONS: THE NEED FOR A DIALOGUE BETWEEN CULTURAL, INDIGENOUS, AND CLINICAL PSYCHOLOGIES

Audrey S. Namdiero-Walsh
Independent Scholar and Researcher, Germany

Meike Watzlawik
Sigmund Freud Universität, Germany

This volume set out to ask a simple but pressing question: *how can cultural psychology strengthen clinical psychology research and practice?* Across the contributions, the answer has been consistent. Culture is not an optional context or a variable to be 'controlled for'. It is a constitutive force in the ways distress is experienced, expressed, and addressed. Psychological phenomena emerge through culturally mediated forms of meaning-making, and without attending to those cultural processes, Clinical Psychology risks misunderstanding the very experiences it seeks to alleviate.

Mainstream clinical psychology has long been shaped by Western epistemologies, diagnostic categories, and therapeutic techniques. While these models have yielded valuable insights, they remain partial and often fail to

Cultural Psychology in Clinical Research and Practices, pages 315–320

doi:10.1108/978-1-83742-213-520261015

capture the plurality of cultural realities or heterogenous ways in which suffering is lived (Henrich et al., 2010). This book responds to those limitations by offering perspectives that emphasise cultural diversity, ethical reflexivity, and political awareness. Cultural Psychology emerges here not merely as an added lens, but as a vital architecture for rethinking both the science and the practice of mental health. Calls for decolonial approaches to knowledge, long emphasized in critical scholarship (e.g., Kirmayer & Pedersen, 2014), align with this vision by challenging the presumed universality of Western categories and by foregrounding knowledge that is relational, embodied, situated, and historically grounded.

RETHINKING THEORY AND KNOWLEDGE PRODUCTION

Several chapters highlight the need to rethink the theoretical foundations of clinical psychology. Semiotic and phenomenological approaches expand our understanding of how individuals construct meaning, especially in contexts marked by suffering or ambiguity (De Luca Picione, Marlino, & Lemmo; Molina & Fossa, *this volume*). Others call for deeper engagement with Indigenous knowledge and nonWestern psychologies, not as peripheral cultural variations, but as equal partners in theory-building (Chakkarath; de Lima Neto & Guimarães, *this volume*). This entails recognizing that knowledge is created within relationships: with communities, with environments, and with the more-than-human world. Such an understanding challenges the linear and hierarchical logic of conventional models, replacing it with a more dynamic, associative or 'spiralic' conception of knowledge development.

Especially Indigenous epistemologies emphasize that knowledge is not neutral or universal; it is alive, connected to land, ancestry, and community, and expressed not only in words, but also in movement, silence, art, music, and ritual. Such expanded notions of language and communication resonate deeply with cultural-psychological theories that view meaning-making as dialogical, embodied, and temporal. Incorporating these perspectives into Clinical Psychology requires not only methodological pluralism, but a willingness to engage in what can be called participatory unlearning: The active dismantling of assumptions that implicitly position Western frameworks as normative (Papa & Takua, 2025).

CLINICAL PRACTICE AS POLITICAL, ETHICAL, AND RELATIONAL WORK

The volume makes clear that clinical psychology cannot be value neutral. Rhodes and colleagues argue that therapy sits within broader questions of justice and should be understood as a form of activist or ethically oriented practice. Therapeutic encounters unfold within histories of power, inequity, and structural violence; they reflect broader moral and political worlds (Fernando, 2017; Kirmayer, 2012; Martín-Baró, 1994; Summerfield, 2008). Work in intercultural settings, particularly with Indigenous communities, illustrates how questions of justice, recognition, and relational responsibility are central to clinical work (de Lima Neto & Guimarães, *this volume*). A stance of humility becomes essential: True dialogue begins with listening, with the courage to sit in silence, and with the recognition that 'the word has an owner', meaning that experiences and narratives belong to those who live them. This might be harder than one thinks, since biases do not only appear openly; they also appear more subtly, which does not make them any less harmful. In this volume, Namdiero-Walsh shows how discourses of whiteness, privilege, and racism shape both social interactions and clinical dynamics, highlighting the ways unconscious bias and social positioning permeate therapeutic practice. From this perspective, therapy is not only a dyadic interaction but also a cultural and political event; relational dynamics, linguistic practices, and embodied expressions all contribute to how therapeutic meaning unfolds (see also Molina & Fossa, *this volume*).

Several chapters show how identity and communication, bilingualism, gender development, and nonverbal interaction shape therapeutic processes as profoundly as any technique (see Sasse; Pang; Blau & Speigel or Rocha, Dias, & Marsico, *this volume*). These insights align with the idea that humans are open systems, constantly shaped by shifting contexts, borders, and temporalities (see Valsiner's preface to this volume). What happens in therapy, counselling or any other psychosocial practice is always embedded in networks of relationships, histories, and cultural narratives.

EMBODIMENT, ECOLOGIES OF HEALING, AND LIVED EXPERIENCE

A number of contributions expand the focus of Clinical Psychology to include the body, environment, and lived experience. Practices such as yoga (Kirschner, this volume), community-based healing, or culturally specific rituals demonstrate how healing is inseparable from embodiment and relationality. Chapters addressing chronic pain, liminality, culturally shaped understandings of truth and delusion, or media-driven self-objectification (Ulmschneider or Vestbjerg, this volume) further reveal that mental health is not merely a cognitive or emotional phenomenon; it is lived through the body, through ecological attachments, and through cultural scripts of identity and value. Interestingly, the increasing interest in body- and nature-based therapeutic approaches within Western contexts, seen in practices such as forest bathing (e.g., Rathmann, 2023), somatic therapies (cp. Feinstein, 2025, for a critical comment on the neglect of those), and embodied as well as embedded mindfulness (e.g., Khoury et al., 2025), suggests a growing recognition that something essential may have been lost in more individualized, disembodied models of care. The resurgence of these practices can be read as an attempt to reconnect with forms of relational, ecological, and embodied knowing that many Indigenous and community-based traditions have continued to cultivate. At the same time, scientific innovation has enabled interventions, such as heart-valve replacement or innovative cancer treatments, that were once unimaginable and have significantly extended life expectancy. These advances represent another kind of relational achievement, built through collaborative inquiry, critical debate, and expanding bodies of evidence. Yet, the very success of such approaches underscores the need for dialogue across knowledge systems, as technological progress alone cannot address the full ecological, relational, and experiential dimensions of human suffering and healing.

This becomes even clearer when considering Indigenous perspectives in which healing is tied to land, food, territory, ancestry, and balance. Cultural Psychology and Indigenous psychologies converge here: both emphasize that psychological life is ecological, emergent, and sustained through networks of relations. Phenomena are always in flux; thus, clinical models must be flexible enough to engage with this complexity rather than impose rigid structures.

METHODOLOGICAL AND PRACTICAL GAPS

Despite meaningful progress in recognizing culture within (clinical) psychological science, and in enabling dialogue across languages and disciplines, aided by translation and global collaboration, significant gaps remain. Many standardized assessment tools continue to lack inter or transcultural construct equivalence, and translation alone does not ensure validity (Kohrt et al., 2014). Local idioms of distress, whether expressed through somatic, spiritual, or relational terms, remain marginal in mainstream research despite their clinical importance (Nichter, 2010). And ethnographic, discourse-analytic, and community-based participatory methods are still underutilized, limiting the field's ability to access the nuanced textures of cultural meaning.

In practice, clinicians often work at a distance from community healers, religious leaders, elders, or social networks that play central roles in local mental health ecologies. Structural inequities in knowledge production persist, with research and authorship heavily concentrated in the Global North. Such asymmetries obscure other ways of knowing and reinforce epistemic hierarchies that the field must work to dismantle.

OPPORTUNITIES FOR FUTURE RESEARCH AND PRACTICE

The contributions in this volume point toward several promising directions. Culturally grounded interventions should be co-produced with communities, not merely adapted for them. Research governance and authorship must reflect equity, redistributing both intellectual property and recognition. Clinical training should incorporate cultural psychology, Indigenous knowledge, reflexive practice, and antiracism, preparing clinicians to work across diverse cultural, political, and linguistic contexts.

Emerging South-to-South collaborations and digital tools co-designed with local users offer new possibilities for innovation grounded in local expertise. Finally, clinical outcomes must move beyond symptom reduction and include measures such as dignity, belonging, social role fulfilment, relational restoration, and community well-being (Dudgeon et al., 2014; Patel et al., 2018). Such metrics align with broader decolonial frameworks that understand healing as a collective, relational, and culturally embedded process.

CLOSING REFLECTIONS

The chapters in this book make one point unmistakably clear: Clinical psychology cannot afford to treat culture as peripheral. The discipline faces a dual responsibility: to confront its blind spots and to reimagine itself through more plural, relational, and ecologically grounded frameworks. Yet there is also an opportunity. By embracing Cultural Psychology's insights and engaging deeply with indigenous and other nonWestern epistemologies, the field can move toward a model of clinical practice that is globally relevant, locally grounded, and ethically engaged.

Such transformation requires humility, participatory unlearning, and a willingness to enter into genuine dialogue – dialogue that is nonlinear, associative, 'spiralic' at times, and attentive to the lived realities of those whom Clinical Psychology seeks to serve. If taken seriously, the insights synthesized in this concluding chapter point toward a more inclusive, responsive, and culturally attuned Clinical Psychology, one capable of addressing suffering in its full relational, embodied, and historical complexity.

REFERENCES

Dudgeon, P., Milroy, H., & Walker, R. (Eds.). (2014). *Working together: Aboriginal and Torres Strait Islander mental health and wellbeing principles and practice* (2nd ed.). Commonwealth of Australia.

Feinstein, D. (2025). Dismissing the body from psychological treatment: Commentary on Tolin et al. (2024). *Clinical Psychology: Science and Practice, 32*(3), 232–236. https://doi.org/10.1037/cps0000275

Fernando, S. (2017). *Institutional racism in psychiatry and clinical psychology: Race matters in mental health.* Palgrave Macmillan. https://doi.org/10.1007/978-3-319-62728-1

Henrich, J., Heine, S. J., & Norenzayan, A. (2010). The weirdest people in the world? *Behavioral and Brain Sciences, 33*(2–3), 61–135. https://doi.org/10.1017/S0140525X0999152X

Khoury, B., Lesage, M., Kasprzyk, A., Sadowski, I., Manova, V., Benchimol-Elkaim, B., Dias Martins, C., Rigas, C., & Rej, S. (2025). Embodied and embedded mindfulness and compassion framework. *Mindfulness, 16,* 1091–1115. https://doi.org/10.1007/s12671-025-02561-4

Kirmayer, L. J. (2012). Rethinking cultural competence. *Transcultural Psychiatry, 49*(2), 149–164. https://doi.org/10.1177/1363461512444673

Kirmayer, L. J., & Pedersen, D. (2014). Toward a new architecture for global mental health. *Transcultural Psychiatry, 51*(6), 759–776. https://doi.org/10.1177/1363461514557202

Kohrt, B. A., Rasmussen, A., Kaiser, B. N., Haroz, E. E., Maharjan, S. M., Mutamba, B. B., de Jong, J. T., & Hinton, D. E. (2014). Cultural concepts of distress and psychiatric disorders: Literature review and research recommendations for global mental health epidemiology. *International Journal of Epidemiology, 43*(2), 365–460. https://doi.org/10.1093/ije/dyt227

Martín-Baró, I. (1994). *Writings for a liberation psychology* edited by A. Aron & S. Corne. Harvard University Press.

Nichter, M. (2010). Idioms of distress revisited. *Culture, Medicine, and Psychiatry, 34*(2), 401–416. https://doi.org/10.1007/s11013-010-9179-6

Papa, X. C., & Takua, C. (2025, October). Dialogue on health and well-being with the Xeramõi Carlos Papa (filmmaker and Mbyá Guarani spiritual leader) and Cristine Takua (writer, artisan, decolonial theorist, activist and Brazilian indigenous teacher of the Maxakali ethnic group) at the Carolina Bori Auditorium. In *Presentation at the 1st international meeting on Indigenous psychology: Health and well-being, university of Sao Paulo and museum of Indigenous cultures.*

Patel, V., Saxena, S., Lund, C., Thornicroft, G., Baingana, F., Bolton, P., Chisholm, D., Collins, P. Y., Cooper, J. L., Eaton, J., Herrman, H., Herzallah, M. M., Huang, Y., Jordans, M. J. D., Kleinman, A., Medina-Mora, M. E., Morgan, E., Niaz, U., Omigbodun, O., … Unützer, J. (2018). The Lancet Commission on global mental health and sustainable development. *The Lancet, 392*(10157), 1553–1598. https://doi.org/10.1016/S0140-6736(18)31612-X

Rathmann, J. (2023). Shinrin Yoku: Waldbaden [Shinrin Yoku: Forrest Bathing]. In *Gesundheitsressource Wald [Health Ressource: Forrest]* (pp. 25–30). Springer Spektrum. Essentials.

Summerfield, D. (2008). How scientifically valid is the knowledge base of global mental health? *BMJ, 336*(7651), 992–994. https://doi.org/10.1136/bmj.39513.441030.AD

Printed and bound by CPI Group (UK) Ltd, Croydon, CR0 4YY
24/09/2026
14968847-0004